50
74
ch 9

W

Revenge of
THE BUSH DYNASTY

Revenge of
THE BUSH DYNASTY

Elizabeth Mitchell

HYPERION

NEW YORK

Designed by Ruth Lee

ISBN: 0-7868-6630-6

FIRST EDITION

1 3 5 7 9 10 8 6 4 2

*To my family
and
to Chuck Fulgham,
beloved soul and favorite son of Texas—
wherever he may be*

ACKNOWLEDGMENTS

The snug schedule for this book brought out the heroic in so many people, not least my editor Leigh Haber, who was able to provide wise suggestions, insightful questions, and clean line edits—all the while dealing with every pestilence known to man from fire to moving offices. She involved me in every edit question, and for that I am extremely grateful.

Her assistant Michele Matrisciani managed to keep her good humor even through the late nights at the office and her enthusiasm was welcome during the most pressing deadlines. David Lott maintained his sanguine attitude while overseeing the production of the book into type and I am appreciative of all of his hard work. I would also like to thank the following people at Hyperion for their support: Bob Miller, Martha Levin, Navorn Johnson, Ruth Lee, Claire Ellis, and Jennifer Landers.

I would like to thank my agent Jane Gelfman for not only being my advocate but my friend. I am not sure which I appreciate more— her bemused approach to situations or her compassion for people. I am grateful to Doug Brinkley, who originally led me to this project. He has always been a loyal friend and champion of mine, and I am glad that he assumes that the rest of the human race has as much energy as he does since that belief pushes his friends to new challenges.

George W. Bush's office was of little help on this project (and seems to suffer a bit from the Bush family allergy to journalists). That said, the governor's many friends and colleagues were uncommonly gracious to me with their time and insights. The best endorsement for George W. Bush is the company he keeps—he seems to have surrounded himself with a multitude of smart, funny, decent people. Many of his friends and colleagues helped me by sitting for long interviews, referring me to other sources, or sending me pertinent clips, but I would like to acknowledge in particular the late Paul Rea, who endured a four-hour interview, provided me with telephone numbers, and helped me get a clear picture of George W.'s oil business dealings in West Texas. I am sure that he will be missed terribly in Midland.

The book could never have been written without the labors of hundreds of journalists throughout the decades who have covered the Bush family. In particular, I would like to thank Herbert Parmet for producing his biography of George Bush; that book was the map for my understanding of the history of the family and contained a trove of great details. The amount of work that went into *George Bush: The Life of a Lone Star Yankee* is staggering but is also a bountiful contribution to our knowledge of American history.

I was carried along by a team of dedicated researchers. Allison Joyner, Priscilla Ryan, Christi Tran, Johnnye Montgomery, Jessica Ricci, Leigh Anne Fitzpatrick, and Lynn Ciecierski spent long hours digging into that part of our nation's past that has not yet been memorized by computers. Likewise, I was blessed to find an extraordinary group of research editors: Barbara Kean, Robert Anasi, Jennifer McCaffery, and Christina Del Valle, who worked meticulously and at breakneck speed to ensure that all was as accurate as could be. They gave far more to this effort than just time and I will always appreciate that.

Other researchers also pitched in to help hunt documents and assemble footnotes, namely Anne Fulgham, as well as Timothy Sprattler, Greg Krauss, and Rebecca Lipchitz.

Susannah Hunnewell has been an incredible friend to me, providing me with a great deal of editorial advice at various stages of the project as well as encouragement. Ned Martel offered his assistance regularly and I took him up on it so often that I am amazed he could maintain his sense of humor throughout. Without Tsalem Mueller, I would have been lost on so many occasions; his support and Rolodex of researchers meant so much. Sean Neary also directed me to helpers when I needed them. Carl Sferrazza Anthony passed along the wisdom of his experience, which I constantly recalled during the project.

I also need to thank my friends for making life easier: RoseMarie Terenzio, Rob Reynolds, Rene Steinke, Craig Marks, Gary Ginsberg, Susanna Aaron, Thalia Field, Darcey Steinke, and Matt Berman. Collin Wilson offered a great example of what it is to write under pressure and eased the anxieties of deadlines with his humor.

Other residents of Big D lent lodging or help to this project, including Kris and Laura Kriofske, Tom Hughes, and Steve and Katie Kenny.

My heroes in all of this have been people who generously offered support to either me or to those dear to me during the time that I have been writing the book, namely Dr. Reuben and Lindalyn Adams, Martin London, Chris Antley, Trish Jones, Darnell Powell, Jonathan Pearlroth, and Rachel Slaton. A book could be written on the unexpected sweetness of each of these people.

Regrettably, I have to thank John Kennedy Jr. after his passing. I hope that this book contains some of the spirit in which he founded *George* magazine: to cover politics in a way that brings the human strengths and frailties of the political players to life. I am grateful to him for having invited me along for that big adventure.

There is no question that a key to the book being written was the benevolence of John, Vicki, and Shannon Crew. They provided me shelter for the longest time—testing the patience of a saint—and without hesitation. More importantly, they were sweet, smart, and fun, and gave me an example of how to live life better.

My parents, Alphonsus and Elizabeth Mitchell, and my brothers—Ed, Sam, and Chris—and their families (most importantly Lisa, Suzanne, and Ann) provided editorial direction and love throughout the process.

Because of the kindness I have received from so many people, I am afraid I may have worn out the words for generosity by this point, and that would be a shame, since nothing can compare to what the following people have given to me: Sally Sebastian and Laigh Langley, Gypsie and Ian Winslade and the Fulghams—Eldon, Sharon, Leigh, Daniel, Anne, and Patrick. They gave to me in every way that it is possible for people to give—from the use of a fax machine to a sense of divine grace, as odd as that sounds. Indeed, if ever I would have any doubts, they are proof that Life is so well provided for.

Finally, I would like to thank Chuck Fulgham, without whom I never would have embarked on this project, and without whom we all must be a little kinder just to make up for the new imbalance in the world.

CONTENTS

W

Revenge of
THE BUSH DYNASTY

INTRODUCTION

I n the last months of the millennium, the American people were
exhausted by the roller-coaster ride of the Clinton presidency, or
at least that's what many of George W. Bush's friends and colleagues believed and, in fact, counted on. They hoped that such national weariness would deliver their man to the White House in 2000.
Almost a decade earlier, after giving his father, George Herbert Walker
Bush, a presidential term, the American people stopped electing father
figures as their chief executives. Instead, they chose a man of modest
means from Arkansas because he seemed to understand them. Like so
many Americans, he claimed to have confronted his demons and quit
causing heartache to those he loved, and it seemed the nation wanted
a president like that; someone similar to themselves, who could feel
their pain as they struggled to get air in a rocky economy.

By anyone's estimation, Bill Clinton led the country into difficult
territory. His conduct forced Americans to quickly recalculate their
standards of morality. People who excused his behavior were compelled to reconstruct a new recipe for good leadership—can a man or
woman still be thought of as a good president even after they've
betrayed their spouse with a White House intern? Those Americans
who condemned him then needed to accept the fact that someone they
despised occupied the Oval Office. If evil had not exactly triumphed
over good, then at least the darker force was traveling in the comfort of

1

Air Force One. For some Americans—particularly the voters and donors who had promoted the rise of genteel George Herbert Walker Bush—the effort of balancing this view of justice with their own upbringing would prove exhausting.

People wanted an easier equation, and so this time around they went looking for candidates relatively free of demons. If, as Norman Mailer has said, every president is an expression of the collective unconscious of the country, then George W. Bush—and even his Democratic opponents Al Gore and Bill Bradley—comes in a fitful dream to the American people when they have grown weary of reinventing morality and monitoring the conduct of their leaders.

There was a time when all of America celebrated its collective sluggishness, when middle-class families clustered around their televisions and, without a trace of self-consciousness, referred to themselves as couch potatoes. It was the first half of the 1980s, and Ronald Reagan offered to stand guard while the American people snoozed, telling us sweet stories all the while.

George W. was not made for that era. His ascent to public awareness needed to coincide with a time when the economy was described as vigorous, when outdoor adventure fascinated, and fortunes were created impetuously in the high-tech world. There was no slack in George W.'s life; early to bed and early to rise, he faced the challenges of dismal existence as if they were segments of a triathlon. He was out running while most of the country slumbered. He could ring a hundred doorbells a day to chat up strangers. While he maintained a schoolbook awe for the presidency, the rest of the population wondered if the office could ever be the same again. Born with a genetic impatience, he took on tasks that seemed tedious to others.

And at a time when the economy was in good health, the country had stopped hungering for a Comeback Kid in its president. The voters did not need a politician who rose from adversity to be an example for them that their own hopes could be realized; they could accept George W. as a candidate, a man who rose from privilege to greater power. His only comeback was from his own spiritual frailties, aided by the unassailable Reverend Billy Graham.

George W. had faced his demons—and even those weaknesses that he acknowledged seemed more humanizing than threatening to his potential to serve as president. He conquered these faults not to make himself a better husband or father, but specifically to be a better leader. When, as governor, he was giving an interview to *GQ*, he gestured to a portrait of Sam Houston dressed as Hannibal in the ruins of Carthage. "The lesson that picture tells you," he said, "is that the difference between making a fool of yourself and being a good governor is whiskey. I've had a lot of defining moments in my life. One of them was quitting drinking. I don't think I was clinically alcoholic. But I'd lose focus, and in order to get elected and lead, you've got to stay focused. I would never have been governor if I hadn't quit."

—

America would be happy with this comeback story—that of a conquering hero of alcoholism—and the citizens seemed relieved too when George W. assured them that he had never been unfaithful to his wife, Laura. They wanted to consider a man for the presidency who would not be toting his darker nature with him.

It seemed, however, that Americans had become addicted to one aspect of Bill Clinton and would hate to see it go—the idea of the leader of the free world as buddy. They liked how Clinton could joke his way along ropelines and hug his way through urban neighborhoods.

But George W. was even simpler fun. The American people saw him as their golfing partner—someone easy to spend time with but who lacked the complications of a bosom friend. And if he wasn't exactly going to set the world on fire with his academic skills or his knowledge of foreign policy, that weakness didn't prove to be a deal breaker for the American public in the early stages of the campaign; the voters had never been greatly enamored with the policy-wonk side of Bill Clinton anyway.

George W.'s only personality flaw that might chafe over time was his tendency to get a little too sharp with a quip; so his handlers struggled to decide how much line to give him, playing between their desire to let him run far enough to work his intimate magic and their fear that he would choke himself on the cord.

There is no profession so simultaneously expansive and solipsistic as politics. While trying to win the right to promote the common good, to improve the society, politicians must engage in an orgy of ego. They spend their campaign days packaging their personalities, spinning their faults, and promoting their talents to the public. Perhaps there was a time when a politician was merely the vessel in which an assortment of policy ideas and public solutions was stored, and the voter simply selected the vessel that contained the highest proportion of his or her own views. But that day has long since passed. Now constituents choose the man or woman they consider most "likeable," hoping that he or she will behave properly when accorded power, a fact clear to George Bush even in his earliest campaigns.

George W. Bush always believed that his father was exactly this sort of extraordinary man who could act with dignity in any situation, and thus should win the highest accolades the country had to offer. George W. not only admired his father, he emulated him, following his path through Andover, Yale, the oil fields of Midland, and into politics. He not only tracked him in the particulars, but even inherited his quirks: he hated to dance, rose at the crack of dawn, and played golf at top speed, just to name a few. But time had shuffled the cards arrayed against him. Instead of finishing schools of privilege—as Andover and Yale were in his father's era—George W. found competitive academic bootcamps. As opposed to his father's experience of glory and challenge fighting abroad for America's protection in World War II, George W. faced the ambivalence of Vietnam from his post in the Texas National Guard. Instead of riding an oil boom to business success, George W. scrambled to gather the shards of his company as it broke into bits on its way down in an oil bust.

George W. grew up in a gray time in which it was difficult to prove one's self a hero. Instead of choosing a controversial path and hoping that history might prove him right, he cleaved to a middle road, anxious to keep his reputation clean for the sake of both himself and his father. He dared himself to controversial views at times, but not regularly. George W. labored to be a good man, even a leader at times, but the greatest risk he took was to submit himself to media dissection by running for public office.

So despite the fact that George W. found himself in the extraordinary position of being the front-runner for the Republican presidential nomination at the end of the millennium, he had actually lived, until

that time, the life of a normal, upper-class man who happened to stride
through a rarefied political atmosphere as his father's son. Thus his
story is composed less of grand events and more of the tone of his
time. When he began running for the presidency, he had served in public office only slightly longer than he had attended Yale.

His father was his hero, and oddly, George W.'s few nagging faults
seemed to have germinated in that deep admiration. Since, unlike his
father, he did not have a litany of accomplishments to mark his excellence, he seemed compelled to boast of successes as if they had been
achieved single-handedly, as if no assistants had helped craft his fate.
He could not trust the world to brag for him; he needed to help the
effort along.

George W. was a normal, upper-class man who would forever be a
child, who had been televised as such since the age of 18 and who would
be photographed during his presidential campaign sitting crosslegged at
his father's feet, smiling impishly like a preschooler. What a strange life
is created for the offspring of a politician who becomes their parents'
asset in a career in public service. The family photos don't just sit in
the albums, or go out on Christmas cards, they are the stuff of political pamphlets and television advertising. The politician's feelings for
their family are regularly written into speeches for Rotary Clubs and
coliseums. A civilian is rarely called upon to summarize a particular
relationship in one bullet point; for a political family, the short declarative sentence covering wide swaths of emotion is second nature. If the
politician experiences nuances to the feeling, those details are shared
only with the very select few who can be trusted to never breathe a
word to anyone else.

Barbara Bush won her role in the theater of political family life at
the age of 39, when George Bush was elected to Congress in 1964. "I'm
sort of used to living in a fishbowl," she told the *Dallas Morning News*
after just a few months playing First Lady of the United States. "I
haven't changed any, [but] I'm getting plenty of visibility. People wave
at you all the time, and they're glad to see you." George W. had grown
up that way, having first auditioned before he was old enough to vote.

George Bush's prominence inspired adoration from his supporters
and hostility from political opponents—and both currents of feeling
directed at the patriarch solidified the relationship among the family

members. They must have become accustomed to hearing the speeches celebrating their familial love, to the photo opportunities, to the glowing welcomes of the party faithful who hosted them at events. They must have felt their affection for one another reconfirmed publicly almost every day. From the time George W. Bush was 18 years old, the children had already learned to huddle together to withstand the barrage of epithets and accusations hurled against their dad. The Bushes were like America during the Cold War: A common enemy created a seamless bond.

On the one hand, America adored the idea of the family. "When you're talking about Clinton fatigue, part of it is that we loved Ozzie and Harriet," said Ron Kaufman, former political director to George Bush. "We really did. People want *Little House on the Prairie* to be real, and the Bushes represent that." Most Americans had regrettably come to the conclusion that such familial love could only be a fantasy. In that context, much of the Bushes' affection for each other came off as exotic, and mere politics could not accommodate a deeper description of the family relationship to explain that level of love, nor could the Bushes find words to convey the nuance. They were forced to sell their familial affection like canned soup. As a result, America seemed to divide into two camps: those who accepted the happy view of the Bushes on blind faith; and those who harbored the creeping suspicion that they were being sold a bromide.

George Bush's former staffers would remark on how the family members talked to each other as if in code—a special language of jokes and jibes that was content-free and thus perfectly suitable for the ears of strangers. The laughter effectively sealed them into their own world. It was an intimacy they could engage in while others hovered. When they teased each other, it was as if they were back in their living room in Midland, Texas.

If the American people had temporarily lost their predilection for electing father figures, it's interesting that in the race for 2000, the voters don't mind having such an archetype close at hand. Two of the strongest candidates in the race for the White House—Geoge W. and Al Gore—were famously proud of their dads. What importance does a strong father have in creating a great president? If recent history offers predictors, then decent male role models breed one-term presidents.

Other than George Bush, whose father, Prescott, commanded respect as a businessman, civic leader, and senator, Jimmy Carter seemed to be the only president in recent history whose biological father was a role model. With a resumé similar to that of Prescott and George Bush, Earl Carter served honorably in World War I, taught Sunday school, served in the state legislature, gave to charities anonymously, and worked hard as a successful peanut farmer and supply store owner.

The difficult father, on the other hand, seems to raise men of political charisma who weather two terms in office. Bill Clinton's biological father, W. J. Blythe, died on the way home from selling heavy machinery across Illinois, when he was speeding toward Hope and the front tire on his Buick blew. Bill was born a few months later, in the same summer George W. arrived in the world. Bill's mother, Virginia, later married Roger Clinton, who was an alcoholic. In the spring of 1959, while George Bush—millionaire and civic leader—was settling the details of relocating his family from bucolic Midland to a posh Houston neighborhood, Roger Clinton brutally beat up Virginia as young Bill phoned his mother's lawyer.

Jack Reagan was a quiet alcoholic. He effectively disguised his problem until his son found him one day lying spread-eagled in the snow on the front lawn. From then on, son Ronald played the role of protector to his dad.

—

George W. Bush has often said that he would be happy with his life whether or not he wins the White House. He does not need the victory to confirm his own worth. He has, by his own account, been blanketed in unconditional love since birth. He is unlikely to jeopardize that affection by demeaning his own ethics to win or to retain power.

Even George W.'s friends describe him as a reluctant candidate. He did not throw himself into the national ring but was pushed by party elders who realized that he had the potential to win. He might not have been anxious to seek the presidency, but the country was ready to have him as a Republican front-runner. As the governor of a state with a population of 18 million, he would possess a solid foundation of electoral votes. He represented a softer Republicanism, abhorring bleeding hearts, but accommodating a certain tenderness on the part of government toward the less powerful and affluent. For the media age, he wasn't a stunner, but he looked vital, handsome enough; one wouldn't feel sad to see him dressed up at state functions. He did not sift his friends to include only the successful but boasted a powerful inner circle inherited from his father. If his business accomplishments had not been entirely of his own making, he had the attitude of success; he believed in his triumphs so completely that he conquered the doubts of others.

George W. would say that his family never placed demands on him, but that his parents expected the best. George Bush's former staffers would remark how they felt that same sort of pressure—their boss's certainty that they would pitch in, behave impeccably, and make perfect decisions. In exchange they would receive his constancy.

Loyalty was the blood of the Bush family—fealty to kin, country, and colleague. No one honored that code more than George W. in his devotion to his father. He believed that his dad's interests overrode those of every man or woman who worked for him, and that advisers and aides should subvert their ambitions for the sake of his father. But George W. didn't limit his cheerleading to simply pushing people on his father's payroll to work harder; he wanted the press to get in line too, and he became infuriated when they balked.

Unfortunately for George W., in the 1992 elections, even his unbridled enthusiasm could not keep his father in the White House. According to friends and his father's former staffers, he accepted that the Bush campaign had its own internal failings. He was infuriated by the infighting among his father's team of advisers and disappointed in his father's reluctance to press his message more forcefully.

But George W. was even more irate at the interlopers: He later publicly acknowledged that he considered the campaigns of Ross Perot and Pat Buchanan that year to be part of a vendetta against the family. Bill Clinton excited his greater wrath for not only beating his father out of another term in the White House, but for conducting his family life while president in a way that could never be depicted by Norman

Rockwell. George W. would love to avenge his father's defeat. To some, his political interest seemed ignited less by passion for the issues than by revenge. "I think we are all motivated by different things," said Torie Clarke, who served as George Bush's campaign press secretary in 1992, "and [the Bushes] will probably get very mad if they ever read this, but I think what [George W.] is doing and how effectively he is doing it has a lot to do with how much he cares about his father. . . Jeb always seemed to have the instincts and the interests, even before his father was 'wronged,' quote-unquote. Jeb always seemed to have the commitment and the passion."

George W. is not alone in wanting to reverse what happened to his father. Much of the money that pours into the campaign coffers of the Texas governor, as well as much of the advice, comes from supporters of his father who are as irritated as the candidate that President Bush was defeated. "He gets the benefit of the doubt from a lot of people because of his dad," said Andy Card, former deputy to the chief of staff in the Bush administration. "He has given us a chance to say, We were right: George Bush was a great guy."

The challenge for George W. lies in defining which brand of loyalty guides him. It seems that everyone who has met President George Bush seems to have deemed him a good man, a decent man, but the question always was whether his loyalty stemmed from strength or weakness. George W. has been described as similarly loyal, and the country is waiting to discover whether that devotion is the transcendent kind that might lead the nation peacefully and prosperously into the next millennium.

I

SON OF SUPERMAN

I f we are to imagine what it is to be George W. Bush—and it is important to cast our thoughts to such speculation so we can predict how he might behave if he were to become our next president—we must first imagine what it would be like to live with the k-constant of George W.'s life, to labor under the assumption that one's father is a bona fide hero.

George W.'s father is not just a decent man, not just a single-threat talent. He is not merely a former college baseball star, the type who could, if he chose, pain his listeners over cordon bleu at the country club with old stories of triple plays. He is not just a wily entrepreneur, not simply a good-looking guy who still charms the gray-haired ladies. You must imagine this: Although George W. Bush was born to his parents when his father was just a college sophomore, George Herbert Walker Bush already had a whole litany of achievements behind him by then. In 1944, only two years before George W. entered the world, his handsome six-foot-two father, George Herbert Walker Bush, stood at attention while the Distinguished Flying Cross was pinned to his lapel. The 20-year-old had won the honor by destroying radio transmitters on the island of Chichi Jima, after being shot down, lost at sea, and rescued within an inch of his life.

The very fact that he had been a U.S. airman in the Pacific at such a tender age was itself a great indicator of his extraordinary New

England mettle. Of course, so many American men had made the exact same decision George Bush had on December 7, 1941, when the Japanese bombed Pearl Harbor. After that attack, the war no longer just rumbling on the dark side of the globe; hostilities were exploding on American seas. The next day, across the country, long lines of volunteers snaked from recruiting stations and wrapped around city blocks. Most Americans feared that more Asian weapons were on the way, targeting everything from the commuter tunnels of New York City to the spans of the Golden Gate Bridge.

With the U.S. at war, it was only a question of when, not if, George Bush would be called to serve. He no longer wanted to continue on directly to Yale, where he had been accepted during his junior year at Andover. Instead he chose battle. Given his character, it was not surprising that he chose action over academics. The war "was against imperialism and against fascism, and I wanted to be on the cutting edge," he has said. He hoped that if he enlisted early, the officers would be happy to train him as a pilot no matter his young age.

But for a boy of his social class, his decision was hasty. The secretary of war, Henry Stimson, in his commencement oration exhorted Bush's graduating Andover class not to jump right into the services. Even Bush's steely New England father, Prescott, had urged his son to change his mind (although he himself had enlisted in World War I directly upon graduation from Yale). Despite the uncommon sight of his father in tears, George Bush went into the trade of kings, becoming at age 18 the Navy's youngest aviator.

George Bush's entry into war tested not just his strength, but also the resolve of young Barbara Pierce, the 16-year-old girl who would be his wife. They met only weeks after Pearl Harbor, at a country club dance in Greenwich, Connecticut. Barbara was back home for the holidays in nearby Rye, New York, on leave from Ashley Hall, the girls' school she attended in Charleston, South Carolina. There she was a good student with a taste for acting. George Bush, from nearby Greenwich, was attending the dance with some friends. Almost immediately, his eye was caught by the tall, auburn-haired girl in the off-the-shoulder dress of holiday red and green. She was bouncing along to the Glenn Miller–style band with his friend Jack Wozencraft. George asked Jack to introduce them. Alas, as George and Barbara prepared for their first dance, the band dropped the tempo to a waltz, and the Andover senior, a rotten hoofer, had to ask her to sit out the song and just talk.

George Bush would later explain the immediacy of their courtship by "the heightened awareness, on-the-edge" quality of the time. After all, the debris in Pearl Harbor was still washing ashore, and most people worried that whatever happiness they were able to find might be the fleeting last rays before more death and destruction. But he was impressed by her exuberance, her lack of self-consciousness.

For her part, Barbara's "heightened awareness" was not induced by wartime fears. She has said that the bombing of Pearl Harbor barely registered with her. Instead, the fever of love she felt was triggered entirely by George Bush, or "Poppy," as he was then nicknamed. "I could hardly breathe when he was in the room," she has said. He asked her what she was doing the following night, and she told him that she would be attending a dance in Rye. He showed up at that event too.

By that time, all of Barbara's family was well aware of her new suitor. She had cooed about him to her mother when she returned home that night from the Greenwich dance. Her mother infuriated her by burning up the phone lines asking around about his background. Luckily, he and his family fared well. At the dance in Rye, her brother James—who had never shown much brotherly affection—cut in on them so that he could send George and Barbara to the sidelines. He wanted to ask Poppy if he would join his private-school basketball team for a showdown against the town kids a few nights later. George Bush agreed but reserved Barbara for a date after the game. He insisted to his parents that he take the car with a radio for that evening in case there was a lull in the conversation. As it turned out, the distraction wasn't necessary. Barbara talked animatedly the whole night; later they would joke that she hasn't stopped talking since.

After the holidays George and Barbara went back to their respective private schools, where they carried on their courtship by mail. She was particularly excited when he invited her to the prom at Andover, which involved a weekend campus stay at a housemaster's home. That night he bestowed a first kiss on her cheek.

He graduated from Andover soon after that in 1942, and went into pilot training, first in North Carolina. A year later, he received his wings in Corpus Christi, Texas, just as Barbara graduated from Ashley Hall. That summer, she was invited to spend over two weeks at the Bush vacation compound of Walker's Point, in Kennebunkport, Maine, to meet the clan and walk the rocks with George in the moonlight. Without his ever asking for her hand, they became secretly engaged.

By the fall, Barbara was attending Smith College in Northampton, Massachusetts; George Bush was in final training before shipping out to the Pacific; and the engagement announcement ran in the *New York Herald Tribune*. Over Christmas of 1943, just before he left for combat, George bestowed the ring.

For the next semester and through summer school, Barbara lolled around Smith, dreaming of her intended and nearly failing all of her classes. Some days she would receive several heavily censored letters from him, mailed from his aircraft carrier, the U.S.S. *San Jacinto*. Often she would go for a month or so without hearing a word. Still she was planning their wedding for Christmastime.

In September 1944, she dropped out of school, right about the same time that, unbeknownst to her, George Bush was being shot down in the Pacific.

She learned of the incident just three days before George Bush sent word through the Navy, assuring her that he was fine, so her anxiety at least was short-lived. The Navy offered him a leave after he had briefly recuperated in Hawaii, but he decided to rejoin his squadron since they had recently lost four pilots. That decision made him late for his wedding. Bar scratched the December 17 date off the invitations and penned in January 6, 1945, as the day that she would marry the first man she had ever kissed. He arrived in New York City on Christmas Eve for the kind of welcome home that would have made even Frank Capra swoon.

He wore his dress blues to their wedding at the First Presbyterian Church in Rye, New York. That night, they went into New York City, where they found time to take in the musical *Meet Me in St. Louis* at Radio City Music Hall. The next morning they boarded a train for the Cloister on Sea Island, Georgia, for their honeymoon.

They spent the next eight months sometimes together and sometimes apart, while he fulfilled his postings at bases in Florida,

Michigan, Maine, and Virginia. By 1945, George Bush was assigned to a torpedo bomber unit planned for use in the imminent invasion of Japan. He feared going on the mission, but was saved when Japan sued for peace in August 1945, after the bombings of Hiroshima and Nagasaki. The next month, he was ready for Yale, and he and Bar moved to New Haven, Connecticut, to begin his studies with the class of 1948.

To accommodate the returning veterans who were eager to get on with their adult lives, Yale offered an abbreviated and intensified version of its usual four-year curriculum. George Bush signed up for the two-and-a-half year program. On the same humid, overcast day that the Yale students enrolled for the first summer session nearly a year after V-J day, George Bush's mother, Dotty Walker, sat with Barbara in the modest apartment on Edwards Street and administered the castor oil that would urge George W.'s birth along. The first son of George Bush was born on July 6, 1946.

In all likelihood, George W. knew his father was a war hero almost from the first pulse of his narrative consciousness. More than 60 percent of his father's class of over 8,000 students were World War II veterans, paying their tuition with the G.I. Bill, as even wealthy George Bush had. During his toddler years, George W. lived at Yale in housing specially built for the former soldiers and their families. Later, his childhood friends would say they were aware of the older George's hero status because of the photographs of him as a U.S. Navy pilot they had seen at his house.

But George Bush did not just rest on his laurels after the war. He went on to excel at collegiate-type activities. He would serve as captain of his Yale baseball team at the NCAA College World Series. He would be Phi Beta Kappa, president of his fraternity, and a member of the secret society Skull and Bones. And that is not to mention the history book's worth of accomplishments awaiting this American political apostle at regular intervals throughout his life, like stations of the cross. "What you'll find about George Bush is that his life is almost too good to be true," George W. has said.

From the first, George W.'s father adored his son and always stood by him. He would say later, after he had been elected to the vice presidency of the United States, that his greatest accomplishment was the fact that his kids still enjoyed coming home. Nonetheless, George W. had to handle the fact that his father would later refer in his autobiography to his first son's birth as a side reference between two em-dashes. ("For one thing, Barbara, young George—he was born in July 1946—and I lived off campus, in a sprawling old house that had been divided into small apartments," he wrote.) His son wasn't and wouldn't be—no matter the heights of George W.'s future accomplishments—the most amazing thing that ever happened in his father's life.

Throughout all of his days, George W. would be trailed by the halo and the shadow of his father. Some of the twinning of mannerisms could be downright spooky to friends. Of course, they shared the same first and last names. Always people would be doing somersaults to distinguish between the two of them. George and Georgie. George Senior and Junior. Big George and Little George. George and George W. His son would frequently have to interject, even into his middle years, that he was not in fact a junior. That he had one fewer name. That he was missing the Herbert. There was one difference. In fact there were many.

—

George W. would publicly define his understanding of that shading later in his political life. Then he would repeat the mantra many times, so that every voter would have the exact same insight into him: "The biggest difference between me and my father," he often said, "is that he went to Greenwich Country Day and I went to San Jacinto Junior High."

To comprehend the meaning of this declaration required that every voter be a bit of a Bush trivia buff. George W. was suggesting that he and his father might be similar men in almost every way, but that they had been profoundly differentiated by their preadolescent schooling, not to mention their upbringing until age 13 in geographically disparate locales. His father had attended a private academy for boys in Greenwich, Connecticut, a wealthy New York suburb, while George W. studied at a public junior high school in the outpost town of Midland, Texas.

Although George W. attended San Jacinto for only one year, his point was valid. While his father had worn a uniform of sweater and knickers to memorize Latin at an institution created by monied parents in the leafy enclave of Greenwich, George W. had gone to a one-story school the color of Pecan Sandies, where they taught Texas history for a year in fourth grade before they taught American history in fifth. George W. wasn't escorted to school by a chauffeur named Alec, as his father had been; he walked or rode his bike or was dropped off by his mother. In other words, until he left San Jacinto and Midland for the eighth grade at the fancy Kinkaid School in Houston in 1959, he lived like most middle-class Americans. He understood people.

And it was exactly George W.'s ability to connect to people—not just to be friendly or polite like his father, but to be, for that one split-second handshake or quip, one of them—that would spell the difference for him on the campaign trails. It wasn't just pundits who would say that George W. was better "with people" than his father. Everyone who knew both of them made the same remark. Friends and colleagues found his father kind and funny, meticulous in his manners, but there was a certain reserve in him, a faint aloofness, like a good old boy under glass.

If geography is destiny, then the most important moment of George W.'s life was the day after his father's commencement from Yale in 1948. His father gunned the engine of the crimson two-door Studebaker streamlined coupe that his father, Prescott, had given him for graduation, peered out the wraparound windows and pointed the nose west toward Odessa, Texas. Both of George W.'s parents had been ripe for this adventure, not least because of a desire to get out from under the thumbs of their respective parents. Bar's mother, Pauline Pierce, was beautiful, fabulous, critical, and meddling. Her father, Marvin Pierce, was witty, frank, and overloaded with work as president of the McCall publishing company. George's mother was kind, athletic, and rigorous; his father dignified, austere, and eager to see his son follow in his path to the doors of Brown Brothers Harriman & Company, where he had made partner and his wife's father had been president. Barbara adored her funny, lighthearted father, but she tangled with her domineering mother and three siblings. "George's mother was a formidable and strong woman, and so was my mother," Barbara told speechwriter Peggy Noonan, "and we wanted to get out from under the parental gaze, be on our own!"

George Bush had grown up in wealth, but of a typically New England variety. The riches protected but did not coddle him; they eliminated all fear for survival but instilled an anxiety of expectation. The family lived in the kind of tony suburb that can boast woods without the wild animals, in a house that was spacious and comfortable but not a rambling estate like those of the Bush's neighbors. His father would be driven to and from the train station each day by Alec, but in a car, not a limousine. The Bushes only retained a cook and a maid, which, some family members liked to point out, was nearly roughing it in that town. Jackets and ties were required at dinner, and Prescott Bush insisted that none of the five children leave the premises on Sunday. He was a stern presence. "The boys were more scared of Dad than I was," George Bush's only sister, Nancy Ellis, told his biographer Herbert Parmet. George's mother demanded high achievement in all of her children, while critiquing them for taking any pride in their accomplishments.

Through the extended clan, the Bushes owned various vacation retreats should they ever feel the need to "recreate." But the places instilled a bracing quality to days of leisure. The hunting lodge owned by Dorothy Bush's father as part of the Duncannon resort in South Carolina, was a particular favorite in the colder months. Nancy Ellis recalled how, as the preamble to a day of quail and dove hunting, they would be awakened "by the most wonderful black servants who could come into the bedrooms early in the morning and light those crackling pinewood fires."

Every summer was spent at the compound of Dorothy's mother, on Walker's Point in Kennebunkport, Maine. While not quite as high end as Bar Harbor to the north, Kennebunkport was, by its very distance from the larger cities of New England, a hub for the wealthy. No one would travel that far north for a week's holiday; the vacationers who chose Kennebunkport were the types who could afford to take a month or even the whole summer for their pleasures. While the days were filled with tennis, golf, baseball, and fishing, the town was no Palm Beach. The icy ocean waters chilled the ankles to aching, the nights cooled to a temperature necessitating windbreakers and sweaters, and the coastline followed small patches of beach to smooth spans of surf-pounded rock, then jagged cliffs that sent the white foam spewing skyward.

Barbara's family was not quite as well off, but they were still upper-class. Her father, Marvin, was a descendent of President Franklin Pierce, and his family had been extremely wealthy until Marvin's birth in the 1890s. At that point, a depression hit their iron foundry, and they lost everything, Barbara's father ending up working to support his parents until their deaths. He also labored to sustain a luxurious life for Bar's mother, Pauline, a former beauty from Ohio with extravagant tastes. Added on to life's bill was the expense of treating the youngest of the Pierce's four children, Scotty, who was found to have a bone cyst in his shoulder when he was only two. After five years of treatment, he was finally cured. Still, they had servants and lived in the better part of Rye in a five-bedroom house.

As a young couple, George and Barbara also would have been expected to settle in the New York suburbs; he could commute to his Wall Street job, while she waved the children off to their private grade schools. But the war had changed George and Bar and their dreams for the early years of their marriage. In war, George found that achievement could be melded to emotion. For a man brought up to win tennis matches and swat homers, battle was the ultimate competition— between the Allies and the enemy, between those who would live and those who would die. In such a clean conflict, he had no reason to doubt the good of the American forces or the evil of the Nazis and Japanese; the moral drama was blessedly simple.

In this global competition, George Bush's side won, and better still, he survived. In fact, through his very survival, leaping from his burning plane into the ocean swells of the Pacific, he became a hero. His two squadron buddies in that maneuver died. That moment of chance introduced George to the mysterious and invigorating experience of defying the odds.

War had also given him time to think. The Prescott Bushes were a frenetic family of sporting and scholastic achievement, which had always been just fine with George. He hated to be alone. In fact, he and his brother Prescott once made a single request on their Christmas wish lists: to be able to share a room again. But in battle, from midnight to 4 A.M., George stood on the deck of the *Finback*, gazing out at the inky night, the brilliant speckling of stars, the wash of sea over the submarine deck and pondered life's trickery. It was perhaps one of the few silences of his life—"God's therapy," he called it in his autobiography. He determined that he would work only with a product that he could see and feel. He could not, he decided, simply shuffle stock slips all day, and then settle onto the 5:15 from Grand Central each evening. He told *Fortune* magazine in the late 1950s that he had decided he wasn't interested in "cut-and-dried jobs, with everybody just like everybody else, getting a job with Dad's help and through Dad's friends."

Bar would trail him on any course he chose. The war had provided her with confirmation that she had found her superman, a husband romantic enough to paint her name on his plane, brave enough to win the Distinguished Flying Cross, and lucky enough to come home intact. If she had been tormented throughout her girlhood by her mother's constant admonitions about her weight and comparisons to her sister's covergirl beauty, here was proof enough that she was a star. George Herbert Walker Bush had chosen her, and now she would follow him anywhere. Her unofficial motto, according to friends, was "Don't mess with George." And he was reciprocally respectful. George W. would later say he "never heard George and Barbara Bush utter a harsh or ugly word to each other, never heard either of them characterize each other in an ugly way."

George Bush's stern Aunt Mary related an incident to Esther H. Smith for the Greenwich Public Library Oral History Project that demonstrated how much Bar adored her husband. One day, soon after George and Bar were married, several women were sitting around Walker's Point and began speculating what it would be like to be First Lady. "I'd like it," Bar said, "because, you know, I'm going to be the First Lady some time." Mary told Smith: "It was because she felt very secure. She felt that there wasn't anybody in the world like George, whom she worshiped."

At first, as George and Bar thought about their plans after graduation, they considered gentleman's farming. A reading of Louis Bromfield's *The Farm* sobered them up with its descriptions of the expense of life in the pastures. While they knew that their families would never fully subsidize them in life, they also understood that their parents would be perfectly happy to invest in any serious endeavor undertaken by their children. To the Pierces and the Bushes, farming would not qualify.

Then Neil Mallon, Prescott's best friend from Yale, offered an acceptable compromise that would provide white-collar adventure. He suggested to George Bush that he try the new frontier for the young: the oil fields of Texas. George Bush had only been to the state briefly when he trained on the limited confines of the navy base in Corpus Christi, so this indeed could be called a daring enterprise.

Back in 1929, Prescott had urged Uncle Neil, as the Bush kids called him, to take over the start-up Dresser Industries, a holding company with a few oil business subsidiaries. Neil thanked Prescott for the good advice by appointing him in 1930 to the board of directors. Now, 18 years later—with the company racking up a small fortune annually—Uncle Neil could look out for Prescott's son too. One of Dresser's subsidiaries, International Derrick & Equipment Company (Ideco), was looking for an equipment clerk in Odessa, Texas. George Bush's job would be to work the counter at the store, sweep out warehouses, and slap rustproof paint on oil drilling rigs heated to over 100 degrees by the unrelenting West Texas sun. The job paid a respectable $375 a month.

Despite the fact that the position sounded modest, Prescott Bush could not complain. He knew the company was sound, since his best friend ran the operation, he served on the board, and had owned 1,900 shares of Dresser for almost a decade. With the war over and fuel rationing ended with it, the oil business was beginning a time of steady growth, and young men with great ambitions for their bank accounts were headed to the oil fields. George Bush was Dresser's only trainee, and with Uncle Neil Mallon as president of the company, there was room eventually to move up—maybe, Mallon implied, to the very top.

So Bar and George W. headed from New Haven to Walker's Point in Kennebunkport for one last draught of the bracing coastal air while they waited for George to find them a house in West Texas. Within a week, the phone rang and he told them that he had found just the place. Bar wasted no time packing up their son and flying down to Dallas, then boarding the single propeller plane—a total of 12 hours of engine roar and airsickness—on their way to their new home.

The family settled in a true outpost of the oil business. Odessa was founded in 1881 as a depot on the Texas and Pacific railroad line. Not long after, a town promoter tried to boost the population by pitching the place as a health resort and education center. That was then. By the time the Bushes arrived, Odessa reeked of oil and gas fumes. As George W. would later say, "It's not exactly a paradise."

George escorted his wife and toddler down the dirt road of East Seventh Street to their shotgun house two doors from a yard full of livestock. The Bush house was split down the middle by a makeshift wall, with a mother-daughter hooker team occupying the other side. The shared bathroom (a luxury given that most of the homes relied on outhouses) was frequently used by the neighbors' overnight guests.

In summer, the place was steamy. Only a screeching window air-conditioning unit cut the Texas heat. The prairie winds blew through the uninsulated walls in winter. But the Bushes did have a refrigerator (a rarity), and soon made friends with their neighbors in the house next door, Jack and Valta Ree Casselman from Oklahoma, and Otis "Ah-tis" Miller from across the street. While George was off at work, Bar was left alone in a strange town with no other focus but Georgie, who became in her words a "slightly spoiled little boy."

Their only friends from back home were Bill and Sally Reeder from Yale who had lived upstairs from them in the New Haven veteran housing and now resided in nearby Midland, the white-collar rival town, with their twin boys. For Bar, it must have felt like traveling from the tundra to the tennis court to visit them, since Midland was noticeably more upper-middle-class.

That first year of roughing it was lonely for Bar. She wrote what she described as boring letters home and was answered with care packages of cold cream and Tide, sent by her worried mother who thought such staples must be rare in that strange frontier. Despite her solitude, Bar and George decided to assert their independence that first Christmas by staying put in Texas for the holidays. On Christmas Eve, she and George W. were waiting to decorate the tree with George, when she heard the sound of a truck engine idling out front. She peered into the gloaming and saw her husband sprawled on the lawn. The Ideco store manager Leo Thomas had unceremoniously dumped him off after he had, as they say in West Texas, "swallowed the crow's beak" after the store's open house—he was flatout drunk. For Bar, Odessa got a little lonelier that night.

In the spring of 1949, after less than a year in Odessa, Dresser assigned George to some of its outfits in California, to help him learn more of the business. The young family lived in a motel in Whittier, the Pierpont Inn in Ventura, a rented house in Bakersfield, and finally an apartment in Compton. George worked first as an assemblyman at Pacific Pumps on eight-hour shifts, seven days a week; then peddled drill bits for Security Engineers Company, both Dresser subsidiaries. By springtime of 1949, Bar was pregnant with their second child.

One day in October, when they were living in Compton, George arrived home early from work. He had horrible news. Bar's mother and father had gotten into a terrible car wreck.

It was a freak accident. Her mother had brought a cup of coffee with her for the drive that autumn day in Rye. She had set it on the seat beside her, but as they drove, the cup started to slide. Marvin reached out, worried the coffee might scald her. The car kept going though, careening right into a stone wall. Pauline Pierce died instantly; Marvin broke several ribs and bruised his face. It was so strange. Bar had just flown back home for her brother Jimmy's wedding a week or so before. She had had a wonderful time. But that trip had been kept short since she was late into her pregnancy.

Now, her father advised her not to travel to the funeral. She was devastated. George's bosses had been so kind, she would later say, in that they allowed him to stay home with her the day after the tragedy; the Bushes knew that job responsibilities often came first. George called their friends in L.A. and they tried to console Bar as best they could.

Two months later, on December 20, the peripatetic Barbara looked into the eyes of a doctor she had only met that day and gave birth to a little girl named after her late mother, Pauline Robinson Pierce. They called their daughter Robin for short.

In the frantic last weeks before giving birth, Bar had arranged to leave George W. with the family down the hall when delivery time came. But the Bushes had been startled one night by pounding at their door. "Call the police," cried the neighbor's children. "Dad is killing Mother!" The Bushes let them in and called the authorities. Needless to say other arrangements were made for George W.

Now everything was fine. George Bush brought Bar and Robin home on Christmas Day. The whole family was safe.

In the late spring of 1950, after the Bushes had spent a year in California, Dresser transferred George back to its Odessa warehouse. The family now knew that Midland was more their kind of town—filled as it was with the white-collar geologists, engineers, lawyers, and company presidents, as opposed to the blue-collar workers, who labored on the rigs and in the fields, living in Odessa. The Bushes decided to make their home in Midland.

The road from Midland International Airport cleaves the desert plains in a straight line to the city of the same name. There are no gentle curves in Highway 20, no hills that require the driver to gun the gas pedal. The asphalt runs exactly as the crow flies, directly from the airport to Wall Street in Midland, an absolute line from Point A to Point B.

The land is so flat it almost leaves a visitor breathless, the peripheral vision unfettered for miles by anything except a Vaseline smear of heat waves. Many of George W.'s friends remember the first time they arrived in Midland to seek their fortunes. They recall a uniform vision: After driving for most of a day across miles of yellow sand, suddenly they spotted a small crop of buildings, like an abandoned metropolis, sprouting up out of the oil fields. The oasis was the Tall City of the Plains.

Nowadays, about 10 miles from the center of town, the first street sign appears, hanging above the road like the mark of a marathon finish line: It says Eisenhower. And as one's car roars past, time and culture seem to rocket back too. Arriving in Midland feels like revisiting an era when Ike was king and Lucille Ball was queen—which is exactly when the Bushes flourished there.

For $7,500, the Bushes bought an 847-square-foot two-bedroom house in the town's first residential development. All the homes were identical, but in a nod to the Texan spirit of individuality, painted different bright hues and canted at varied angles on their lots. Lining the block, the houses looked like dyed eggs in a carton, which earned the neighborhood the nickname "Easter Egg Row." The Bushes' home at 405 East Maple was light blue, and George W. quickly made friends with the boy in the colored egg next door: Randy Roden.

The arrival of the East Coast Bushes in town was not a unique event but part of a postwar trend. "All the Yankees are moving in," the

25,000 locals chuckled to each other. And the Easterners showed up in droves. Dottie and Earle Craig Jr. hailed from Yale and arrived in August, just months after the Bushes. The Liedtke brothers, Bill and Hugh, had both earned degrees from Amherst College and the University of Texas Law School. There were John Ashmun, Toby Hilliard, Hopie and Jimmy Ritchie, among others.

The Texans too were young and ready to work hard to make their fortunes: John Overbey lived across the street. C. Fred Chambers, Steve and Anne Farish, Liz and Tom Fowler, and Betty and Murphy Baxter all became great friends.

So what could have been a lost, slightly lonely adventure of daring (like life in blue-collar Odessa) was transformed into Ivy League on the Prairie, like campus life with kids. If the landscape seemed a little bleak at times, the Easterners could plant trees and grass. They would name their streets after their Ivy League alma maters—Harvard and Princeton. They would raise money for the Midland Community Theater, where folks with a dramatic bent performed. They would upgrade the YMCA from an old grocery store so that all of the kids could race their electric trains there. And just like at school, they would have cliques, because there were so many friends to choose from.

And for a kid, Midland was like an oversized playground. During the Bushes' stint there, the population increased rapidly, yet everybody kept their doors unlocked and their bicycles on the front walk. Unlike other suburban kids in America, George W. never had to see town sprawl as the death of beauty. In Midland, no prized tree would fall victim to the developer's zeal, no lovely wheat field would be mowed to make way for a residential cul de sac. As George W. grew, Midland spread further on all sides, not like a steamroller, but like a gentleman laying down his coat for a lady, the carpet of turf set out over the prairie sand step by step. The paved roads just grew longer as tracks for bike races. At the modern high school stadium, the braver kids could hang by their knees from the highest support beams like bats, and three movie theaters opened downtown that would often show Buck Rogers for nine cents.

George W. would spend his formative years surrounded by prosperity, but to a certain extent, Midland wealth was hidden. Since building a home over one-story makes little sense in a land of heat and sand-storms, the mansions hid their extravagances under their petticoats—squash courts were constructed below ground, swimming pools tucked behind high fences. Since there was no significant body of water nearby, riches couldn't be displayed in schooners and cigarette boats.

Every morning, at the crack of dawn in those early days in Midland, George W.'s dad, still just a salaried employee, would head out the door in his high-water khakis, short sleeve button-down shirt, and madras belt with matching watchband to sell a Reed-Roller bit to a tool pusher out in the Odessa oil fields. That oil field worker would have every reason to buy a Hughes bit instead—after all, it was the industry favorite. But more often than not Bush would take another dollar out of Howard Hughes's tiny pockets, because the driller, who had never left the oil field in his life, would be so charmed by George Bush, he'd spit his tobacco juice onto the rig floor and call it a deal. And that was because George W.'s father could *communicate*.

All the kids in the neighborhood were crazy about Bar, who had a quick wit and knew how to keep score in baseball. She was easy to approach. Many of George W.'s friends remember her out in the park or yard, surrounded by youngsters. "If I had to go talk to somebody about my troubles, it would have been her," said one of George W.'s childhood friends, Terry Throckmorton.

Every Sunday, the Bushes attended church led by Dr. R. Matthew Lynn, a minister who was a recent transplant from Houston. George W.'s father would head over to the First Presbyterian church to teach the junior high kids. Although he had been raised an Episcopalian, he and Bar would worship with different Protestant denominations depending on what town they were in. At First Presbyterian, George was the only man offering instruction at the time, but he would make catechism extremely masculine by illustrating religious principles in that Yankee accent with stories of his time in World War II, all the while looking so clean and cool, as if he had just stepped out of the shower.

They would drive over for "coffee and" at the Craigs', then have hamburger cookouts in the evening, with the kids racing around, dogs barking, and the men (all in their mid-20s) scuffling in touch football scrimmages in the dirt lot near Midland High School. George Bush would always be quarterback. His son would arrive at the games with Bar and then stand there watching, hanging on to Robin's carriage.

Like all slightly idyllic moments in life, those early days in Midland didn't come about completely by chance. The Bushes built their own happiness; they organized their joy. And they were helped by the blessed isolation they found in the oasis in West Texas where global cares never intruded. The town was filled with Texas-style optimists and the Bushes fit right in. Bar's mother had always pined for what she did not have, waited for the moment her ship would come in, and ignored the pleasures of her adoring husband and fine home. Bar learned from that negative example. "You have two choices in life," she would write in her memoir. "You can like what you do, or you can dislike it. I have chosen to like it." Through force of will she had been able to collect a lifetime of "wonderful" moments and "precious" friends.

George Bush, at the time, was still controlled by his desire to win at whatever undertaking he chose. "All my life, I'd worked at channeling my emotions, trying not to let anger or frustration influence my thinking," he explained in his autobiography. His children would rarely see either emotion in him.

George W. too seemed to share his parents' optimistic view from a young age. "Whenever I came home [George W.] greets me and talks a blue streak, sentences disjointed of course but enthusiasm and spirit boundless," George Bush wrote about his son in a letter to a friend when the family was still living in Odessa. "The great thing is that he seems to be very happy wherever he is and he is very good about amusing himself in the small yard we have here . . ."

George took the helm of the first fund-raising drive for the Midland Community Theater when they broke ground on the new stage across from Dennis the Menace Park. In late April 1951, the Midland dads organized and played the First Annual Martini Bowl at the junior high football field complete with mimeographed programs. The Midland Misfits took on the Lubbock Leftovers, and in the karmic conclusion that seemed the essence of West Texas at the time, the game ended in a tie. When a baseball field was needed for Little League, George Bush grabbed a shovel and dug a diamond with the other fathers.

Global concerns did not greatly intrude on this population, most of which had already completed their service during World War II. The summer that the Bushes first moved into their light blue Easter Egg, more than 60,000 North Korean troops marched into South Korea. The only signs of trouble out in Midland were the roar of the B-36 Intercontinental bombers flying overhead.

But underscoring the melody of suburban bliss was the hum of anxiety among the men who worried that their success was just one dry well or government regulation away from bankruptcy. The men had uprooted their loved ones and brought them to this bleak desert outpost for one reason: to make millions of dollars. No one could claim that silver pot, however, without a gamble.

When the Bushes arrived in Midland, prospects were good because of the untapped oil-rich land and demand for fuel during the postwar growth. Still, the competition was fierce. A seven-year drought had sent area farmers scrambling from the cantaloupe fields to the oil business. That meant almost everyone in town was in the same industry—whether as an operator, a leaser, a manager of a pulling unit, or a field supplier. Every Midlander's hide was riding on whether or not they would hit a gusher. Most people knew what it was to have a sudden rush of cash, but they also knew that the unpredictability of the business guaranteed hard times. That was when government stepped in and regulated the industry, such as closing down wells for natural gas emissions.

In late 1950, George Bush too "caught the fever," as he called it, and entered the high-stakes oil game. He resigned from his salaried work with Neil Mallon to start his own company with his neighbor from across the street, John Overbey. That's when he learned the real lessons of West Texas business relations.

If the Bushes had a nickel for every time they said throughout their political lives, "Midland was the kind of place where a handshake was your contract," they could have financed another offshore drilling expedition in Dubai. That statement said a man's word is his word. It evoked down-home trust. But the handshake wasn't just sealing the deal on a milk tab at the corner grocery store or ensuring that the lawnmower a person had his eye on would still be at the yard sale when he got back with his cash. These handshakes had fortunes riding on them. It was as odd as if Wall Street were run on high fives.

Let's say George Bush had sent a landman to the Ector County courthouse for Bush-Overbey to check who owned the mineral rights to a section and dispatched him all the way out to the rancher's place to ask if the family might be willing to sell or farm out that land. If the rancher shook hands on that agreement, it would mean that he wasn't going to just swing his screen door open for Gulf Oil 20 minutes later. The handshake said finder's keepers. It said the one who hustles first wins. It said timing was everything.

Not that George Bush didn't get burned from time to time. His partner, John Overbey, wrote him a letter in 1986 reminiscing about their early days in the business. He recalled one deal in which George Bush haggled with a rancher by phone to buy a piece of land for $150 an acre, and then suggested he and the rancher telegram their agreements to each other. The rancher said no. "My word is my bond,"he assured George Bush.

"You, having been indoctrinated in the oil patch myth that a handshake was all the contract you needed," wrote Overbey, "agreed to forgo the exchange of telegrams." Within days, the rancher sold the land to another buyer for $1.50 more per acre. So much for the bond of the man's word.

But the fact that the Bushes would forever repeat as certainty that in Midland, "Your handshake was your contract," was to say that they, the eternal optimists, liked the myth that West Texas offered. They would tell all of their friends and constituents about that utopia of trust for as long as they lived. From time to time, the town lived up to their dreams.

—

To the kids in the neighborhood, George W.'s father was fun and extremely likeable. While he worked long hours, he was home slightly more often than the other dads. He and Barbara always tried to show the kids some new skill, guide them to some new interest. They seemed to feel that a kid had to do more than just be strong and healthy.

When George Bush began prospecting on wells with John Overbey, he would take George W. and his friend, Randy Roden, out to the fields to watch the drilling. The boys slept in the back of the station wagon, waking up every once in a while to see the big blackened machinery against the long horizon of the Texas fields. It was called sitting on a well. The boys were thrilled.

Some time after George W.'s grandfather was elected to the U.S. Senate in 1952, George Bush took the boys on a field trip to Washington, D.C., to see the heart of government. He took them to the statue of Nathan Hale and the Iwo Jima monuments, regaling them with patriotic talks about the meaning of both places. His misty-eyed love for the principles of the nation was evident. They went to Prescott and Dotty's elegant town house in Georgetown for lunch. Randy had never seen finger bowls before. George W.'s grandfather was grand; he didn't roughhouse with the boys. At the end of the day, they took in a Washington Senators baseball game; that team would later move to Arlington, Texas, and become the Texas Rangers. George W. would become one of the investors.

II

THE PRINCE OF THE PARK

George and Bar adored their kids. Mrs. J. A. Ebeling would remember how on Halloween, her neighbors from across the street at 1412 Ohio Avenue would come by trick or treating: Georgie and the toddler Robin waited on the porch while their mother crouched in the bushes, beaming.

Then the Bushes were blessed again on February 11, 1953—just over three years after Robin was born—by the arrival of John Ellis, whom they called Jeb. A week or two after the birth, George and Bar went on a trip. It was just after they came back, on an early spring day, that Robin woke up listless.

"I'm either going to lie on the bed and look at books," Robin told her mother that morning, "or lie in the grass and watch cars go by." She had always been softer in temperament than George W., but she was a feisty girl too. As her father described her, "She'd fight and cry and play and make her way just like the rest."

Bar was immediately worried. She hurried Robin to their pediatrician, Dr. Dorothy Wyvell, who took a blood sample and told Bar to come back with George that afternoon. Bar had not noticed the small bruises on Robin's legs.

A teary-eyed Dr. Wyvell—and that emotion had been so surprising on her, since she was such a strong woman with her dark, chiseled features—sat George and Bar down for a talk. She gave them two pieces of advice on how to deal with their daughter's very advanced leukemia (for God's sake, George and Bar had never even heard of the disease): Number one, don't tell anyone. Number two, don't treat her. "You should take her home, make life as easy as possible for her, and in three weeks' time, she'll be gone," Dr. Wyvell said. No leukemia patient had ever recovered.

George and Bar didn't heed either part of their doctor's advice, except they did keep the truth from George W. and Robin. Almost immediately, their friends at the country club were discussing the tragedy; their pals Earle and Dottie Craig talked about the disease with Dottie's surgeon father, who was visiting. And as for treating her, the night that Dr. Wyvell gave the Bushes the diagnosis, George called his uncle, Dr. John Walker, a former cancer specialist who was president of New York's Memorial Hospital. He urged them to take Robin to its Sloan-Kettering Institute in New York. "You could never live with yourselves unless you treat her," he said. In fact, instead of three weeks, they won six months more of life with Robin.

From George W.'s six-year-old perspective the comings and goings during that time must have seemed so mysterious. One day, they were a happy family with a brand-new baby brother, and the next morning, they had splintered off in all directions. For six months, he rarely saw his mother. When she did come home briefly a few months after her abrupt departure, she spent all day holding Robin, tickling her, reading to her. His mother would snap at him when he tried to horse around with his sister. His father drifted in and out of his life. His baby brother stayed sometimes with family friends in Midland and sometimes in the Bushes' home with a house-keeper caring for both of them.

When the school year started, George W. was back at Sam Houston Elementary School. His parents had been up in New York with Robin. For some strange reason, all the kids in his class that mid-October day knew that the Bushes were coming to pick him up. He was carrying a Victrola with Bill Sallee to Mr. Bizilo's office when he saw his parents' green Oldsmobile pull into the dirt parking lot. He ran to ask his teacher if he could go see his mother, father, and Robin. She said yes.

When he got outside, he could see them all in the car. But as he got closer, he realized that Robin wasn't in there. His parents let him

into the car and told him that they had something to tell him. Robin
had died, they said, of a disease called leukemia.

But when did you know? he kept asking.

For a while, they had to admit.

But why wouldn't you tell me? He asked so many questions, and
he just couldn't understand why they hadn't said *anything* for all of
that time. It wasn't *fair.*

From the adults' perspective, George and Bar, both then in their
late 20s, had been living a peripatetic double life—between Ganny and
Gampy Walker's beautiful Sutton Place apartment and their Ohio
Avenue house in Texas. Sometimes the oil man Eddie Chiles would
fly Bar and Robin back to New York. Meanwhile, they had a new
baby at home.

In March, just before the Bushes received the news about Robin,
George and John Overbey had merged their company with that of
their friends Hugh and Bill Liedtke to create Zapata oil. (They wanted a name for the company that started with an A or a Z so it wouldn't
get lost in the phone book, and the film *Viva Zapata* was playing
downtown.) Starting the new enterprise hadn't been easy. George
asked his uncle Herbie and his Wall Street banking firm, G.H. Walker
& Co., to help him find investors for his half of the $1 million to buy
8,100 acres in the West Jamieson Field of Coke County for prospecting. So George was either sitting vigil up in New York, or down in his
Midland office worrying, or on his knees praying at the First
Presbyterian church in the early morning hours with Dr. Lynn a pew
behind him, begging God's grace too.

And sometimes, Robin looked so well. "Where's the little girl who
was so sick?" the folks at the bank had asked George when he stopped
by with her one day. He stood there looking down at the top of his
daughter's blond head, and she was radiant. No one could have known
that if her platelets were low enough, she could just start bleeding and
they wouldn't know when she would stop; that her father was even
afraid to help her blow her nose because that could set it off; that she had
spent parts of her days in an oxygen tent; that he had stood watching the
IV line of blood running into her veins until he couldn't take it anymore
and had to excuse himself to use the bathroom (Bar had joked that
Robin would think her daddy had the weakest bladder in the world).

They couldn't have known that she would die a few months from then, on October 11, after the New York doctors had tried desperately to close the holes in her stomach, with her devastated mother by her side and the pictures of the two brothers she called supermen taped to her headboard. That a few days after, Dotty Bush and the Bushes' friend from Yale, Lud Ashley, would bury her in the plot her grandfather bought her in Greenwich alongside all the imposing mausoleums. He had planted a beautiful hedge, a tree, and a bush there—the latter to make her feel at home—to set it off as the resting place of a gentle little girl.

George and Bar tried to move right on with life; in fact they played golf with Bar's father in Rye the day after Robin died.

They had been so strong through the ordeal, but at different times. Ashley would visit Sloan-Kettering as often as possible, even stopping by at 2:00 in the morning after a night on the town, yet he never saw Bar cry during the hospital stays. That was her rule, no crying in the room so that Robin wouldn't be frightened. Then George was a rock afterward, coaxing Bar to visit with her friends, holding her while she sobbed in the night.

But one of the odd things about political life was how this wrenchingly vivid time in the Bushes' life was edited over the years—not to exactly avoid the pain of the period—but to excise the freakishness that is part of grief. So that when Bar later told about the experience in her quick biography upon entering the White House, and then penned it herself in her autobiography, she didn't include the details that seemed so piercing in her 1988 *Texas Monthly* account of Robin's death: that she had always suffered from airsickness but hadn't gotten nauseated when she took Robin to New York, and she never would have that discomfort again; that during the following June, she and George had gone for checkups since they both were sure they were suffering some major physical ailment.

"At least it wasn't your firstborn and a boy at that," one grieving Midlander told Bar when she returned to town after the death. She would remember that awful comment for decades, but the rest of their friends in town were superb—donating blood during Robin's illness to replace the pints she required. They came in droves to pay their respects. Only a month after Robin died, the women at the Midland

Service League appointed Bar to serve on a committee to find a location for the "Little Shop," a store to raise money for their good works. She hadn't been much of a ladies' craft type in the past. As Dottie Craig said, when Bar was assigned earlier to sew baby clothes for newborns at the hospital, "I don't think she was much of the layette type." But there was wisdom in the girls getting her involved in one of those projects, since she threw herself into the task for a year. It was during this time that 28-year-old Bar's hair began turning gray.

But mainly, Bar had the boys. She was going to love the heck out of them, make up for those lost months.

George W.'s irreverent seven-year-old perspective on the tragedy helped ease George and Bar's pain. She remembers his asking her which way Robin had been buried. "What difference would it make?" Bar asked.

He had just learned about the earth's rotation, he told her. "One way she'd be spinning around like this"—he demonstrated— "and one way like this."

Another time the family had gone to a football game. George suddenly blurted out, "I wish I were Robin." All of the adults nearby shifted uncomfortably.

"Why do you wish you were Robin?" George asked his son.

"I bet she can see the game better from up there than we can here," he said.

But George W.'s close childhood friend, Randy Roden, remembers the more anguished side too. He was sleeping over at the Bushes one night not long after Robin died when George W. woke up with nightmares. Bar came in to comfort him. "[The death] was a sad and disturbing thing in my life as a child," said Randy. "It was devastating for the Bushes. I'm sure I knew that from overhearing my parents and other adults talking. I'm sure I heard them say, 'Can you imagine? How horrible!'"

Even at the time Randy noticed that George W. became more attentive and concerned about his mother. "You would naturally say to the oldest son, 'Watch out for your little sister,'" Randy said. "Nobody's trying to do anything to him. But if it's your job to watch out for your little sister and she dies, then maybe you feel like you didn't do such a good job. Nobody ever told you that, but certainly it would affect your world view in terms of how easy it is to protect people from things. He probably felt some need to protect his mother after that. You know, you don't want to lose your mother after everything else. You wouldn't want it to be repeated."

One sunny day, less than a year after Robin's death, Bar broke that spell. With the windows open and the curtains blowing in the breeze, she heard young George telling his pal he couldn't go play. "I have to be with my mother—she's so unhappy," he said. That's when she realized that she had to let him be a child.

Neil would be born a year and a half after Robin's death, on January 22, 1955. Then Marvin arrived on October 22, 1956. The household was full of boys, but hanging over them, literally, was the portrait of Robin that Dotty Bush had given the family, a Rubenesque painting of the young angel. George W.'s friend Terry Throckmorton eventually gathered the courage to ask who the little girl was in the picture in the living room. "That's my sister who died," George W. told him.

In a letter to his mother a few years after his daughter's passing, George Bush acknowledged the pressure that portrait presented: "I sometimes wonder whether it is fair to our boys and to our friends to 'fly-high' that portrait of Robin which I love so much; but here selfishness takes over because every time I sit at our table with just our candlelight, I somehow can't help but glance at this picture you gave us and enjoy a renewed physical sensation of closeness to a loved one."

—

In the mid-fifties, the family moved to a custom-built house on 2703 Sentinel Avenue. George W. could walk through the den and out the back door, past the swimming pool and two-car garage to a child's version of heaven: a gently undulating expanse of park, with the grass clipped to perfect ballplaying length. (Their collie, Mark, had the run of the place for a few years—until he was mysteriously dognapped.) McCall Park was vast enough that you couldn't quite make out the basketball hoops on the other side, but small enough that any parent would be able to spot their child dashing across on little legs. A small crop of trees offered oasis. When the rainstorms came in the spring, the field would become a four-foot–deep pond, and thousands of frogs would arrive to screech through the night. The boys who had BB guns raced out for shooting practice. Most boys would stuff firecrackers in them. Said Terry Throckmorton, "It was gruesome."

Other days you could stand in the park and see a sandstorm approaching like a brown tidal wave. The hardware store sold gas masks for protection but the kids would just race through, then earn dimes for sweeping up after.

The Bushes lived in this low-slung ranch house when George W. was between the ages of 9 and 13 and played baseball for the Midland Central Little League Cubs on the diamond just visible out the den window. He played pickup ball every other available moment with Terry, Kelly, Dick McFarland, and the O'Neill brothers—and all of the kids ran in and out of the Bushes' for glasses of water.

Boys with sports at the center of their lives operate on the basis of a simple hierarchy: If you are well coordinated and not a hothead about losing, you are a star. If you are gawky or a baby, you are out of the loop. All of the good athletes run together. If you are on a Little League team, you care about winning. If you are playing hotbox in the backyard, you care about grace and speed. If you are in school, you care about recess.

George W. played sandlot football in those elementary school years. Even decades later, when his father was head of the CIA and Jack Hanks and Randy Roden were lawyers in Washington, they would get together and George W. would reminisce about what a great team that was—as if it were Knute Rockne and Notre Dame. He liked to romanticize those times.

During the spring, the boys at Sam Houston showed up early to play first-come, first-served baseball. George W. always made sure he nabbed his fair share of the "flies" and "skinners" that Principal Bizilo, in shirt and tie, batted out to the field of students. George W. was scrappy. He was just a pleasant, aggressive person, as his third grade teacher Austine Crosby recalled. He had a look in his eye, as if he understood what was going on. His friends knew he had a kind of smart-aleck streak.

Then there is the semiotics of field positions. For most of his Little League career, George W. was the catcher. He wasn't very tall for his age but he was stocky—even kind of pudgy; he didn't get lean until late high school. He was also always very aggressive. A catcher is involved in every play for almost every game. George W. was fearless, if not the most talented catcher.

George W.'s father certainly taught him to love baseball. As a toddler, George W. would take in the games at Yale. In Midland, his father played catch with him in their backyard, and he even coached the Cubs in what is now a parking lot of Angel Stadium when George W. and Joey O'Neill played on the team their first year. Mrs. O'Neill remembered the boys coming home with their baseball caps sticking to their heads because of scabs. They had been trying to emulate Mr. Bush, who could go out for a fly ball, drop his head forward, and make the catch behind his back down at belt level. George W. would later recall one of the most poignant moments of his life: when his father told him that he was good enough that his father no longer had to hold back on throws. And baseball confirmed their bond. "Georgie aggravates the hell out of me at times (I am sure I do the same to him)," wrote George Bush to his father-in-law, "but then at times I am so proud of him I could die. He is out for Little League—so eager."

Bar had kept score for her husband's games at Yale, right through her pregnancy with George W., when the coach moved her behind the screen at home plate for her safety. She now kept the tallies for her son. Even when he was governor, she still treasured a collection of scorecards from every game he played in Little League. George W. couldn't help but notice his mother's keen interest.

When George W. wasn't actually on the playing fields, his father would set out shoeboxes of baseball cards and shoot trivia questions at his son and his friends. What George W. lacked in real academic passion, he made up for in his skill at memorizing stats. He and Terry, whose father, Bob Throckmorton, was head of Midland Little League, dreamed of playing in the majors. They collected Coke bottles for the money to buy Topps cards. George W. owned valuable Yankee cards, but was a passionate fan of the New York Giants. He came up with the idea of pasting the Topps cards to postcards and mailing them to the players in spring training to get their autographs. George W. already knew how to sweet talk.

The notes would say things like, "Dear Mister, I sure do hope you make the All-Star Team this year," when the player had never been among the top 50 in the league.

Every day after school, he and Terry would race home to see who had sent their cards back. The project was secret; they would never tell the other kids at school.

Terry and George W. played triple headers of nine-inning hallway baseball at the Bushes, using a Ping-Pong ball and paddle. They played swimming pool baseball with a golf ball. Some days they would just sit on George W.'s bunk beds, beneath the display of pennants, and rattle off nine-inning imaginary games against each other, using the stats on the backs of the cards.

"There's no way you could get Mickey Mantle out," they'd taunt each other.

"You're a has-been pitcher."

The school fed their passion too. During the World Series, they could watch the games during rest period. Decades later, when George W. was on the campaign trail to become the president of the United States, he would be asked by a child what his favorite book had been in his youth. He couldn't remember a single title. The only books Terry could remember their reading was a mystery series that George W. had come across somewhere. The setting was the world of baseball.

For most kids, this single-minded devotion to a sport might suggest a sort of frivolousness, that George W. only cared about games. But as with so many aspects of his life, he would turn his diversion into a vehicle for adult success. In the late 1980s, when he appeared on a sports talk show to promote the Texas Rangers, the major league team that he then partly owned, he was challenged to name the starting lineup of the New York Giants in 1954. After only a slight pause, he reeled off the whole list. The new boss of the Rangers showed himself to be a star, because of the time he'd spent with Terry Throckmorton, memorizing the backs of Topps cards.

—

From age seven, George W. trekked to Camp Longhorn on Inks Lake in the Hill Country outside of Austin each July to join 500 other boys and girls in what was essentially a month-long recess. Former University of Texas swim coach Tex Robertson, who then was in his mid-40s, founded Longhorn on the simple belief that nothing was more glorious than swimming (he had broken Johnny Weissmuller's record in college) and no praise was sweeter than that emanating from a camp counselor to a kid: *Attawaytogo!* The style was no frills—the place was built of World War II surplus. In the waning days of the session, each kid would be expected to swim a mile course—out to a buoy and back—which George W. did with ease. He even made campfire boy—kind of a best boy of the day. Doro and Neil became Attawaytogo kids too.

George Bush loved the camp so much, he brought the slogan back home to Midland—*Attawaytogo!* he would say around the house. On parents' day, he convinced the adults to climb on a launch to watch the kids' sailboat race. The launch sank. All the parents climbed out, soaked and laughing.

The family never coddled the kids at sports. One summer, George Bush's younger brother William—or "Bucky" as he was called—convinced his high school buddy Fay Vincent, who later became commissioner of baseball, to go with him to work on one of his brother George's oil rigs down in West Texas before they started college. Fay thought it was a great idea. They could get in shape for football season and come back ready to kill bear. George Bush didn't want anyone to know that the new roustabouts were relatives, so he just plugged them into regular shifts without saying a word. Unfortunately, the guys on the crews got the idea when Bucky's team on the overnight shift was sacked because they hit clay and no one tried to fix the drill but instead sat idle until dawn. Only Bucky got hired back.

That's how Fay and Bucky came to be in West Texas. The telling moment for Fay was when George W.'s Little League umpire couldn't make it to a game and Bucky—six foot five and 280 pounds in high school—got called to help. You might think he would have gone easy on his nephew, George W., who Vincent remembers as being extremely mature for his age. But instead, when George W. got up to bat: "Strriiiiike Ooooone," Bucky yelled. Then another swing. "Striiiiiiiiiiike Twoooooooo." Then, would he really do it? "Striiiiiiiiiike Threeeee. You're OUUUUT!"

"I'm sorry, George," was Bucky's only concession to family ties.

The Bushes could be elegant and objective about sports, because there would always be another game. There would be so many games over their lifetimes. Fay remembered coming home with Bucky to the Bushes' house after a double date with two local girls. They were horsing around, playing a ferocious game of carpet bowling in the living room, when George and Bar heard them on the intercom and came in to join the fun, wearing their pajamas.

But their pleasure in games didn't overshadow their passion for winning. As one friend who had watched vicious games of family Ping-Pong said, "I was surprised there still was a ball."

That competitive spirit began with George Bush's mother, Dotty. She was a great athlete, famous for once hitting a home run, rounding the bases, and then unceremoniously heading off to give birth to George Bush's brother, Prescott. At Walker's Point in Kennebunkport, all of the grandchildren would flock to her house to see her, despite any trepidation they might feel about encountering their stern grandfather. In a Mother's Day tribute that George Bush wrote to the family matriarch in the *Greenwich Time* newspaper in 1985, he remembers the many games she taught him as a boy—solitaire, bridge, anagrams, Scrabble, charades, golf, swimming, baseball, tennis, tiddlywinks.

Still, she hated athletic boasts. One day young George Bush came home from a tennis match and said he was off his game.

"Don't be ridiculous," his mother snapped. "You don't have a game."

George W. idolized his grandmother, and she adored him back. Once when comparing his grandmother to his mother for his mother's biographer, Donnie Radcliffe, he said, "My grandmother is an unbelievable person, one of the most gentle, kind souls I've ever met."

George Bush was aware of that tender side when he wrote a letter to his mother when the family was still in Midland after Robin's death. He bemoaned the missing softening agent in the family: "We need a doll house to stand firm against our forts and rackets and thousand baseball cards. We need a cut-out star to play alone while the others battle to see who's 'family champ' . . .

"We need a legitimate Christmas angel—one who doesn't have cuffs beneath the dress . . .

"We need someone who's afraid of frogs.

"We need someone to cry when I get mad—not argue . . .

"We need a girl . . .

"We had one once—she'd fight and cry and play and make her way just like the rest. But there was about her a certain softness . . .

"Like them, she'd climb in to sleep with me, but somehow she'd fit.

"She didn't boot and flip and wake me up with pug nose and mischievous eyes a challenging quarter-inch from my sleeping face . . .

"Her peace made me feel strong, and so very important."

—

Even at that young age, George W. was noticed for who his parents were—not treated differently exactly, not pampered, but noticed. George and Bar were PTA cochairmen and that set them apart slightly. They were more involved than the parents who visited the geography classes at Sam Houston Elementary School to tell their tales of travels in the oil business. The Bushes had won fame by converting a football locker room, which former Abilene Christian University All-American Tugboat Jones had built and then abandoned, into the first interschool library. The Bushes were heroes for that.

So their status made the situation somewhat tougher for Principal John Bizilo when the fourth grade teacher, Mrs. Frances Childress, led young George W. down the outdoor walkway to his office and presented the sheepish boy for paddling. Bizilo had made the rule that teachers couldn't paddle because they might go at it too hard. "What has he done?" Bizilo asked Mrs. Childress.

"Just *look* at him."

George W. had etched sideburns, a mustache and a goatee on his face with ball-point ink. "I told him that I was his principal and that it was my responsibility to see that there weren't any disturbances created in the classroom," said Bizilo. "Since he created a disturbance he was wrong. So, anyway, he accepted it." Then, after the paddling, Bizilo sent George W. off to the washroom to scrub at the nearly indelible ink.

His mother would probably be able to detect the traces when he returned from school that day. As far as anyone could fathom, George W. would have taken her chastisements hard. He was a pretty sensitive kid, according to his friends. At that age, he would get teary before he would ever give her any back talk.

His parents would never lean on him too hard to be something more than he could be, but they were full of expectations. They assumed he would be well behaved. They knew he would be bright. It was only a matter of time, they were sure, before he grew up to be a success. They were as certain of that ultimate validation as he was that they were the best parents a boy could ever have.

—

In the mid-'50s, when George Herbert Walker Bush was just past the threshold of 30 and Zapata was thriving if not booming, he was kicking back after a little badminton game with Curtis Inman, an oil operator. He uttered the words: "I want to be in politics." What was his dream? The governorship? The presidency?

No, the presidency was not what George Bush had his eye on. "I want to be an ambassador," he said.

The Bush family, which traditionally had been a clan of bankers and industrialists with a strong civic streak, entered the political arena in the middle of the century. Prescott Bush had been running the Greenwich town meetings for 20 years, not to mention his civic duties. In 1950, at age 55, he ran for the senate in Connecticut as a fiscal conservative bent on reigning in the New Deal Democrats. He lost by a squeaker to incumbent William Benton. But two years later, he was elected to fill the state's other seat when Senator Brien McMahon died. That same year, the Midland's Young Republicans Club convened for the first time in that staunchly Democratic district—state, for that matter. George Bush helped raise funds for Eisenhower's presidential landslides as Midland County chairman of the campaign.

Only two weeks after the first anniversary of Robin's death—and that day was noticeable, since Bar began the tradition of spending those 24 hours in somber reflection; she would later say she was even sanctimonious about it—George spun off an ocean drilling venture, Zapata Off-Shore, worth $4.5 million. The Bushes were wealthy enough before. After all, the Sentinel house had been custom-built, with one of the few swimming pools in town; they belonged to the country club; and they could afford to spend August every other year in Maine. But this was the beginning of big money, and big money meant one thing to George Bush—not a flashy car (the cigarette boat would come later), and not a license to squash his Andover and Yale friends when they met for reunions. No, big money only meant that George Bush could follow the path that his father, then Andover and Yale had laid out for him. It meant he could enter politics.

No politician, his father Prescott had warned, should be elected to office penniless. That meant he *needed* the election victory too much, because he needed a paycheck. That led to corruption, compromise. George Bush had hoped to make money fast enough to have good fighting years in him for the political trenches. By the end of 1954, Zapata had 71 wells producing an average of 1,250 barrels a day.

The big payoff for Zapata Off-Shore came three weeks after the company was founded, when George Bush signed a contract with a gruff but kooky engineer, R.G. LeTourneau, from Vicksburg, Mississippi, to build the *Scorpion*, a three-legged drill that could plumb new depths in the wild new world of offshore drilling. The plan was for LeTourneau to build the drill on his own—with an advance of $400,000 from Zapata. If the rig failed, LeTourneau had to pay back the cash; if it worked, he would get more than $1 million paid over three years and 38,000 shares of Zapata Off-Shore. By 1956, the *Scorpion*—the industry's first electric self-elevating jackup drilling platform—was ready to roll in Galveston.

On the morning of March 20, 1956 Zapata president George Bush and his ten-year-old son, George W., stood on the deck of the nine-million-pound steel barge to officiate at the launching ceremonies. They were both wearing white carnations with the Zapata ribbon hanging down. Unfortunately, that particular rig sucked saltwater into its gear boxes. But it was soon reconfigured and the *Scorpion*, and then the *Vinegarroon*, and then the Maverick brought the oil industry into the future. It also made George Bush wealthy. That year, the Junior Chamber of Commerce named George W.'s father one of the "Five Outstanding Young Men of Texas."

By the end of the decade, George Bush had revised his ambitions. Now instead of lounging after badminton with Curtis Inman and spinning dreams of an ambassadorial posting, he was drinking sake with his friend C. Fred Chambers when he officially declared his hopes for elected office. His plan was to be a senator like his father. He had won freedom from financial worry—enough money in fact that he could have fun investing in Broadway musicals. He had achieved in all the ways one could hope to: in battle, in civic duty, even in the hierarchy of his church as an elder.

Oddly enough, for George W.'s own political career, that last year in Midland had been important too: He had been able to spend that crucial tenure at San Jacinto Junior High. He even had run his first campaign—for student council in seventh grade—and won against his Little League team's first baseman.

Now after three years commuting between Midland and Houston, George Bush decided to buy out the Liedtke's interests in Zapata and move his family to Houston to what would become the launch pad for his political life. Baine and Mildred Kerr found a 1.2-acre lot around the corner from their own home, and the Bushes hired an architect to build what George W. later described as a "fancy" place with a pool and a small baseball field.

He started eighth grade at the private Kinkaid school, where the thirteen-year-old immediately demonstrated athletic ability and became a class officer. Social life—mainly in the form of dances at the Shamrock Hotel—was orchestrated by Madora Masterson, a party planner who would put together invitation lists and arrange escorts for the offspring of wealthy Houstonians. The change in tone from Midland was shocking to George W. "One day at Kinkaid a guy walks up to me after practice and says, 'Hey, you want a ride home, Bush?'" he recalled to *Texas Monthly*. "I was waiting for the bus. This was an eighth grader, who might have been fourteen at the time, and he was driving a GTO—in the eighth grade! I remember saying, 'No thanks, man.' It was just a different world."

A girl was finally added to the string of male children with the birth of Dorothy—called Doro—on August 18, 1959. And George Bush started to slip from the daily life of the family into the world of politics. While his wife cared for the brood of five, he traveled three times around the globe, an accomplishment he would later boast about during his early campaigns.

"I had moments where I was jealous of attractive young women, out in a man's world," Bar told her biographer, Donnie Radcliffe. "I would think, 'Well, George is off on a trip doing all these exciting things and I'm sitting home with these absolutely brilliant children, who say one thing a week of interest.'"

Bar held down the fort with steely decisions. "She'd say, 'All right, this is the way we're going to do it or you go to your room,'" Doro would later tell Bar's biographer. "She's understanding, she'd listen to reason, but somebody had to set the guidelines, otherwise there'd be chaos."

She wouldn't wait for George Bush to come home and lay down the law. "I don't think that's any good," the *Washington Post* reported her saying. "I don't think your husband comes home, exhausted from work, and you say, 'Well, go sock Marvin.'"

Still, George W. couldn't fail to notice how laborious his mother's life had become while running the household almost single-handedly. "This was a period, for me," she has said, "of long days and short years; of diapers, runny noses, earaches, more Little League games than you could believe possible, tonsils, and those unscheduled races to the hospital emergency room, Sunday school and church, of hours of urging homework, short chubby arms around your neck and sticky kisses; and experiencing bumpy moments—not many, but a few—of feeling that I'd never, ever be able to have fun again; and coping with the feeling that George Bush, in his excitement of starting a small company and traveling around the world, was having a lot of fun."

Even the eternally optimistic Bar was broken by this period, virtually raising the children alone. While they were financially secure—George Bush was already a millionaire—Bar would make references to this time as being one where she didn't feel they could really afford to enjoy luxuries.

George W., now a teenager, was left sometimes to play proxy for his father and Bar would come to miss him terribly when he eventually went away to school. He was more than just the sharp-witted kid with whom she could trade jokes. He also came to her aid during emotional crises. Once he had to drive his mother to the hospital when she started having a miscarriage, the *Washington Post* reported. George W. comforted her through the pain and sadness, then tried to serve as confidant when he picked her up the next day. His mother remembered him turning to her seriously. "'Don't you think we ought to talk about this before you have more children?'" he asked.

III

THE COMMISSIONER

OF STICKBALL

George W. recalls the day in Houston he first learned that his father's legacy had become his fate. He was walking up the drive to the family's house, when his mother came out to greet him. "Congratulations, son," she said. "You got into Andover." He had been accepted to start in the autumn semester of 1961 as a sophomore.

Phillips Academy at Andover, the all-male preparatory school in Massachusetts, was legendary in the Bush clan as the brine from which his father first rose like Apollo, back in the early 1940s. There, George Bush became captain of the varsity soccer and baseball teams, a deacon at the chapel, and president of the fraternity-like club, the Greeks. When the Japanese bombed Pearl Harbor in the middle of George Bush's senior year, he gilded his legend by vowing to put off Yale and enter the war. His sense of duty was honed at Andover, whose understated motto was *Non Sibi*, not for one's self. That message, as George Bush would say, was "inculcated" into him.

Now, George W. was expected to ship off to test himself against that record book. If George W. understood his parents' desires through their "expectations" of him rather than their demands, then attending Andover was not exactly optional. His father and uncle had attended the school. His cousin Prescott was already enrolled in the class of 1963. Andover would introduce him to the sort of young men who could grow with him as best friends and professional colleagues through his adult years. It would help him springboard into the even more "expected" Bush tradition of attending Yale. But Andover was a more unusual proposition for George W. than it had been for his father. George Bush had merely moved a few hours north of his town of oak and maple trees to another New England hamlet of oak and maple trees. His son, by comparison, had to fly halfway across the country to a state with an entirely different climate and accent.

In the bleak days of a Massachusetts mid-January of 1960, three Andover faculty members had huddled with the admissions director, grading every applicant from 1 to 5. The higher score meant rejection. Once those scores were tallied, three points were automatically knocked off if the student was an Alumni spawn. About one-fifth of the boys were accepted. At Kinkaid, George W. had been a fair student but a true athlete, and class leader as a member of the student government. He made the cut.

Everyone knew Andover was tough. The school was built on Puritanism. A 26-year-old Calvinist named Samuel Phillips Jr. founded this academic Outward Bound—a rigorous institution with a survival-of-the-fittest ethos—in the late 18th century. He had been tormented by the "decay of virtue, public and private" and convinced his father and preacher-uncle John to finance a school where young boys could learn "the great end and real business of living." Paul Revere engraved the Calvinist wisdom, *Finis Origine Pendet,* on the school seal: "The end depends on the beginning." As the galvanizing motto for an elite collection of students who hailed from the wealthier homes of America, and then the far reaches of the globe, that statement could be read over the intervening centuries either innocently or cynically.

The school quickly gained influential supporters. Only nine years after the academy opened, George Washington addressed the student body from horseback. He enrolled his beloved nephew there and covered tuition for his eight grandnephews. Phillips's uncle John, sensing a successful enterprise, started neighboring Phillips Exeter Academy in 1781. Almost 100 years later the blood rivalry between the two institutions sparked when Andover demolished Exeter in their first football match. For the next century and beyond, that competition—like the rivalry between Midland and Odessa—would provide entertainment, foster ambition, and help define the opposing sides. And it would offer George W. a perfect field for his cheerleading personality.

Andover was notoriously tough on its charges. One legend—apocryphal or not—described how, at the turn of the century, the senior class (some 90 students) defied the wishes of the headmaster by attending a circus in the nearby town of Lawrence. When they came back to campus, they found eviction notices nailed to their doors. With a sense of independence that vanished by the early 1960s, the students flouted the headmaster's fury again by taking the train to New Haven and enrolling at Yale.

Headmaster John Kemper, who oversaw the school during George W.'s era, was not so involved in the lives of his students. But still he fretted about how to teach his young men a sense of humanity and public service. A former West Pointer, he was beached by peacetime on the shores of academia. For eleven generations, the Kempers had served in the army, going all the way back to the Pequot Indian War. "I never would have resigned had I known Korea was coming," Kemper once drawled in his affected Harvard accent. "I loved the Army with a passion."

While still a "sand-rat lieutenant," he headed up a school to help enlisted men cram for the West Point exams, and was so successful that West Point pushed him to get a History degree at the height of World War II. In 1942, he received his master's degree from Columbia University. An Andover trustee noticed Kemper's organizational abilities when he was commissioned by the Army to coordinate a group of historians to tell the story of the war. The trustees of Andover tapped him in 1947, and by that time, he was ready to serve.

Now, in 1961, he was a recent widower—having lost his beloved wife, Sylvia, to cancer at the beginning of the school year—and battling the already insidious careerism in the teenage minds he helped mold. Every boy was obsessed with college—would he get his first choice? Kemper worried over this trend. "There's just not enough emphasis on the old dream of simply being a good father, a good man," he lamented. He fretted over how to teach his young men a sense of humanity and public service—a goal George Bush would clearly appreciate.

"The spirit of man is neglected in this school," Emory Basford, the veteran chairman of the English department griped to *Time* in a 1962 cover story that featured Andover. "These boys admire managerial things. Even when they collect clothes for the poor, it is done as a study in organization. . . . This has become a strange, bewildering, killing place."

When George W. arrived on campus in the fall of 1961, that obsessive academic competition must have been the most bewildering of all Andover's new aspects. The lack of female companions must have run a close second; the nearby Abbot school for girls provided some consolation, but the coeds were not even allowed to exchange letters with the Andover boys. Finally, the New England winters provided a chilly welcome to a boy from the Texas plains.

George W. was accustomed to being separated from his parents for at least brief stints—work often carried his father far from home, and even his mother occasionally left the kids in the care of housekeepers, for example, when she and George moved to Houston months early to oversee the construction of their house. But when George W. left for Andover, Bar missed her son terribly, and wept when she received his first letter, which began: "Last weekend was the greatest in my life . . ." George W. loved his siblings, but he would not have anguished over the separation, since they were not his peers: The next oldest, Jeb, was just eight when George W. started prep school.

The personality and temperament of the typical New Englander would not have been unfamiliar to George W., since he understood the New England character from visiting his grandparents in Greenwich and in Rye, and from spending stretches of every other summer with the whole clan in Kennebunkport.

But the competitiveness in the classroom—not on the baseball diamond—was a completely new experience for him. "Without a great deal of effort, George had probably done pretty well at San Jacinto," said Randy Roden, who applied to Andover at the encouragement of the Bushes and started at the same time as George W. "[At Andover], you were not automatically going to be the star of the class just because you could read. That was kind of a shock."

There in the rolling hills of Massachusetts, George W. was competing not just against the other boys but against the standards of his old man. The pressure was internal. "Dad never tried to impose his will on us," he told a reporter. "He never tried to make me the lead halfback on the football team. He was careful about that." But his father's glow was so strong at Andover, he became a trustee during George W.'s junior year. His three-year term would be extended to lifetime office. When George W. went back to an Andover reunion as an adult he confessed to having been terrified of failure, since this was the institution so beloved by his father. "It's a natural challenge that George would have found it terribly difficult to live up to his father's achievements," Randy said. "That was the task—just [because of] the magnitude of his father's achievements and also of the myth and the lore that goes with it."

—

Randy remembered all the faculty being so happy to see big George that first day of school. He and Bar drove George W. and Randy around the enormous campus, introduced them to old teachers, and took them to dinner.

George W. was assigned to a single in Bancroft Hall. There were still old coal bins in the basement where the students of a past era left briquettes to pay their tuition. The dorm was maintained, with an emphasis on silence, by Mr. Thomas Mikula, a math teacher. "He was a real quiet man," remembered fellow dorm mate Peter Schandorff, who went on to Harvard and became a long-time friend of Al Gore. "He wanted it to be real quiet."

Each day at Andover began promptly with breakfast at 7:05 in the Commons, followed by 7:50 compulsory chapel led by Dean G. Grenville Benedict. "G-Squared," as the boys nicknamed him, was a ubiquitous figure in their lives. He ran the assemblies, handled the discipline problems, and even served as the college counselor. "He was sort of like Adlai Stevenson with an attitude," Schandorff remembered. His manner was distant and he spoke a cryptic, dignified dialect all his own. "Abjure the hypotenuse," he would say, which meant don't walk on the grass. At prom time, he warned the boys to "avoid the vernal urge." No boy would dream of crossing him. If he told you to go to the library, you went. His tone left no room for talking back.

After chapel all 847 boys would lope off to classes in their jacket-and-tie ensembles, a jumble of tweed and madras jackets, Shetland sweaters, oxford shirts, striped ties, flannels, white socks, loafers and Wejuns. A boy who wore black sneakers stood out. Lunch was followed by athletics and more classes before it was back to the Commons, tray in hand, for supper. After eating, the guys spun off to various clubs, bands, and campus publications. In his sophomore year, George W. joined Spanish Club as well as Phillips Society, an organization that took on good works in town.

After the clubs had dispersed for the night, every boy faced a minimum of five hours studying. Any extracurricular activity after dinner, even a game of backgammon or dorm-room chitchat, meant early morning hours hunched over a book, with the slight nausea of exhaustion. Officially, it was lights off at 10:00. There were no radios for students who weren't seniors and no television for anyone. Some of the dorms had working fireplaces, but it could be brutally cold at night: After hours, the school turned the steam radiators off in some dorms. In others they rattled and hissed like dragons.

Andover could be a steely place: One of the first things each kid did after they registered at George Washington Hall was go to the infirmary for a physical fitness test of climbing and jumping. Then the nurse examined each student's skin and drew a circle around the dotted smiley face that best represented his acne curse. There was the fire drill to learn: Outside each dorm window hung a hook on a rope. The faculty gathered the boys at an old abandoned building. Each kid had to climb up a ladder three stories high and shimmy down a cable. During junior year, every guy was put through the paces to win a "silver." Each student had his hands strapped together and was thrown into the pool, where he remained for 35 minutes while faculty watched him sink or swim.

—

In that kind of forbidding environment, George W. fell back on his wit to survive—that's what earned him the nickname "Lip." He had inherited a rapier tongue from his mother, and continued to hone it with his siblings. "We tried to be disrespectful on a regular basis," joked brother Marvin later. With his father, George W. could be bratty, Randy Roden remembered, but he would never be seriously disrespectful; he would joke hard to get his point across, to communicate what he wanted to his father without really saying it.

The other Andover students learned to fear his ribbing. They only made fun of George W.'s twang for one day, a classmate recalled, before he put them in their place out at the ice-cream truck after dinner.

Aside from the twang, George W. didn't seem much like the usual Texas transplants to Andover. Tom Seligson, a classmate, recalled that Texans usually had a lot of money and their own refrigerators in their rooms. But George W. never seemed to flaunt his wealth. In fact, he exhibited a certain openness, an unselfconscious friendliness that seemed to be a regional trait.

He could be touchy when he wasn't up for joking around. But he wasn't socially cruel like the other guys could be. He could be part of the in group but he wouldn't resort to the snobbish meanness that sometimes characterized it. That was a family violation. "The biggest crime we could commit growing up was to be malicious toward someone else—finding a vulnerable spot, make fun," Marvin would say.

As in all high schools, the student body fractured into cliques. Jocks and academic achievers ruled. George W.'s athletic clique was among the in-crowds—after all, this was a school that spent $3,000 a year on athletic tape. But there were also grungy kids with dirt under their fingernails who loitered in the art center, and peacock dressers with charge accounts at the Andover shop. There were activist kids just wading into the Civil Rights protests, and other students who endured four lonely years, suffering the rough sports and hiding out in their dorm rooms.

None of the cliques was racially diverse. The color barrier had been broken at Andover in the late 1800s when the school accepted its first black students, but George W.'s class only included a couple of black kids. That lack of diversity may explain why the civil rights struggles going on at the time barely registered with his classmates. In the school paper, the *Phillipian*, a student reporter described an "eye-opening" talk by a Mississippi attorney in 1962, and wrote the piece with a telling number of exclamation points: "The ratio of dollars spent for educating a white child to the amount spent for a colored child is four to one!"

If there were any group George W. didn't really get along with it would have been the peaceniks, said his classmates; or he might have gotten ticked off by the "green book-bag crowd" that would arrive early to pump the Benner House jukebox full of quarters on weekend nights so the *Brandenburg Concerti* would blast through the campus burger joint until curfew.

But George W. could also be a peacemaker. Friend John Kidde remembered that George W. would sometimes ignore dining room social rules and sit down casually at a table with boys that his own group would ordinarily have snubbed. But not George. He'd make some joke, usually at a teacher's expense, and then say, "Don't you think that's true, Herbie?" And Herbie would look up, hardly believing that he was being spoken to and say, "Yeah, I think that's right." And before you knew it, they'd all be talking. George W.'s friends could be nice, but they weren't that outgoing. For the most part, George W. was an easy guy to like.

Everyone on campus had nicknames: "Jock," "Moondoggie," "Joe Traveler." One student, Tira Chai Kambhu, critiqued the heterogeneity of the Andover population by listing his nicknames as "Gross Foreigner," "Cherokee," "Yellow," and "Chink."

George W. bonded early with Clay "Opie" Johnson, a quiet, gentlemanly kid from Fort Worth who could shoot from outside. George W.'s other big buddy was John "Ho-Dad" Kidde, a California surfer type who was blond, funny, and imperturbable. Don "Vermin" Vermeil was a joker too; that's why George W. picked him to room with his junior year. They were assigned to the worst space in the dorm—a 10-foot by 15-foot box off a six-foot-long hall. They made each other laugh constantly. Another friend, Logan Everett Sawyer, was a better athlete than the rest of them—a kindly jock with no nickname more catchy than "L. E." Then there was quiet Rob Dieter, who barely registered on his classmates' radar, but who would go on to room with George W. during their four years at Yale.

George W. was a near-jock. He was too funny and sharp to earn the full-fledged title. And frankly, he wasn't skilled enough on the field. He liked being onstage, being a cutup. "Whether he was secure or not secure was not clear," said Tory Peterson. "He was a little bit of a chameleon. He picked up some of Tommy [Eastland]'s stuff but it didn't fit him."

George W. didn't appear to come from circumstances grander than those of his classmates. A kid's background was hard to determine at Andover. Unlike life at the Kinkaid school, where a kid could drive his wealth, the Weejuns and madras jackets were an equalizer of sorts. Schandorff recalled that the son of the prime minister of Somalia, for instance, prepped at the school to hone his English before heading off to a New England college. He had 16 wives at home, but only a few lucky boys knew that fact or got to hear his stories of feminine wiles.

But there definitely was an aura of politics on a grand scale about George W.'s clan. During the school year, his fellow Andover students would be walking up to Bancroft and see the gleaming black limousine parked out front with its senatorial license plates, which read Connecticut 2. Grampy was visiting.

George W. invited friends to the big family Thanksgiving at his Grandfather Prescott's home in Greenwich, Connecticut. The talk, at least in that first year of Andover when Prescott was still in the senate, would be politics. Not policy or theory, but personalities: Who was making work hard for Senator Bush and who was easing a negotiation. In conversation, the president wasn't some august figure but simply another player in the game, John Kidde remembered. And George W. could keep right up. He seemed to know who the Washington players were.

—

No one could be quite sure when the sarcasm started at Andover. But by the spring of 1962, in George W.'s sophomore year, a new form of negative chic was so entrenched on prep-school campuses, even old codger publications like *Life* were commenting on it. "Negoism," some guy at Exeter dubbed the perspective—a pernicious, infectious form of pessimism.

Some of George W.'s classmates thought Tom Eastland was the one to first introduce the evil Esperanto to Andover, and helped spread it to all of the cliques. Eastland was always so facetious. Before he got to Andover, he had done a few years at the Fay School, which was rumored to be even more oppressive. As a result he had developed an early and abiding aversion to the Establishment. He eventually got kicked out for lighting up a cigarette in his Andover dorm room during a week when the faculty was still mulling over what to do about his "underachieving."

But before he got expelled, he taught the class of 1964 its lingua franca. Say it was a rainy day and a kid walked into the Commons and skidded onto his back on the slick floor, Eastland would turn to the next guy in line, and sneer, "Oh, he's quite the guy!" Or say a kid got up at chapel to announce the tribulations of the chess club, and he was all enthusiasm and stutters. An Eastland follower might lean forward and whisper into the ear of the smirking friend in front of him, "He's really *in* there." Which meant he was so far *out* from the ninth ring of coolness. The tone caught on fast, and it even had foreign language derivatives. *Pas si jolie,* they said of Mr. Bill Markey, the young French teacher.

The new lingo had a certain edge, yet it certainly wasn't powerful enough to get the students into any disciplinary trouble. It was a safe outlet of angst. But the attitude's even more satisfying aspect was that, if all of life at Andover was approached with sarcasm, then no one would know when a boy really cared. If the boy injected a "Quite the guy" about some other poor sop, he could be sure, for that moment, that everyone was chuckling too hard to focus on his own degree of teenage gaucheness. The sarcasm gave the boys the liberating illusion that they didn't mind the harshness of Andover a bit.

That was the dragon waiting to sark (the verb derived from sarcasm) George W. when he arrived, all Texas two-talk, in 1961.

"Look at the snow!" he yelled. It was late October. A large storm was just blowing in and he ran outside. He had never seen the stuff. "Look at the snow!" he shouted with childish giddiness as his purposefully jaded classmates looked on. It was like a mouse dancing the cha-cha in front of a bored cat. The *Life* article noted how an expression of simple joy could be grounds for ridicule. "If I ever said, 'Gee! It's a nice spring day!'" one Andover student told the reporter, "I'd be laughed right out of the quadrangle."

But here was Bush, tongue out, racing around. "George was unembarrassable," noted one of his classmates, Sam Allis.

George W. seemed the polar opposite to all the *Life* article was exposing. "This is a world of madness," one student leader at a prep school lamented to the reporter. "There are no values to depend upon." An athlete at the Hill School exclaimed: "Take one good look at the world and you'll see there's no interest in decency, only in power and in pushing the other guy around."

Life suggested that the prep school population—the leaders of the next generation—were rejecting the values of their parents. Of course, the magazine could have been just stirring the pot—giving parents something to rattle their sleep after they had leafed through blissful candids of the Kennedy clan. How's that for a scare story? Those brats who you are paying $1,800 dollars a year to educate don't believe in you or your stinking religion or your rotten sense of right and wrong. They lie awake in their beds in their ivy-covered dorms, cradling *The Catcher in the Rye* and thinking about how corrupt you are.

But that reporter even got an anonymous Andover coach, a ten-year veteran of the school to assess the situation: "They're running scared. More than anything else they are afraid of making a mistake with their lives and they feel threatened on all sides by mistakes they're sure they'll make."

One reason for the students' anxiety was probably the nature of prep school itself. For the years that their son is enrolled, parents resign the daily tussles and pleasures of raising him to a resident faculty of 101 strangers. Without that diurnal contact, a parent's role becomes essentially like a holiday cruise director's—"We're going to meet in Palm Beach for Christmas break."

Since high school students are not the most generous conversationalists, mothers and fathers come off as headline seekers: "Did you make varsity?" "How are the grades?" "Did you hear from Harvard yet?" No wonder Andover felt like a pressure cooker.

Then there was the fact that a boy's very admittance into the school implied that the administration expected him to be a leader. The idea of going to Harvard or Yale was bred into him. But the other fear of failure came from the new levels of competition in the nation's preparatory schools.

George Bush had excelled at Andover and at Yale, and George W. hoped to live up to his standards, but a case could be made that he was competing on a far more challenging course. All the academic hurdles at those institutions had shifted upward between those two generations. After World War II, almost every young American hoped to get a college diploma, and many more applicants could afford higher education because of the G.I. Bill. The number of college applications swelled. Unless the preparatory schools could produce students with high test scores, those elite institutions couldn't sell themselves as conduits to the best universities any longer. To find smarter pupils, the prep schools started to scour the country for talent in all of the social classes. "Today my daughter graduates from Foxcroft. Tomorrow my chauffeur's son graduates from Groton," one uppercrust Bostonian sniffed in *Time*.

In George Bush's era, almost every Andover boy was accepted to his first-choice college—particularly Harvard and Yale. By George W.'s time, just over half won a place at their top pick.

The students in the *Life* article blamed their education itself for their pessimism. "Freud is the real culprit," an Exeter boy said. Other students added: Darwin, Camus, Sartre, Melville, Salinger, Arthur Miller, and Robert Penn Warren. All of those thinkers and writers had second-guessed everything. No good deed was done as an expression of virtue; it was a survival instinct, a latent sexual perversion, or a meaningless act.

But George W. seemed immune to any intellectually inspired soul-searching. "He did not lay back on his bed and ponder the mysteries of the world," said Seligson. "He was not reading Camus and planning to be the next Jackson Pollock. I don't think he was particularly introspective. I don't think he is particularly introspective now."

The *Life* article gave voice to students' complaints about the computerization of America, which was just taking off in government and research work. "Everything has turned into numbers to go into IBM machines. . . . But who we are and what we feel never shows up on the cards," said one malcontent. "And our fathers? Just numbers on bank accounts, tax reports, Social Security—and a big number covering family life: the 5:19, followed by martinis."

George W. could not imagine feeling that way about his father. His dad had driven his Studebaker past Greenwich, past Wall Street, to the baking earth of Midland, struck black gold over and over until he had sated his every monetary wish. In Houston, he lived the life of a successful executive with country club memberships and a million dollars in the bank, but he still traveled the world overseeing offshore rigs.

He went up in helicopters to see what wreckage hurricanes had left of his multimillion-pound drills. He was still the kind of man whose fate could be determined by such storms! And even with that muscular business to engage him, he was at the brink of putting it all aside for the even riskier adventure of running for political office. Certainly George W.'s father was exactly the man that the Negoists yearned to be. "I wish," a lanky Andover senior told *Life*, "that it were the days of the great West, when a man could go out and prove what he was, just *out* of what he was."

Life could have been spinning the theory hard, but there was something to it. "By the time I graduated," Seligson remembered about the infectious sarcasm in his conversation, "it was hard for me to speak a simple declarative sentence."

—

Later in life, George W. would be forced to prove, and his friends would be at pains to explain, that male cheerleading wasn't for losers. Not at Andover. There was nothing feminine about screaming your lungs out for the ol' Blue and White. In fact, there was competition to be on the squad. You had to *try out* to win a white sweater, and over half the guys who wanted to get on got cut. Most of the guys played at least one varsity or junior varsity sport.

George W. had even made *head* cheerleader. He was determined to infuse a little life into his squad. As the *Phillipian* fretted, when George W. was a senior: "Last year the student was lost. He stumbled blindly to a game, if he even knew there was one, mechanically watched, and rarely emitted a short cry of emotion. The leaders of school spirit, the cheerleaders, failed to show any emotion or instill any."

George W. would change the way students thought about victory. But despite his pride in the project, he had enough West Texas in him to see the humor, the challenge in making siss-boom-bah hip: "We're going to work hard next year and try to make it an honor to be a cheer-leader," he told the *Phillipian* at the end of his junior year.

His decision was based on a cool-headed assessment of what lay ahead that fall: He knew he was too small and not good enough to make varsity football. He'd be happy to play JV where the guys didn't take it too seriously and he was actually considered tough enough to play defensive lineman. And he didn't want to be left out. "He just loved being in the midst of stuff," explained Randy Roden. "It was better than being on the bench."

George W. had spent a fair amount of time warming the wood. He'd made varsity teams because he was an enthusiastic athlete, but he didn't usually start. In fact, on varsity basketball, he, Clay, and Vermin, along with Ahlmquist, Doc Downing, and Greenberg, called themselves the Chinese Boundits, because their sole job seemed to be rebounding the ball for the good players at practice.

Coach "Deke" DiClemente had adored George W.'s father, even making a big deal out of it when George Bush came to one of the practices. Deke loved George W. too, and everyone worshiped Deke, a champion among men. He was the teacher voted best "Wit" by the senior class and that golden aura pervaded the squad: The basketball team, gushed the yearbook the *PotPourri*, was "great in other ways which won-lost records cannot indicate."

"A guy who just mopes his way through . . . boy, that's almost a sin," one student told a reporter, describing the mixed possibilities contained on a 436-acre campus. That could have been George W.'s motto.

In the fall of his senior year, the title of head cheerleader carried some institutional prestige: George W. was elected one of the representatives at-large of the Student Congress, an organization that looked great on applications but accomplished little more than learning how to use Robert's Rules of Order. By the beginning of October, the real fun began. Instead of just belting out hokey chants and forcing the guys to holler back, George W. would riff. He had that megaphone—The Lip amplified to the whole football field!—and he would just talk, puncture the pompous people and make jokes about the other team. Kidde remembered trying to concentrate in the varsity huddle and hearing George W. telling the fans in the stands parts of a conversation Kidde had been having with him the night before. Kidde couldn't help but laugh to himself.

Then George W. and the boys took it to the next level. They invented skits. At the Saturday morning assembly that first weekend of October, the cheerleaders posed as the "sports gang," duded up in motorcycle boots and garrison belts, and carrying beer cans. They came up with tough-guy names for the team: the body contact men (football), the foot-fighters (soccer), and the hit-and-run men (X-country). If the rest of the school didn't go to the games and support the team, one of the cheerleader thugs threatened, the gang members were going to mess with them. Sartore even carried a blade. The students loved it. The next week, inspired by a teacher's speech on "predatory females" downtown, the cheerleaders appeared in assembly in drag and vamped around, trying to lure the school to the stands that day. As the *Phillipian* burbled: "The effect has been incomprehensible."

The downside to being so school-positive was that it wasn't completely clear to all of their fellow classmates whose side George W. and his friends were on: that of the students or the faculty. Every year, Chaplain Baldwin picked six or seven guys to be deacons whose job it was to take daily attendance in the chapel after the last bell tolled and the massive oak doors were closed. As his father had been before him, George was a deacon, along with L.E. and John Kidde. Baldwin was smart about that: He picked guys who were naturally part of the in crowd. Nerds had no power. The cool kids would run roughshod over them. So the Godsquad had authority over the rest of the students. They were usually benevolent, letting students cover for a friend who overslept. But not always: A boy once got kicked out of church because under his suit and tie, he was wearing a striped shirt instead of the required white one.

On Saturday nights, the only fun available was the cartoon and movie shown in the assembly hall. If you cut class or got caught with an illegal radio, your name went on a list and you couldn't go to the screening. That was the high school equivalent of being sent to Siberia. The cheerleaders took advantage of the large movie audience to fuel school spirit. They would stand up before showtime and lead the crowds in cheers and songs. They read football scores from across the nation, and all the kids would roar their reactions to the news: "Minnesota, 28! Wisconsin, 21!" *Yaaaaayyayyyyh!* "Alabama 35! Mississippi 17!" *Booooooooh!* There was no rhyme or reason to the response. It was funny, kind of surreal, but people didn't really know if the cheerleaders saw it that way.

The cheerleaders would get everyone chanting: *Group Guts! Group Guts!* It meant something more visceral than one for all and all for one.

It meant share the bloodlust for victory, let that be the driving narrative of the whole Andover experience. *Group Guts! Group Guts!* Even the little acne-ridden losers felt like they belonged for one moment with the square-jawed, witty, sarcastic, prep-school stars who tended to come from the massive frontier states of Texas and California, or the good-old-boy birthing grounds like the South. For that one moment, the school was bonded in this half-facetious display of enthusiasm.

But it was definitely not a joke to George W.'s crowd if a kid violated the one golden rule that every boy attend the Andover–Exeter game. Seniors who had the *audacity* not to go would be met with boos when they came slumping in to the Commons to join the food line. One year, two such boys came to lunch and the entire dining room began to hiss. It was 238 against 2. A milk carton went flying and pelted one of them. Then another. Even the acne-ridden losers were joining in! Some of them would think about it later and feel like jerks for joining in the assault. Most of the square-jawed stars would never consider it again. And if there was a downside to all of that rah-rah school spirit, it was contained in that barrage of milk cartons: It sought to humiliate the guys who would rather not go to the Andover–Exeter game. The enthusiasm inadvertently sought to make everyone conform.

In the early weeks of senior year, the faculty began complaining that the cheerleaders were having "too many rallies and skits!" Dean Benedict even said the cheerleaders should "take a good look" at whether their theatrical antics were bringing more attention to themselves than to the teams. If Bush and the boys had become the stars, he said, the skits should end. The faculty argued that having a rally every Friday on Flagstaff Court, plus the skits at Saturday's morning meeting, could detract from the Super Bowl of rallies: the torchlit pagan riot with the burning "A" up on Andover's Sam Phil vista on the eve of the Exeter football matchup.

Benedict got what he wanted. His lecture that day ran long, the cheerleaders didn't have time to do their assembly bit, and the turnout for the foot-fighters' big victory over Mount Hermon was, in the sharp opinion of the editors at the *Phillipian*, "pitiful."

The *Phillipian* came to the cheerleaders' defense, writing that "George's gang has done a commendable job, and now is not the time to throw a wet blanket over cheerleading."

So Bush and the boys amped it up for the big rivalry that first weekend in November. Everyone tramped up to Sam Phil and yowled their heads off. The next day they headed out on buses to the Exeter campus and stole the rival's banner by snaring it with fish hooks. But the football team got trounced. Enthusiasm couldn't change events on the field.

The more productive side of such enthusiasm was that George W.'s social power could be put to use for more serious endeavors. His class was nicknamed the "Lush Class" because of the drinking in certain dormitories. Guys would bring back bottles after visiting friends at Harvard, then guzzle them in the wooded acres around the school. The policy against alcohol was strict: If you knew that your roommate drank, and he got caught, you were both out. For the most part, George W.'s friends say they never saw him imbibe on campus, but most guys drank a little.

The drinking had gotten so out of hand in certain dorms that class president Dan Cooper became concerned. More than two dozen students could get busted. So he went to Kemper and made a deal; if he could get a couple hours' grace period for the guys to dump their booze, the school could go ahead and—with the blessing of the student leadership—conduct room-by-room searches. Kemper liked the idea.

Now the only problem would be getting the students to actually follow through. So Cooper went to George W., the social leader without portfolio. "I didn't know what George would do," said Cooper, "but I knew he'd motivate them to do the right thing and make it seem it wasn't anything but fun. He was always up for lark and he made it into a kind of celebration, hamming it up."

Seniors poured gallons of booze down the janitor's drains in the dorm basements, leading to jokes about the alcohol content in the town's water supply. The class of 1964 ended up with the smallest percentage of students ever expelled.

—

Tom Seligson remembered looking out his dorm window one Friday afternoon a few weeks later and seeing Joe Freeman walking up the path. Freeman yelled to him, "The president's been shot." Later, Seligson went to chorus and found the door locked and a sign posted: "I don't feel like singing." Randy "Reno" Roden was in the gym.

"Kennedy's been shot," a kid told him. Randy thought they were talking about Sean Kennedy, one of their classmates.

The Ivy League early acceptances had just arrived in the student mailboxes. Peter Schandorff had just gotten into Harvard, and Dick Broadhead got into Yale. They were going back to Dick's room to celebrate. They didn't care if they got in trouble, so they turned on WBZ in Boston, Radio 103, even though it wasn't the legal hours to listen. The DJ was playing the Singing Nun. Suddenly a newscaster broke in and said that the vice president had been shot at in Dallas. Then a few minutes later came the bulletin about the president. One kid raced outside, wrapped in a Confederate flag, cheering on the main quad between Foxcroft and Bartlet Hall. Another student yelled, "Ding, dong, the witch is dead."

On November 22, 1963, Bar Bush was at the beauty parlor getting her hair done in Tyler, Texas, and writing a letter home. Back in September, George Bush had become the first declared Republican candidate for the 1964 senate elections—a Goldwater Republican— and the two of them were now on a several-city campaign swing. George came to pick her up and they flew on a Mr. Zeppo's private plane, which he disembarked in Fort Worth and then flew the Bushes back to Dallas. They had to circle while they waited for the second presidential plane to take off. Later that day, George Bush called into the Federal Bureau of Investigation to report a rumor he had heard that James Parrott, who may have been a student at the University of Houston, had been talking of killing the president. The FBI visited Parrott's house after Lee Harvey Oswald was arrested, and cleared the student of the allegations.

George W.'s roommate that year, John Kidde, remembered talking about the tragedy with him in the room that night. In the days of Camelot, George Bush had boasted, "Just wait till I turn these Bush boys out," the *Austin-American Statesman* would report decades later. "[George W.] was very upset about the tragedy," recalled Kidde. "It touched him kind of deeply. I was more shocked that someone would assassinate the president. He was more, you know, it was like somebody he knew."

On Saturday, Deans Blackmer and Benedict led a chapel service and then dispatched everyone to classes. That was the Andover way: The academics must go on. But there was no movie that night, and on Monday, even Andover had to observe the national day of mourning declared by President Johnson. Kemper led a service that morning, and all the students clustered around six television sets to watch the mass and burial.

On Tuesday, the long Thanksgiving weekend started, and George W. brought Kidde to his grandfather's house for the holiday. Prescott Bush had retired from the senate the year before, due to ill health. The atmosphere was formal as usual. As George W. later said: "One always wore a coat and tie to dinner." The whole clan played touch football out in somebody's backyard.

Not too long after that, probably on the other side of Christmas vacation, Kidde walked into the suite at his dorm, America House, and found a book that wasn't on any syllabus lying on Lip's desk. "What the hell is this?" Kidde asked.

It was Barry Goldwater's treatise, *The Conscience of a Conservative*. "My parents gave this to me," George W. told him. Kidde was shocked his friend was reading just for himself.

That summer, Dean Benedict had sent Kidde's parents a letter: "I see no hope of John's getting into Stanford, it said." Nothing in the world meant more to Kidde than getting into Stanford, and his dream had been machine-gunned with one stiff sentence.

What the hell have you been doing? Kidde's parents had demanded. He'd come back to Andover that fall determined to turn his fate around, which earned him the nickname Gary, as in Gary Grind, study bug.

Kidde had applied to be a proctor to add extracurricular credits to his college applications. He and George W. were assigned to America House, the farthest outpost, 15 minutes from the main quad, down near the girl's school, Abbot. They had to run just to get anywhere on time.

George was set on going to Yale, the Bush alma mater since he'd been born there in New Haven, and gone to Harvard–Yale games with his grandfather throughout his childhood.

The Bush blood was Yale Blue. But Benedict had damned his chances too—told him he'd never make the cut. Much later in life, George W. would explain to a television interviewer that his true first choice had been the University of Texas, but once Benedict put up that challenge, he'd been forced to prove him wrong. Kidde remembered it a little differently: They used to commiserate that Stanford and Yale respectively were the only schools that appealed to them.

But George W. was no great student. He would vividly remember when his sophomore year English teacher asked the class, for their first writing assignment, to pen an essay on something that had made them cry. He had searched a new thesaurus his mother gave him for a synonym for *tears*. He came up with *lacerates* and used it in the first sentence of his piece. The teacher pressed so hard writing the zero in his composition book, the indent showed through to the other side.

Most of the students worshiped Thomas Lyons, who taught a rigorous course in American history. When reporters questioned Lyons about his former pupil years after George W. graduated—when he was governor of Texas—Lyons offered no comment. The governor had written him a fond two-page letter on the occasion of the teacher's retirement. George W. must have learned that there was no easier way to disarm a critic than to compliment him or her. His father had been an addictive note-writer, trundling stacks of stationery with him through life so that a few spare moments might be given to jotting down a quick greeting, soothing a bruised ego. That gesture or tactic would serve both men well in political life.

James Lockhart III, a classmate, remembered George W. working hard in Spanish class, but the language didn't come easily. And Kidde himself recalled that the only time he saw George W. got really steamed was over the criticism of a faculty member. "He came home and he was real ticked off. He felt he was getting a raw deal from one of his professors and he was trying to get good grades and get into Yale."

So here they were, sweating it out trying to get into their colleges, barely keeping up, Kidde thought, and George was reading a book for pleasure? No one did that. Hardly anyone even cracked a newspaper. There just wasn't time. Kidde asked George W. what the book was about and George W. sketched out Goldwater's ultraconservative philosophy, and explained why his family was so interested.

A month later, Kidde asked him again about the book because he hadn't seen it lying around and thought maybe George W. had given up. But he had plowed through. "He got it read because, he said, his dad was interested in it and thought George ought to read it," Kidde remembered. "And he respected his father so much, he made time for it."

But even deeper in the story was that the support for Goldwater passed not just from father to son, but from grandfather to father. In the spring of George W.'s junior year, Prescott had made news by condemning New York governor Nelson Rockefeller—a former friend and a candidate for president—for his divorce and remarriage. At a commencement address at the Rosemary Hall girls' school in Greenwich, Prescott likely shocked the audience of cloistered, prepschool females by using the forum to thunder: "Have we come to the point in our life as a nation where the governor of a great state—one who perhaps aspires to the nomination for president of the United States—can desert a good wife, mother of his grown children, divorce her, then persuade a young mother of four youngsters to abandon her husband and their four children and marry the governor?

"Have we come to the point where one of the two great political parties will confer upon such a one its highest honor and greatest responsibility? I venture to hope not."

It wasn't exactly the usual commencement "Seize the Day" speech. That moment affected George W. so profoundly he would cite his grandfather's critique of Rockefeller as one of his main memories of his political legacy, in an interview with his father's biographer, Herbert Parmet. "There is a philosophy that is the basis for a political philosophy laid down; you know, family unit, the old family values theme," he said. "I can remember my grandfather going after Nelson Rockefeller for his divorce . . . which at that point in politics was taboo. . . . There is a concept that you are responsible for your behavior. You can't shirk off your problems on somebody else. You must handle them yourself. There is the individual code of honor and respect for your neighbor. There is a religious undertone, and a very strong religious sense for this. I guess what we have all inherited is the basis for political philosophy, if we're political people."

The idea that personal conduct, particularly in family life, could be the basis of political leadership was a strong chord played throughout George W.'s pursuit of higher office, particularly when he decided to run for president in the year 2000. George Bush had always run on the premise that his close, all-American family was a great asset to him as a politician. But George W. would further the notion, announcing almost from the first steps of his exploratory committee that he had been faithful to his wife—a direct challenge to the legacy of President Bill Clinton's promiscuous conduct. If his grandfather's denunciation of a politician who had caused such familial mayhem was righteous, then perhaps its opposite was true. Perhaps an elected official who had stayed faithful deserved to be president.

With Prescott's denunciation, the Bushes became Goldwater supporters. George Bush's 1964 campaign echoed almost every one of Goldwater's main policies in *Conscience of a Conservative*. Just as Rockefeller's personal conduct would spell the end of Prescott's political support, the friendly appeal of Goldwater would seal a bond with George Bush that could weather any previous ideological differences.

Just before graduation, Randy Roden was driving in a car with George W.'s father when Bush brought up Goldwater. "He's such a hateful warmonger," Randy snapped. He wanted to pick an argument, even though he had only seen Goldwater's television ads.

George Bush turned to Randy. "Well, I can't imagine why you would feel that way," he said. "I know him personally and he's a very fine person." Randy was humiliated by his graciousness. But Randy saw the point of not limiting friends to those who share the same perspective. Still the *New York Times* review of the new conservative bible had noted: "[Goldwater] is a pleasant man, but not that pleasant."

—

In the spring of senior year, when Andover campus was bathed in the new warmth of the season, the trees were in blossom, and all of the rigors of academia were about to disappear with matriculation, stickball was a revolution. Played on five fields simultaneously, each dorm fielding a team, it was as complicated an organizational feat as anything the school officially sanctioned. Yet the students ruled.

A tennis ball, a broom handle, and a dream—that's all George W. really had when he was appointed to the high post in the Stickball League in the spring of 1964. The tournament had existed in previous years, but the moment Dan Cooper, the class president, stood up at the school assembly and began the "To Tell the Truth"–style introduction of High Commissioner "Tweeds," all of the guys knew stickball was going to be big that year.

George W. "Tweeds" Bush got up in his top hat and shades. His friends said he had planned to say only a word or two about the League, but he just started talking. Everything that came out of his mouth was outrageous. The guys started roaring with laughter, and he kept riffing, telling them all of the arcane rules they would have to abide by that season under his command as commissioner of stickball. He must have done a half hour. He introduced the rest of the commission: Frank "The Thumb" Hight, as chief umpire; Mike "The Couch" Campbell, as league psychiatrist; and J. C. Morgan, as official scribe. He pledged honesty and fairness in all his dealings with the league. The guys hooted at that.

What about the rumors that you are closely related to the notorious "Lucky" Luciano? Mike Strauss quizzed him at the press conference that Tweeds held after the assembly in the trustee room.

"I don't consider anyone who's been deported a relative, " Tweeds replied.

After dinner, you could stroll out to one of the fields, and everyone would be playing in their handmade T-shirts with irreverent team names scrawled on their backs ("Go Nads! Go Nads!" the fans of one team shouted)—even the terrible athletes. That was the point. It was an organized way to smash all of the cliques for one blissful month.

And George W. played that up. Alan Wofsey remembered being unable even to begin to catch the ball. The other guys kept coaching him to just close his hands if the ball came near him. One time, he did just that, and made an out. George W. stopped the game and led everyone in a standing ovation.

George W. could forget his own athletic challenges with stickball. Officially, he was a third-string pitcher on the varsity baseball team. Kidde remembered how badly he wanted to make the cut. But that squad wasn't exactly glorious. "Actually the team was probably the worst squad that Coach Harrison has ever coached and it certainly did not live up to previous Andover powerhouses," the yearbook noted. George W.'s big contribution was teaching the guys how to chew Tootsie Rolls and spit the brown juice on the ground so it looked like they had chaw in their cheeks.

The lackluster baseball squad just left more excitement for stickball. George W. dreamt of stickball dances, films, and cards, but never quite got them off the ground. But the students loved him for what he had done—even decades later. In that daunting institution, with its academic rigors and its Benedict-ine discipline, the kids finally had fun. "George took responsibilities that others didn't want to take—even stickball," said Tory Peterson. "To get a whole school to do something that made them want to be there and love it."

—

The college acceptances started arriving in mailboxes just after spring break that year. Kidde cut class the day the acceptances were due from Stanford. He sat in front of his mailbox for an hour. When he ripped the package open in the student-faculty lounge, everybody burst into a big round of applause. They knew how much he had wanted it.

George was off the wall when the Yale acceptances came in, Kidde remembered. Thirty students from Andover planned to attend, and George W. was one of them.

George W.'s acceptance, despite Benedict's dire prediction, did not surprise his classmates. "Fred Blimp, the Dean at Harvard, used to talk about good fourth-quarter men," said Schandorff. "Somebody's got to be at the bottom of the class and why not someone that will give us five million dollars and won't jump out the window the first time he gets a D."

—

The prom, with its tropical theme, was coming up the first week of May. The summer between junior and senior year, George W. had met a girl named Debbie Taylor, walking the beach in Kennebunkport. She was beautiful and bubbly and from California. She had a little of that edgy sarcasm too. They got to talking and it turned out she had known John Kidde on the West Coast.

Throughout the year, George W. would ask Kidde about her, and he and Debbie talked a few times on the telephone. When George went out to visit John for a week over one of the vacations, George took Debbie out on several dates. When prom time came, Debbie wasn't surprised that George asked her to go, although she wouldn't have

been shocked if she hadn't heard from him. Since she had some colleges to visit on the East Coast, she made the trip. George Bush's date
for that same Andover prom twenty years earlier had been Barbara
Pierce.

For a student's years at Andover, dating was basically put on hold.
In tenth grade, all of the boys were required to take dancing lessons—
to learn the rumba, the mambo, and the cha-cha. George W. hated to
dance just as his father had. In fact, his parents' first encounter was
sitting out a waltz at that dance in Greenwich.

The school scheduled tea dances every so often with nearby girls'
schools, including Dana Hall, in Wellesley. But the organizers seemed
intent on throwing students into a state of angst about the nature of
romantic selection. The day of the dance, a bus would pull up at the
top of the hill and 30 girls would file out. The matron would line them
up by height. The boys would be waiting at the bottom of the slope,
also arranged by height. Then the boys and girls would join up in that
order and those would be the couplings for the night. Each guy had
to escort that height-selected girl back to the bus at the end of the
evening. So the Andover boys would stand in the line, count over to
their pairing. If the guys didn't like the looks of the girl, they flipped
quarters to trade with the guys to their right or left.

The tea dances thrown by the clubs were a slight improvement,
since a club officer could choose which girls' school to invite. The club
president or officers also got to assign the dates. Spanish club, which
George W. belonged to all three years, had the reputation for the best
tea dances. But none of George W.'s friends remembers him dating
much.

The whole weekend of the prom was packed with events for the
visiting girls. Debbie and George went to watch a lacrosse game. For
the prom itself Debbie remembered wearing a bright yellow dress with
a long matching coat. She kept up with George W. for a time after the
prom. She thought he was funny, but she didn't seem to be smitten.
Truthfully, the boys felt more comfortable after the girls left. They
could return to their familiar gripings about life without girls and
behave like boys, rather than gentleman, again.

They could act out their vernal urges through extra enthusiasm on
senior pranks. One day the faculty discovered Mr. Markey's Mustang

parked in the Copley Wing of the library; the place looked like a car showroom. John Kidde was in on that one. Someone floated balloons to the ceiling of the chapel and left e.e. cummings's "The Balloon Man" on the lectern. One prankster set up a graveyard on the main quad with the names of every student from the original class of 1964 who had left Andover.

The Right Reverend Hobson from Ohio gave the commencement address that year. Its only memorable message was: Do it with class. As soon as the ceremony ended, John Hay, the football captain, revved his motorcycle and drove it right down Main Street—through the mob of faculty in black robes, the dads in seersucker suits and the mothers in linen dresses—to symbolize that the Andover shackles had been broken.

For George W., Andover had been an important three years. He had found friends, like Clay Johnson and Rob Dieter, who would go on to room with him at Yale all four years—and beyond—as well as dozens of other New Haven–bound friends who would make that transition to college easy. Years later, when he went back to his hometown of Midland to work in the oil business, Randy Roden and L. E. Sawyer would arrive about the same month. They too would stay friends. John Kidde and Don Vermeil would offer support for his political bids.

In the yearbook, he was not chosen as "Most Likely to Succeed"— his father hadn't won that category either—or "Politico," but he had made "BMOC." If he had not excelled by academic standards, he had certainly survived the first leg of his father's own journey through life, and did it "with class."

He could not help that the times had shifted under him. While his father planned his enlistment in the last six months, the Andover class of 1964 congratulated themselves on being the "first upperclassmen to eat in an unproctored dorm during Spring Term."

Circumstances were simply more prosaic, but so were his fellow students. George W. served as glue to a society of conformists. "There were no crusades for changes from the *status quo*," the yearbook editors wrote. "This low-pressure class didn't lead any riots or experience any civil wars, but it had a special light spirit of its own."

One of the final editorial pages of the 1964 *Phillipian* observed that school spirit—George W.'s magic contribution to Andover—was the most important ingredient in their young lives. "Being a name instead of a number is a noble aim, but the class of '63 overextended itself in its cult of the individual," the paper scolded. "Personal freedom led to lack of organization, chaos, and apathy. . . . Perhaps the class of '63 can be praised for its individuality, but this year's seniors deserve credit for proving that normalcy is as successful as malignant nihilism."

Here was the power of being a friendly guy.

George W.'s father's legacy at Andover had familiarized him with life at the school, but it had not made any of the requirements easier. He was still forced to earn his own place on campus and he had done so—not through achievement in either academics or sports—but through his outgoing personality. One of the more significant aspects of the time that George W. spent at Andover was how he personally was not as memorable to his classmates as was the fun he concocted, which they all enjoyed—stickball and cheerleading. When his classmates cast their thoughts back to those spring days of swinging a broom handle at a tennis ball, they remembered gratefully how George W. had brought that pleasure to them, but more importantly, they recollect their own fun in the game. Such a magic trick is exactly what is needed when a politician sets his volunteers fanning out into the agony of a political campaign, and George W. had it at the tender age of 18.

IV

BOY ON THE

BUSH BANDWAGON

"We promise not to work you to death. In fact, we're going to make a GAME out of this, AND THE NAME OF THE GAME IS WINNING."

— from a Bush volunteers bulletin for the 1966 congressional campaign

When George Bush was still an undergraduate at Yale, he reportedly posed an intriguing question to his father, Prescott. They were driving back to town after a round of golf with Uncle Herbie and George's friend from Andover and Yale William F. Howe Jr., later named George W.'s godfather.

The crew had stopped for gas, and while they were waiting, George Bush looked around the station. He said to Prescott, "If you were in politics, would you get out of the car now and go shake hands with everybody?"

"His father thought a minute and said, yes, he probably would," recalled Howe. "I thought, what an interesting question to ask his father."

George Bush's query not only illuminates his early fascination with retail politics. It also begins to bore into the koan: How does one tell the difference between a good person and an active politician? The two are nearly indistinguishable, since a politician must behave like a good person in order to win votes. George Bush would always be a perfect example of this condundrum: Was he one of the kindest men in America or one of the nation's savviest politicians? If he was both, then in what ratio?

In his later years in the political ring, George Bush would complain about the cynicism of the press, who always seemed to second-guess his actions, and George W. would rage that certain journalists failed to understand that his father was virtuous to his core. But the press was simply grappling with the discomfort caused by the fact that so many of George Bush's lovely qualities—such as his habit of writing letters to strangers and his policy of not fostering enemies—were also politically useful. His father sold himself to voters more as the kind of man who would make a trustworthy and talented manager of a district than as a revolutionary with a vision. As such, voters' personal feelings toward him mattered more than they would with a Barry Goldwater or Ronald Reagan. Constituents wanted assurance that Bush's kindness was earnest, not manipulative.

The gas station anecdote reveals that Bush was savvy to the theater of political friendliness at an early age. If a stranger popped out of his car at a gas station and greeted everyone with deep enthusiasm no matter their rank—from the manager to the mechanic to the attendant—each worker might consider the man a little odd, but they might also think, "What a nice, friendly guy that is! What an unexpectedly kind thing to do in this cold world where everyone races around, caring only for themselves, not paying a lick of attention to anyone else. He just got out of his car and said hello."

If a politician leapt from his car to greet strangers, the gas station employees would feel similarly warmed, but the motivation would clearly be different: The politician would be in pursuit of votes; he not only would want all those workers to cast their ballots for him, he would want each of them to talk him up to their friends. He would hope that just that one stop at the gas station might mean the difference of 50 votes down the line.

George Bush always carried stationery with him and wrote letters to acquaintances in every spare moment. He would pass this habit on to Jeb and to George W., who began penning note cards in profusion during his first campaign for congress in 1978. When a civilian writes a note, he or she hopes to impart good feeling to the recipient. When a politician pens a card, the motivation is the same, but he or she hopes the karmic wave might carry further. The politician wants to set off the ripple effect of thanks which will eventually lead to higher vote tallies on election night.

The family took care to leave as few enemies in their wake as possible. While good people would make karmic purity a goal, a politician is *required* to be a peacemaker. He or she can't afford to let anyone remain hostile to him or her for long, since those enemies can rise again decades later to take revenge. Former staffers to George Bush would note how, after he severed a work relationship, he would invite the alienated employee to be part of his personal life—asking the person to dinner or golf, including them on his list of pen pals. He earned credit for being one of the world's kindest men to the degree that he showed this concern. But the practice also had its strategic merit. George Bush would last several decades in the political arena before an unappeasable and infuriated Ross Perot helped take him down.

Over a half century after George Bush asked his father that question at the New Haven gas station, there is ample testimony from their acquaintances that the former president and his son George W. are caring people. "There is a Christian innocence to George," his cousin Ray Walker, a psychoanalyst told the *L.A. Times.* "His life has been without moral ambiguity. He feels he has been granted goodness and that his success proves the goodness was warranted." The question is, which came first: Was the kindness of two men rewarded with public office, or did they "care" their way into power? Does it matter? Or has retail politics taken the place of God in making some of our more ambitious fellow human beings more considerate, kinder people?

—

In early December 1964, William F. Buckley published a postmortem on that year's elections in his *National Review* magazine. He invited George Bush, who was paradoxically the new Republican star after losing his first campaign that year for the Senate, to contribute. Bush argued that the reason Lyndon Johnson steamrolled Barry Goldwater in

November was not just the result of an extended period of mourning for the slain Democratic president John Kennedy. The "nut fringe," he wrote, had been too sharply critical of the liberal welfare state. The party had to reposition itself, he urged: "We should repackage our philosophy. Emphasize the positive, eliminate the negative. . . . Conservatism can and will survive—it needs to be practical and positive."

George W. would absorb those words, perhaps by osmosis: Just after the 1998 Texas governor's race, when he was celebrating his historic second-term victory, George W. gave an interview to the *Dallas Morning News* speculating on who might carry the Republican banner in the presidential race for 2000. "It's going to be somewhat difficult for the Republican Party to project a positive and optimistic national agenda until they get a candidate in the year 2000 who is positive and optimistic and conservative," George W. told reporter Wayne Slater, who noted "'positive and optimistic' was a characterization George W. frequently used to describe himself."

George W. would often say in later years—and his friends would say too—that the legacy of the Bush family was the clan's commitment to public service. But what is underestimated in assessments of the family is the tradition of hard-driving, showboating, image-spinning, even sometimes name-calling, retail politics that George W. learned at his father's knee. That education began in Houston.

When George Bush first moved his family to Houston in 1959, he immediately began introducing himself into the circles (or in that Democratic state more like a pie crust's quarter edge) of the Republican party. He was definitely a business success as the founder and president of an *international offshore* drilling company when offshore drilling was still in its infancy. He worked multimillion-dollar deals, jetting off to exotic places like Borneo and Trinidad. He even drilled the first offshore well in Kuwait.

In 1963, he tried to bring some of that corporate, wave-of-the-future savvy to the Republican party in his district. As GOP chairman of Harris County, he went on a mission to modernize operations: They got a new headquarters, hired a full-time executive director, and started a research library, and a county newspaper just for the party. They even paid some girls to punch all of those party records into computers.

No one took on those kinds of projects without dreaming of a payoff in the future. Everyone knew George Bush was going to run for something.

He went to Jack Porter, a bigwig as former head of the Texas GOP, to ask if he should get in the race. Porter didn't exactly give him a rousing cheer; all Bush would be able to say when, in that autumn of 1963, he announced his candidacy for the senate from the Capitol Press office was, "He did not discourage me."

That didn't sound so great; but Porter was in a bind. He knew the oil man Jack Cox, who most recently had run for governor on the Republican ticket, would likely jump into the race too. That's why George Bush had started so early. He wanted to be sprinting down the first turn before the other candidates even got in the blocks.

At that first press conference, George Bush laid out his positions: He opposed Kennedy's civil rights bill, particularly the public accommodations section, because he believed it would damage the constitution. Only moral persuasion could change race relations in America, Bush said. The nuclear test ban treaty was too soft, in his opinion. But mainly he was opposed to any government intervention in state affairs—that, he assured the voters, would put him in direct debate with his likely opponent, Democratic Senator Ralph Yarborough. Who would he support for president? Goldwater—all the way. In fact, his positions echoed almost all of Mr. Conservative's. But, George Bush said, any Republican better than Kennedy would get his help.

George Bush's whole point, he told the press that day, was to start early to make his name known. His promoter, Hal Hazelrigg, public relations man, stood at his side. Yes, George Bush was all cattle and no hat—hero to his family, friends, shipmates, business partners, varsity baseball squad, Sunday school classes, Little League outfielders, but to no one else. The general public didn't know his name. Of course they would come to like him, support him in time. They just hadn't met him yet.

George Bush did believe in public service, basically because he had no doubt that he was a good man. He would watch out for the voters; he wouldn't cheat or manipulate. He had taken on dozens of extensive and probably tedious good works projects in Midland just to make the community sturdier. Power wasn't what motivated George

Bush. He was an achiever. He didn't pursue leadership roles because he needed to squash the little people but because he felt most reassured of his worth by occupying the top post in any organization: team captain, fraternity president, CEO.

But to rise to the top of civic life, George Bush would have to make himself famous. Broad fame is bestowed in only a few ways. Either you pull off an extraordinary feat in an arena the public is already watching—as Willie Mays or General Patton did—or you never miss an opportunity to angle the spotlight on yourself and use the moments in which you find yourself in the beam to boast about your accomplishments. Unfortunately for the ambitious George Bush, he had been scolded away from bragging by his mother. She insisted that her children only brag about the *team's* accomplishments, not their own. So George Bush had to try to win fame a third way, by befriending so many people that he actually *would know* absolutely everyone. Already the Bush family Christmas card list was the stuff of legend, loaded as it was with the names of every friend and acquaintance who had ever exchanged a handshake with Bush. The fall of 1963 was the turning point for George Bush: He was setting out on the road to put the nation on his Christmas card list.

That's why he started early.

Life was lonely for Republicans in Texas. But then, in the first months of the new year, George Bush saw an opportunity to whittle away at the Democratic majority, when Lloyd Bentsen, a possible Democratic challenger, dropped out of the primary. Bush decided he could question that withdrawal as a way of casting suspicions on the party as a whole. He had to do it! There was no way he could win without chipping the soft edges off that Democratic iceberg in Texas! So he used Bentsen's desertion to make people feel the leg-irons of LBJ's political chain gang; there was nothing Texans hated more than being told what to do or how to think.

So in early January, at Ivan Irwin Jr.'s house in Dallas, Bush told the dinner guests that he believed that the only reason LBJ had persuaded Bentsen to drop out was to knit that fractious Democratic party together. The Democrats weren't even getting to decide if they *wanted* a conservative Democrat, *it was being decided for them!* Then he threw in something for the reporter from the *Dallas Times Herald* to carry out to the people. "Our Negro citizens, citizens of Latin heritage, union rank and file, farmers and ranchers, and members of other common-interest groups now realize that their votes have been bought," he said. "And bought with grandiose promises of something for nothing."

That ought to shake a few votes loose.

A month later, Jack Cox, oil man and former collegiate lightweight boxer, launched his own campaign. Bush, who had lapped him for six months, popped off that Cox was rolling into the race at the last minute. "He reminds me of Harold Stassen. I think he's running because it has gotten to be a habit."

It was a little strange for Bush to rough up Cox like that, since only two years earlier he'd been the pusher supporting Cox's habit: Bush had served as the Harris County finance chairman for Cox's bid for governor. But now, when a group of Bush supporters at a Dallas meeting ripped into Cox before the primary, George joked, "I'm pleased to detect a certain amount of anti-Cox sentiment." And when someone suggested that this election might require poll watchers. Bush smirked: "Get big fellows."

It wasn't surprising that politics required the candidates to cuff each other around a little, but what did raise eyebrows was that George Bush, the notorious gentleman, would seem to take to the grappling so easily. Since his mother had sternly ruled out bragging as a way to assert one's ego, politics was a perfect outlet for George Bush to finally express all the pent-up self-confidence he had probably stashed away. (Amazingly, even after he had risen to the heights of political power as the leader of the free world, he insisted at the opening of his presidential library that having such a permanent tribute was embarrassing because of his discomfort with boasting.) But public service itself was structured in just the right way to serve as an ego escape valve: Running for office meant competing for a chance to help large numbers of people. Thus, he could pass off his aggression as simply a side note to being a true competitor, and his self-promotion as the necessary work to reach the grander virtue of public service. He could bat Cox around because he was such a good citizen.

Cox returned the favors, accusing Bush of being bankrolled by Eastern sources, particularly anti-Goldwater Republicans. Bush was forced to parade around a photo of himself with Mr. Conservative, just to prove Cox wrong. The primary on May 2 left no clear victor, so a run-off was called for early June.

Bush couldn't seem to help himself. He'd gotten the bug to scrap around with his opponents and he couldn't shake it. He started taking swings at Yarborough just weeks before the Republican runoff. On April 13, he brought up charges against Yarborough regarding an old campaign gift made by farm financial wizard and later convicted swindler Billie Sol Estes. Bush pounded the charge, but the Department of Justice found nothing untoward in the donation.

On Saturday, June 6, Bush beat Cox in a landslide and started the full-time campaign to take on Yarborough. "Bush is pleasant to talk to," the *Texas Observer* wrote in its endorsement of him, "and he admits to having normal feelings for the poor and the dispossessed, although he does not let these feelings interfere in any way with his steadfast convictions against the issues." With Bar nursing a cold by his side, Bush told supporters that night his victory was one for "responsible conservatism."

—

Over that summer vacation before Yale, George W. helped his father in Houston. Every Sunday, his father's top campaign men, Martin Allday and Jimmy Allison Jr. would come by the house for hamburger cookouts to discuss developments. After the primary, George Bush had flown out to Midland to convince Allday to join the team full-time as campaign chair. Allday had a wife and kids, not to mention a law firm of which he was partner, but he said yes. Bush could convince him of anything. Allday's one demand was that Bush hire on Jimmy Allison too.

Allison had power with the Texas press since his family owned the *Midland Reporter-Telegram,* and he had recently been elected president of the Press Association. Allday figured that Allison could work wonders making the introductions to editors and columnists around the district. Also, he was a marvelous organizer.

Allison wasn't hard to persuade. He was going through a divorce and was only too happy to be distracted by life on the campaign trail. The gentle, dark-haired, dark-eyed Texan soon bonded with the candidate to such an extent that even decades later, their friends still spoke of their relationship with awe. But what the friendship between George Bush and Jimmy Allison represented more than anything was an era, and even a specific set of circumstances, that allowed two pals to participate in politics as a gentleman's avocation. Allison never spun Bush into something he was not. He constantly encouraged his friend to be more himself.

The discussions at those Houston barbecues centered on how to better organize precincts. George Bush had always existed on the crest of the modernization of politics. Easter Egg Row in Midland, his precinct, had been one of the first to computerize its voting list. For the 1964 race, the Bush team emphasized the importance of a sophisticated network of support; in 154 out of the 254 counties, they recruited a campaign chair and sometimes even a finance chair to help their effort. In certain towns, voters had never previously considered casting a ballot for anyone but a Democrat. John Tower had been the only Republican to win statewide office since Reconstruction, when he secured Lyndon Johnson's Senate seat in 1961 after LBJ became vice president. But with Bush's campaign, they would have a choice. When George Bush served as Harris County chair, he had recognized how crucial that framework was for the future of the GOP. Now the manager-as-politician would put the groundwork to use and for decades to come.

In July, the candidate, Barbara, George W., and Jimmy Allison headed off on a bus trip through Texas. "The Bush Bandwagon" traveled to eight or more towns a day with the Black Mountain Boys from Abilene opening the program with country and western tunes. The Bush Bluebonnet Belles, a group of female supporters, sang in town squares: "The sun's going to shine in the Senate some day/George Bush is going to chase them liberals away."

At first George Bush was a little awkward. He could be slightly formal. The local press homed right in on the problem. When someone from the campaign told him to go shake hands in the J.C. Penney in Brenham, for example, he walked in and asked for the store manager. That gave the guys in the press a hoot! Bush always had to start at the top.

But to boost himself, George Bush could only be comfortable promoting the team—whether it was the Republican party or his family. In that first campaign, his wife and children became not just relatives but selling points. "From St. Martin's Episcopal Church which they

attend together, to backyard barbecues, to sports which are an important part of their lives," one of the campaign flyers read, "this close-
knit family exemplifies the ideal of American family life."

—

At the time George W. entered Yale, he looked eerily like his father
when he had been in college—the heavy brows hanging right over the
smallish eyes, the crescent moon smile, the thatch of brown hair. But
George W. was the rougher version. In the drama of the doppelganger,
he seemed like he could have popped the "Herbert" version on the chin.

George W.'s father had achieved so much on the all-male campus
(and in only two and a half years!). He had played on the varsity soccer and baseball teams—even been captain. He had secured Phi Beta
Kappa, the presidency of Delta Kappa Epsilon, and a tap inviting him
into the secret society of Skull and Bones. He had even served as the
president of Yale's United Negro College Fund.

George W.'s grandfather too had been a Yale man—had played
first base for the varsity team and been tapped for Skull and Bones.
Years later, the university had invited Prescott to be a trustee. Then in
1962, one month after ill health forced him to announce his retirement
from the Senate, he received an honorary law degree from his alma
mater in the same ceremony in which President Kennedy was
bestowed his. "You have served your country well," the citation for
Prescott Bush read, "and personified the best in both political parties."

Prescott, who was 69 years old when George W. entered Yale, carried that sense of dignity in his physical being. At six foot four, and
with steely blue eyes, he still cut an imposing and elegant figure when
he visited the campus. George W. was so awed by him, he even held his
quick tongue in the man's presence—an act George W. reserved for
very few people. "I recall his being very, very proud of the fact that
his grandfather was a public servant," said classmate Donald Etra.
Prescott was always friendly, of course, always asked George W.'s
friends about their studies, their sports. But to the other students, he
seemed to be some kind of soapstone monument.

When one of George W.'s classmates, Lanny Davis, who would later
become legal counsel to President Bill Clinton, learned that he had been
accepted into Yale, his ultraliberal father told him approvingly,

"Connecticut is home to Senator Prescott Bush. Even though he is a Republican, he stood up to Joe McCarthy." Later, when Congressman George Bush visited his son at his residential college of Davenport, Davis told him, "My father was a great admirer of your father's."

Almost half of the students at Yale had gone to prep school, and they formed a powerful clique on campus. Either they knew each other from Andover or Exeter or Deerfield, or they had faced each other on the prep-school sporting fields. George W., Rob Dieter, and Clay Johnson decided to room together that first year and would remain together throughout their stay.

George W. and his friends did traditional Yale things. On Mondays, a bunch of guys would sometimes go over to Mary's to see their friend sing in the legendary all-male group, the Whiffenpoofs. George W. competed for the famous intercollege Tyng Cup on Davenport's sports teams, and worked on the house's Social Council to concoct amusements for the other guys.

To devise fun wasn't very hard for George W.'s clique: There was the time Clayton Day Jr., a carrot-topped freshman, tried to collect enough dimes to go see his girlfriend in Reno, Nevada. That endeavor made national news. According to Robert McCallum, George W. and his friends dreamed up the fund-raising idea of putting on a tackle football game, without pads, there on Old Campus with members of the freshman team. Everyone threw a dime into the mug to watch that bruiser.

Like the other prep-school guys, George W. was breaking out from under the thumb of intense authority and, of course, drinking was part of the fun. Russell Walker remembered staggering home with George W., seriously drunk sometime in their freshman year. They had just dropped off their dates—arranged by Russell—at the fleabag motel where they were staying in downtown New Haven. "Let's rock and roll," George W. shouted. "You rock and I'll roll." He dropped to the ground and tumbled toward home.

—

In the third week of September, George Bush finally got one of those great breaks candidates dream about: The former Dallas County Democratic Chairman Ed Drake announced that he was putting together a group of Democrats for Bush. There was that soft ice Bush had been looking for. But a skirmish soon developed, with Democrats calling on Drake's group to resign from the party, then other Democrats calling on the critics to resign. It was definitely getting ugly, and Yarborough had taken command in the polls.

Yarborough popped off that Bush was an oil importer, so George had to hire an auditor to pore over ten years of financial records to verify that he had never imported, nor produced oil outside of the United States. The John Birch Society accused Bush of being a commie (because his father-in-law was an executive at McCall's, which published *Redbook*). Yarborough added that George Bush was nothing but a carpetbagger. "I would have been born in Texas but I wanted to be close to my mother," George Bush said, making light of the attack.

Then on November 1, the Sunday papers reported that Yarborough had told his supporters in Houston that George Bush was "the darling of the John Birch Society." That was rich! Everyone knew that the ultraconservative John Birchers had never been big on Bush.

The night before the election, an anxious George Bush was scheduled to make his final television appearance. He was at the Houston Club getting a massage with Martin Allday. For weeks, LBJ had been accusing Goldwater of being a bomb thrower, and Yarborough borrowed the tactic, leveling the charge at Bush. "Doesn't he know, atom bombs create leukemia?" Yarborough ranted.

The gap showed in the polls. Allday, as the campaign chairman, was desperate. "George," he said, "you know, if you wanted to, you could turn this whole bomb thing around on him. You could say, 'I understand leukemia more than most people. I lost a daughter to it.'"

Bush would have none of it. "Martin, I don't think it's appropriate to bring my kids into it." Yet the broadcast that night featured his wife and five children.

George W. came down from Yale for the weekend to be with his family in Houston for the big night. Even Prescott and Dotty traveled from Connecticut. The night before the election, George Bush lay awake in the early hours. "It was just nervousness—like pregame symptoms," he explained.

At the Hotel America on November 3, George W. tallied his

father's results on the big board while 300 supporters looked on. George Bush did well—better than Goldwater, who had been demolished by LBJ; in fact stronger than any other Republican candidate in the state's history. Still he never pulled ahead of Yarborough. George Bush watched the returns on television too, while his giant father slumped, head in hand, like an inconsolable Max von Sydow. "I don't mean to be ungrateful," Bush said as he watched Yarborough's returns climb, "but I'm a competitor."

Yarborough claimed victory around 9:30 P.M. "[George Bush] ought to pick up his baggage and go back where he came from," said Yarborough. He called the campaign "one of the vilest in history."

Bush did not concede for two more hours. Bar and George W. stood by him as he visibly tried to choke back his emotions. "I tried desperately to think of someone else I could blame for this and I came to the conclusion there is no one else to blame but me," he joked half-heartedly.

"I just don't know how it happened," Bush told reporters. "I don't understand it. I guess I have a lot to learn about politics."

"I literally ached for days after," Allday would remember decades later.

George Bush later wrote that he had been bitten by the campaign bug during that election, and in less than two years he would let it lead him back to the campaign trail.

George W. would use his father's reaction to that election as an example of resilience. "My father had a great disappointment in not winning the Senate seat," his Yale friend, Robert McCallum, told a reporter. "But this is what you do, you bounce back. So you're down, you just get back up. His attitude was, you gave it your best shot."

V

DUKE OF DEKE

It was over Thanksgiving break, probably in George W.'s freshman year at Yale that his friend from Andover, Jim "Juice" Lockhart, remembered George W. setting the bar for his college high jump. They were heading out for Thanksgiving on the train from New Haven after partying like lunatics leading up to the break. Then George W. suddenly got serious. "I'm going to make something of myself at Yale," he told Lockhart. It was a strong statement. Lockhart felt that George W. was consciously making the declaration in front of someone else. "So he couldn't backslide," Lockhart said. After he made the proclamation on the train, George W. started to play baseball and went on to become president of the fraternity Delta Kappa Epsilon—began to "do some things rather than pure partying," said Lockhart.

George W. was fresh from watching his father's losing race for the Senate. On the campaign trail, he had watched as every Republican that could be smoked out of the backwater towns of Harris County praised his father at the "Bush Bandwagon" rallies, telling the voters why his father was a good man who deserved support. Even at his father's defeat, he would have seen how all of the volunteers and headquarters staffers were devastated. In their hearts, the better man had lost. How could George W. have failed to be influenced by the glamour of that?

If he had wanted to make his mark by winning an official leadership position, he would have been thwarted. Yale did not have significant student government. The only office a guy actually could get appointed to was class secretary or treasurer in senior year, but that only involved overseeing the class business after graduation. Instead, George W. would have to try to achieve along a similar path to his father's—sports and fraternity life. To hit the academic apex was pretty much out of the question. But George W. could continue to distinguish himself in the role that he had discovered at Andover, as social leader.

Luckily, Little George, as his friends at Yale preferred to call him, liked everybody on campus—every guy, that is, except the intellectual snobs, the name droppers; all the guys except the ones who attacked him in his last years about some position his dad had taken publicly. He just *personalized* what people said about his father, his friend Ken Cohen said.

But some attacks *were* personal—as if the critic had lost sight of the fact that his father was not just a politician but a parent too. The Reverend William Sloane Coffin, the chaplain at Yale, was a contemporary of George W.'s father and a fellow Skull and Bones member who had gone on to be an icon on campus. George W. went to see Coffin soon after his dad's 1964 defeat. "I knew your father," Bush recalled Coffin saying, "and your father lost to a better man."

"You talk about a shattering blow," Barbara Bush told the *Washington Post* decades later. "Not only to George, but shattering to us. And it was a very awful thing for a chaplain to say to a freshman at college, particularly if he might have wanted to have seen him in church. I'm not sure that George W. ever put his foot again [in the school chapel]." Coffin has said he was probably joking. George W. maintained the wound.

Still, until a Yalie crossed him in precisely that way, Little George gave them a shot. "George W. is not duplicitous," said Robert McCallum. "He knows what he thinks and is willing to tell you. He's teasing you, teasing himself. He teased me about being a southerner, being too serious, screwing up on the basketball court. You know, like, 'That was a good pass you made . . . right to the other team.'"

George W. got to know the guys at Yale. He asked questions. He remembered not only their names, but a little detail about each of them, such as what their father did, or where they liked to vacation. Every friend would later talk about how impressive that personal memory was; what a sign it was of the way George cared. One famous story had him proving that his class of pledges to Deke was aware of the importance of the brotherhood, by listing off all 50 names on command. And truly, no one else was walking around committing that stuff to memory. The best any other pledge could do was recite four or five names. So George W. did care that much more than the next guy. But for him, it had to be just like memorizing baseball cards—a trick he learned from his dad.

In sophomore year, George W. and his roommates were assigned to a wood-paneled suite with a fireplace in Davenport, a lovely residential college with about 250 students. Down in the gorgeous dining room, the food was good, and guys would congregate there for long discussions. George W. was specifically nonintellectual. His whole family was this way. "We could play like we discuss books and stuff around the dinner table," he would tell David Marannis as an adult, "but that's just not the way it works. We're really more doers."

Instead, he liked to hold court, offering witty insights about the people walking by. He could be so funny—the guys would be crying with laughter. But his jokes also showed intelligence. Lanny Davis used to kid George that his "big secret was how smart he was and he didn't want anybody to know it."

In his sophomore year, George W. pledged his father's fraternity, Delta Kappa Epsilon, with Dieter, Johnson, and another student who had been assigned to room with them at Davenport, Callister "Terry" Johnson Jr. Yale only had six fraternities at the time. None was a major force on campus, but if a guy had the money for the initiation fee, joining a fraternity was a good way to solidify a sizable clique within the democratized college system. Deke had the reputation of being the most athletic and rowdy fraternity; its detractors would say cruder and crasser. It also was the largest and boasted the longest bar on campus, open around the clock. The house had no living quarters, but the brothers could gather for a good meal a couple of times a week, stop by and play pool, and throw loud, sweaty parties every Friday or Saturday night.

The Smith girls would show up and everyone would try to do as much as possible before Sunday. Curfew for the girls was midnight in the dorms, but at Deke, the parties could go on all night. Lanny Davis remembered George W.'s friend Roland Betts doing "unprintable activities with young women there, in certain scenes that I envied," he said. Unlike the southern fraternities, the ones at Yale paid no penance in community service for their hangovers. The purpose of the fraternities was purely social.

The Dekes certainly could pound beers—there was no question about that. On initiation nights, the martinis would flow and guys could get bowl-hugging drunk, but the situation never turned dire. Yale men would down Green Cups at Mary's or grain alcohol punch at Jonathan Edwards.

George W. smoked. In fact, his habit caused one of the only scenes he could remember of open disagreement between his mother and father on a discipline issue. "I was eighteen or nineteen at the time and she got upset and told me I shouldn't smoke," he told Donnie Radcliffe. "I remember my father clearly saying, 'Barbara, who are you to tell your son he shouldn't smoke as you so deeply inhale your Newport?' I guess she stopped smoking when she saw all her kids start."

Drugs were not at all prevalent at Yale then. If anyone did smoke pot, they would do it surreptitiously. No one seemed to recall George W. doing drugs. But Russell Walker said that by the end of senior year most people had tried it. "I'd be surprised if George didn't," he said.

Ron Rosenbaum, writing in the class of 1968 reunion book, explained the clear difference between their class and the ones below. "Marijuana didn't really appear until senior year," he wrote, "mainly in the form of rumors about, say, the guy across the hall who maybe had a girlfriend at Sarah Lawrence who read him the passage from Mailer's *Armies of the Night* about marijuana and sex and talked him into trying them together. But meanwhile, the sophomores were already doing bong hits of hash and the freshman were dropping acid, climbing to the top of Bingham Hall and conversing with the stars."

—

"He just didn't have his heart in making money anymore," Aleene Smith, George Bush's secretary at Zapata, told a reporter. Her boss had never gotten over his 1964 loss to Yarborough. Within months of that defeat, Bush listed himself as one of the plaintiffs in a suit to redraw the 7th Congressional District, in Houston. The plaintiffs won. Now the new seat was an open contest and George Bush wanted to try again.

In early February 1966, he filed as a Republican candidate for Congress. What had George Bush learned from 1964? Start fast and firm. Even though public relations man Hal Hazelrigg had been by Bush's side from the first breath of that senate campaign, Bush had never really lofted up into the public consciousness. Even in the last weeks, he struggled with the "George Who" question.

This time, he would define himself. He would draw such a vivid, complete portrait, no candidate would be able to damage his image in the last minutes of the campaign the way Yarborough had. George Bush called on Harry Treleaven, a vice president at the powerful ad agency J. Walter Thompson, in New York City, who had handled such popular clients as Ford, Pan Am, and Singer.

Bush decided he wouldn't run part-time. A campaign was too tough and too important to be conducted on the edges of job responsibilities. During the 1964 campaign, he took a leave of absence from the company. This time he would resign as CEO of Zapata Off-Shore. Of course, that might make the financial situation tight: George W. was the only child in college so far, with the other four trailing behind. But Bush decided that $1.1 million extracted from Zapata should leave them in fine shape. He called Allison to join the team full-time.

Advertising would be the rocket fuel of the campaign. In May of 1966, Treleaven traveled to Houston to get a firsthand look at his client and his likely opponent in their native habitat. Luckily, the leading adversary, Frank Briscoe, was in the middle of a Democratic primary. The consultant was able to dissect the opponent's ads, his sound bites. Briscoe came off as a good guy, but Treleaven gave his assessment to George Bush straight: Briscoe "seemed uninteresting, even boring, completely lacking in warmth or color." The consultant committed his sentiments to paper in a report that would seem pertinent over 30 years later to George W.'s own go at the presidency in 2000: "Bush is strongest and [his opponent] weakest in the personality department . . . the likability quotient favors Bush."

Bush and his advisers analyzed the candidate's chances. Texas was still Democratic and Briscoe had no obvious flaws aside from his sleepy personality. Only the charm of George Bush and superior organization at every level could win him this election. So on May 9, 1966, Allison, Treleaven, and Bush sat down to formulate the "12 Basics of the Bush for Congress" campaign strategy, a roadmap that was maintained with little variance through election night.

Number one: "Make people aware of George Bush." The campaign had commissioned two polls before Bush declared, and found that 38 percent of the voters in his district didn't know who he was. Not only would the campaign change that fact, its legacy would provide nepotistic coattails over thirty years later by making famous the George Bush name.

Second: "Issues aren't a factor in this race." When placed side by side, Bush and Briscoe did not differ much on the main legislative matters of the day. But rather than describe the hairbreadth difference to the voters, Treleaven and Allison decided that the voter "responds to the complexity of government by withdrawal rather than by increased interest and effort." Better to ignore the fact that government office ultimately involves decision-making based on beliefs. Instead, base the race on personality.

Third: "Advertising should feature the man, not the label." In the Democratic stronghold of Texas, Bush had no choice but to separate himself from fierce party identification. His advisers suggested that he staunchly defend his right to be free of any clear party affiliation, thus giving rise to Bush's regularly evoked retort: "Labels are for cans."

Fourth: "Don't attack by trying to fault the Democratic Party." Bush had learned this truth the hard way in 1964. There was no use taking swipes at LBJ in the same state where he owned a ranch. Likewise number five: "Attacking Briscoe's record would be futile."

Sixth: "Bush has to get the 'emotional vote' to win." Treleaven and Allison needed to convince voters that they *wanted* to give Bush the victory, that Bush was their buddy asking for a favor and the voters would do anything to grant it. This was where George Bush's friendly manner would be the great advantage.

Seventh: Bush's background can be exploited. Put a positive spin on the whole eastern, Ivy League, madras watchband, rich-boy image. "He has a *variety* of experiences behind him—unlike his opponent,

who has been stuck in one place and in one kind of job all his life."
Treleaven wanted Briscoe to come off like the kind of man who, if he
were sent to D.C., wouldn't know which "spoon to pick up."

Eighth: "The advertising must appeal to younger voters." Bush
already had the oldster set sewn up. He needed to take on a segment of
the great unwashed.

Ninth: "A special appeal to women is called for." Women were at
the time—and still are—more likely to ignore party labels when voting. That sector of independent thinkers was what the Republican
frontiersman needed to win. In the later months of the campaign, the
Bushes' seven-year-old daughter, Dorothy, starred in an ad with her
father especially tailored for female voters. He kissed Doro then sat
down for a campaign chat. "The next sixty seconds are just for you
ladies," he told the camera, then explained why he wanted to be the
congressman for the women of that district. Treleaven and Allison
hoped for a particular interior monologue from the ladies of District 7:
"He would be *so* disappointed if he lost," they wrote, "and—well, no
woman with a heart could let *that* happen!"

Tenth: "Bush should not play it cool. He should work up a sweat
and it should show." Bush should "create fighting underdog image,"
advised Allison and Treleaven.

Eleventh: "The advertisements must present Bush as a man of
action who will be heard from, who will get things done."

Twelfth: "The advertising should accentuate the positive and never
be defensive. We must act, not react." The campaign slogan would
imply adventure, entertainment. The team devised the film-poster–style
pitch: "Elect George Bush to Congress—and Watch the Action!"

For two months, George Bush flickered on the Houston consciousness. On George W.'s twentieth birthday, an abbreviated version
of his father's television ad "family" aired. The full commercial had
played two months before: The voice-over introduced each of the kids
as they ran by the camera on their way to a convertible. They were all
"going on the Bush Bandwagon!"

"Okay gang—pile in!" Bush cajoled.

Starting in late July, George Bush invaded the collective thought
bubble of that district. He was everywhere: He loomed on a billboard, a windblown color silhouette against a stark white back-

ground, waving. Then he'd appear up ahead on another billboard, his jacket hooked on his thumb, his hands on his hips, practically panting from the effort of trying to win the votes of Houstonians. If you turned on the radio, you'd hear the brassy opening bars of "Seventy-six Trombones" and then George Bush's voice telling you he wanted your support. Twelve of those ran a day! If you turned on the TV after the middle of September, you were bound to encounter an ad—they ran on all three networks from the *Today* show in the morning to the late-night movie. There were buttons, banners, 24-foot posters, car tops, newspaper ads. The pamphlets boasted endorsements from Dwight D. Eisenhower and Mrs. W. Howard Lee, otherwise known as the glamorous actress Gene Tierney. George was ubiquitous. He even had an "exact time" message for people to call. *George Bush gives you the time of day.* The voters couldn't escape him; they wouldn't want to!

Then, about a week after the tsunami that was George Bush's campaign hit maximum velocity—when the whole district was blinded by the confetti of George Bush bumper stickers and pamphlets, when the whole district was hunkering down for the remaining two months of that high-intensity publicity slam—Frank Briscoe finally opened his campaign for the general election.

Three weeks after the first George Bush advertisements ran, a phone survey showed that an astounding nine out of ten people had seen the ads. A full 92 percent could recall parts of the message without prompting, and 99 percent of the voters viewed George Bush favorably.

Briscoe began criticizing Bush for overspending on advertisements.

On November 8, 1966, George Bush won his first political seat with 58 percent to Briscoe's 42 percent. He had worked 18 hours a day, seven days a week, to achieve this success, and managed by the end of the campaign not only to have become a congressman but also a household name.

In the new family tradition, George W. marked the tallies on the blackboard at headquarters. George Bush, down to his shirtsleeves, kept calling up Prescott and Dotty in Greenwich: "Gosh, Mother and Dad, it looks like we're ahead," he'd yell over the din of his supporters. A little after 10 P.M., Briscoe conceded, saying, "I have been elected to practice law." The Bush headquarters went wild. Everyone hugged. Jimmy Allison cried, he was so happy.

—

After George Bush was sworn in as a representative, Allison and Treleaven set to paper the history of the 1966 election strategy, entitled "Upset: The Story of a Modern Political Campaign." Indeed, it was the cookie cutter, if inadvertently, for a multitude of races through the rest of the century.

"Political candidates are celebrities," noted Allison and Treleaven in their postmortem. "And today, with TV taking them into everybody's home right along with Johnny Carson and Batman, they're more of a public attraction than ever."

It seems strange now to think of George Bush as being one of the pioneers of modern, commercial-driven campaigning. Still, despite the success of his pitch—as superman, wonderful guy, cool-headed businessman—even in that 1966 campaign, one could detect the seeds of that pernicious problem that he would struggle for decades to solve. How could a man who was essentially a nice guy find a graceful way to convey his power to his constituents? And if that trial could be seen anywhere it could be detected in the shooting script for one of his final 1966 ads.

The controversial idea was to create a moody commercial, one that got into the head of a candidate on the eve of an election. It started with a voice-over musing about all the paths not taken during the campaign, "I'm wondering if I said the right words, if you really understand how much I care . . . ," George Bush ruminated.

The telltale sign of George Bush's future troubles with image management was the script's stage directions: "Walks toward us with his small poodle, unleashed. He is lost in thought."

—

While his father prepared to serve as representative to the United States Congress, George W. was presiding as president of the illustrious Delta Kappa Epsilon, the same post his father had held at Yale. The position mainly required overseeing the budget and serving as spokesman. George W. took his duties seriously. His most famous act as president came in December of 1966 when he helped boost holiday cheer. As Christmas and Hanukkah approached, George W. realized that Deke was running low on yuletide spirit. So he and a couple of other brothers tried to lift a wreath from a storefront one night. The cops nabbed him and he got charged with a misdemeanor. Later, the charges were dropped. The next year, he publicly threw his support behind branding in fraternities. Under the headline "Disgrace on the Row," the *Yale Daily News* had condemned the fraternities for violating their own rule against branding, beating, and mock sex acts. The fraternity presidents, under the auspices of the Inter-Fraternity Council (IFC), had agreed that brotherhoods should have to face temporary closure or a $1,000 fine for any violation. But when the *News* exposed the continuing tradition, none of the fraternities would accept the punishment. George W., as a former president, defended branding in the *New York Times* by saying that the mark was "only a cigarette burn." The question still stood as to whether that discomfort would be worth enduring for the sake of joining an official clique.

In truth, the procedure was more of a psychological test than a physical one. During initiation, the guys pledging Deke would be shown a four-inch red-hot steel brand. When they turned their backs for the procedure, something more minor would be substituted. "I don't know if I still have it, but I had a little Delta on my back," said Jim Lockhart, a Deke brother.

The fight came down to whether a bunch of guys who wanted to drink together could engage in silly rituals beforehand. George W. would come down on the side of tradition, on male ritual. The campus scolds were not amused. "Initiations, formal or informal, which are brutal or degrading in any way have no place in a recognized undergraduate activity," the editors at the *News* wrote. Such practices imperil the reputation of the house, the worth of the IFC, and are inexcusable impositions on new members." George W. was never much for accommodating the scolds. He chose to support the continuity of tradition and to downplay the importance of the gesture, rather than question why it was so important to continue branding students in the first place. Deke ended up paying a fine under $1,000, and branding was dropped the following year.

These antics were partly just the normal hubbub of college life, partly the runoff of testosterone on an all-male campus. Everywhere you looked at Yale, it was guys. All these men drinking together, playing sports, competing in classes, cheering on the football team. They couldn't help but bond. During the week, hardly anyone dated, so if a guy got depressed, his only choice was to talk to his buddy about it. The environment wasn't touchy feely, but if a Yale man was looking for *action* . . . if he could come up with something someone could *do* to help him out, to keep him from being depressed, to get him out of a bind, then he knew he could count on one of the guys. He could count on them for the rest of his life.

The weekends were girl time. Then a Yalie might hop in his car and go on a road trip to see his sweetie at Vassar or Smith. A Yalie could date Quinnipiac girls over in Hamden, or Albertus Magnus gals just up the road in New Haven itself. Some guys even went out with the teens from the local high schools.

George W. wasn't known as a big dater. Almost none of his friends considered him a romantic. He just would not abandon himself that way, they said. But George W. had been enough of a Casanova to put himself in the worst trouble he ever had with his father. George W. had been working as a roughneck on an oil rig just offshore Houston one summer, and the days were ticking down to when he would have to go back up to New Haven. He missed the girl he was dating when he was out there on the rig, and wanted to make sure he saw a little more of her before he had to leave town. He quit the job before his employer was through with him.

"Before long I was called to my father's office in downtown Houston," George W. told CBS talk-show host Charlie Rose. "He simply told me: 'In our family, and in life, you fulfill your commitments; you've disappointed me.' And that was it." George W. had let romance fill his head and he lost his way. The Bushes didn't stand for that.

Still, George Bush had enough of a soft spot for young infatuation, or perhaps just a deep belief in his own unconditional love for his son, that he took the couple to the Houston Astros game that night.

When George W. returned to Yale after the Christmas break his junior year he had big news for his friends—at least the information was shocking to *them*. To George W., it seemed less monumental. He and his girlfriend, Cathy Wolfman, a neighbor from Houston who had gone to Smith and visited him a couple of times at Yale, were planning to be married that summer. The engagement to "pretty" Cathy Wolfman had been written up in the *Houston Chronicle* on the first day of the New Year with a picture of the two of them sitting cozily with nothing but a large pillow between them.

To get engaged while in college wasn't in itself so out of the ordinary. "Most college women looked at senior year as a time to find a husband," said Lanny Davis, who himself got married in his junior year.

But many of George W.'s friends and fraternity brothers didn't even know he was seriously dating Cathy, let alone choosing to spend the rest of his life with her. He did not talk about her very often, and she had only visited a couple of times. George W.'s friend Donald Ensenat vividly remembered walking along in front of the fraternity, when George W. announced the news to him. Ensenat was stunned. "Personally," he told him, "I think you are too young." George W. didn't discuss the issue further.

But while the engagement might be startling given the two people involved, there had been a precedent set. The relationship so echoed George W.'s parents' history that even some of his friends noticed. Cathy had been a Smith girl, as Barbara was, although she transferred to Rice University for her last years. George W. was 20 years old, the same age his father was when he married Bar. They made the decision over Christmas vacation, the same holiday season when his parents wed. They planned to spend senior year in New Haven together just like his parents had.

The two became enamoured with each other when Cathy was home in Houston recuperating from a skiing accident. Her mother had divorced her father and was now remarried to the owner of an eponymous high-end clothing store, Wolfman's. Cathy attended the prestigious private high school, St. John's, where she was an outstanding athlete. She went to Smith, then eventually enrolled at Rice, where she majored in economics and participated in the Elizabeth Baldwin Literary Society. Gene Tierney's daughter, Tina Cassini, told the *Dallas Morning News* that some young people in their flashy social scene may have looked down a bit on Cathy because her stepfather was a merchant, but George W. definitely was not among them. He loved the bubbly, erudite, athletic girl who got along so well with adults.

—

The Vietnam War crept into the consciousness of the Yale men slowly, but soon invaded their every waking thought. Every year, the students were required to submit their transcripts to see if the academic deferment still held. If a guy had failed, he had to reenter the lottery. The test was easy but the idea unsettling. The academic draft deferment for graduate students was canceled for good on February 16 during their senior year; only medical students were still exempt.

As a jock who crossed different cliques at Davenport, George W. was drawn into the harangues over the issues of the day. "We would debate the war," remembered fellow Davenport resident Don Etra. "We would debate the role of Dr. Spock and Bill Coffin protesting the war. We would debate the fact that there were tanks rolling down the main street of New Haven because of potential civil unrest. We would debate what the best course of action was for handling the war if you opposed it."

The arguments about Vietnam took all sorts of bewildering twists and turns in an environment where most people fancied themselves remarkably bright, and where the stake in the debate was life itself:

"My duty is to country, I would serve if called."

"My duty is to God, I would refuse to serve."

"God would want me to fight this moral war."

"I am a conscientious objector."

"But if someone came into your house and shot your mother would you kill them?"

"Of course."

"Then you're not a pacifist."

In the fall of their junior year, Robert Birge remembered sitting in George W.'s room and talking to Perrin Quarles, one of their classmates, who had been vocal in his support of the war and had left Yale early to fight. "[Quarles] came back to visit on leave and his stories were so shocking and horrible, he had a bigger impact on us than anything that we saw on TV," said Birge. "Just knowing somebody who had switched so dramatically. That had a very big impact on me. . . .

George's attitude was that basically you've just got to do your duty. I never understood that [rigidity] because he was so open and free in many other ways, but this was something that was very important to him: responsibility to one's country."

George W. always supported the war, from those days in his junior year when debate flourished but the academic deferment kept the men safe from actually putting their lives on the line, to graduation, when a Yale man's views determined whether he would be boarding a plane for Vietnam or sneaking over the border to Canada. "The big issue for us was what were we going to do," said Birge. "We spent a lot of time agonizing about that. I really think that one of the big impacts of the war on people my age going through college was that it made you look at the short term rather than the long term, and the short term was to get through it and survive. . . . George was very proud of his father's service in World War II, and it was a matter of honor to him to serve."

Birge was more conflicted than his friend. He thought that young men who escaped to Canada were pursuing a perfectly reasonable option. He ended up serving in the Air Force, but reluctantly. "George [W.] was much more forgiving about the decision to fight in Vietnam. I would not call him right wing," said Birge. "He would have a good discussion about it and have good points, but he thought my attitude was inappropriate."

George W. expressed his views passionately. "I can remember him telling me why I was chickenshit for not just going into the Air Force or the Army and doing my job like I'm supposed to. Just letting me have it," recalled Birge. "He was never shy about telling people where he stood and where they should stand." But despite the aggressiveness of George W.'s opinions, Birge marveled how George W.'s likable manner overrode any annoyance. "I remember thinking, 'If I had heard this from other people, I'd be punching them, but I'm listening to you,'" he said of George W.'s critique. "So he automatically carries a certain amount of respect. His demeanor is very effective, and that's a gift."

Many of George W.'s closest friends were as pro-military as he. "George W. and I had no objection to military service," said Etra. "I believed in the stated purposes for the war and the goal of battling communism. Therefore I saw no moral or ethical or intellectual reasons not to serve if called."

"I knew he was going to be in a military air program," said Robert McCallum. "I remember his views as to duty to country. If he was troubled [about the mission of the war], that was a blur. If George W. had received a draft notice, he would not have, as Bill Clinton did, sit down and cry. He would have said, 'That's what I have to do.'"

They had friends who were drafted and some who volunteered. A good percentage of the class was in ROTC. Only 9 percent of Yale students who voted supported Lyndon Johnson and his policies. George W., according to his friends, cast a wary eye on protesters. His father's position was similar. While he defended the right to freedom of expression, he ranted against the mayhem caused by demonstrations. In the spring of 1968, George Bush introduced a bill to remove any federal worker from employment for five years if they were convicted of a civil disorder. He was right-wing enough that year to earn a 67 percent approval rating among conservatives.

The fact that George W.'s political views were accommodating to government positions is not surprising. Although life-and-death issues were being debated all around him, he saw politics from the inside out. While students at other schools were discussing revolution, his father was campaigning for and maintaining traditional political involvement. As a result of remaining on the Establishment side of politics, George W. was allowed to live a fairly trouble-free life: He wasn't arrested for civil disobedience, just picked up for wreath stealing. He wasn't shot at, like the Kent State students, he was chastised by the *Yale Daily News* for branding.

Yale uniquely insulated him from the mayhem as well. Unlike Columbia University or Kent State, the students at Yale were relatively tranquil. Lady Bird Johnson contended with nothing more threatening than the backs of 1,200 silent students when she spoke on Freshman Commons. California governor Ronald Reagan fared even better when he visited as a Chubb fellow in December of George W.'s senior year. He received a standing ovation. Reagan whispered to an aide that the Yale students were "surprisingly quiet and receptive."

"The Yale student is concerned, but not too much," wrote journalist Tom Herman in his 1968 classbook. "He signs up eagerly for the Political Union which will not ask him to take a stand on issues and affords him the chance to hear front-page stars, but spurns the activist associations, perhaps fearing that membership in action groups may harm him in later years."

—

While the rituals of the 168-year-old secret society Skull and Bones are strictly guarded, one graduate of George W.'s class, Ron Rosenbaum, uncovered a trove of secrets (whose veracity he would endorse to varying degrees) for a 1977 article in *Esquire* magazine. The society appears to have been imported from Germany in 1832 by a Yale senior, William H. Russell, who befriended a university student there who was one of the club's leaders. Years later, Russell established a trust for the society that financed, among other perks, the maintenance of Deer Island, a wooded resort on the St. Lawrence River in upstate New York, for the group's more elaborate encounters.

If the secrets Rosenbaum uncovered are to be believed, George W. was waiting in his room in Davenport on tap night in April of his junior year when he heard a loud thump on the door. When he swung it open, he was greeted by a senior Bonesman who clapped him on the shoulder and shouted, "Skull and Bones: Do you accept?" That Bonesman was likely Victor Ashe, whose parents had been great friends of Prescott and Dotty Bush down in Hobe Sound, Florida, where both families had vacation homes. (Ashe would later become the mayor of Knoxville, Tennessee, and George W. would stump for him in a losing campaign for the senate.) George W. readily agreed to be one of the 15 elite members of campus to enter not only The Order that year, but the many generations of a powerful, watchful brotherhood. According to lore, he may or may not have also been given a financial gift of $15,000 from the Russell trust to use in whatever way he pleased.

With that clap on the shoulder, George W. was finally fully invited into the world of his father. So much of George Herbert Walker Bush's life had been touched by Bonesmen. His father, Prescott, was a member of the Secret society. It was Bonesman Henry Stimson, former secretary of war, who had given the commencement speech at Andover that day in 1942 when George Bush decided against all odds to throw himself into the conflict. Bonesman Neil Mallon gave him his first job at Dresser in Texas. It would be Bonesman Bill Buckley who invited him to help redirect the Republican Party by showing his insights in *National Review* after his losing 1964 senate campaign. Supreme Court Justice Potter Stewart would swear in his Bones brother, George Bush, as head of the CIA and then twice as vice president. Just to name a few members of The Order his father had regularly turned to in life.

The Tuesday after tap night, George W. would be instructed to "wear no metal" when he showed up at the sepulcher-like structure for his first meeting.

According to the reconnaissance of a rival society, File and Claw, the Bones headquarters boasts an arched vault on which are painted a skull, Masonic symbols, and a German slogan: "Who was the fool, who the wise man, beggar or king? Whether poor or rich, all's the same in death." Here at last was an institutionalized anti-snobbism—that still could enjoy elitism.

To all the Bonesmen, the diversity of the organization is key to its power. While the fraternities could forge friendly bonds, frat brothers were basically self-selected by common interest. In The Order, the members were chosen for their *varying* perspectives. Understandings were built across social and racial lines. "It's a much smaller group," said Robert McCallum, "so there's no place to hide. You've got to deal."

Yale would provide George W. with a vast network of male friends who would help him politically and in business throughout his life, just as Andover had. He would maintain the buddies from sports and the brothers from Deke. But some of his closest friends were those from Skull and Bones. "Of all societies none is more glorious nor of greater strength than when good men of similar morals are joined in intimacy," reads one Latin maxim of the club.

Just before senior year, all the new Bonesmen traditionally travel to Deer Island where they meet the secret society's alumni and their families. Only the Bonesmen know for sure who attended the year George W. first arrived.

In September, the Bones members shared first their biographical histories, and then their sexual sagas. George Bush told the stories of his married life with Bar back when he first joined The Order. Rosenbaum wrote about the power of this initiation for Yale men, particularly of his era and earlier: "Idle, preppie Prince Hals suddenly became serious students of society and themselves, as if acceptance into the tomb were a signal to leave the tavern and prepare to rule the land. Those embarrassed at introspection and afraid of trusting other men are given the mandate and the confidence to do so." George W. reportedly spoke of his relationship with his father.

George W.'s ambitions for himself were extremely personal. "He wasn't like Strobe Talbott [who went on to be deputy secretary of state in the Clinton administration], where being the big guy on campus was absolutely critical to his view of himself," said fellow Bonesman Robert Birge. "He was much more introspective than Strobe. The issues that were important to him were not at all how he was perceived by others. [His issues were] what he was going to do with himself, how was he going to make a living, what was he going to do in terms of his relationships with women and people ten or twenty years down the road. It was very important to him that he be responsible and have a positive impact [in the world], but not that he be in the spotlight. So it's absolutely surprising to me that he would want to run for president."

Before senior year, Birge thought of George W. as spontaneous, a party animal. "When you got to know him as just another student at Yale, he did not come across as a serious person," said Birge. "But when you really got to know him, he was."

—

In November 1967, after a five-day "Hate Princeton" rally, the Yale men traveled down to New Jersey to reengage the school's rivalry with the Tigers. Yale hadn't beaten Princeton in eight years. Rain soaked the field, and all the guys huddled with their dates, drinking hard to beat the bitter cold. George W. and the boys were counting on Deke brothers halfback Calvin Hill and quarterback Brian Dowling to save the Yale reputation.

Late in the last quarter, with Yale leading 29 to 7, a call came down from further north that Cornell had beaten Dartmouth, which meant that the Bulldogs were about to win the Ivy League title.

At that moment, one shot of sun lit up the visitors' stands, and about 30 Yalies raced across the field and clambered up the goalposts. The campus police nabbed a half dozen. Don Ensenat remembered George W. being escorted down the field with a cop holding each arm.

The perpetrators were brought down to campus police headquarters and told they had ten minutes to get out of town. George W. still hadn't returned to Princeton thirty years later. But the guys who managed to get away dragged a 15-foot chunk of the crossbar into the locker room and presented it to coach Carmen Cozza.

What a beautiful moment that was! All of the guys just out of their heads with joy at victory. Wasn't Yale great! All the buses and cars rolled back to New Haven like they were floating aircarts all the way up I-95. The Bulldogs had redeemed themselves after the slights of even three years before. "It was one of the last things you could grasp onto that was frivolous and yet 'important'—to avenge [Princeton star fullback] Cosmo Iacavazzi for sending footballs into the Yale stands at the Bowl [after scoring two touchdowns]," remembered McCallum. "Get your mind off of whether you would kill someone or not in Vietnam."

—

Over that Christmas break, George W. called the Texas Air National Guard recruiting office in Houston to inquire if there were any openings. In the latter part of December, he had met Lieutenant Colonel Walter B. Staudt, who friends told him was the man to call about applications. Yes, Staudt told George W. on the telephone, there were slots available. On January 17, George W. took the officers qualification test at the United States Air Force Recruiting Station in New Haven.

During that same period, George W.'s father was also becoming more involved in evaluating the situation in Vietnam. Right around the time George W. was meeting Staudt in late December, George Bush left on a fact-finding mission to Vietnam conducted at his own expense. He had planned since September to go as soon as Congress was out of session. In his newsletter earlier in the fall, he wrote that he had disagreed with President Johnson on many aspects of his Vietnam policy; for one, he wrote: "I frankly am lukewarm on sending more American boys to Viet Nam. I want more involvement by Asians."

On the trip, George Bush met with top U.S. commanders in Hawaii before flying to a hotel in Saigon. From there, he choppered to military sites in Vietnam, from the Mekong Delta south of Saigon to the coastal town of Danang. He met with U.S. ambassador Ellsworth

Bunker and with Robert W. Komer, the head of the U.S. pacification program, along with other officials. "I'm convinced [the South Vietnamese army] are improving," George Bush said. "A lot of our kids don't mind being in the field and fighting alongside them at all."

What struck George Bush most was how distorted the U.S. press coverage had been. Those damned media people had made the South Vietnamese seem barbaric, the U.S. bunglers, and the war a ubiquitous terror in the lives of the Vietnamese. Instead, he was surprised by how business in the cities just carried on as usual. "When I came home I read about the shelling of Danang—front page big deal," he wrote in a typed letter uncovered by biographer Herbert Parmet, "and yet I was there that night—slept thru the whole thing—was shut down on one runway maybe for an hour—no one was killee [sic] and yet reading the paper I thought I might have been in the Bataan siege for heaven sakes." But in the countryside, George Bush saw that despite the ready smiles of children, people's lives were more affected. An elderly farmer just hoped someone would fix his road.

Upon George Bush's return to Houston, he took the peace activists to task for portraying the military men as heartless hawks. "I wish you could have seen our young pilots in the carrier briefing room as they discussed their hazardous mission over the flak-ridden skies of Hanoi," he told reporters at a press conference in Texas upon his return.

But he had come back a bit more sympathetic to young people protesting the war at home. Before the end of January, he met with students in Washington to hear their concerns. He even gave a speech to Republicans in Houston saying that the activists were voicing their beliefs for moral reasons.

On the Air Force officers qualification test that George W. took that same month, he had received 25 percent—a score that was barely passing. He did a little better on the navigator aptitude test, with 50 percent. His best performance was on the "officer quality" section, for which he received 95 percent.

Over the years of his political career, the fact that George W. had been accepted into the National Guard infuriated his critics, primarily because he always suggested that he had not benefited from favoritism, or even luck, but that he had been one of the few young

men *willing* to fill the need for pilots in Texas. While the pilot training and Air National Guard service that followed were by no means
easy, pleasant experiences, they were a far cry from being sent into the
infantry. George W. explained that he had decided on the National
Guard because he was eager to learn how to pilot a plane, just like his
father, and did not want to simply be sent into the trenches in Vietnam.
That meant that George W. got exactly the military situation he was
looking for, an uncommon luxury in that era.

He insisted that his father never directly intervened on his behalf
to gain him a slot in the Guard. "Governor Bush did not need and did
not ask anybody for help," George W.'s campaign spokesman for his
presidential bid, Scott McClellan, told the *Washington Post*. "President
Bush has said he did not seek any help for his son in getting into the
National Guard."

But in 1999, the former lieutenant governor of Texas, who during
the Vietnam era oversaw the state's National Guard, stated in a deposition that a friend of the family had approached him in late 1967 or
early 1968 to put in a word for George Bush's eldest son. Ben Barnes,
who in 1968 was a 29-year-old Democratic wunderkind as lieutenant
governor, said that oil man Sidney Adger, a longtime friend of George
Bush from Houston, asked for help getting George W. accepted.
Barnes had then called Brigadier General James M. Rose, who was the
head of the Air Guard.

The statement arose after a deposition Barnes gave for a wrongful
dismissal lawsuit against GTECH, a company that runs lotteries and
for which he was a former lobbyist, going before the Texas courts in
1999. Barnes was called as a witness to explore the allegation that
GTECH was allowed to keep their lucrative state lottery contract
because George W., when governor, wanted to keep Barnes quiet
about the National Guard question. George W. was also subpoenaed
in that lawsuit.

In 1998, during George W.'s reelection campaign for the Texas
governorship, his friend from Midland, Don Evans, who would go on
to serve as national finance chair for the 2000 presidential bid, went
to see Barnes to ask if he remembered anyone asking for special dis-
pensation for George W. He was particularly concerned about a story
circulating that George Bush had approached Barnes at the

Bluebonnet Bowl in December 1967. Barnes assured him that he had not been contacted by any member of the Bush family, but that he remembered hearing from an oilman from Houston who urged him to help George W. become a pilot in the Guard.

In Bush tradition, George W. followed up with a note, this one to Barnes on September 9, 1998, underscoring the important points of the meeting. "Dear Ben," he wrote, "Don Evans reported your conversation. Thank you for your candor and for killing the rumor about you and Dad ever discussing my status. Like you, he never remembered any conversation. I appreciate your help."

Barnes's recommendation of George W. to the Guard in 1968 would have been enough to get him in. That April, the lieutenant governor had been made an honorary lifetime member of the Guard. George W. would not have needed his father to contact the National Guard officers directly to benefit from his power and prestige since George Bush was a well-known political force in Texas. Across the country, almost every young man who did not want to be sent as cannon fodder to Vietnam—yet who also did not want to be a conscientious objector—was begging his state representatives to help him get into National Guard programs. Jim Lockhart turned to Senator Hubert Humphrey for assistance with Navy OC3.

Lanny Davis said that it's obvious that George W.'s name helped get him in. Lanny himself had been trying to petition his senator to find him a slot in the guard for some time, to no avail. Finally, when his wife got pregnant, a parental exemption saved him. Still he doesn't think George W. sought any favors. "He says he did not get help from his father and I totally believe him on that," said Davis. "The reason I believe him is that I'm totally convinced that George would not have a problem being up-front about that. If he'd called his father and said, Hey, could you make a few calls for me to get me into a guard unit, he would admit it." That spring of 1968, many of George W.'s friends, even those from Skull and Bones, would be unaware that he had found a possible placement with the National Guard; apparently he never told them.

—

Outside the ivy-covered sanctuary of Yale, the world was in disarray that spring of 1968. In Paris, students packed the avenues nightly to lob rocks over the police barricades while ten million workers struck in solidarity. Soviet tanks rolled down the cobblestone streets of Prague to suppress the mobs of protesters. Even Yale was threatening to change. Those last few years, the dinner-table talk intensified about whether or not women should be accepted into the university. "George W. and I knew it would change the fabric of the school," said Ken Cohen.

The Yale men had just returned from spring vacation on March 31 when Lyndon Johnson announced that he would not run for reelection that November. "I thought that was a cop-out," said Etra. The other presidential candidates had all declared their support for continuing the war. By abandoning the presidency, Johnson had left the young American men to deal with the draft and the ambiguities of Vietnam.

A few days later, Martin Luther King Jr. was assassinated. For almost the first time, the students at Yale actually took to the streets, even if it was only to join an angry memorial for the civil rights leader on the town green.

Representative George Bush himself had begun to show a more activist side on racial issues. In March, he pushed his home state to adopt "For Mexican American Texans—A Future of Fair Play and Progress," a series of guidelines to bring more diversity to state government. Now, in the aftermath of the King assassination, George Bush faced a vote on the civil rights open housing bill.

George Bush's views on civil rights issues had evolved over the decades. His family had always worked for causes that helped black Americans, and he had been the head of the United Negro College Fund at Yale. But those philanthropic efforts were below the radar. In 1964, Bush ran adamantly against Lyndon Johnson's civil rights bill, arguing that its passage would violate the constitution and that only moral persuasion could end prejudicial practices in the United States. He echoed his constituents' own opposition to the bill, but presented the view in a cloak of reason. He laundered their ugliness. He condemned Martin Luther King Jr. as a radical, but still reached out for minority support by saying that the Democratic Party had failed minority voters. That year he only managed to win 3 percent of the "Negro or Latin" precincts and joked about how there had been no groundswell.

In the 1966 campaign, he inched a little further toward racial issues when he declared: "I think the day is past when we can afford to have a lily white district." He used the Bush passion of baseball to build a bridge. In Houston, the softball and Little League teams had been all white. Some league organizers approached Bush and asked him if he would fund a black all-girl team. The George Bush All-Stars desegregated the sport in that city.

ﾗ   The trip to Vietnam, though, had infused passion to George Bush's views. He could no longer abide the fact that black soldiers were putting their lives on the line in Southeast Asia, yet were treated as second-class citizens in their own country. Although his constituents fiercely opposed the open housing bill, he voted with nine other Texas Republican congressional representatives and the House majority for it.

Immediately, the Bush family home was flooded with hate mail and crank calls. A week after the vote, Representative Bush flew to the Memorial-West section of his district to give a speech. The crowd started hooting, screaming obscenities as he spoke. But instead of pandering to the crowd in any way, Bush decided to take a stand. "Somehow it seems fundamental that a man—if he has the money and the good character—should not have a door slammed in his face if he is a Negro or if he speaks with a Latin American accent," he said. The catcalls gave way to applause and soon George Bush was looking at a sea of standing supporters.

He later described the event as the greatest moment in his political life.

—

George W. finalized his plans to join the Texas Air National Guard on May 27, during a special trip to Houston. He visited Lt. Col. Walter B. "Buck" Staudt at his office and told him that he wanted to learn how to fly "just like his daddy." At the time, there were two openings in the guard, but two men were just finishing their training and another was waiting to be transferred. Still, Staudt made room for George W. He was sworn in by a captain.

"Nobody did anything for him," Staudt told the *Los Angeles Times*. "There was no goddamn influence on his behalf. Neither his daddy nor anybody else got him into the guard."

Another 150 applicants for all the Texas Air Guard posts, including ground crew, waited on a list kept by Sergeant Donald Dean Barnhart, according to the *Los Angeles Times*. He told the paper that it could take up to a year and a half for an applicant to move up to placement. That's because basic training at Lackland Air Force in San Antonio was usually completely full. Lloyd Bentsen III, the son of the man who would eventually challenge George Bush in the 1970 election, was also in the group, as was the son of then-Senator John Tower and at least seven Dallas Cowboys.

George W. flew back up to Yale. In those tumultuous times, the prom had been canceled due to insufficient interest. On June 5, George W. and his fellow Bonesmen headed up to Deer Island to share one last inculcation before being thrown out into the real world. Someone turned on the radio while they were driving north. *The coffin is being loaded onto the plane for the trip back . . .* the announcer said. They thought it was some kind of reprise of the 1963 assassination. Then they realized it was Bobby. "George W. was stunned and horrified like the rest of them," said one Bonesman.

"I was appalled and shocked," McCallum recalled. " I was thinking where the hell are we? There was devastation after devastation to the psyche of the country."

"I did feel that the confluence of Pope John the twenty-third and President Kennedy was indeed Camelot," remembers fellow Bonesman Don Etra, "and then the events of the Kennedy assassination and the Martin Luther King death were pulling asunder the fabric of what had been a much better world at least politically and socially back in 1963, and there was [further] deterioration from 1963 to 1968."

The Bonesmen spent three or four days on the island in brotherly bonding with no other distractions, including telephones. The closest television was located at the Alexandria Bay saloon. Ken Cohen took a boat there to watch the replay of the shooting. "I don't think he would despair for his own safety as much as he would despair for his father's," said Ken Cohen.

That Sunday, June 9, the class of 1968 gathered in Woolsey Hall for the baccalaureate address. President Kingman Brewster Jr. started with a reference to the recent assassination: "Until last Wednesday morning I hadn't expected to talk about this. But in a way, perhaps I had; because I had intended to talk about the frustrations of always having to be against things, somehow never having a chance to strike a publicly significant blow in terms of what you are for. In the aftermath of Wednesday's shock, I realized that there is a connection between violence and negativism. Destructive violence, particularly murderous violence, is the ultimate negative. It is the supreme dramatic cry of the 'anti-.'"

Brewster went on to praise the class for its ability to remain positively focused, considering the times, and gave credit primarily to its student leaders. But most of Brewster's words were dedicated to dealing with the conundrum the draft presented to young men. He spoke of those who would serve gladly and those who would go to jail for ducking the draft. "Many others feel they have no choice other than to approach the problem of military service in much the same spirit as a tax lawyer," he continued. "They are left to weave their way down the narrow line which divides proper avoidance from improper evasion. . . . Perhaps the crudest evidence of the distortion of motivation which is induced by an unconscionable law was the clearly discernible increase in applications to the Divinity School this spring. This coincided with General Hershey's edict that college graduates would lose their deferments and would be called in order of seniority."

In early May, nine students from the class of 1968, including Strobe Talbott, began circulating a petition against the war. "As long as the United States continues to wage its war in Vietnam," the statement read, "we cannot, without violating our consciences, allow ourselves to be conscripted into the armed services of our country." Some of the students who signed did go on to serve in the war. Ken Cohen remembered that he and George W. were among the few who didn't add their signatures.

George W.'s father did not linger for the commencement festivities. He was unopposed for reelection in 1968, but he was working as a surrogate for, among other political figures, Richard Nixon, who was running for the Republican presidential nomination. Terry Johnson would later tell the *Washington Post* that George W. was somewhat hurt by his father's hurry. "[George W.] hung out with my family for most of the two days," Johnson recalled. "I remember as his dad left, he made some comment about [wishing his] dad didn't have these other obligations. 'I wish, it would have been great if my dad could have been here during the whole time.'

"It wasn't said in passing," Johnson told the reporter. "Everybody wants their family there sharing with them. . . . He's very aware of the toll that public service takes on the family members."

To George W., personal relationships were all that really mattered. Fellow Bonesman Britt Kolar, who had volunteered for U.S. Navy Intelligence, remembered how he agonized over what to do about his girlfriend now that he was going overseas. Perhaps thinking of George and Bar, George W. greatly encouraged him not to sacrifice the relationship just because he was headed to war. "Don't cut this off just because you might die or something," George W. told him. He recognized that decisions couldn't be made based on fleeting circumstances. "He is a romantic in that respect," said Kolar. "He values human relationships above anything else, and that is a romantic notion."

George W.'s own engagement had been put off the previous summer. Unlike Bar, who waited patiently in Rye for her man to return from the service, Cathy Wolfman was headed to D.C. on her own while George W. went back to Texas for basic training.

So much of George W.'s effort to live the kind of Yale experience that his father and mother had enjoyed had been thwarted by the nature of his own era. He had become the president of Deke house like his father, but the fraternities weren't as popular as when his dad had been Deke president; his dad never would have been pulled into a politically correct tussle over branding. George W. was confronted with a war, but rather than enjoying Yale on the other side of military glory as his father had, he was forced to wrangle with the fears and ambiguities of Vietnam and postpone his plans for his future to a date sometime after military service. The world awaiting him after graduation was not enjoying a postwar boom, but a cultural apocalypse.

Some of the guys in the class of 1968 felt that no one could really understand what they faced in these struggles. "The classes after us had certainties to choose from . . . ," wrote Ron Rosenbaum 25 years after graduating, in the Yale Class of 1968 reunion book. "Look by contrast at the kind of choices *we* faced when we were about to graduate: war, protest, jail, exile, or writing extremely complex soul-searching letters to our draft boards that could later come back to haunt us."

Still, those years at Yale, before the fallout for draft decisions hit, seemed like something of a refuge in the chaotic time. "Like so many of our classmates, I had so enjoyed college," said Etra of the melancholy that made this particular commencement so difficult. "There was clearly a considerable amount of sadness that we would—the class would no longer be together."

By the fall of 1969, the era to which George W. belonged at Yale was wiped clean from the campus. Robert McCallum, back for law school, found that the events of the summer, particularly the riots at the Democratic convention in Chicago, had transformed the political style. Where in the spring he and George W. could feel at least accepted in their fierce patriotism, by fall McCallum felt like an alien, with his army reserve buzz cut. Students no longer viewed pot as a mysterious and exotic high, but instead passed joints openly. As fate would have it, George W. had escaped to the far more conservative climate of Houston, Texas, before any of his views would be challenged—not just by talk—but by lifestyle itself.

V I

PILOT IN SEARCH OF

A CO-PILOT

By June of 1968, George W. had a bachelor's degree in history from Yale, but little idea what he wanted to do with his life. He arrived back at his parent's place in Houston that summer, assigned to the Texas Air National Guard. Like all healthy young men of the time, that requirement was just about all the future plan he needed. Such an assignment was far preferable to being sent to Vietnam as a member of the infantry. While there was a slight chance that his unit could be called up to serve in Vietnam, he would be able to trust that in all likelihood he would not be dying in the rice paddies of Southeast Asia, since Texas National Guard units were not regularly sent overseas.

When George W. registered for pilot training, he was told the basic course of the next six years of his life all the way up until May 26, 1974: He would report to basic training from July 14 to August 20 at Lackland, where he would be introduced to the military life of discipline and restraint. Normally, a recruit would then report to a base until he began further training. But George W. had already been set on a course for pilot training. He would be given a discharge as an enlisted man from the Texas National Guard, until he reported for his year-long Air Force training on November 25 in Valdosta, Georgia.

The discharge would allow him to work on another project: While George W. was finishing up his studies at Yale, Jimmy Allison, his father's friend and political consultant, had offered to hire him as an aide for the last months of the Senate campaign of Edward J. Gurney in Florida. The military training he was granted conveniently left his schedule more flexible during that time.

After graduation from the pilot training program in December 1969, he would return to Houston to serve out his six years in the Texas Air National Guard Reserve. Until that time, he didn't have to worry about a career path. He had signed a form when applying for pilot training that committed him to one continuing passion: "I, George Walker Bush, . . . have applied for pilot training with the goal of making flying a lifetime pursuit and I believe I can best accomplish this to my satisfaction by serving as a member of the air national guard as long as possible." He would not actually live up to that promise, flying only a few times after he left the National Guard, but for the time, that statement could serve as an enforced form of direction.

He would only have to start contemplating an actual career path in early 1970, when the Guard would thin his schedule down to only a few days a month. That's when he was, by his own description, lost. That was also, coincidentally, the only period that he lived off of his father's precise grid. He would seek the help of his father's friends, but he could not mimic his father's path the way he had with Andover, Yale, and the military service. At age 24, his dad had been headed to Midland to work the oil fields. It would take George W. five more years to get back on the George Bush track and head to Midland himself.

"People keep talking about George discovering his way after a certain time," said one Yale classmate. "In our era, [to be lost was] not unheard of, and there are also people who've never wandered back on the path. Most people just keep wandering."

While George W. acknowledged how aimless he was during this time, what is more striking is how lost his father was also. If a politician could be said to be without direction while always tethered to service in government, then through those years—from early 1970 stretching as far as 1979, George W.'s father too seemed to lack clear purpose. His only mission seemed to be serving Richard Nixon, who played loyal George Bush like a puppet throughout that era. First, Nixon convinced him to give up a solid congressional seat to make a risky—and ultimately losing—run for the senate, then he sent him on an obstacle course of brief and far-flung federal jobs, from ambassador to the United Nations to liaison to China. George Bush had always prided himself on his devotion to friends and superiors, and his deference to Nixon was loyalty's most dangerous symptom. "A total Nixon man—first," President Nixon acknowledged approvingly about George Bush, when he and secretary of the treasury George Shultz were hashing over appointments in the early 1970s. "Doubt if you can do better than Bush."

In a time of national upheaval, George Bush locked on to the one point of apparent stability in the nation—the president, or rather the man who occupied the presidency. He would follow that North Star no matter where it took him, right up until the time Nixon became one of the main causes of the nation's disarray. George W.'s life also became entwined in the servitude to Nixon: He would work for Nixon candidates in statewide elections; he would even be picked up by plane to take Nixon's daughter Tricia on a date. Ultimately, he would suffer mightily from the criticism aimed at his father, who had been asked by Nixon to serve as the head of the Republican National Committee after the burglars had been caught breaking into the Watergate hotel. George W. would watch from the liberal bastion of Harvard while Superman picked his way through the debris left after he bequeathed his loyalty to the wrong man. For the first time, his hero father would be caught on the other side.

Early in the summer of 1968, the extent to which Richard Nixon could disrupt George Bush's life was still beyond anyone's imagining. At that point, George W. never would have been able to dream that his hero father would be forced to absorb national criticism during one of the worst scandals in the nation's political history. At the time, being George Bush's son was still a guarantee of kind treatment. Lieutenant Governor Ben Barnes acknowledged that hearing from George Bush's friend Sidney Adger caused him to place a special call to Brigadier General James M. Rose, who in turn helped George W. get into the National Guard. Rose would continue to recommend George W. for promotion throughout his military career.

While George W. was, by all accounts, a friendly, conscientious, enthusiastic pilot, and probably deserved good reviews, his rapid advancement must have been aided by the warm glow surrounding the star congressman's son. In 1968, George Bush won such strong reviews as a representative, no one had the courage to challenge him in the election that year. He would run unopposed in November—one of the reasons George W. and Jimmy Allison were free to help another candidate that fall.

For most Texas Air National Guard recruits, basic training was just the first step toward becoming an officer. Trainees often would pass through that program and then complete a rigorous officer candidate school before even being considered for promotion to second lieutenant, but Lieutenant Colonel Walter B. Staudt greenlighted George W. for advancement right after basic training. Tom Hail, the Texas National Guard historian, reviewed George W.'s service records decades later for a special exhibit when he was governor. Hail reportedly found the automatic promotion to second lieutenant unusual. "I've never heard of that," he told the *Los Angeles Times*. "Generally they did that for doctors only, mostly because we needed extra flight surgeons."

While the specific criteria that the National Guard in Texas set for advancement at that time is apparently unavailable in the archives, the *Los Angeles Times* discovered documents itemizing standards for promotion into pilot training for the National Guard in general, only one of which George W. met. A manual from the adjutant general's department stated that the requirements for advancement included a high-school diploma, 18 months of military service including six months of active duty, and completion of officer training. Another set of criteria, reported by the *Times*, spelled out three ways that a guardsman could become a second lieutenant. The guardsman could take a 23-week officer training program, a nine-week training "reserve component special officer candidate course," or complete eight weekend drill periods and two summer camps. George W. pushed through to the pilot training after just five weeks of basic training. The application to the special pilot instruction asked for the cadet candidate to itemize previous military training and flying school instruction. George W. just answered in the negative in those boxes.

As Hail pointed out, some recruits won automatic advancement because of their special qualifications, such as medical training, but George W. lacked unique skills. The form requested the applicant to list courses taken in flight training, meteorology, navigation, mathematics, physics, and electronics. George W. wrote *none* in those boxes. He could only boast a Yale history degree and a series of summer jobs: as a messenger for James Baker's law firm; a ranch hand at the XX outside Williams, Arizona; a roustabout for Circle Oil in Lake Charles, Louisiana; a sporting goods salesman at the Sears in Houston; and a bookkeeper at the First City National Bank, also in Houston.

Based on that resumé, the National Guard contracted the Air Force to train George W. as a pilot for the 147th Division. Usually the Air Force hesitated to take any recruit who hadn't proven himself first in more extensive military training, since educating a pilot was expensive, but the Air Force waved George W. along. David Beckwith, one of George W.'s former press aides for the presidential campaign, reportedly insisted that George W. was quickly accepted into the program because, unlike other young men of the time, he was willing to go through the training.

Staudt was clearly excited to welcome George W. to the 147th Division of the Texas Air National Guard. Because a captain had sworn him in the first time—and no pictures had been taken to commemorate the event—Staudt staged a second swearing-in ceremony for the congressman's son at which he administered the honors. He wanted to have a picture of himself welcoming the young Bush boy.

George W. reported to Lackland base in San Antonio on July 14 for the regular course of basic training and finished toward the end of August. At that point, he was assigned to help the mechanics at Ellington Field Air National Guard base in Houston until his pilot training began in November. But within a week of his completion of basic training, he was granted a leave to work as an aide for his father's friend and political consultant, Jimmy Allison. The campaign was the Florida senate race of Edward J. Gurney.

Jim Martin, who was then the top aide to Gurney, remembered Allison telling him about George W. "We were looking for someone to get the media on and off the plane, into their hotel rooms, and back up again at six A.M.," Martin told the *Washington Times*.

"I've got someone in mind," Allison told him. "[Bush's] oldest son. He's getting out of Yale, just like his father. He's getting his license to be a pilot, just like his dad."

According to the *Washington Times*, Martin remembered being thrilled at the idea of having a clean-cut son of a Republican star on the payroll. He reportedly recalled thinking, "How much will we have to pay him and how soon can he start? I went in and told Gurney and his reaction also was, 'How soon can he start?'"

On September 3, 1968, George W. was discharged as an enlisted member from the National Guard. He joined the campaign as an aide. Staudt recommended him for commission to second lieutenant the next day. In October, Brigadier General James M. Rose, the same man who had been contacted by Lieutenant Governor Ben Barnes to help George W. get into the National Guard, informed George W. of that commission. From September until after election night, he would only need to report to the base once a month.

Edward Gurney was a three-term congressman going up against Democrat LeRoy Collins, a former governor and one of the best-known politicians in Florida, a Democratic state. The state hadn't elected a Republican senator since Reconstruction, and Gurney had little name recognition. His victory was less than assured.

The Florida campaign could not have been further ideologically from the world of hand-wringing Yale peaceniks that George W. had left behind three months earlier. It seems amusing that fellow students from Yale would consider George W. relatively apolitical, when by the end of that summer after their graduation he was chaperoning journalists on one of the more strident Republican campaigns in the country.

Gurney did not agonize over whether or not fighting in Vietnam was justified. He absolutely supported U.S. intervention. In a time of Vietnam furor, the handsome 54-year-old had a political strength to back up his hawkish views: He was a bona fide war hero, having won the Silver Star and the Purple Heart in World War II. He still toted a foam rubber seat cushion with him on his campaign stops so that an aching hip wound wouldn't cause him too much trouble. His views too had been forever shaped by battle.

He believed that the U.S. needed to go in "hot pursuit" of the enemy in Laos and Cambodia. America should order the Soviets out of the port of Haiphong, he said; then we should "unleash our navy and air force on the port."

"I say he's doing business with dynamite," his opponent, Collins, retorted.

No, said Gurney, his Maine accent tumbling from his dropped jaw, just look how well it worked in Cub*ar*.

He followed a strategy that was remarkably similar to the one George W. became famous for implementing in his own gubernatorial races: Gurney pared his platform issues to just three that he ferociously hammered so that the voters would have no doubt where he stood. In Gurney's case, he wanted to get tough in Vietnam, end Lyndon Johnson's heavy domestic spending, and restore the nation to "*lawr* and order," including making Washington, D.C., a model city with more cops on the beat.

As a campaigner, Gurney was fierce, never softening his image for the sake of the voters. When Collins criticized Gurney for missing meetings of his Congressional committees, Gurney only retorted that Collins didn't understand the competing schedules of committees; Gurney did not disclose the fact that a good portion of his missed votes occurred during the previous spring in the month following his son's suicide.

George W. also was able to see in Gurney the power of a more conservative candidate than his father. The local press noted, for example, that Gurney adamantly opposed the open housing bill that Representative Bush had voted for. In October, Ronald Reagan traveled to Jacksonville to endorse Gurney and tape a campaign advertisement, demonstrating that he was closer to that wing of the Republican Party than to George Bush's more moderate version.

On Election Day, November 5, George W. celebrated Gurney's historic victory. The tough campaign had broken the Democratic Party's domination of the state's politics. Richard Nixon too had easily won the presidency. Collins mourned for his beloved state of Florida, which had "followed a national trend . . . to deeper conservatism. It seems the mood of our times."

At that point, Gurney took the rhetoric down a pace. He told his supporters at his election night celebration that partisan politics would now be shelved.

This was how a campaign was won: By never wavering from the

political message and by tuning the rhetoric to the public mood. Gurney would go on to be Richard Nixon's most ardent defender during the Watergate hearings; the administration funneled specific questions for him to pose to witnesses that would help Nixon's cause.

—

On November 25, George W. was sent to Moody Air Force Base in Valdosta, Georgia, for pilot training. Although he had been promoted to second lieutenant back in September, Lieutenant Colonel Walter B. Staudt decided that a picture needed to be taken of his commissioning George W., so he staged another ceremony. George W.'s father traveled from Washington to pose with them in Staudt's office.

Sixty-five pilot trainees—or "pods," as they were nicknamed— were accepted into the program that session, including a number of military men from Iran, Germany, Denmark, Sweden, and Norway. Several officers' sons were admitted. But of all the pods, George W. seemed to be the only guardsman. Usually, the Air Force would not train a recruit right out of basic training, since the year-long program was expensive, and a military man that untested might end up wasting taxpayer money if he failed or was dismissed for disciplinary reasons midway through the training. David Hanifl, another trainee who was in the same clique of bachelors on base as George W., seemed annoyed by his buddy's unique status. "Basically we knew George was there on a special deal," he explained. "It was unheard of that a taxpayer would be paying that much to train someone. Normally you don't send someone who is totally green."

The ease with which he had been accepted into the program was unusual. "You had to pass a lot of tests," Colonel Ralph Anderson, a fellow trainee, told the *Los Angeles Times* about the usual requirements. Anderson had served in the air force before getting into the Air National Guard. "I went through ROTC at Ohio University. I had to do all the air force qualification tests, and I had to go through a private pilot's license program at Ohio University and pass a physical. And finally there was a selection board."

Still, Anderson didn't hold the apparent favoritism against George W. "I liked him a lot," he told the *Los Angeles Times.* "He was a real outgoing guy, a good pilot and lots of fun. He was a leader. He took things on and got them done."

Hanifl remembered George W. standing out from the start, since he had lost his luggage in transit from Houston to Georgia. He endured the sweltering classrooms in his dress blues while he waited for his khakis to be found. Although most of the other pilots soon recognized the special circumstances under which he had been accepted for pilot training right out of basic, they couldn't help but respect his skill once he began work in the classroom. He scored high in the academic areas and displayed real talent for reading pictorial presentations of the functions of planes. "How do you read this crap?" Hanifl asked him.

"That's one thing I was always good at," George W. said, "reading charts." Whether dealing with batting statistics, aircraft radar or later Midland land rights diagrams, George W. always demonstrated an ability to sift through data and consider it analytically. The mechanical information for pilots was presented in Programmed Text Learning to make memorization easy. First there would be a paragraph on the altimeter. Following that would be a list of statements:

This instrument has a spring.
This instrument has a spring and stirrup.
This instrument has a spring, a stirrup, and the butterfly.

By the end, the pod should have memorized the entire makeup of a plane. George W. excelled at this, since he had proven from his earliest days that he had a proclivity for committing information to memory.

The day usually began at 6:00 A.M. and dragged on until 6:00 P.M. Half the day was spent in the classroom and the other half up in the air. The first six weeks were spent training on a T-41 (otherwise known as a Cessna 172). Every time a pilot went up, a superior would be on board to make sure he ran through the checklist. If he missed even one task, he would be downgraded. Everyone was nervous about making it through that Initial Progress Check (IPC). "I thought George W. was pampered," said Hanifl. He remembered a certain aggressive check officer who so frequently downgraded pilots for even minor infractions, he earned the nickname "Rodney Red Pencil." Hanifl didn't remember George W. ever having to fly with Rodney, which Hanifl considered a lucky coincidence.

The senior instructors too seemed to be aware of George W.'s family connections and, Hanifl said, seemed to seek out contact with George W. According to Hanifl, they would hint to the scheduling officer that they wanted to fly with Bush. They were probably looking for a promotion to field grade officer or colonel status, and an officer effectiveness report didn't have enough detail to make one good officer stand out from another. "There were only so many ways you can say outstanding," said Hanifl. A recommendation from another source could help their case, and a popular politician would be the best booster of all. Hanifl theorized that they might be hoping for a word of praise from George W.'s congressman father.

A few weeks after IPC, a pilot was required to take a superior up for the final check. If the pilot failed that test, he would be gone. For George W., failing the pilot training program would be disastrous, not only because he would need to devise another way to complete his military service at a time when the Vietnam War was raging; but also because being kicked out would bring deep personal humiliation. His position in the pilot program was high profile—the staged swearing-in ceremonies certainly indicated that—so a failure would be noticed by more than just his immediate superiors. In the past, he had been worried about not meeting his father's standards at Andover, as he admitted at his twentieth reunion, because of what the school meant to George Bush. Certainly, he must have fretted about failing pilot training, since his father's history as a hero pilot was even more important to the family. About half of George W.'s pilot training group flunked out during the final check, but George W. passed.

Around the third or fourth month at Valdosta—as the number of troops in Vietnam were hitting their peak of 543,400—a one-star general from the guard came to the base just to say hello to George W., just to check in on him and give him an "attaboy." Hanifl said that the visit confirmed that George W. was special to the most powerful people in the guard. They cared about what became of him.

George Bush also must have been feeling that the most highly placed people had his interests at heart. President Richard Nixon had shown a unique concern about the congressman's future. He hoped to consolidate Republican strength on the Hill during the midterm elections and was looking for fresh faces to unseat some of the more vulnerable Democrats across the country.

Nixon knew that loyalty was the bonus he got with Congressman George Bush, the representative of the moderate Republican district that included the thriving city of Houston. Because Bush's campaign in 1966 had relied so heavily on television advertising, he was a well-known political figure in Texas. The fact that no one had opposed him in 1968 only confirmed his power, and Nixon had to respect that strength. The president also liked Bush personally, since he considered Bush different from the usual "Ivy League bastards" populating the political world. Bush had worked in the West Texas oil business—a tough, mostly male industry where people of different classes jockeyed to make vast fortunes. He knew what it was to grapple for a paycheck, and Nixon could appreciate that scrappiness.

What is harder to understand is Bush's devotion to Nixon, who lacked the country-club charm and kindly wit that usually drew the congressman's professional friendship. Bush himself described Nixon as "kind of pulled back a little bit, tough and cold. He was always kind of . . . standoffish is the word. There certainly was no buddy-buddy approach, at least with me. There was never a totally relaxed camaraderie on any relation I had with him at all."

But George Bush's attachment to Nixon seemed to be less personal than patriotic. Richard Nixon was the president, and George Bush had grown up with a deep respect for the institutions of government, almost to the point where he was a pushover for any request emanating from the corridors of power. "It's hard to say no to the president of the United States," he would lament to Bar years later, when he returned home from a Nixon meeting at which he had been given the short-straw job of head of the Republican National Committee.

Nixon tapped into an archetypal role for Bush—that of mentor. Bush had always gravitated to such avuncular figures, including Neil Mallon, who guided him through the oil business, and Uncle Herbie, who helped pull together the financing for his initial drilling projects.

This time, the president of the United States was offering to assist him with reaching his coveted goal of becoming a senator, and George Bush would not weigh whether or not he liked the man's politics or his "tough and cold" personality when deciding to accept Nixon's guidance. In this case, he chose poorly, since Nixon led him into dangerous territory.

But Bush was always loyal to his mentors, almost on a first-come, first-serve basis. Bush sealed his attachment to Nixon in 1952, when the vice presidential candidate arrived in Midland for the first political event Bush ever organized. Nixon, then on the ticket as Eisenhower's number two, arrived at the Midland airport for a reception, and George Bush was there to greet him and play host. Alas, a bunch of protesters were also waiting, holding up signs and yelling. George Bush boiled over. He certainly wouldn't have any of that incivility—and certainly not on his watch! He raced over to the hooligans and tore up their signs.

The bond between Nixon and Bush grew over the decades. Nixon helped at fund-raisers for Bush in 1964. George Bush shared Harry Treleaven, the p.r. man who masterminded his 1966 election to congress, with Richard Nixon for his makeover to win the American public's love in 1968. That year, Nixon put Bush on the short list of his vice presidential candidates, but lamented that he was too green to make the cut. Instead, George Bush joined the small team of surrogates campaigning on the presidential candidate's behalf after the Republican convention.

Leading into the 1970 election, Nixon was salivating at the chance to end the career of Senator Yarborough, the liberal Democrat from Texas. Yarborough had been described as "the undisputed political leader of populist liberal forces" by a Texas historian. But the politics of the Lone Star State were shifting to the right beneath the senator, and some observers thought the time might be right to topple him. The situation just needed to be tested. George Bush would be the lever.

In May 1969, Nixon summoned Bush to the White House for a 40-minute chat about senate prospects—the same format he used for other Republicans he was sending into the midterm political trenches. Not long after the meeting with Nixon, Bush told the press that he had commissioned a poll to test the temperature for a run for the Senate. He was invited out to San Clemente that summer for even lengthier talks about the race. By early July, Bar was saying that her husband was definitely planning a Senate campaign. Harry Treleaven was put back on the case of crafting Bush's image for 1970. But political observers wondered about the Bush camp's level of confidence that they would achieve victory. Jimmy Allison Jr. had gone to work for the Republican National Committee. Ordinarily, he would be expected to take a leave to help Bush, one of his closest friends, on this important campaign. But Allison stayed put at the RNC, a decision that would later be interpreted as confirmation that those in the know understood the race to be a losing cause.

Richard Nixon was letting George Bush take a run for a seat that was far less than a sure thing. Back in Connecticut, Prescott thought his son was crazy to throw away a four-year-old congressional career on a race against a two-term incumbent. George Bush was in the process of making an extremely risky political move, and those who loved him best knew it.

—

While his father was entering more treacherous waters, George W. was happily serving out his time at the Air Force pilot training program. He loved being a pilot—operating the high-tech equipment and enjoying the young Turk persona that came with it. In the spring of 1969, he flew his plane to the Wisconsin wedding of Britt Kolar, his fellow Bonesman. His parents were also there, and George W. showed up wearing his flight suit. It was obvious to his friends that he thought the whole pilot persona was cool. "He told me he loved [flying]," said Yale friend Don Etra. "He showed me pictures of himself in front of his plane."

George W.'s own wedding had fallen apart the year before. At first, the couple had postponed their plans to marry in the summer between junior and senior year. Tina Cassini, a friend of both George W. and Cathy Wolfman from Houston, told the *Dallas Morning News* that she thought the two just drifted apart when they were attending separate schools. Other friends hypothesized that they just got cold feet since they were so young. George W. reportedly said that once the engagement was postponed the first time, he knew that they would not be marrying. When fellow Bonesman Robert Birge was asked what he thought of Cathy Wolfman, he demurred. "I don't want to say," he replied, implying less than fond feelings from the Bush camp.

George W.'s service in the National Guard pushed the possible wedding date even further into the future, since the application indicated that candidates for the pilot cadet program were not allowed to marry until after their graduation. That restriction would have postponed their wedding until after December 1969. While Wolfman was working down in Washington, D.C., she met Roderick Young, a graduate of Stanford who went on to receive his MBA from Harvard. In May 1969, they were married.

"I loved [George]," Cathy Wolfman told the *Dallas Morning News* three decades later. "But I have no thoughts of 'what if'—no regrets. It's been too long, and I'm happy as a clam." George W. told the newspaper that he always "thought the world" of her.

Although George W. described himself as a ladies' man during that time, his fellow trainees don't remember his having many dates over the 53 weeks of pilot training. The only significant occasion of courting seems to have been when President Nixon flew a plane down to the base to pick up George W. for a date with his daughter Tricia. George W. only romanced the president's daughter that one time.

His parents remember his social life as being more active, since they witnessed a few courtships when he invited a series of dates up to the family compound in Kennebunkport. The Bush family members often asked friends to join them on Walker's Point, so the invitations themselves weren't so significant, but clearly he wanted to audition girlfriends for the clan. "He brought some lulus to Maine in those days," Barbara Bush told a reporter. "They were very nice, but it would only take a day before he would decide they wouldn't fit in with the family."

For bachelors on the base, the best place for parties on Saturday nights was either the nearby Holiday Inn or the officer's club. Not much revelry took place in the nearest town of Valdosta, Georgia, which was a ten miles away and dry. The officers could go to Jacksonville, where there was a large population of secretaries looking for a fun night out. But at the officer's club, the town girls would pack the dance floor, and the pairing off was almost enforced. If a girl didn't have someone to escort her by 10:00 P.M., she had to leave. Everyone would do lots of drinking and dancing.

The trainees had few weather delays that year, so the class finished its most rigorous requirements about six weeks early. That left a lot of free time for the pilots to horse around. George W. hooked up with an extremely outgoing young woman who he would only identify later as "Judy." According to Hanifl, George W.'s parents were less than thrilled about his choice of girlfriend. He said that, in general, the military men were warned to watch out for the town girls, who wanted to find a man to marry and would hook them in however they could. The Bushes, Hanifl claimed, let their son know of their displeasure.

George Bush was scheduled to be the speaker for the group's commencement that December. He was billed as a former war hero and pilot, but he also had been a regular commentator on the Vietnam War over that past year. His office had issued five formal public statements on the conflict. Three or four days before the commencement, George W.'s parents arrived for a visit.

Hanifl remembered seeing George W. soon after the Bushes arrived and finding him disgruntled. "I went to see him and he was just kind of depressed," Hanifl said.

Hanifl claimed that George and Bar Bush had ordered George W. to end the relationship with Judy. "My parents just said that I'm breaking up with my girlfriend," George W. allegedly told him. "His parents had the attitude that he had been isolated from the real world."

George W. graduated from Air Force pilot training on December 2, 1969. Theoretically, the 28 pilots who passed were now trained to fly any type of aircraft, after taking some specialized instruction. Depending on a pilot's class standing, he had a variety of assignments to choose from, ranging from flying in Vietnam to working as a pilot instructor in the States. The pilots who ranked lower would have fewer options to choose from. About a half dozen of the pilots went for tours in Vietnam because they wanted to fly the highest-performance craft they could find, and those planes were overseas. George W. did not participate in the selection of assignments since he was scheduled to head back to the Guard in Texas to complete his service. He would not be faced with the decision of whether or not to immediately serve in Vietnam.

Nine months earlier, in March 1969, the Texas Air National Guard had put through the request to have George W. reassigned for training on the T-33A and F102 fighters as soon after his graduation from the Air Force program as possible. He went from active duty, during which he was required to live on the base in Valdosta, to inactive duty, during which he reported to the base in Houston about once a month. George W. would now have to face decisions about what he wanted to do with his life, since his new military schedule allowed him enough free time to work another job as well.

—

George Bush knew his own plans for the next year. He was on the brink of declaring his Senate run, and in the traditional Bush style of melding friendship and politics, the family Christmas card list that year was massive. In mid-January, George Bush met with Nixon one last time before making his official announcement the following day. The talk, almost from the start, was that if Bush could beat Yarborough in the Senate race, he would be Nixon's vice presidential candidate in 1972.

George Bush had done a good turn that was paying political dividends in early 1970. Back in 1968, on Nixon's inauguration day, he had left the Republican festivities early to go out to Andrews Air Force Base to bid good-bye to the exiting Democratic president, Lyndon Johnson. Bush felt he owed such a courtesy to Johnson as a Texan and in tribute to the collegial way Johnson had dealt with him over the years. Johnson had seemed to feel well-disposed to Bush from then on. Perhaps in acknowledgment for Bush's graciousness, Johnson had not stepped in to endorse Yarborough in the senate race. Once again, it would be very difficult to tell the difference between a good man and a savvy politician.

Unfortunately, the race was getting more complicated. A new fighter was entering the ring. Lloyd Bentsen began waging a feroc' challenge against Yarborough for the Democratic nomination. I 1964, when Bush used Bentsen's departure from the race to cc LBJ and the Democratic Party, now he would wish Bentsen moderate businessman from Houston who had also Distinguished Flying Cross in battle, Bentsen was too m' The press would dub the race "Tweedledum" versus "T

—

In March 1970, George W. moved back to Houston and house-sat for his parents while they were on the campaign trail. A local paper reported that he planned to go to law school in September at either the University of Texas or the University of Houston. He was later rejected from UT, a difficult school to get into where apparently the Bush family name had no sway. After that, he would be forced to hatch another plan, abandoning the idea of law school entirely.

George W. was getting strong compliments from his military superiors. He started flying "alerts" from Ellington Field, scanning the Gulf Coast borders for enemy attacks and soaring over the oil fields of Texas to protect the refineries. The National Guard sent out a press release trumpeting their newest star and his first solo flight: "George Walker Bush is one member of the younger generation who doesn't get his kicks from pot or hashish or speed. Oh, he gets high, all right, but not from narcotics. . . . As far as kicks are concerned, Lt. Bush gets his from the roaring afterburner of the F-102."

George W. went right along with the pitch. The solo flight was, in his estimation, "really neat. It was fun, and very exciting. I felt really serene up there."

In a not-so-subtle plug for his father's campaign, the Texas Air National Guard public relations office added: "Lt. Bush is the son of U.S. Representative George Bush, who is a candidate for the U.S. Senate seat of Senator Ralph Yarborough. The elder Bush was a navy pilot. Lt. Bush said that his father was just as excited and enthusiastic about his solo flight as he was." While National Guard spokespeople later explained that they frequently tried to trumpet the accomplishments of their more high-profile recruits—not just George W.— the plug confirms that he was notable to his superiors as the son of a politico.

On June 23, 1970, George W. finished combat crew training. Now he was only required to take the F-102 Delta out a few times a month. Bush claimed that he tried to volunteer just before the end of the instruction for an overseas stint, called the "Palace Alert" program, which could have sent him to Vietnam as an F-102 pilot for three to six months. "I did [ask]—and I was told, 'You're not going,'" Bush told he *Washington Post.*

But George W. had to have known that the expiration date was eady set on the F-102s. Therefore, although he insisted that he tried to fight in Vietnam, the facts suggest that he must have known that the very program he was pursuing through the National Guard precluded him from serving overseas. Most of the F-102s had been retired from overseas duty beginning in late 1969, and even the National Guard was phasing out its F-102 instruction. In fact, George W.'s very unit in Texas was being shut down the week after he finished combat training. "Had my unit been called up, I'd have gone . . . to Vietnam," Bush insisted. "I was prepared to go." Almost as soon as George W. was fully qualified to fly the F-102 in combat, the plane was obsolete. He would later say he had not been sent because the United States had "wiped out" the North Vietnamese air force by the time he was ready to go.

Ironically, both candidates in the 1970 Senate race—Lloyd Bentsen and George Bush—had sons in the Texas National Guard. On Election Day, November 3, George W.'s stature in the military would surge when the guard nominated him and Lloyd Bentsen III for promotion to first lieutenant. Brigadier General James M. Rose, the man who originally had been contacted by Ben Barnes about George W., put through the paperwork. George W.'s commander wrote up a report that strongly endorsed a man who was by all accounts a dutiful officer. But the assessment seemed extremely complimentary for someone who had put in such a short stint of service—just over a year.

"[George W.] clearly stands out as a top-notch fighter interceptor pilot," wrote George W.'s commander Lieutenant Colonel Jerry Killian, noting George W.'s participation in a weapons deployment drill. "Lt. Bush's skills far exceed his contemporaries'. He is a natural leader whom his contemporaries look to for leadership. Lt. Bush is also a good follower with outstanding disciplinary traits and an impeccable military bearing. Lt. Bush possesses vast potential and should be promoted well ahead of his contemporaries." The appointment officially went through four days later.

With George W.'s assignment to the reserves worked out, and the question of further service overseas settled for him because of the retirement of the F-102, George W. was left to figure out what to do with his life. He rented a bachelor pad at the swinging apartment complex, Chateaux Dijon, in Houston. He played all-day games of volleyball in the pool, drank beer, and dated.

That summer, George W. joined his father's campaign against Lloyd Bentsen, who had won the primary.

On a military form, he would later describe his role on the campaign as that of a "surrogate candidate" for his father. He traveled across the state conducting interviews and giving speeches on his dad's behalf. He also helped with the Bush college internship program, which brought 30 students from Texas to the Houston headquarters for three weeks and then took them out on the trail for another three weeks. With Vietnam raging and the country engaged in continuous cultural wars, a Republican campaign was not the most popular cause for young people. During the intern recruitment, the Bush team told the students that they only needed to have a desire to work on a political campaign to come on board for George Bush; they did not have to believe in the Republican platform—or even the candidate. As it turned out, the interns who joined in a state of ambivalence about the party found themselves enchanted by gentle George Bush.

The bus would pull into a town square and the students would pile out to hold a Bush rally. Sometimes they would only be met by one supporter, so they would go over to the local radio station and George W. would do an interview for his father. At 24, he was already smooth on the air, handling most of his father's campaign questions with ease. Nancy Ippolito, a former intern, remembered the guy they called "Geo" as seeming old for his age. He was quiet and serious, never even using slang in the interns' presence. He would ride the bus with the young people in the program instead of flying in the campaign plane, but would not go drinking with them or do anything else that might reflect badly on his father. When he campaigned he rarely joked with constituents, but would shake their hands, then drill his pitch about his father's issues. Still, his youthful side showed at times. In Houston, the Bush team took part in a fund-raising walk on a particularly hot day. The good-looking candidate's son whipped off his shirt and strolled bare-chested behind George Bush.

Above all else, Ippolito was impressed by George W.'s absolute devotion to his father. "He pushed his causes more out of family loyalty and 'we stick together' than being one hundred percent on line with his father's positions." she said. "We didn't know anyone who liked their father at that time," she added, referring to the tumultuous era, and George W. clearly loved his dad.

Robert Mosbacher Jr., the son of George Bush's friend and frequent fund-raiser, had been working on the George Bush campaign since the fall. When the intern program started, he helped select the participants. That year, Mosbacher's mother, Jane, had been diagnosed with leukemia. George W. got word that she was about to die when they were on the road. He was the only appropriate person—a family friend and an adult at 24 years of age—who could tell Mosbacher the news.

As Mosbacher remembered the moment, George W. chose to introduce the matter by first telling his friend a joke. When Mosbacher started laughing, George W. suddenly turned serious and told him he needed to get back to Houston immediately to see his mother who was ill. Rob rented a car and drove right to the hospital. She died soon after. The Bushes all attended the funeral.

"He handled it in absolutely the best way he could," said Mosbacher. That use of humor, even in the face of tragedy, seemed reminiscent of the jokes George W. made as a boy to keep his mother laughing after the death of his sister Robin—asking how she was buried, envying her view at the football game. The jokes didn't deny the heartbreak, they just eased the pain.

—

In 1966, George Bush's congressional race was built on personal image, not policy; but in 1970, he tried to make the senate campaign more issue oriented. He proclaimed that he had donned the cloak of conservatism, but as the months unfolded, he put forward a confused platform with an overabundance of ideas. He warned Bentsen at the start of the race that if the Democrat planned to run to Bush's right, he "was going to step off the edge of the earth." He did indeed campaign on the conservative's staple of law-and-order issues, but that was just one ingredient in a jambalaya of political positions, ranging from liberal to odd. Even then, he struggled with the "vision thing."

How could voters be expected to remember George Bush's views on Election Day, when he had put forward so many? During that campaign, he declared that he supported family planning, environmental protection, and gun-control legislation. Toward the end of the summer, when he was trying hard to woo the youth vote, he proposed downgrading the penalty for marijuana possession from a felony to a misdemeanor. He supported Nixon's call for day-care centers. He boosted legislation to bring more Spanish-speaking leaders into government councils. He supported an "all-volunteer army" to fight in Vietnam. In the spring, he produced a travel guide for students warning of the penalties against drug possession in various countries. In a press release, he talked about the need for "meaningful and forceful action against those who bomb and make bomb threats." He gave heartfelt speeches about busing, inflation, ethics.

On the trail, Bush boasted how effective he had been in Congress. He'd introduced or cosponsored 167 bills in his four years. Only 22 of those bills had passed, including an exemption for sporting ammunition from gun control, tax incentives for companies who used pollution-control equipment, and new penalties for people who used dangerous drugs such as LSD. "I say in 1970 you've got to be positive, to be for something," he railed. "And I'm for block grants, decentralization, revenue sharing, greater protection for society as a whole, and a return to fiscal sanity."

There wasn't an issue that George Bush had not weighed in on. His slogan was "George Bush: He can do more," but he was doing far too much for any voter to clearly understand his perspective. This campaign was the polar opposite of the Gurney campaign run by Allison, where the candidate stuck to his few tough stances and won.

Nixon did what he could to help Bush by stumping in two Texas cities toward the end of October. In Dallas, the public-school students were let out early so they and their parents could go see the president. When George Bush traveled on to his next stop, at the Midland-Odessa airport, he described the thrill of having the president speak on his behalf. "I hope I never get so blasé," he said, "that I don't feel the tingly feeling I know you feel when the president is near."

Unfortunately, Nixon had also shown his support by sending some of his men to Houston during the campaign to give Bush a $106,000 donation. The contribution was paid mostly in cash, out of his secret

"Townhouse Operation" fund. That money would ghost George Bush's political reputation in the years after Nixon was forced to resign.

At the last rally, in Houston, George Bush was cheered on by George W., Prescott, Dotty, the college interns, an entourage of professional athletes, and 2,000 screaming supporters. But away from that corner of his home city, Bush was being further undermined by a round of endorsement ads for Bentsen featuring John Connally; that move would earn him the undying enmity of the Bush family.

By midnight on Election Day, the guests at George Bush's headquarters were emotionally destroyed. Bentsen had won—53 percent to 47 percent. George Bush had lost not only the Senate race, but with it the life he had so enjoyed on the Hill for the past four years. He seemed to have bottomed out at the age of 46.

Jimmy Allison blamed himself for the loss, worrying that he had not left the Republican National Committee to help more with the campaign. He and Harry Treleaven left the main reception area, snuck into an adjacent office, and cried. Jim Oberwetter, one of George Bush's most loyal fund-raisers, went under the stairs to weep in peace and George W. was there in tears too. George Bush's sister, Nancy Ellis, remembers calling Bar, who could not stop crying. "It will be okay," George Bush told his sobbing daughter, Doro, who was then 11 years old. "Oh, no, it won't," she pouted. "I'll be the only girl in fifth grade whose daddy doesn't have a job."

The Bentsen team had used Richard Nixon's appearances against George Bush, but he would not blame his mentor. "I can't find anything to blame—not the president, not my campaign workers, not finances," he said. "I'm looking introvertedly and I don't like what I see. I must've done something wrong."

He struggled to remain upbeat. "I've got a house, a wife, some kids, and a dog here in Houston," he said. "A man doesn't need much else."

Still, he was none too happy about his exit from elected office. "I had a depth of feeling about being in the Senate," George Bush told the *Dallas Morning News* about a month after the election. "It was not just one alternative of something to do and if that didn't work, then there were plenty of other things I'd have in mind. It was not just ambition.

It was the feeling that the Senate is the zenith of politics, of public service, the best a person can be."

"George Bush doesn't get mad when he loses," said Jim
Oberwetter. "He gets blue."

A month later, Nixon rewarded George Bush with the post of U.S.
ambassador to the United Nations.

—

In May 1972, George W. went to work for Jimmy Allison again.
George W. had tried other jobs during his time in the reserves without finding work that he actually enjoyed. He never ventured far
from the network of Bush family friends. Since he had no specific
occupational passion, finding him a job within the clan never proved
too difficult. George W. was willing to try any job for at least a little
while.

For almost a year, starting in early 1971, he worked at Stratford
of Texas, an agribusiness company started by Robert Gow two years
earlier. Gow was a friend of Uncle Herbie's son, Ray Walker, from
Yale. When George Bush ran Zapata, he had hired Gow, who eventually moved up to president of the company after George Bush left.
George W. was a management trainee, required to wear a coat and
tie every day to work. "We weren't looking for someone," Gow told
the *Washington Post* about how he brought George W. aboard, "but
I thought this would be a talented guy we should hire, and he was
available."

For Stratford, George W. would fly across the United States and
even to South America looking for greenhouses the company could
buy. He would put in a weekend of duty with the reserves once or
twice a month. One of his commanding officers noted how useful his
work with Stratford could be to public relations for the Texas Air
National Guard: "He is on the managerial staff of this diversified company and tells the story of the Air National Guard and the USAF to
the public at every opportunity," the commanding officer wrote. But
George W. was bored and apparently began talking about leaving
within his first months on the job. He departed Stratford nine months
after he began.

Then he considered running for the Texas legislature. The idea was pondered seriously enough to make brief mention in the paper. He ultimately decided against making the run.

The politician on Allison's dance card in 1972 was first-time candidate Winton M. "Red" Blount, a 51-year-old construction company millionaire from Alabama. When George Bush had served in Congress, he would be invited by the White House to play doubles with Blount on the tennis courts hidden behind the trees and rhododendron bushes on the South Lawn.

Blount enjoyed the good graces of Nixon, having served on his cabinet as postmaster general, expanding the job's usual duties by reworking its bureaucracy. Nixon allowed Blount to resign from his cabinet duties to help win the president a Republican majority in the Senate. Blount was challenging Senator John J. Sparkman, a Democrat with 36 years of experience on the Hill. As in Florida, the work of aiding a Republican candidate was all uphill, since the state had never even held a Republican primary. George W. became Blount's political director.

The post required that George W. be transferred to the Alabama National Guard for the duration of the campaign. He wrote a letter to his commanding officer, making the request, signed simply "George." The courtesy was promptly granted to him; he was told he should report to Lieutenant Colonel William Turnipseed upon arrival in Alabama. "Lt. Bush is very active in civic affairs in the community and manifests a deep interest in the operation of our government," wrote one commander in an evaluation.

George W. was chastised once during that period. He was briefly suspended from flying because he failed to get one of his required physicals, due to the fact that his doctor was in Houston.

Blount was great with numbers; unfortunately he was not so good with people. And Sparkman had a gift of extraordinary charisma. "My, that's some boy you got there, Tom," the silver-haired smoothie would drawl to a constituent. "They shoot up like weeds, don't they?"

Sparkman boasted of his insider power, telling the crowd at one campaign stop about legislation he had introduced that had brought federal funds to build a new hospital near Birmingham. "Now the fellow in charge of that agency has to come before my committee for his appropriation, and he personally came around to my office to speak to me about that hospital," said Sparkman. Then gave a wink and a chuckle. "I come to know all of these people and, believe me, it's quite helpful. Let me tell you, seniority is not out of style."

For Blount to match such ease would have taken more than a little coaching. He just did not have the necessary geniality. Despite the fact that the post office looked more efficient to government types, voters out on the trail reacted badly to his resumé, since they were still steamed about the rise in postal rates. Blount won the state's first Republican primary against former representative James D. Martin with a decisive 61 percent to 27 percent, but his total vote was only an anemic one tenth of what Sparkman received in the Democratic primary.

Perhaps echoing the strongly conservative bent Allison and Bush had found so fruitful in Florida, the Blount billboards across the state were tough: "A vote for Red Blount is a vote against forced busing."

" . . . against coddling criminals."

" . . . against welfare freeloaders."

Sparkman, however, was shrewd. With Richard Nixon running so far ahead in the polls in Alabama, the incumbent made an effective case for why voters should split their ticket: They could not afford to have northerners in key committee posts—no matter what the party—and a shift in the Senate's majority would mean just that. Richard Nixon won reelection. Blount was demolished. The lesson of Blount's campaign was that even if a candidate kept strict discipline to staying on message he couldn't win an election if personal charisma was lacking. The candidate had to either make friends with the voters or face defeat.

George W. enjoyed the work so much that his Uncle Jonathan Bush, who had always been active in campaigns, told the *Washington Post* that he was sure his nephew was going to become a political consultant.

———

George Bush was an equivocator with his kids. If they needed direction, he would listen to every side of the issue and never actually weigh in. He wanted to "let them think it out for themselves," Bar would explain.

George W. told David Maraniss that during this time he was trying to "reconcile who I was and who my dad was, to establish my own identity in my own way." One night, when George W. was staying with his parents over the Christmas holiday, he took his 16-year-old brother Marvin to a friend's house and they got drunk. When they were driving back, George W. hit a neighbor's garbage can, which stuck to one of the wheels and clanged all the way up the driveway. Marvin was clearly lubricated. His father, who was reading in the den, was not pleased. He sent for George W.

"I hear you're looking for me," George W. said when he walked in. "You wanna go *mano a mano* right here."

Apparently, the tension was high. Jeb tried to step in and ease the situation with evidence that George W. was not as lost as he seemed. Months before, George W. had applied to the University of Texas Business School for the fall and been rejected. Jeb announced that George W. had also applied to Harvard and been accepted. George W. hadn't told his parents because he wasn't sure he wanted to go. "You should think about that, son," his father told him.

An article in *GQ* reported that he told his parents, "Oh, I'm not going. I just wanted to let you know I could get into it." But he did start in the fall of 1975.

Although George W. was known to carouse, his friends claim his drinking at the time wasn't out of control. They also say they did not see him doing drugs. "He wasn't that wild," one of his Houston friends, Doug Hannah, told *Texas Monthly*. "We were such cheap-skates back then that if someone's parents were willing to pay for our liquor, we would go over there, have dinner and drinks, and play Jeopardy until it was time for someone to drive us home."

Still, George Bush thought his son needed a fuller perspective on life. He signed him up to work for an organization called PULL (Professionals United for Leadership), of which he was honorary chairman. Located in one of Houston's tougher areas, PULL was run by Bush's good friend, former pro-football player John L. White, as an effort to get minority kids the kind of mentoring and role models they needed.

George W. arrived in torn khakis and a bombed-out car. He took the kids on trips to prisons to show them the danger of leading dissipated lives. He played basketball with them. The *Washington Post* reported that he would even teach them not to run if they saw a police cruiser go by. Everyone who worked at the program loved George W., but no one more than Jimmy Dean, who was around six years old at the time. He and George adopted each other. Jimmy would wait on the steps for George W. to arrive in the morning, tag along with him all day, and hang on his neck during meetings. Many years later, George W. would find out that Dean had been killed by gunfire.

The work at PULL tapped directly into George W.'s most natural and powerful impulses. He was at his best helping someone who was struggling. "He would love to see some underdog with the right cause overcome some giant with maybe not quite the right message," said his friend in later years, Charlie Younger. "If someone was bashing a minority, he would demand, why do you think that way? All people have worth to George. A president of an oil company might not be as honorable as someone who is a roughneck on that drilling rig." He would frequently get misty at stories of goodness overcoming evil. "Things where people overcome odds to succeed really tug at his heart," said Younger.

George W. stayed with PULL until the Harvard term began in October 1973. His Bones brother Britt Kolar remembered George W. loving PULL and the power he had in those kids' lives. But one of the counselors advised George W. that he could have a bigger impact on low-income, minority youths like these if he went to Harvard, earned money and prestige, and then tried to help them. The school would also give him the discipline and "structure," as his mother described it, that he needed to be successful. In order to attend Harvard, he also needed to be discharged early from the Texas National Guard. He was easily released since he was only six months shy of completing his full stint, and the F-102s were already obsolete.

—

At the time George W. was joining PULL, his father was receiving his next assignment from Richard Nixon. The president summoned Bush to Camp David for a private tête à tête. The rumor in Washington was that Nixon was looking to fill the Republic National Committee chair. No one would have wanted that job. On June 17, burglars had been caught trying to break into the Democratic National Committee offices at the Watergate complex. That was the time bomb yet to go off.

The more immediate concern about taking the job was that the post was about to get politically gruesome. Richard Nixon was eager to clean house at the committee—drive out the eastern establishment and bring in some new western faces. The head of the RNC was sure to be a prime target for party vitriol.

Before George Bush left for his meeting with Nixon, Bar begged him not to take that post if it was offered.

Richard Nixon had recently embarrassed George Bush when Bush was serving as ambassador to the U.N. Bush had been a fierce advocate for Taiwan continuing as the representative nation for the two Chinas in the United Nations. Then, about six months into the job, George Bush read in the paper that Secretary of State Henry Kissinger had gone on a secret mission to Beijing. The U.S. government's policy quickly shifted to U.N. status for both Chinas.

George Bush went along with the idea out of loyalty to the president, but when the council's final negotiations were reached, communist China was a U.N. member and Taiwan was expelled. When the Taiwanese stalked out of the assembly, George Bush rushed after them to offer condolences. The incident was a true embarrassment to George Bush, since it made him seem far out of the loop of the more important diplomatic negotiations of his country.

When he returned home from his Camp David meeting with Nixon, Bar's worst fears were confirmed. "Boy, you can't turn a president down," he told her. Bar told Donnie Radcliffe that George Bush would say that overseeing the party's business during that time was like "being married to a centipede and it kept dropping shoes."

Andy Card, who was then head of the Massachusetts Republican Party, remembered George Bush coming to his state at the height of the scandal to urge business as usual in the party's outposts. He was scheduled to give a talk, and the local organizers had set up chairs for 600 people. Only 60 supporters came. But George Bush breezed in, greeted everyone, and delivered a rousing speech. He was so convinced that there needed to be a viable two-party system that he wasn't going to get down about something so silly as attendance.

"You can't imagine the tension," Eddie Mahe Jr., who was serving as political director of the committee, told the *Los Angeles Times*. "There was never any good news. Bush was the epitome of the good trouper. At staff meetings, he'd tell everyone to hang in there. Then privately, he'd be very distressed. He would moan: 'What is going on?'"

George W. had arrived at Harvard Business School, perfectly comfortable to stand out as an individual. "This was HBS, and people were fooling around with the accouterments of money and power," one of George W.'s former girlfriends, April Foley, told the *Washington Post*. "While they were drinking Chivas Regal, he was drinking Wild Turkey. They were smoking Benson and Hedges and he's dipping Copenhagen, and while they were going to the opera, he would listen to Johnny Rodriguez over and over and over and over."

But he could not have anticipated the fallout in Cambridge over Watergate. He said that he found it "claustrophobic, intellectually and physically."

"You know Harvard Square and how they felt about Nixon," explained his aunt Nancy Ellis, who lived in the area, to Donnie Radcliffe. "But here was Georgie, his father head of the Republican National Committee. So he came out a lot with us just to get out of there."

———

When Richard Nixon was forced to resign on August 9, 1974, many observers thought the time had finally come for George Bush to be rewarded for his loyalty to the party with an appointment to vice president. But the Townhouse Operation donation Richard Nixon had given to George Bush's 1970 Senate campaign had come to light in the many months of Watergate investigations. Although no one could prove that the donation was illegal, the connection to Watergate was too close for the American public to stomach. President Gerald Ford passed him over for Nelson Rockefeller, the same man whose presidential ambitions Prescott Bush had worked to end.

"Yesterday was a real downer," Bush wrote in a letter to his friend Lud Ashley. "I guess I had let my hopes zoom unrealistically, but today perspective is coming back and I realize I was lucky to be in the game at all."

George Bush's colleague at the RNC was more blunt. "[George Bush] thought he had it," Mahe told the *L.A. Times*. "He said they could shove the RNC job."

In an odd twist on the embarrassment George Bush experienced at the U.N., he requested a posting as liaison to China from President Ford. George Bush had been around the globe many times as an oil industry CEO, as congressman, politico, and diplomat. Bar, who had stayed behind to maintain the homefront during all her husband's travels, would now be taking her first trip abroad.

VII

KING OF THE PERMIAN BASIN

George W. graduated from Harvard in 1975 with the discipline he needed to get into business, but without a clear idea of which industry to enter. He knew from his work at Stratford that he didn't want a "coat-and-tie job," with its stifling formality. On the way down to visit a friend's ranch in Tucson, he stopped off to see his old friend Joey O'Neill III in Midland. In the 1950s, Midland was experiencing a time of steady growth because of the end of the war's oil embargo and the new prospecting in the West Texas fields. When George W. visited in the mid-seventies, the region was riding a boom. An Arab oil embargo had made domestic oil even more valuable.

In the 1950s, the United States produced more oil than the country could consume, but the price still depended on consumer demand. Since the Organization for Petroleum Exporting Countries (OPEC) was formed in 1960, U.S. producers had been at the whim of the now 13 Arab countries that set the world oil prices. Those nations can afford to set the price low, since they have so many productive wells.

The ratio of domestic to import use started to shift to a state of near equilibrium in the 1960s, then the nation's dependence on foreign oil increased. The turn in oil production—where we started consuming more than we produce—began in the mid-seventies. Whether business was good or bad for Midlanders all depended on where those

OPEC countries set the price of oil and how much foreign oil was being allowed into the United States.

George W. had always admired the way his father took the risk of moving to Odessa and Midland to seek his fortune, and in the economic climate of the mid-seventies, that gamble to try the oil industry could be even more profitable. Over the next decade, 18 new office buildings would rise from the desert sand in Midland, the population would almost double, and bank deposits would grow from $384 million to nearly $2 billion as all of the new oil money poured into savings accounts. By the early 1980s, Midland was the richest town in America, with the highest per capita income and the highest level of Rolls-Royce sales. Odessa, the town nearby, led for retail sales volume.

George W. realized that this was where he, a favorite son of Midland, could build his own business, and in that economic climate probably flourish, without having to crawl slowly up the ladder. Like his father he wanted to run for political office; building a fortune quickly could help ensure his independence from special interests. The West Texas style suited his own temperament. At Harvard, he had not abandoned his maverick streaks of snapping his gum in class and showing up in bomber jackets. In Midland, he could work on a cud of tobacco and wear cowboy boots with impunity.

He would build an entire life—including a business, a wife, and a political campaign—within only two years of arriving in the Tall City of the Plains. Each decision would be based on a certain impetuousness, as if he were quickly trying to make up for the years he'd spent meandering as a pilot in the reserves. He would construct an existence almost identical to his father's early life, with a few exceptions. Instead of waiting to build his fortune before running for office, he put himself forward as a candidate before he had put together his first drilling fund. The losing campaign that resulted would teach him the lesson once and for all that a politician cannot run without a resumé. In that congressional race, he did well in Midland County but was less successful in districts where the voters had not known him since he was a child and did not see him on a daily basis. In Midland, he was beloved because of his parents and his personality.

He brought excitement to the West Texas suburbs with his eccentric personal style and reckless sense of adventure. He was a good friend to those in his circle who hit hard times. Later in George W.'s life, when he moved to Washington and operated in a more rarefied atmosphere of power, he could come off as testy and arrogant. But in Midland, those qualities were rarely exhibited. His ego must have been content. He has said that if he were to die tomorrow, he would want to be buried in Midland, and that must, to some extent, be a marker of how he felt most comfortable there, most like himself, at his best. Lying on the grass in the backyard at night with his buddies—Joey O'Neill, Donnie Evans, and Dennis Grubb—looking up at the stars, and listening to John Anderson on the radio, yodeling in his Texas twang, "And they were swingin'. . . . " Life seemed sweet. The wives would be laughing and talking in the kitchen.

Although George W. was following his father's path, he had found a protected isolation in the oasis of West Texas. By 1980, George Bush was vice president of the United States and George W. ran a small oil company named Arbusto. On an average day, George W. could be found in the early morning running at the high school stadium. When his father came to visit, the place would be encircled by secret service agents, the surrounding streets closed for transit—it was just a boy and his father out for a run. But after Air Force Two had lifted off, and his father headed back to Washington, D.C., George W. was back to being the king of Midland.

It all began after he graduated from Harvard, when he pointed the nose of his 1970 Cutlass west, and headed from the Northeast like his father had, for Midland, the city whose motto is The Sky Is the Limit.

—

Five hundred million years before George W. trod the terrain of the Permian Basin, that land of West Texas was a vast ocean. When the waters receded, they left only hundreds of thousands of miles of desert. That was the sunbaked landscape that George and Bar had found in the early 1950s and that George W. returned to over 20 years later. The region boasted a seasonable climate but no comforting natural beauty.

"Midland–Odessa is pretty horrible geographically," confessed George W.'s childhood pal Randy Roden, who spent his formative years in the Permian Basin and came back in the mid-seventies for more. "Any place that's known by its *geologic* designation—that gives you your first clue."

Most of the people who settled in Midland, including George W., were looking to make money in the oil business. As a result, their world view was shaped by the values and risks of the industry. "Anywhere else in America, you would say, 'I own a piece of land,'" observed Roden. "There, they would say, 'Oh, you own the surface.' Nobody cares about that stuff on the top; it's what's underneath [that counts]."

Indeed, Midland's land rights stack up like a prospector's Napoleon. A prospector might buy the mineral rights to the oil or the gas; they might purchase the land at 4,500 feet or at 8,000 feet. A different person might own each depth. As many as one hundred people can own parts of one square mile, or section. The history of Midland is writ miles down in the earth, of rights sold or inherited, of the oil that sat undisturbed for decades while prospectors poked about at a depth just above.

The oil lies trapped beneath shale or under hillocks created by the shift of a geological fault. Water usually lingers under the oil—since it is heavier—providing the pressure that pushes the riches toward the surface. The geologist predicts the location of the deposits. The landman checks maps of the land rights at the county clerk's office and then tracks down the owners and strikes deals. The engineer rigs the drill to puncture the shale and decides when it's time to put down pipe. The roustabouts run the rigs; and the investors pay for the drilling on the gamble that either their investment will evaporate if the well is dry, or they will be paid dividends for up to 30 years—maybe more—on a gusher that just won't quit. George W. would become a landman.

In Midland, a person's fate is determined by how lucky he or she is at picking the right place to put down money. A farmer can see his ill fate in a dry season that gradually withers the crops. A fisherman knows by the empty nets that the schools are depleted and it's time to go into construction. An oil man might go for years without a good well, then plunge the bit into a vast reserve. Of all the professionals to compare him to, the oil man is most like a stockbroker in cowboy boots. George W. would not be lucky at choosing drilling sites during

the time he lived in Midland, but he would be fortunate in the help he
gained from his friends.

He had two main contacts there: his father's beloved pal, Jimmy
Allison Jr., and another dear friend, the lawyer Martin Allday, both of
whom had worked on George Bush's early campaigns. Allison, after
watching from the sidelines at the Republican National Committee
while George Bush lost his 1970 senate campaign, had eventually
returned to Midland. His father had died about six months before
George W. arrived in town and Allison had inherited the *Midland
Reporter-Telegram*. Allday was now an oil and gas lawyer. George W.
wanted to get into the oil business however he could.

Another friend Nick Taylor rented his garage apartment to George
W. It was a real bachelor pad with magazines and newspapers carpeting
the floor and his bed held together with an old necktie. Having him
nearby, Taylor could look out for him, and George W. seemed to enjoy
being around a real family. When Nick's boy was just two years old,
George W. taught him how to shake hands. Look the guy in the eye,
George W. explained to the toddler, and hold your hand firm.

Martin and Patricia Allday tried to introduce him around to the
other folks in town. They would invite him over for dinner—maybe
ask some young belle over too, to meet the town's newest bachelor at
her mother's request. Paul Rea and his wife were often invited along.
Paul Rea was a geologist who worked for the private fund of Bill
DeWitt from Cincinnati, then for the investment company of his son,
Bill Jr., and his partner Mercer Reynolds. The oil part of Reynolds
DeWitt was called Spectrum 7.

So Allday and Rea would hash out George W.'s prospects over
cocktails—how he could get into the "bidness." Allday and Rea determined that the only place for George W. was as a leasebroker, or landman. George W. didn't know the technical end—he wasn't a geologist
or an engineer—and he wasn't a lawyer. It was a process of elimination. Rea got the feeling that George W. saw the oil business as a way
to make enough money so he could go into politics. His parents had
taught him that a man shouldn't pursue his own ambitions until he had
provided for his family first. His grandfather had always said that a
politician shouldn't run for office without building savings, or he
would be too dependent on special interests for reelection.

To learn the business, they said, he should tag around with a broker and take classes at the Permian Basin Graduate School, where local geologists, engineers, and lawyers passed on their expertise to one another.

To find a landman with whom he could apprentice, George W. stopped by Boyd Laughlin's law office for advice. "Buzz Mills and Ralph Ways," Laughlin advised George W., according to Nick Taylor, who had stopped by the same day. "I don't know two men who have more fun in the oil business than those two."

Buzz was one of the smartest mineral men around, with a deep drawl and a flattop. Ways constantly chewed a cigar. They agreed to let George W. set up shop in their office. The phones rang constantly with prospectors shopping deals.

Buzz and Ralph took George W. to the county courthouses and showed him how to look up land records—to see who owned the surface and the lower levels, and where they lived. Then they trained him in the way to make a deal. It was all talk—sweet and straight. You'd go up to some rancher and tell him why you wanted a go at his land and how much you would pay. Usually, the rancher would go for the deal, because he needed the cash. But sometimes you would find a prickly rancher, and then you would have to keep bird-dogging him, or else just drop the deal and move on to another piece of land. That was part of the lesson of the oil business. You couldn't get down about a no. There was always another piece of land to drill. But you had to be friendly if you wanted the rancher to reconsider—you couldn't give off the whiff of anxiety because then maybe he would think you were up to no good. You learned that you'd better not show up in a coat and tie. And you understood pretty quickly that the world was not made up of only Ivy League graduates who summered.

If the landman worked a deal with open property adjacent, or if he heard about another good prospect, he could pick up his own leases here and there. George W. had the remnants of an educational trust fund set up by his parents—about $13,000—burning a hole in his pocket, and since the job as landman paid about $100 a day, he could easily afford to begin investing.

In the mid-seventies, it seemed like a new independent oil company was starting every 24 hours. George W. opened his own operation,

Arbusto, in the first half of 1977. Like his father, he gave his company a Spanish name—the word means "Bush." Back in 1953, his father had insisted that his own oil company name should start with an A or Z so it wouldn't get lost in the phone book. The new name met that criteria. George W.'s 20-year-old brother Marvin teasingly called him J.R.

Starting a company cost George W. relatively little, since there was no overhead until active operations began. Basically, an oil man could begin collecting money from investors for a drilling fund when he had nothing but the idea that the geology on a particular parcel of land looked promising. George W. didn't even begin drilling operations until 1979, since the prospect of running for Congress intervened in the meantime and set him temporarily off course.

—

From the moment George W. arrived in Midland, he established himself as a favorite personality, with his quick humor and exuberance. An old driller named G. W. Brock also trained at the stadium where George W. often took his early morning runs. Every time George W. lapped him, he'd reach and over and tug down Brock's pants. "I'm so glad that SOB finally left town," Brock cooed to a reporter.

If George W. missed his morning training, he would jog a fast-paced five miles at the YMCA during lunch hour. Paul Rea would be there, and George W. met some other guys his own age, including oil men Don Evans and Dennis Grubb. Charlie Younger, an orthopedic surgeon who used to live catercorner to him on Ohio Street when he was a kid, also ran there. They had known each other in the old days, but only peripherally, since Younger was five years older. Younger too had left Midland for school. He vowed to never come back, but ended up missing the town's camaraderie and sense that you could really effect civic change. He never felt trapped there; he could always drive to the airport and escape for a while if life got too slow or the weather too hot. Midland was a perfect town to use as a place to work, and then go elsewhere for bigger fun and beauty.

He and George hit it off right away because they loved to joke. "We like to stick a needle in each other," said Younger. George W. dubbed him the "Young One" or "Fingers," as in two fingers. He earned that name after a little too much Tequila on the way from

Midland to Lubbock one night. The guys called George W. "The Bombastic Bushkin," as a tribute to his crazy high energy. The four guys who ran every day christened themselves "the greyhounds," since they ran like dogs at the racetrack.

George W. was the most spontaneous person any of those guys had ever met. He played golf like it was polo, just speeding from hole to hole, whacking the ball without teeing. If a decision needed to be made—from where to go eat later on, to how to react to a campaign snafu—the question wouldn't linger on the table for more than a few seconds. "This is what we've got to do," he'd say, and he'd be off—out the door before his buddy could climb out of his chair.

He was hilarious, but he'd blurt out any funny line he had—even if it cut too deep. He didn't think the effect through, how the person might take the joke.

He thought it; he said it. Done.

Most of the time, that impulsiveness meant fun. When George W. went to visit his parents in China the summer of 1975, during his father's tenure as U.S. liaison to that nation, he had bought a few suits that were cheap and fit strangely. He wore them on the rare occasions that he dressed up. He also picked up a pair of slippers. His friends constantly razzed him about how much he wore them.

After dinner at his house one night with L.E. and Penny Sawyer and Don and Suzy Evans, when they were all a little warmed up from the wine, the girls were teasing him about his slippers. He'd had enough. "I bet I could beat you running the track—even in these slippers," he said.

They took him on. So they all trudged out to the track and the three of them went racing off into the darkness. George did win. But his slippers were ruined forever. At least that was fun. He was making some fun happen.

In his family, he was a hero for this impetuous quality. "We all idolized him," his sister, Doro, told the *Washington Post*. "He was always such fun and wild, you always wanted to be with him because he was always daring. . . . He was on the edge.

"We'd go out in the boat at night [in Kennebunkport] and that was always an adventure. Now, if we went out in the boat at night with Neil, you know that was fine because he's a boatsman, my brother

Neil, and he knew everything about it — and still does. George, on the other hand, it was more of a kind of a wild risky thing because we're not sure that he, you know, could manage the boat as well."

Donnie Evans remembered a similar story involving an airplane. He told David Maraniss that less than a year after George W. first got back to Midland he came over to Donnie's house and told him he wanted to take a single-engine Cessna for a little joyride. They drove over to the airfield and got in the plane. Then George W. realized he didn't have a clue how to fly a Cessna.

"The guy didn't even know how to start the thing," Evans reportedly said. "That was a bad omen. Finally we get it started and roll down the runway, and he tries to take it straight up like a jet! We go into a stall, buzzers are going off. I say, 'Give it some gas!' We finally get it airborne, and he decides he better turn around and go back. I can tell he's nervous, but he says, 'Okay, Evvie, got it under control.' We come down and he lands half on the runway and half on the grass. And then he pats my leg and says don't worry, and he takes it up again. This time he's so scared he says, 'Hey, let's fly around Midland.' He had to get his confidence up. Somehow we got back safely. He's never flown again."

George W. had vowed on his Texas Air National Guard application to make flying a lifetime pursuit, but obviously he needed to abandon that promise. He later explained that flying was too dangerous if a person didn't practice regularly and he couldn't afford the risk.

For rowdy times, the guys would all throw parties at one of their houses or head over to Odessa. Midland had fewer watering holes. In fact, all decadent activities were frowned upon. Even in the late 1990s, a story would circulate in town that one of the convenience stores insisted that *Cosmopolitan* magazine be wrapped in brown paper to obscure its lurid covers.

From the early '40s through George W.'s first years back in Midland as an adult, Sheriff Ed Darnell ruled the town with a big gun and an unwavering hatred of all things blue and bawdy. Patrol officer "Preacher" Roberts continued the aversion, standing watch over the younger set. One local resident remembered that on one occasion a rapscallion showed up at town hall trying to file to open a porn shop. The policeman said that such a venture was impossible. The guy insisted that not only was it possible, he had a license to do so. There was nothing the police chief could do.

The first day the porn shop opened, a policeman arrived with a big dog and stood right outside the door. He stayed there all day until closing time. The next day he was back at his post, and it continued that way until the porn proprietor got the message and packed up. He probably headed to Odessa, which ended up as the drainage ditch for Midland's seedier impulses. As Michelle, a topless waitress from the Doll's House on Highway 385 in Odessa told a local paper decades later, "There aren't no [nude] bars in Midland because they don't believe in having fun."

George W. always demonstrated a knack for dodging the counterculture. He had just missed the more radical days at Yale; camped out in conservative Houston for the early 1970s; and then lived for his early adulthood in this haven of relatively clean living. He had law and order bred into his bones.

—

George W.'s decision to run for Congress in 1978 surprised just about everyone he knew. He obviously had been interested in politics from his father's campaigns and the work he did with Jimmy Allison on the elections in Georgia and Florida, when he was in the National Guard. In 1976, he was the 19th District coordinator for Gerald Ford's presidential bid and, among other duties, traveled to Lubbock to introduce the vice presidential nominee Bob Dole. But his friends thought he hadn't really *mulled over* the idea of running for Congress himself; he just hurled himself in. It was another example of his impetuousness. He couldn't resist the good timing of an open seat, the coordination with his father's own ambitions, and the prevailing mood in the district that made a Midlander a potential winner for office.

"I remember him sitting around our kitchen table talking about this and we were saying: Why do you want to do this?" Joe O'Neill told the *Washington Post*. "He looked around the table and said, 'Are you gonna do it? Are you gonna do it?' And of course none of us wanted to. He said, 'Well then, I am.' "

The Andover boys too had seen that side of George W.—the way he was willing to take on the responsibilities no one else wanted. His impulsiveness helped him start a project, and then he would become diligent in his impetuousness. He insisted on seeing any idea through that he had committed to, no matter how shaky the foundation. He would make up his mind quickly, and then live with the consequences. So, once he decided to run—however hastily—he never stopped working for victory.

His path had been cleared by the fact that his father had decided from China not to pursue the Texas governorship in 1978; George W. wouldn't have wanted to run in the same election cycle. George Bush had considered the idea but ultimately realized that after 18 months in Beijing he was too out of touch with politics in Texas. In late 1975, President Gerald Ford had wired him asking him to return to the states to helm the CIA, an agency that had suffered terribly that year when congressional investigations exposed it to be on a renegade course.

George Bush was intrigued by the challenge of cleaning up the reputation of such an important federal agency. He had felt isolated in China, where Bar said he missed his regular phone calls most of all. Taking over the CIA would mean being in the middle of the action, however controversial. Still, George Bush called George W. to ask whether he and the other kids—who were all at ages when their peers would likely be critical of the CIA—would give their blessing. Most of George Bush's friends and political advisers had told him that the position was a dead end, a way of effectively ending his career in elected office. But George W. called his father back and told him to do it. "Take the job and come home," he said. "We want you home."

George Bush was commissioned as director of the CIA in December. He grew to enjoy the job because of its intriguing concerns and the diligent people who worked there. When Jimmy Carter won the 1976 election, George Bush offered to stay on past inauguration day. But Carter chose to put his own person in the job, and on January 20, 1977, when power transferred to the new administration, George Bush was forced to resign.

He headed back to the private sector in Houston. Ross Perot, a fellow Texan who had made a fortune facilitating Medicare payments through his company Electronic Data Processing, flew up to Maine when George Bush was vacationing there to offer him a job overseeing a Houston oil company. But Bush turned him down. Instead he focused on increasing his bank account through investments and corporate consulting fees, and building his reputation as a civic leader, all the while looking for his next opportunity in national politics.

For George W., the congressional contest in West Texas was just too good to ignore. George Mahon, the granddaddy of Texas politics, announced in the summer of 1977 that he was stepping down from his congressional throne. He had ascended in 1934 and never been shaken off. He had just grown grayer and more revered as the longest-serving member. Thirty years after he first arrived on the Hill, he was made chairman of the House Appropriations Committee. When the nuclear bomb was being built, only half a dozen men were on the committee allocating the secret $2 billion budget. Mahon was one of them.

George W. never could have seriously challenged Mahon if the old man had decided to stay on. But when Mahon announced his retirement July 6—coincidentally George W.s' 31st birthday—the Bombastic Bushkin recognized the beauty of the timing. An open seat had presented itself and he had no daily commitments elsewhere. Timing was key! Plus, some Midlanders were begging him to run—or at least they encouraged him to get in the race. In Lubbock he was getting encouragement too. Bob Blake, a longtime friend of his father's from the Midland Martini Bowl, took him to Mahlouf's Fine Apparel for Men and Women to buy him a running-for-Congress suit. He would need one now that he was an official candidate.

George W. surveyed the field of possible opponents. Everyone expected 48-year-old Jim Reese to make a go for the seat. Reese was a former television sportscaster and ex-mayor of Odessa turned stockbroker. In the 1970 senate race, he had helped George W.'s father at a campaign rally at the Midland–Odessa airport. In 1976, he ran as a Republican against Mahon and won a hearty 46 percent of the vote. That election was a kind of test spin for Reese; he was just taking out the Benz before he actually inherited it. In 1978, Reese presumed that the seat was his. Then Junior went and complicated things.

The 20 miles between Midland and Odessa, which had always been a sunbaked stretch of no-man's-land, had grown even hotter over the previous four years. The wealthy Scharbauer family, one of the most powerful clans in the county, donated 600 acres to the University of Texas on which to build a branch. Midland and Odessa fought over which town would get to claim the school. The final verdict was that both towns would claim ownership, if Midland would vote itself into Odessa's tax district to foot the bill on construction. After the tax bill went through, Odessa said, "It's time to be selfish." They claimed the branch as their own. Midlanders never got over their fury, and there wasn't even time to take a deep breath by 1978, when this election was upon them. To many Midlanders, there was no way on God's flat earth that a former mayor of Odessa was going to represent them in the nation's capital.

In Midland, George W. had the help, not only of his closest friends and business associates, but of his father's network from decades earlier. The rest of the district was less well stocked. In Lubbock, he could turn for help to his father's friend Bob Blake, but he mainly built his staff in that area from scratch. He found a young lawyer and accountant named Mike Weiss when he was touring a shopping mall in Lubbock shaking hands. Weiss liked what George W. had to say at that brief encounter in a men's clothing store and invited him to stop by the office some time. George W. showed up the next day and they sat down for a talk that stretched on for hours. Weiss signed up as George W.'s campaign manager.

If George W. could pull off a victory in the primary, his main opponent on the Democratic side would likely be 35-year-old Kent Hance, the district's state senator. Hance was the ultimate good old boy from Dimmitt, a skinny charmer with a lazy grin who had been raised on a wheat farm. When one of George W.'s older friends from Midland heard that George W. was going to be facing Hance in that down-home region, he had one question. "Do you have any boots?"

"No, but does he have any shoes?" George W. retorted. Ultimately, it became obvious that Hance and George W. were very much alike in that they had been inculcated into the political world since they were children. They inherited their political passions from their parents. But Hance was a down-home Texan—he knew how to charm voters and connect to the issues that concerned them. George W. would learn most of what he needed to know about retail politicking watching Hance out in the field.

Hance had loved politics since he was a kid. On primary day, his parents, Raymond and Beral, would let the fields fend for themselves so they could drive into Dimmitt for the big event. In Castro County at the time, primary day was the campaign moment that mattered, because practically everyone in the state was a Democrat. The Hances would make a whole day of it—go shopping early and then eat dinner. As dusk fell, they would stroll into the town square, which was packed with people gossiping about the campaigns. Someone would be marking the returns from all of the district's little hamlets on a chalkboard. Hance would stand there, mesmerized, watching the numbers roll in and the faces of the people as their political horse took the lead or fell to the back.

If a politician swung through the area to stump, Hance's mother would take Kent down to watch. No one had television. This was entertainment. In class, he would get in trouble for reading while the teacher was talking; he just couldn't put down his biographies of the presidents, particularly Eisenhower. He would sit listening to his father and uncles grumbling about politics. The only role of government was to deliver the mail and keep the Communists out, they said. FDR knew the Japs were going to bomb Pearl Harbor, but he let them do it so everybody would be mad enough to go to war. Boy, they got passionate! They were furious and suspicious of everything. That's what drove their political beliefs. The Bushes weren't like that.

When young George W. Bush popped into the race, Hance hadn't yet decided whether he was going to run or not. The election that got Hance into the state senate—against 16-year incumbent Doc Blanchard—had been a grueling experience. He was ready for a rest and his seat was uncontested. He could get real work done down in Austin. But if he chose to run for congress, he would have an advantage over George W., since his senate district substantially overlapped with the U.S. congressional district.

George W. focused first on Reese in his campaign. What we need is decent representation, he told the reporters who had assembled at 9:30 in the morning out at Midland Regional Air Terminal on July 19 for the announcement of his first political campaign. George W. had convinced Donnie Evans to volunteer as campaign chair and Robert McCleskey, a childhood friend who was now his accountant, to prepare his Federal Election Commission filings. The 31-year-old George W. told reporters that he'd always aspired to public office.

George W. implied that he would be a more businesslike representative in Washington. George W. believed in reducing the size of government and people's dependence on it, he said; but more importantly, he believed in the oil business itself. Almost all of the policies he laid out that morning were tuned to the ears of the Midland oilman.

His proposals were crafted by sincerity, not guile; after all, they were exactly the issues that he, as an oil man, cared about. America, he said, needed a wise energy policy and the deregulation of oil and natural gas prices. But more important, Washington, D.C., needed to get a swift education in the risks of petrol production—how the independents and majors staked everything on gambles that could crash on them, and how even so, the government was always calling their cards at inopportune times. "I'm idealistic enough to think some good can be done," George W. said. He later would say he ran specifically because of his antipathy for the policies of Jimmy Carter, who, of course, had also relieved his father of his duties at the CIA. With that, George W. was off and running, in fact racing to catch a plane down to Odessa to kick off the campaign from that city too. George W. had learned from his father that campaigning was a contest of endurance and energy, and he would get off to a quick start.

If George W. had any thought that he would be able to keep the issue of his father out of the 1978 race, the reality was spelled out in the first sentence of his announcement coverage. "The son of former CIA director George Bush has entered the race for the congressional seat held by retiring Rep. George Mahon, D-Tex.," read the wire story from Midland on July 20. The reporter had asked George W. whether or not his father would be campaigning on his behalf. No, George W. told them, he would seek the advice and support of his father, but was off to the races by himself.

He could not afford to associate himself closely with his father for a couple of reasons. As a novice politician, he needed to show that he was running because he himself wanted to, not just as a nepotistic act. His dad had lost his last statewide contest in 1970 and then disappeared from the Texas scene, so he was associated more with politics as usual than the prairie voters liked. George W. needed to come off as one of them.

That didn't mean he wouldn't rely on some of the family's support. His 22-year-old brother Neil, in a triumphant victory over dyslexia, had just finished his bachelor's degree at Tulane. He was now at postgraduate loose ends. He decided to help George W. and moved down to Lubbock, setting himself up at a rolltop desk in headquarters as the county campaign chair. Ruth Schiermeyer, the vice chair of the Republican Party in Lubbock, loaned him her garage apartment. He was as disheveled as any recent college graduate. When he moved to another Lubbock pad later in the campaign, Schiermeyer asked him if he needed any supplies; how about any bedding? "Oh, I'll just cover up with my coat," he told her.

Pitching in was Neil's style. George W. remembered how, when they were younger, his mother would chirp, "Who's going to mow the lawn?"

"Three of us were diving under the couch," George W. recalled. But not Neil. "I'll do it, Mom," he'd say. He was the supreme volunteer.

Neil was so oddly open—just completely naive. Everyone who worked on the campaign would remark on that quality. Some would also grumble that he wasn't the most useful addition to the team. But he was sweet. And he just loved his family. In high school, he would *ask* his younger brother Marvin to tag along to parties. He idolized George. And both George W. and Neil adored their parents. It was almost a little weird. Didn't those kids ever rebel?

"When you have a young man, twenty-two years of age, that's the time that Mom and Dad are not the smartest people in the world," Schiermeyer marveled. "That was nowhere in George's attitude or Neil's attitude. You never picked up any negative at all." Later the other kids came down briefly to stuff envelopes and hand out flyers. They all knew the grassroots techniques from working for their dad.

A couple of other candidates also declared: Republican Joe Hicox, a retired air force lieutenant colonel from Shallowater, and Democrat Morris Sheats.

Even a month and a half into George W.'s campaign, in late August, Hance still wasn't sure whether or not he would join the fray. He had been surprised when he first read of George W.'s announcement in the newspaper. At the time, Hance said, he didn't know who that Bush boy was. Finally, he decided that he would rather have a say in national issues than just state ones. Before he declared in September, Hance went around for two weeks letting the key players know he was getting in to the congressional race and dropping out of the state senate to do so. He stopped by Arbusto to see the Bush boy and told him his plans, while Ralph Ways just sat there chewing his cigar. Hance thought George W. seemed like a nice enough guy.

—

George W. was no Casanova as far as his friends can recall. He rarely dated the same girl for long but not because he was off to another one. "Any time he would date a girl more than two or three times, and he had an inkling that they might be serious for a relationship," said Charlie Younger, "he was out of there."

Still, Younger says he didn't leave a lot of broken hearts. He was a little too off-the-wall to be a dream date—a man who was slow to pick up the check for his friends and had a Worst Dressed Award named after him at the local country club. "[George W.] wasn't exactly presidential timber yet," his friend Joey O'Neill told the *Washington Post*. "It took some coaching for us to get the girls to go out with him." He tended to go out with party girls who just wanted some fun and matched his own frenetic energy.

Then, one night toward the end of July, Jan and Joey O'Neill invited the new congressional candidate over to a barbecue. It was just going to be the three of them, plus Jan had invited one of her best friends, 30-year-old Laura Welch, who was visiting from Austin. Laura had grown up in Midland, and her parents, Harold and Jenna Welch still lived there. Her father was a successful architect and contractor in Midland; her mother a devoted bird-watcher and office holder in the Midland Naturalist Society. Laura was an only child.

In fact Laura had been raised only blocks from George W. She had attended the same playschool, attended the same junior high, served in the student council, lived in the Chateaux Dijon in Houston at the same time, and yet George W. says he does not remember meeting her before the barbecue. The Bombastic Bushkin, known for his get-to-know-you style, his extraordinary memory for names and a person's favorite vacation spot, never got around to knowing Laura Welch. On the other hand, Laura says she knew who George W. was from grammar school onward, and of course she was aware of his family.

Perhaps he had overlooked her because she was quiet. At San Jacinto and Midland High, the Welch's only child was known as a good student with a sweet smile. She was popular and dated quite a bit in high school while he was off at Andover. She went off to Southern Methodist University in Dallas for her bachelor of science and got a master of library science from the University of Texas at Austin. At the time she and George W. met, she was working as a librarian in the independent school district in Austin. Many of her friends from Midland were from her parents' generation.

Most of George W. and Laura's friends had known them both separately—most since childhood; one of her best friends was Susie Evans, who was married to George W.'s friend Don, for example. But only the O'Neills had thought to set them up, and even they weren't sold on the idea because they thought the personalities were so different. Laura never showed interest in the proposition either. Whenever the O'Neills brought up the idea of fixing them up, she would brush it aside. She really didn't want to get involved with a political family.

"I would never have matched them together," said Younger, who remembered Laura from childhood and whose mother became close to Laura later on. "Laura is more ladylike. She was the teacher-librarian-type lady and George was more the rambunctious reveler and a rambler."

A few weeks after the barbecue, the O'Neills were surprised to hear that George W. and Laura were still in touch. Part of the attraction, friends say, came from the fact that Laura was independent and elusive; at 31, she was still in no hurry to settle down.

"There wasn't some mom pushing Laura off on George," said Younger.

Then, their personalities complemented each other's. They were so different, they could enjoy a fifty-fifty power dynamic. When he got too loud, she could calmly rein him in. He could inject a little swagger into her docile existence and she loved that he made her laugh.

Barbara Bush insisted that her son had fallen head over heels in love. "He was struck by lightning when he met her," she told *Texas Monthly,* "calling back to Midland every minute. And then one day he said he was going home. I think he had called [Laura's house] one day and a man had answered." George W. told the magazine he did not recall the incident.

Friends say that timing was the key to why the relationship turned into marriage. George W. was tired of being the devilish bachelor. He was probably sick of feeling like the fifth wheel, weary of showing up at his married friends' houses with his dirty laundry to sweet-talk his friends' wives into helping him do it.

"My personal explanation is that he was ready to settle down. She came along and he came along, and each of them applied," said Younger. "I think the timing was a critical factor, because both of them were at a crossroads in their lives. He was ready to settle down and think about a family and have a decent lady to make a life with. Call it fate, destiny, whatever, but they came along and crossed at the right time."

They were engaged five weeks after they met. "We don't agonize over decisions," Laura told the *Dallas Morning News* years later. "We just do things. Obviously—we married three months after meeting."

George W. and Laura were wed at 11:00 in the morning of November 6, 1977, at the United Methodist Church in Midland, the same week "You Light Up My Life" topped the charts. In a land of big weddings, theirs was decidedly demure. Laura wore a long-sleeved, street-length crepe de chine dress with blouson bodice and pleated skirt. A gardenia corsage was pinned to her waist. Her cousin Robert and George W.'s brothers served as the ushers. Younger thought they decided to "low key it" since they had so many friends. "It would have to be either a huge wedding or a little wedding, and neither of them wanted a huge wedding," he said.

But the Bush family also had never been inclined toward big weddings. After all, George and Bar had been so casual about their own event, they simply crossed off the date they intended to get married and wrote in the day George would be back from overseas.

Don Etra remembered flying from Washington, D.C., the night before George W.'s wedding and meeting up in Dallas with George W.'s grandmother and a few others for the trek to Midland. They were all seated on the puddle jumper to West Texas when the luggage truck backed into the fuselage and damaged it. George W.'s grandmother refused to be late for the rehearsal dinner at the Midland Hilton. "There is no way I'm going to miss it," she said, and chartered another plane.

At the luncheon reception at the Racquet Club, Bar stood to give a toast, but George W.'s father said nothing. It had been the same at the wedding of Jeb and Columba in 1974, where Bar rose to speak from the heart and her husband stayed silent. Indeed, George Bush was as layered as the land of Midland—a man who could write sentimental poetry about the meaning of family in Maine but seemed to feel too uncomfortable to share an intimate tribute in public.

George W. and Laura spent their honeymoon in Mexico and then rejoined the campaign trail in his white Bonneville upon their return.

The relationship between George W. and Laura was always traditional. After they were married, Laura stopped working despite the fact that George W. was running for office full-time instead of earning a regular paycheck. She devoted herself to volunteer projects and eventually to raising their daughters. Neither George W. nor Laura, it would seem, would describe each other as soul mates. "I don't really like that 'best friend' thing," Laura Bush told the *Dallas Morning News*. "George is my husband and not my best friend, necessarily. We obviously have a very close relationship. But like most couples, we probably mainly talk about our children, our pets, the most mundane things that happen in our lives. We don't have a lot of policy discussions where we philosophize."

Laura was in fact the perfect political wife. She gave her first speech in junior high when she ran for student council. She had taken on the project of putting together the student handbook.

She would never be outspoken or interfere in her husband's plans for his political future. "In general, I don't give George advice," she told the *Dallas Morning News*. "I will every once in a while, but not really. For one thing, I know he doesn't really want my advice, just like I don't really want his. I think marriages are a little bit better when you're not constantly telling who you're married to something. I know George has got plenty of people who want to tell him things. I don't need to be one of them."

When they were married, her mother-in-law gave her only one piece of advice: Never criticize your husband's speeches. Laura tried to abide by the rule, but one night during the 1978 campaign, she and

George W. were driving back from an event, when he said to her, "Tell me the truth: How did it go tonight?"

She told him it hadn't gone very well. He drove the car right into the garage wall, and she never insisted on truthfulness again.

As to her own public appearances, when Laura and George W. married they made a deal. He promised never to ask her to give a speech herself, and she vowed to start jogging with him. She never went jogging, and within months, Laura was giving her first speech on George W.'s behalf in Muleshoe. "She was scared to death," said Ruth Schiermeyer.

Hance remembered thinking, when he heard Bush was getting married, "He's a smart son of a bitch to do it now, because if he waited until after the campaign, she might not want to have anything to do with him."

VIII

THE TIRELESS CANDIDATE

L ong after the 1978 campaign had ended, Kent Hance, a Texas
Tech graduate, would gloat that George W. had one of the finest
educations a man could receive—from Andover, Yale,
Harvard—and that Hance had successfully turned that fact around and
made it work against him.

Down in West Texas, the usual standards of achievement were seen
as immaterial, or even viewed as a negative. Voters cared more about
whether or not their representative understood them and would carry
their concerns to Washington than they did about whether or not he
would impress the other legislators in D.C. George W. learned that lesson quickly and irrevocably while putting in "windshield time," driving the straight, sun-drenched highways across the Permian Basin in
search of votes. Suddenly, the areas that had given him the biggest challenge in his life, namely academics at Andover and Yale, mattered far
less than the skills he had learned on the cheerleading squad, as commissioner of stickball, as fraternity president, as a Little League coach,
and at PULL. The ability to rally support, to make people feel comfortable and happy, and to convert helpmates—these were more
important than any history class he might have taken back East. He

needed first to connect to people before they would entrust him with their interests. Luckily, that charm had always been one of George W.'s greatest strengths.

Still, in 1978, George W. was not quite the smooth politician he would become 16 years later as governor of Texas. He needed a little work to get as down-home as his opponents. He was smart, funny, friendly, but he had not completely shed his Northeast edge or his Houstonian cool. Even his pronunciation marked him as an outsider in those rural Texas towns: He would say Lubb*ick* instead of Lubb*ock*, and *raw*ther rather than *rather*.

His father had decided in 1966, during his congressional campaign, that it was important to portray himself as a man of action, to come across as a person who would be able to bring what seemed like an inexhaustible amount of energy to bear on his work in Congress. His son took a page out of that playbook. His first television ad showed him jogging—a man on the move.

Hance punctured that image. The jogging played perfectly into Hance's game plan, which was to point out whenever possible that George W. was an out-of-towner. No one jogs in Muleshoe, one Hance campaign supporter joked, unless they're trying to get away from someone. The constituents laughed along with him.

In fact, the older George Bush's playbook proved nearly useless to George W. in West Texas in the 1978 campaign. George W. did take a few cues from his dad, though: Namely, he used a few of his father's local contacts to initially staff the team; like his dad, he scribbled follow-up notes to the voters he met, not to mention those he was not able to meet in person when swinging through their neighborhoods. George W. put the famous Bush energy to good use as a frenetic, energetic campaigner, and he even tapped some out-of-town donors who were friends of his father from the oil business and from the United Nations. But the persona that had played so well for George Bush in Houston during his 1966 congressional campaign—that of a responsible, young businessman with a passion for honesty—did not now work well for George W. outside of white-collar Midland. In Lubbock and the hamlets in between, it was clear that George W. would need to devise his own strategy. By the end of the campaign, he learned how important it was for a Texas politician to be a good old boy.

Not only did George W. have to strike out on his own in terms of the structure of his campaign and his own political persona, he actually needed to distance himself somewhat from his father to have a chance at taking the district. The region was heavily stocked with Ronald Reagan Republicans. They liked the California governor's swagger, his antigovernment rhetoric, his tough talk. He had already organized heavily in those farm regions. George Bush and Ronald Reagan had not yet officially declared their candidacies for the 1980 presidential nomination, but most political observers knew that they both would be running. The West Texas supporters of Reagan certainly did not want to give George Bush any advantage at securing the presidential nomination, and if his son became well known in those parts, or worse still, got elected to Congress, George Bush might gain an extra boost in 1980. They did not want to see that happen, and indeed, the Reagan supporters could even use the congressional campaign against their opponent, attacking the father through the medium of the son, which is what they ultimately did.

Despite his father's popularity as a congressman, George W. had to face the fact that his dad did not offer true coattails to him. At the time that George W. announced he was getting into the contest, his father was in Houston, serving on corporate boards and managing his portfolio, as he put together his 1980 race. He had been out of elective politics for the seven years since he lost his senate race in 1970. After that, the older George Bush had become increasingly identified with the Establishment—in fact, with the two institutions that were absolute bastions of the Establishment: the United Nations and the CIA. In West Texas, where the politics of suspicion that Kent Hance's father and uncles subscribed to and mouthed off about was quite common, such connections could only hurt George W.'s candidacy.

Later in the campaign, Hance made an issue of all the money that had come into Bush's campaign from sources outside the district, including such donors as General Douglas MacArthur's widow, who lived in the Waldorf-Astoria Hotel. The media would report the stories, which were meant to highlight the idea that George W. was a carpetbagger invading the district with the support of his East Coast Establishment friends. George W. responded to this charge by saying that of the 3,000 people who had given money to his campaign, 63 percent were from the district, a statistic that probably did not serve to reassure voters. He then compounded his mistake by publicly encouraging absentee voting, which was viewed by some as another way of seeking support from his cabal. These miscues taught the emerging politician the importance of local support and the limit of high-flung connections, and he must have remembered the lessons in future political endeavors.

George W. ran on a platform that favored the oil industry, that looked for government to stop hampering people who were willing to take risks in that important sector. But that first campaign in 1978 had much of the same feeling as his father's early efforts. George W. was offering himself more as a responsible representative than as a revolutionary. He did not get into politics with the fury of his Republican opponent, Jim Reese, or for the love of the game that Hance clearly exhibited. Instead, he seemed to be running because he knew how; because he could; because it would be enough to be an honest politician; because the timing was right.

Only later, when George W. ran for governor of Texas in 1994, with Karl Rove by his side as adviser, would he seem to remember the lessons he learned from Jimmy Allison Jr. and the campaign in Florida: how important the "vision thing" was to achieving victory. He would see firsthand from his father's 1992 presidential bid how damaging the lack of a coherent platform could be.

He didn't appear to have any high-powered advisers in 1978. Instead, the campaign was staffed with friends. Donnie Evans, Joey O'Neill, and Robert McCloskey—all from Midland—helped out. Contemporaries of his father, such as Ernie Angelo and Bob Blake, pitched in too. He recruited Mike Weiss, an attorney and accountant with no political experience, to oversee operations in Lubbock. George W.'s wife, Laura, attended coffees on his behalf and famously gave her first speech, which—in her recollection—opened all right but dissolved into rambling. She shook with anxiety as she spoke. But it was their first year of marriage—in fact, by election day, they had known each other for a mere 16 months—and she seemed happy enough to help her husband realize his ambitions.

The primary campaign in West Texas, with its circus of big personalities, was hilarious at times. Republicans and Democrats were
thrown together for five-way debates. Party affiliation really didn't
matter that much in those parts, since prairie politics dictated that
every one of the candidates be some version of conservative. But
charm did count a great deal, especially since politics was considered
practically a form of entertainment in West Texas, something Kent
Hance knew well.

In the debate format, Hance had the hands-down advantage and
he knew it. He first recognized his own skill as a debater in the
Democratic primary against Morris Sheats, a local preacher. At one
debate, an audience member said to Sheats, "You're a nice bright guy,
but Washington is a lion's den. What are you going to do when you get
down there?"

Sheats answered with the Biblical sentiment about how the lions
must lie down with the sheep. The audience murmured its support.

Then Hance broke in. "What he's not telling you is, the sheep
didn't get much sleep that night." Everybody roared, and he knew he
had won them over. It was all about timing.

During the 1978 congressional race, a question about gun control
came up in a debate at the Kako Center in Lubbock. So the candidates
went down the line.

First, Bush said he was against gun control.

Hicox said he was *really* against gun control, upping the ante with
his passion.

Sheats said that not only was he against gun control, he would
never vote for any measure of any kind.

Then Reese followed up, saying that he would introduce a bill
outlawing anyone from ever again introducing a gun control law.
Never mind that such an action wouldn't even be legal.

Hance was next. Bush looked down the line at him, just smiling,
snickering. He was waiting for the next escalation. Although he was
serious about politics, he was not so puritanical that he could not see
the humor in the kind of wild rhetoric that was being thrown around
because five candidates were trying to one-up each other.

Hance looked out at the crowd, smiled, and drawled, "Not only
am I going to fight any law controlling guns, but if they do pass one,

I'm going to personally come over to your house and help you keep your guns." The crowd cheered and George W. just shook his head and smiled at Hance.

In the Republican primary on May 6, none of the candidates gained a decisive victory, but Bush did beat Reese by around 800 votes, which then mandated a runoff. Hicox followed far behind. Most observers of the West Texas political scene were surprised that Reese hadn't won, since he had established himself as such a stellar candidate in the 1976 election cycle when he nipped at the heels of distinguished congressman George Mahon. But George W. had campaigned harder than anyone had expected, impressing even Reese with his tirelessness. And as it turned out, the election depended a great deal on geography. For the Republican primary, all of the candidates were clustered in the Midland/Odessa area. Of the two districts, Midland was larger, so George W. had the advantage.

"We're going to be polite and dignified in this campaign," said Bush about the next leg of the journey. "[I will] not slam my opponent there [in Odessa], because I need their votes in November." He described his campaign strategy to the *Midland Reporter-Telegram* as, "No secrets. Hard-performing organization workers. Personalities."

He said that Reese had "insulted the voters" when he told them that Bush's support derived from people who mistakenly thought they were voting for his father. "We don't need Dad in this race," Reese had commented defensively. "We don't need anybody in this race except the people in this district."

—

George W. kicked into high gear during the weeks leading up to the runoff on June 3. Six days a week, he drove his white Bonneville out to the distant towns, mostly hitting the malls. He was utterly tireless. "You could schedule him for a six A.M. breakfast and an eight P.M. coffee," Mike Weiss, his Lubbock county chair, said.

"That's the good thing about politics," George W. enthused about the joys of political coffees and travel to far-flung towns, speaking in sentences as jagged as the ones his father was famous for. "The days are all different. Part of it's the mental, but part of it's the stamina to keep going." He confessed, "I'm glad we're not running statewide."

During this phase of the campaign, George W. walked the neighborhoods with the hot sun beating down on him, knocking on more than 65 doors a day. If no one was home, he'd leave a handwritten note, like his father had taught him to do. "Our whole thing is to keep it positive," he told a reporter, echoing the Buckley advice given to his father in 1964. "People are tired of negative politicians. . . . I'm convinced people are looking for somebody to say, 'Here's what's good.'"

Charlie Younger recalled that George W. loved life on the trail. He liked meeting people. He was a sponge, soaking up facts about little geographic areas, about the people who lived there.

He had always had that strong personal touch. "He's very persuasive," Robert Birge, his friend from Skull and Bones, explained. "He's always been very effective not only one on one, but one on ten. I've always admired his ability to interact with people and his effectiveness in getting his point across. He does it with an intelligence that is masked by his sense of humor. He doesn't come across as being as smart as he is, so he's that much more effective."

After all of those years floating around Houston during his tenure with the National Guard, George W. had finally found a mission that constantly engaged his curiosity, that capitalized on his greatest strengths—personal charm and stamina—and that didn't require him to sit in an office at a dreaded coat-and-tie job.

—

Agriculture was the big issue on the campaign trail that year. In 1977, a group of farmers, worried over the drop in food prices, started the American Agriculture Movement. The group turned more radical on April 12, 1978, when Congress voted on a farm bill that would provide "parity," or price setting, for various crops. The farmers thought that the bill looked certain to pass, but was suddenly defeated.

"There must be some reason why a hundred congressmen would change their votes in three or four hours," said an Ag movement supporter whose sentiment provided the rallying cry for the movement. The farmers blamed the sudden about-face on a new international policy group, called the Trilateral Commission formed by millionaire David Rockefeller.

That group was composed of bankers, elected officials, and intellectuals from Japan, Europe, and North America who met to reconsider the roles of various first-world nations in maintaining global stability now that the United States was not the only economic superpower. What must have been hard for the Ag movement members to understand was how over 300 of the wealthiest, smartest, most politically powerful men and women in the world could gather in one place and not cook up anything more intriguing than heady policy papers meant to impress one another.

The movement grew in strength. By February 1979, hundreds of Ag movement tractors had camped out at the Mall in Washington, D.C., and stopped traffic on and off for days. In Lubbock, one of the hotbeds of the Ag movement, the farmers went wild when the local paper accused them of employing tactics similar to those used by striking workers at a nearby meat-packing plant. The farmers showed up on their tractors and threatened to block newspaper delivery by circling the offices for four hours. The farmers finally backed down when the editors promised to print their side of the story the next day.

Agriculture issues were not George W.'s strongest suit, particularly against Reese and Hance, both of whom were sons of farmers. Still, George W. said he would go after Hance "tooth and toenail on the farm issues." Reese said he remembered an event that they both had attended early in the campaign at a farm in Dimmitt. George W. arrived and flat-out told the waiting crowd: "You know, I've never been on a farm." Reese observed that George W. got a few dirty looks.

George W. found that he had at least one other liability. His father had become a member of the Trilateral Commission in early 1977, about six months before George W. started his campaign. If the United Nations and the CIA seemed bastions of the Establishment to West Texas voters, then the mysterious Trilateral Commission completed the portrait of George Bush as a man devoted to stealing power from the working man and funneling it into the hands of the elite. The opponents of George W. and his father would use the Trilateral Commission as a weapon against them both.

On the campaign trail, the farmers would corner Hance and ask him, "So what do you think about the Trilateral Commission, Kent?"

Hance would just sort of step to the side of the question—not really come out and say anything specific but just get all of those potential voters mulling over the bigger picture. "Well, I don't know anything about that," he would say. "But let me ask you this: What were the prices of corn and cotton and wheat before the commission was established, and what were they after? And that's what you should be thinking about." The farmers would just look at him and nod. That was all that needed to be said.

Over those many months of the campaign, guys would come up to Hance and slip him cassette tapes. They would tell him he *ought to listen to this,* with a half-mournful, half-knowing expression tugging at their features. The tapes were copies of a recording of a retired general talking about the Trilateral Commission and how dangerous it was. By the end of the campaign, Hance had *stacks* of these tapes. Of course he listened to the recordings. He picked out some of the choice buzzwords and inserted them into his speeches. Then the farmers in the audience who already had listened to the tapes could nod knowingly and say, Here's our man. Hance could demonstrate his allegiance to them without ever actually declaring it. That was the brilliance.

In the late days of May, J. C. Lewis, described in the *Midland Reporter-Telegram* as a farmer from Guymon, Oklahoma, and Clarence Warner, also of Oklahoma, suddenly arrived in town for a press conference at the Midland Regional Airport. They reiterated to the reporters and the large crowd of farmers gathered there that George W. Bush's father was a member of the Trilateral Commission and that George W. had said that he saw nothing wrong with the organization. On the contrary, they said, the commission was the beginning of the creation of a one-world government set to break farmers and the workers of the United States.

George W. had witnessed attacks on his father before: He certainly had known about the hate mail slipped under the door at his parents' house after his father had announced his support for the Civil Rights Act. He also would have heard the stories during his father's first campaign about John Birch Society members accusing his father of being a communist; they had thought it stood to reason, since Bar's father was an executive at *Redbook*. But here was criticism of his father's patriotism, and it had been instigated by George W.'s own run for office. It would have seemed both cartoonish, because of the conspiracy these two men from Oklahoma were spinning about his dear old dad, and painful, since they were going after him in public.

While the *Midland Reporter-Telegram* failed to make the connection, both J. C. Lewis and Clarence Warner were more than just a couple of guys from out of state who wanted to weigh in on the congressional race in Texas. J. C. Lewis was actually the retired military man featured on the tape now circulating among the farmers, which had made him a bit of a celebrity in those parts. He had been invited down by Roz Haley, one of the leaders of the Agriculture Movement there.

Lewis had earned a bachelor's degree in history from Panhandle State University in Oklahoma and a master's degree in international affairs from George Washington University. He tended to open his talks with the compelling introduction, "I'm not a joiner. I don't think I'm a radical. I'm not a member of the John Birch Society or the Communist Party. I think I'm somewhere in between. I've joined three things in my life: my church, the United States Air Force, and the American Agriculture Movement. I love my God. I love my country. I love my family."

Clarence Warner was not just any old boy from Oklahoma. He had been Ronald Reagan's farm states coordinator in 1976 and in fact had been a candidate for chair of the Republican National Committee that same year. At the 1976 Republican convention, Warner helped round up Reagan delegates while George Bush's biggest booster, James Baker, was fighting to secure Ford delegates.

Reese had worked for Reagan in 1976 as his county chairman for the Republican presidential campaign. When Reese ran that year, Reagan threw him his support. Now, in the 1978 race, Reagan's political action committee made a $1,000 contribution to Reese. Reagan himself wrote an endorsement letter that was mailed out in the district. Then, when Reagan was visiting in Amarillo, Reese went down to meet him, and they taped a campaign commercial together for the district.

Some political observers couldn't help thinking that Reagan was trying not just to boost a longtime ally, but to squash the rise of a Bush in a Reagan stronghold, especially given the context that it was 1978 and George W.'s father was already preparing to vie with Reagan for the Republican presidential nomination. Without question, Reese and Lewis's attacks on George W. were a case of guilt by association. While the stated intention was simply to give Reese an edge against George W. in the district primary, there was no doubt that it also was setting the stage for the presidential nomination battle.

George W. fought back fiercely over the charges that his father was somehow un-American. "[My father] has the highest security clearance, and ran the CIA during its most troubled times," he said. "Against tough congressional inquiries, he stood firm so as not to weaken the CIA. . . . When it comes to the integrity of my father, I will fight back. They are trying to slam me by slamming my father."

"The Trilateral Commission thing enraged [George W.]," remembered Charlie Younger. "He puts his father on a pedestal. That was his pop-off valve. He's the oldest son. He feels he's the big brother and it's his job [to protect his dad]."

For his part, George Bush worked behind the scenes to quiet his son's attackers. "Daddy Bush got a little mad at me," J. C. Lewis explained. He was told by Gerald McCatheren, an Ag movement leader in Hereford, Texas, that George Bush had called him and said he had a message to pass to Lewis. George Bush said that Lewis, a former military man, had no right to be talking about the Trilateral Commission. "And my point was, what rights did I give up because I was in the military?" said Lewis. The farmers in Hereford told Lewis that Bush said he wanted to take Lewis on. So Lewis called George Bush's office and asked him to do just that on national TV. Lewis never heard from him again.

The last few days before the runoff were filled with attacks against George W. by the Reese camp. Reese said that Bush was trying to "capitalize on the rivalry between Midland and Odessa. . . . This divisive effort has been counterproductive." He also questioned the existence of a company George W. had owned with his accountant, Robert McCloskey. Reese said that the business, called Field Services Inc., wasn't even listed in the phone book. George W. defended himself, saying that they had sold their interest months earlier and that the new owner worked from home and that's why it wasn't listed.

Next, Reese seized on the carpetbagger issue. "[George W.'s] a personable young man from back East who apparently has been misleading the people about his West Texas background," Reese told TV viewers in his campaign ads. "[He has] a bright future in politics somewhere, but it's not out here."

In this instance, George W. tried to counter with humor. The day before the runoff, he held a press conference. His one regret in this campaign, he told the reporters, was that he wasn't born in Midland; but at the time, he thought it was more important to stay close to his mother and "she happened to be in New Haven, Connecticut." The line was lifted directly from his father's 1964 campaign.

George W. wanted to change the way politics is run in the United States, he said. "This may sound corny," he explained, "but one of our intentions in getting into this race was to elevate the status of politics. . . . Leadership is not over-emotionalizing the issues."

For the first time in George W.'s life, Karl Rove—the man who went on to become his political guru in his gubernatorial and presidential bids—arose as an issue. Reese sent a letter to his supporters, which read, "I am very disappointed that George Jr. has Rockefeller-type Republicans such as Karl Rove to help him run his campaign." Reese was trying to emphasize the notion that George W. would vote like a moderate Republican if elected to office, but also perhaps there was a subtext that George W. was inextricably linked to the Trilateral Commission, since David Rockefeller, Nelson's brother, founded the organization. George W. retorted that Karl Rove was a "twenty-seven-year-old guy who works in my dad's office in Houston. He has never been to West Texas and he has had nothing to do with my campaign. I doubt that he even supports Rockefeller."

In those last days of the campaign, the Reagan PAC threw another $2,000 to Reese. George W.'s father told the *Washington Post* at that time: "I'm not interested in getting into an argument with Reagan. But I am surprised about what he is doing here, in my state. . . . They are making a real effort to defeat George." The *Post* years later reported that Bush even complained to Reagan directly about his involvement in the campaign.

—

The first thing George W.'s supporters saw when they walked into campaign headquarters on Saturday, June 3, was a beer dispenser tagged with a "Drink me first" sign. The place was decorated with red, white, and blue streamers, and the volunteers passed around white straw boaters with Bush hatbands wrapped around them. On the back wall were pictures of the campaign. Against one side, Glenna Krumboltz stood writing the returns on a chalkboard. Everybody started streaming in just after 7:00, when the polls closed. Within the hour, the place was packed. Reese's numbers kept getting closer.

A rock and roll band started to tune up in the parking lot. Finally George W. and Laura arrived. George W. delivered his victory speech in the stuffy room at 9:00 P.M.

He joked that he might live to regret jumping the gun since some of the precincts hadn't reported. He said he planned to mend the feud between Midland and Odessa. Then in a slightly odd endorsement of his opponent for the general election and also an accurate prediction of Hance's party switch seven years later, Bush told the crowd: "Hance is a good man. He just happens to be in the wrong party."

George W. then flew to Lubbock for the victory speech there. By 10:30, the Midland police radio was reporting "Things are getting rowdy there."

A reporter reached Reese at his home. "I guess it's obvious the Lord has something else in mind for me to do." Given the tenor of the campaign, it was not surprising that he failed to volunteer to help George W. in the general election.

—

George W. and Hance agreed on the big issues for the district: beating inflation, controlling government spending, and supporting the oil, gas, and agriculture industries. But ultimately, the race was decided on the question of style.

The big difference between George W. and Hance came down to who could "out good-old-boy" the other. Toward the end of the summer of 1978, they both were campaigning at a fair in Muleshoe. After the program was over, they both walked out to the parking lot. George W. and Laura were ahead. They came across a guy whose truck wouldn't start. George W. started trying to help him.

Then Hance came up. "What's wrong?" he asked.

The guy told him. So Hance went to his own car and got some jumper cables. He hooked them up and George W. said good-bye to everyone and drove away.

Once the car was started the guy marveled at how kindhearted both candidates were. "You both are so nice," he said.

Hance shot back, "Yeah, but I got the jumper cables."

—

On Labor Day weekend, Jimmy Allison, who had been battling leukemia for some time, died of pneumonia in Houston. All the way up to his death, he never lost interest in the political game. Peter Roussel, the press secretary on Bush's 1970 campaign, remembered visiting Allison's hospital room that last summer he was alive. Roussel stopped by with Jim Baker, who was running for attorney general of Texas. Allison struggled to sit up as they entered. "Hey fellas, what do the polls show?" he asked.

Three weeks before Allison died, Rollan Melton, a columnist from Reno, Nevada, visited the hospital the same night George Bush came by. Bush and Allison talked animatedly and intently about all the goings-on in the Bush family. Then George Bush got serious. "Well, I wonder about the outlook . . ." he began.

"It's like this, George," Allison told him. "I've got the leukemia that won't back off."

George Bush started to cry, then Allison wept too. Later, Melton encountered Bush out in the hall. Bush described his parting words to Allison. "I just told him, 'Jimmy, we've come a long way together. There's a lot farther to go. Just remember, I never had a friend I thought so much of.'"

George W. was one of the pallbearers along with his father at the funeral. It was not only the loss of a friend, but the end of a gentler political era for the Bushes. George Bush's early campaigns were guided by the advice of a man whom he loved and admired. When he went out on the trail with Allison, they would enjoy the pleasure of not just pursuing a say in the political direction of the country, but the joy of time spent in long conversations on campaign buses. Allison never tried to manipulate George Bush's politics; therefore his friend could rest easy knowing that he had never compromised his own principles to win.

In later years, George Bush would hire professionals to create his campaigns for him. While some of these men and women grew friendly with their client, they never were revered by Bush to the same degree as Allison was. And Bush would also end up hiring some advisers, particularly in the 1992 race, that never stood by him the way George W. and others thought they should. Allison had never lost sight of his mission, which was to get his dear friend elected to office. After his death, the Bushes would be forced to figure out the Machiavellian politics of modern campaigning on their own.

George W. got a strong taste of this new world just before the 1978 election, when friends of Hance badly damaged his standing in the Lubbock region by capitalizing on what was either an error by George W.'s team, or, as Ruth Schiermeyer tells it, engaging in "dirty tricks" campaigning.

In early September, Schiermeyer was sitting at her desk in Lubbock headquarters when a good-looking young man who was the Bush chairman at Texas Tech came in and slapped a copy of the school's newspaper down in front of her. He had run an ad, without getting approval, that announced a youth volunteer event at the home of Jim Granberry, the former mayor of Lubbock who had endorsed George W. back in the Republican primary. The ad announced "A Bush Bash." Come for "free beer and music," it said.

Schiermeyer felt sick. After years spent helping the underdog campaigns of area Republicans, she knew this was trouble, since the Lubbock district was highly conservative and pushing beer on college kids would be seen as a sign of decadence. Other staffers didn't think the ad was so bad since most politicians served alcohol at their events; they just didn't advertise it. The young volunteer definitely didn't seem to think he had caused a problem. To Schiermeyer, he seemed completely nonchalant. The event was held as planned and ended by 8:30 P.M.

The trouble didn't hit right away. But, on November 2, just five days before the election, Kent Hance's former law partner, George Thompson III, sent a letter to 4,000 members of the Church of Christ in the area. He denounced Bush for using beer as a lure to students to gain votes. The Lubbock paper reported the mailing, copies of the letter were placed under windshield wipers at the churches, and the county conservatives buzzed with talk of the event.

George W. went ballistic. "This is the only place where we served beer," he told the press. "It is an isolated incident. . . . [Kent Hance's] campaign has been funny. First he attacked my family, then my background, and now my morals."

Hance's reply was smooth as the West Texas highway. "Maybe it's a cool thing to do at Harvard or Yale . . ." he drawled.

"That is harking back to my education," George W. countered. "He won't campaign on the issues, and that's going to hurt him." Everyone could see Hance knew how to push George W.'s buttons.

The people who worked on Bush's campaign took a dim view of the actions of Hance's law partner. But they also said that they saw the depth of their own candidate's virtue in the turmoil. Instead of engaging in tit for tat campaign tactics, George W. decided to take the high ground.

Hance owned some land near Texas Tech that he leased to a bar called Fat Dogs. If it was bad to serve beer to college students at a campaign event, then surely, George W.'s supporters reasoned, it was bad to profit from carousing by leasing property to a bar, or at least it was hypocritical to attack George W. for his campaign's lapse. Many of George W.'s supporters stopped by his headquarters right after the letter went out, urging him to let the press know about Fat Dogs. The paper would only report the lease deal if George W. made the accusation himself.

Some of George W.'s campaign workers were surprised by his sangfroid. He was known for his shoot-from-the-hip style. Mike Weiss, the campaign manager in Lubbock, says he was often astounded by the complete spontaneity of George W.'s actions. Once Weiss had come to him with a different negative article in the university paper and George W. immediately picked up the phone and started dialing. "What are you doing?" demanded Weiss.

"I'm calling them."

"Can't we just have at least a thirty-second conversation about this?" Weiss asked.

But George W. was already talking to the reporter, telling them everything they had wrong in their story.

Now Ruth Schiermeyer begged George W. to call the paper and point out Hance's connection to Fat Dogs, but he refused. "Ruthie, Kent

Hance is not a bad person and I'm not going to destroy him in his home-town," he told her. "This is not an issue. If I try to destroy him to win, I don't win." George W. had seen how much his father had been hurt when competitors tried to pull him down. He knew the pain that such attacks caused his family. He had learned enough from his life as a politician's son to know that such smear tactics damaged more than they achieved. From a purely strategic perspective, he must have understood that a slash-and-burn campaign could only hurt him in the long run.

Several years later, Schiermeyer was on a plane and found herself sitting next to a political adviser connected to Democratic politics in the region. They were talking about the old days of politics in Lubbock when he said, "Do you remember . . .?" and he named the intern from 1978.

Schiermeyer said, "How can I ever forget? He was our campus coordinator who ran the Bush Bash ad at Texas Tech."

"But do you know who he was really working for?" the adviser asked.

"What do you mean?" Schiermeyer replied.

"Who was paying him." Then the adviser pointed to himself. "He was working for me." He went on. "Do you know who drew the ad?"

"Who?" asked Schiermeyer.

He said, "Me." Schiermeyer said that she never told George W., but she did pass the word on to Weiss. If true, the information would show that George W. was defeated, in part, by a dirty tricks campaign, and even Democrats from the time find the story likely. That first time out, the candidate who still "was idealistic enough to believe that some good can be done" might have been undermined by true campaign trickery.

Hance claimed he didn't know that his law partner was going to write the letter. Decades later, he said he didn't think the mailing really hurt George W.'s campaign. He said George W. was already behind in the tracking polls, and the mailing just gave George W.'s campaign staffers a good excuse for losing.

—

The voting on November 7 was extremely heavy. Some say the deep interest in the Bush versus Hance pairing drew voters out. Others contend it was just the clear weather after several days of rain. For the first time in Midland, Mickey Mouse and Donald Duck were unable to receive votes. Write-in candidates had to be registered beforehand.

George W. cast his vote at San Jacinto. When the grade-schoolers in Midland had held a mock vote the day before, he was the decisive winner. One student, clearly parroting the views of her parents, gave him her support because "he seems nice on TV." Another student rewarded him with a vote because "he has been running for Congress for a long time." In fact, with his early declaration, George W. had been running longer than most presidential candidates. Back at headquarters, George W.'s supporters were calling people throughout the district to get out the vote and found that those who had actually met him on the trail were the ones already won over to his side.

George W. conceded to Hance at 11:00 P.M., even when he had an 8,000-vote lead. The rural areas hadn't reported yet, and he knew he would get killed there. "I have to congratulate you," he told Hance by telephone.

Hance told him he owed him one. He had run against guys who never conceded. "We got to be friends during the campaign," Hance told the paper. He had ended up winning 53 to 47 percent. The results reflected the geographic realities of that campaign; just as Midland was larger than Odessa, and that had contributed to George W.'s defeat of Reese, Lubbock dominated the district and so Lubbock's own candidate, Kent Hance, had dominated. But more important, George W. had never been able to crack the rural areas; he was not a farm boy and that would cost him. Still, he had fared well compared to what political observers had predicted for the unknown candidate with the famous name.

When Weiss and his wife, Nancy, went to George W. and Laura's house the next day, Weiss figured he would find the candidate in a full funk. "I thought we would sit around acting like we lost the city championships, or like we were at a funeral," he said. Instead, he found George W. joking around, bursting with energy, headed down to the campaign office to get the place cleaned out. "I think I just lay around on the couch," said Weiss. He put his own spin on the situation. "Arguably, you don't *lose* a football game, you just run out of time." True to his frugal ways, George W. ran the campaign in the black.

Ruth Schiermeyer said she thought she had mononucleosis for three weeks, because she was so depressed. "I just couldn't believe that this fine, decent, honest young man had been defeated by untruths," she said. "When the Trilateral Commission that had absolutely nothing to do with George W. Bush is one of the big factors, a 'beer bash' that didn't happen was one of the factors, instead of it being leadership issues." As it happened, George W.'s father resigned from the Trilateral Commission a month before the election in 1978, and J. C. Lewis would support George W. in the presidential race for 2000.

The race quelled George W.'s hunger for politics for a while. He didn't seem to have any urge to get back in right away. But he had learned to never get out good-old-boyed again. When next he ran for office, campaigning for governor in 1994, he made sure that he had a resumé to run on and a loose demeanor to please the voters.

His focus moved elsewhere. He now had a wife whom he needed to support, no regular salary of any kind, and he and Laura wanted to have children. That meant buckling down to business.

Many of George W.'s friends and political aides came to bless the day he lost in the congressional race. If he had won, they argue, he might have found himself cloistered away in D.C., with no chance to build a vision and no opportunity to prove himself as a businessman. After all, part of the problem in 1978 was that he had run without any track record to show the voters, so there was little to talk about but his daddy. By the time he ran for governor in 1994, he would have a few business accomplishments to boast about, and he would be able to capitalize on the fame of his name without carrying along its baggage.

IX

PRODIGAL SON OF THE PRAIRIE

George W. would remark many times over the years that he had a good eye for catching "users"—people who angled near him so they could gain a perk from his dad. He must have been invited to so many parties in his early middle age because of his inherited notoriety, been coaxed for so many rounds of golf, asked out into the Texas hill country on such a number of hunting trips. Sometimes he probably just went along for the ride, staying careful, monitoring his words so that when they percolated up weeks later in his host's cocktail party conversation—with George W. far out of earshot—his recycled commentary would not embarrass his family. He must have gotten to the point where he could smell the bargain on these new friends.

But in the life of a famous son, there are also the men and women who serve the opposite function. Instead of leeching off his fame, they hurry ahead to lay down the red carpet for his triumphal journey through the years. Oddly enough, they don't seem to seek any direct personal benefit from their gesture. They usually hail from an older generation, and their work is offered in the name of history's greater drama. They understand the inevitability of the famous child's ascension and even help pave the way, so that when the biographies are written—with probably no mention of their names—no questionable glitch will mar the narrative. That is gift enough for them. They will be happy enough knowing that one story of a leader's rise went off as sweetly as such sagas used to go in their grade-school history textbooks. The famous child might not even be aware of the work the carpetlayers do—at least George W. Bush never seemed to be. Perhaps he thought the fortuitous meetings and sudden saves were typical for a person over the course of a life, or that luck was on his side. But the helpers who actually assist the famous son's journey are the handmaidens of history, and it would appear that several resided in Midland.

—

The first well George W. sunk money into came up dry. "Oops!" he recalled thinking. "This is not quite as easy as we all thought it was going to be."

But a lesson of the oil industry is to keep trying. The biggest discovery ever made in the continental United States was in the fields of East Texas. Dad Joyner drilled dry holes there all of his life until he was an old man. Then he hit the gusher. That was the message: If a hole came up dry, an oil man should just move on to the next one. You never knew.

George W.'s Uncle Jonathan, who headed a New York investment firm, J. Bush & Company, helped put his nephew's drilling fund together in 1979, primarily with his own clients. He was also simultaneously helping George W.'s father raise money for his presidential bid, since George Bush had launched his presidential search committee at the beginning of the year and declared himself a candidate on May 1. Jonathan said George W.'s family connection never became part of his pitch for Arbusto, although the name association couldn't have hurt him. "[George W. was a] very hard-working guy, and he had a darned good little company," Jonathan reportedly said. "Everybody liked dealing with him and it wasn't a hard sale, frankly."

Still, many of the early investors were friends of the family. "I remember when he was just starting in that oil business and Johnny brought him around," said Fay Vincent, who had met little George when Vincent spent the summer as a roustabout at Zapata. "I was running Columbia Pictures and he said, 'Would you invest?' I invested twenty-five thousand dollars because I felt very indebted to his father and to the family for being so nice to me. . . . I knew it was a crap shoot and I can't say I was terribly surprised that it wasn't a huge success."

The first Arbusto offices were located in the Petroleum Building—the same place where George W.'s father started Zapata in the early 1950s. In Arbusto's first year of active operations, George W. pulled together a pot of $565,000 and kept drilling—no big gambles, just small, low-risk attempts. One of his first investors was Philip A. Uzielli, a new acquaintance of George W.'s father. Uzielli was also a close friend of Jim Baker's from college, but George W. said he didn't know that until later, after Uzielli had upped his stake. Baker's intimacy with the Bush family was strong enough that he was not only considered "little brother" to "big brother" George Bush, he was Bush's 1980 campaign manager.

Uzielli lost money on that first deal, but he had few regrets. He told the *Dallas Morning News* in 1994: "I originally invested in some wildcat drilling Arbusto had in New Mexico. It was disastrous—through no fault of George's. The good Lord just didn't put any oil there."

—

In early 1980, George W. punctuated his schedule running Arbusto with sidetrips on his father's behalf for the primaries.

He would swagger into Republican functions—from Massachusetts to Iowa—ready to exhort the voters to choose his dad over Ronald Reagan, Howard Baker, or John Connally, the other front-runners. George W. looked remarkably similar to his father. Both men had the same hand gestures, same mannerisms, even the same erect posture. But George Bush's staffers were shocked by the difference in George W.'s presentation. Two years earlier, he might have been too Ivy League for the campaign trail in West Texas, but for the snow-covered hamlets of New England and the Midwest, he was a little too Lone Star. He wore cowboy boots that branded him a Westerner (they also helped him stand a little taller as he was three inches shorter than his father). When he talked, a thin, brown syrup from his chewing tobacco would ooze out of the corner of his mouth. When he was out of the crowd's earshot, he'd curse like a roughneck.

In his speeches, he hit the key points six-shooter style. Bam! Bam! Bam! The issues would lie decimated on the ground. He seemed more conservative than his father. He was excited about gun freedoms, family responsibility, and against 'bortion, as he called it. Few rhetorical flourishes and little friendly banter spiced his speeches. He talked to his points and was gone.

His brothers and sister gave more of their lives to that campaign than he did. Jeb resigned from a bank job in Venezuela to work as a surrogate full time. Neil and Marvin each took a leave of absence from school to oversee the New Hampshire and Iowa efforts respectively. Doro made the biggest sacrifice. When George Bush told her that she needed to hone a particular skill if she wanted to contribute to the election effort, she enrolled at the Katherine Gibbs secretarial school in Boston. After improving her typing during a three-month-long course, she joined the campaign. For Bar, the 1980 effort was a turning point in how she was viewed by her children. After years of being asked what she called the "peanut butter and jelly questions" as opposed to the policy ones, she finally earned her children's respect as a politico in her own right.

That didn't mean the kids still wouldn't tease her mercilessly, and she joked right back. George W. was her favorite sparring partner. But if he jabbed too hard, either at her or another unwitting target, or got too cocky, she would roll her eyes. He would rib his father too. People on that campaign noticed there was something slightly more competitive about their joking. The teasing would escalate on both sides until it was at the brink of taunting. "I think there were times they'd rather he maybe bit his tongue or zipped his mouth," George W.'s friend from Midland, Charlie Younger, told Patrick Beach of the *Austin-American Statesman*. "He'd just stay right out there on the edge. He'd never hop over, but he'd lean over. Mischievous."

Jeb, on the other hand, tended to be more of the intellectual sounding board for his father. He breezed into the events like an executive ready to make his presentation to stockholders. He was a businessman politician, engaged in the gentlemanly exercise of securing votes.

In addition to Reagan, Connally, and Baker, Bob Dole and Phil Crane were fighting for the nomination. Congressman John Anderson, although a Republican, was running as an Independent. Bush was deeply encouraged by the Iowa primary. He had pulled off a surprise victory and made the cover of *Newsweek* for doing so. But almost immediately, his campaign fell under the treads of the Ronald Reagan tank. The California governor not only had the requisite charisma to win, he had built a grassroots juggernaut over the last half dozen years or more. Although George Bush would make 850 campaign stops in 329 days that election cycle, he couldn't beat the army Reagan had commissioned in the field.

Even when the outcome of the primary season became obvious, even after campaign manager Jim Baker knew George Bush's presidential hopes had been ground to dust, Bush would not give in. He had put in too much effort. His thousands of handwritten notes to potential voters covered the United States like snowfall. Plus he had accumulated a hefty campaign debt, and he needed to at least continue the pantomime of running so that he could collect federal matching funds. The Reagan supporters despised him for refusing to officially admit defeat when he knew his cause was a losing one. In their opinion, he was only dragging on the standing of the real candidate, and they could not forgive him for coining the term "voodoo economics" to describe Reagan's fiscal policy during a speech in Houston.

Ernie Angelo, chair of the Reagan campaign in Texas, remembered the moment word came down at the Republican National Convention in Detroit that George Bush would be Ronald Reagan's vice presidential nominee. The Texas delegation was irate. "When [Bush and Reagan] ran against each other in eighty, there wasn't a lot of good feeling," Angelo remembered. "The 'voodoo economics' deal in Houston really grated on Reagan and it was a pretty tough campaign. In Texas, I did everything I could to keep it from being an anti-Bush effort, because I felt that we needed to have everybody together, and I knew that Reagan would carry the election early on.

"A lot of the Reagan people here in Texas were really anti–George Senior. They were not very happy when Reagan picked him," he explained. "They felt like that was somewhat of a betrayal. There was still carryover that they thought [Bush] was too liberal, and he would not support Reagan's philosophy—it would be a bad thing for the Reagan revolution. And I can't say that Reagan didn't feel the same way for a long time—up until the time they decided to pull together. His respect for Bush grew as they got to know each other and worked together."

Bush had outspent Reagan in Texas by ten to one, but Reagan carried all but about seven of the districts in the state. Bush had campaigned aggressively in the last weeks, and the Bush delegates never dreamed that their man had a chance to serve as vice president. "[Bush] knew that he had gotten pretty out of character when he went after Reagan the way he did," Angelo observed.

Angelo was on the floor of the convention center in Detroit when word came over his earpiece that Bush had been selected. He let the delegation know the choice, then herded them all up to a hotel suite. "We very nearly had a rebellion," Angelo said. "Governor [Bill] Clements gets up and tells our delegation why they have to support Bush, and he's not even getting their attention."

Andy Card went to the convention as a whip for the New England Bush delegates. He was so discouraged about his man's rejection for the presidential nomination that even before Reagan announced his choice for vice president, Card, along with Leon Lombardi and Paul Celucci, got into their cars and started driving to their hotel. Out on the highway, word came over the radio that Bush was the probable vice presidential nominee. Card pulled a U-turn and started speeding back to the coliseum.

It was around midnight and the Texas delegates buzzed with talk of how they could stage a walkout on the vote, when Bush's name was called for the nomination. Angelo realized that he needed to rally the troops. "It's been said that it was one of my better impromptu speeches," he acknowledged. "I was really mad because here they were, getting ready to embarrass the state, the candidate, and everybody. I gave them a tongue lashing. The main thing I remember saying was, 'You've been supporting this guy [Reagan] with your blood and sweat and tears for the last six or eight years—some of you ten. You've put everything you had into getting him to this point, and now the first official decision he makes, you're going to jump ship and embarrass him. You can't do it. You are to be on the floor and vote for Bush, or don't come to the floor, stay up in the stands.' Three or four stayed up in the stands. It was a really bitter primary, and they thought there was a big ideological gap there. So it was a hot night." When the moment came on July 17 to welcome Bush onto the ticket, the Texas delegates as well as the rest of the Reagan devotees were in line, if not exactly enthusiastic.

From the start, the Reagan people did not trust the Bushes. They put a couple of aides on the trail with George and Barbara leading up to election day, just to monitor their activities and make sure they didn't stray from the party line. They had no reason to fear. George Bush made clear to his whole staff that there would be no backbiting, naysaying, or name-calling when it came to the Reagan people. He would be loyal and even absorb the totality of Reagan's positions—even his penchant for "voodoo economics."

For a man who prided himself on stamina, George Bush had to face the fact that Ronald Reagan had outrun him. George W. testified to the endurance of the Gipper at the January 20 inaugural. His father was so exhausted, he said, from keeping up with Reagan's pace, that he was the grumpiest George W. had ever seen him at the inaugural balls that night.

—

With his father safely ensconced in the highest echelons of power, George W. focused full time on his own life in Midland. In addition to working to expand Arbusto's operations, he and Laura had wanted to start a family for some time.

They knew they loved kids. George W. had served as a kind of surrogate parent to his younger siblings growing up; after all, he was an official adult when his sister Doro was still just a young child. At PULL, he had forged that intense bond with little Jimmy Dean and the other mentees. He also was an extremely popular Little League coach when he first moved back to Midland. He and L. E. Sawyer commanded a team called the Bankers that implemented an unusual strategy. The town took its Little League seriously enough to hold tryouts for draft picks, and a 12-year-old cost more points than a 10-year-old. L.E. and George W. decided to "build for the future" and took only the outstanding younger kids. The Bankers were demolished that season, finished 0 and 14, but they had a great time.

George W. and Laura also had seen how much his parents adored being grandparents. Jeb and Columba already had two children, George P. and Noelle.

Unfortunately, George W. and Laura were not having much luck conceiving. Eager to start their family, they applied to the Edna

Gladney Agency in Fort Worth to adopt. The process was within weeks of being completed when they received the extraordinary news that Laura was pregnant.

They were thrilled. Still, neither of them seemed ready to believe their good fortune. "I didn't decorate [the twins'] nurseries until I had them," Laura would tell the *Dallas Morning News* years later. "It' s a little bit of an afraid-to-count-your-chicks-before-they-hatch philosophy that I have."

George W. too seemed unable to put aside his fears. Over the years, he had been uncommonly kind to another YMCA runner, John Kirwan, and his son, Daniel, who had Down Syndrome. When George W. got wind that one of the women at the Y tended to look down on Daniel, George W. began going up to him publicly and throwing his arm around Daniel, announcing that the boy could boast he had the most important people as friends. The woman's attitude began to change. When George W. went running, he would sometimes invite Daniel and then jog slowly beside him. He would sit with them at football games. Kirwan had decided to push his son's education with the hope that it would make his life more complete. He enrolled him in an intensive program called the Institute for the Development of Human Potential, based in Philadelphia.

Now, with Laura expecting, George W. went up to Daniel's mother at the track. He was curious, he said. What were they trying to achieve with her son? What could be possible? "Nothing short of excellence," said Daniel's mother. John Kirwan thought George W. was worried that, because he and Laura were relatively older parents at age 35, perhaps their child would be born with defects.

The twins were born on November 25, 1981. They were named Jenna and Barbara, after both of their grandmothers. George W. handed out cigars to all of his friends. "He was on cloud nine," said Younger. Several of George W.'s friends would say that the birth of his daughters was the most important thing that ever happened to him.

—

The price of oil peaked at an extraordinary $35 a barrel in 1980, then the value just started giving out, staggering slowly down to nearly nothing. The oil men in Midland knew that ups and downs were part of the business, so the idea was just to ride out the trouble.

When the price of oil drops, producers not only contend with the immediate loss of revenue from sales, but also with the decline's effects on their bank loans. To put together a drilling deal, an oil producer may need cash quickly, and he has only one thing to use as collateral: the amount of oil estimated to be pumped out of an active well. But if the price of oil has recently fluctuated, the bank will value the collateral at its lowest price.

In 1982, George W. was still confident enough about the future to hire an extra engineer, although he already had a full staff of about ten. He received a big, new cash infusion from one of his first investors, Philip Uzielli, through his company Executive Resources out of Panama. Uzielli put up $1 million for a 10 percent stake in Arbusto, even though George W.'s company only had a total book value of $382,376. Uzielli said he was willing to overlook that discrepancy because he wanted to provide George W. with the money he needed at a crucial time, and because Uzielli was willing to bet that the price of oil would recover. George W. said that only after this investment did he find out that "Uzi" was a close friend of James Baker, who had become Ronald Reagan's chief of staff.

By May, George W. became convinced that he needed to change the name of his company. Friends were kidding him about failing Ar-*bust*-o, and he needed to attract more investors. The family name couldn't hurt that effort, so he rechristened the operation Bush Exploration Company; then the money people would know who was running the place. In August, the company planned to pull together a drilling fund of $6 million. They barely managed to scrape together a sixth of that. When his father was working with the Liedtkes over two decades earlier, $1 million had been a fine goal. Now it was too little to start any serious drilling.

George W. worked hard to woo investors. That was his main focus; he cared less about the appearances of the company. Framed pictures still sat on this office floor because he never bothered to hang them. Some of George W.'s 1982 investors had ties to his father, such as William H. Draper III, who helped with the 1980 campaign fund-raising. He put $172,550 into the Bush Exploration pot. George W.'s grandmother and Marvin's godfather also contributed. By the end of that year, George W. had accumulated $4.7 million dollars' worth of investments, including the capital from Uzielli.

Unfortunately, drilling did not go as well as planned. By the next year, George W. had 16 wells that only produced 47,888 barrels of oil. The team didn't even try to put together a new limited partnership; they held out no hope of raising the cash. They kept drilling with the money they had. By April 1984, Bush Exploration had drilled 95 holes, nearly half of which were dry. By comparison, his father had hit oil with all 127 wells he drilled in the mid-'50s.

George W. had been named the director of a new financial institution called United Bank of Midland. He turned to that bank for help in the same year and was granted a loan of $372,000 for Bush Exploration, as well as a personal $275,000 mortgage.

—

That year, George W.'s old friend from his first days in Midland, Paul Rea, received a call from his client, Bill DeWitt Jr., who wanted to talk about restructuring Spectrum 7. DeWitt realized that with his other business ventures—Coca-Cola, radio stations, and restaurnts—he was too busy to really work his oil interests in Midland the way he should. He asked his geologist for ideas on who might handle the business side of the oil properties. DeWitt would be coming down to Midland with Mercer Reynolds and a couple of the Reynolds, DeWitt directors, and would like to meet with anyone Rea thought could be helpful. Rea thought immediately of George W.

Bill had gone to Yale and then Harvard five years before George W. attended those schools. Rea hoped the Ivy League match up might work.

The story of Rea's association with the DeWitt family resonated with the spirit of Horatio Alger and would become important to the saga of George W.'s future business success. Back when Rea was a boy, he had gone to work for Bill DeWitt Sr., when he was an owner of the St. Louis Browns. Rea began working at the stadium when he was around 10 years old, selling score cards. He worked his way up to the concession stands, then in high school became an usher and finally a ticket taker. He went off to get an economics degree, and after graduation went back to work for DeWitt, who hired him as a business manager for the Browns' minor league team down in San Antonio.

Over the years that he worked in Texas, Rea would gaze up at the people in the box seats and wonder what had made them so much money. Oil, they told him. He asked how to get into the business, and they suggested as a geologist or engineer. He never forgot that advice. After he was drafted into the Korean War, he used the G.I. bill to get a geology degree.

When Rea started operations as an independent, Bill DeWitt Sr. would call occasionally to check on business. He had been hired by Powell Crosley to be the general manager of the Cincinnati Reds and pulled together one of the greatest teams in the history of baseball. Pete Rose and Tony Perez started in the farm system there when DeWitt was in charge, and the team won the 1961 pennant. When Crosley died that year, none of his heirs had the slightest interest in the team, so DeWitt borrowed the capital to buy it himself. In 1968, Rea went up to the World Series in St. Louis and ran into DeWitt. DeWitt told Rea that he had sold the team and now had a pile of money for a good oil deal if one came up. Rea found a big-ticket lease for DeWitt. Either he would lose everything or make a fortune. Luckily, they hit a gusher. DeWitt put the income from the well into a family trust for his son and two daughters. Meanwhile, Bill DeWitt Jr. was wending his way through Yale and Harvard.

When DeWitt Jr. finished his education, he started watching over the business aspects of Rea's oil prospects from Cincinnati. DeWitt Sr. passed away, and DeWitt Jr. and the family stockbroker, Mercer Reynolds, decided to start up their own firm, Reynolds, DeWitt Company. They ran a mutual fund and brokerage accounts. They bought Coca-Cola of Cincinnati and Dayton, snapped up some radio stations, and even dabbled in restaurants. The firm became uncomfortably busy, and that's when DeWitt Jr. called Rea and asked for his advice on hiring someone for the oil side.

Rea called George W. and told him DeWitt was coming down and they should meet. George W. already knew from Rea that DeWitt was a Yale and Harvard man, and—from George W.'s detailed knowledge of baseball history—was aware of the family's connection to the game. So they all went to lunch at the rooftop restaurant in Rea's building, looking out onto the farthest reaches of Midland. The whole crew from Cincinnati turned out to be Ivy Leaguers—including Reynolds—so the talk was friendly as everyone traced the connections of shared schooling and vacation spots. It turned out that DeWitt's father had been chummy with Uncle Bucky—so it really was a small world. In terms of personalities, DeWitt wasn't the *landman* type. While he didn't match George W.'s outgoing demeanor, he was reserved but extremely smart. They weren't much alike, but they complemented each other.

About a week later, DeWitt called Rea to say he wanted to set up the business side of Spectrum 7 down in Midland and wanted George W. to run operations for them. Rea called George W., who was excited. He would get to keep his staff and just work with a bigger pile of money from all the Reynolds, DeWitt investors. His original Arbusto investors, like Uzielli, would finally get some payback. This was prepackaged salvation.

There would be few changes in operations, but all of them would be pleasant: For example, George W. would now work more with Rea, who was named president, and they would move into new office space in the Midland National Bank Building. The merger went through in February 1984. George became the third largest owner of Spectrum 7, with 16 percent of the stock. He was given the titles of board director, chairman, and CEO. Spectrum 7 assigned engineer Jim McAninch a company car and wanted George W. to take one too, but he wouldn't do it. He was perfectly happy with his Buick station wagon.

George W. had been extremely lucky to find a way out of Arbusto's difficult times without having to shop the business himself. The *Dallas Morning News* discovered that George W.'s company performed far better for itself than it did for its drilling fund investors. George W.'s limited partners reportedly invested a total of $4.66 million but only received a distribution of $1.54 million. The company itself—80 percent of which was owned by George W.—invested $102,000 and received back $362,000. The profits from the wells also paid for office operations, making the total payout for George W.'s company $678,000, according to the *News*. The limited partners didn't mind the loss because they could take a large tax write-off.

For many people putting money in oil, even if they lost, they won. Tax advisers in those days would steer their clients into a small oil investment to give them a deduction. In the early 1980s a tax break was needed. In 1979, the highest bracket was taxed at 70 percent; three years later, the level was 50 percent.

For Bill DeWitt, the appeal of merging with Arbusto, however, was mainly that he would be gaining a business manager in George W.—one with a winning personality and a reputation as an honest broker in West Texas. He also liked the deal because he would be providing his investors with a large hedge opportunity.

Spectrum 7 operated 180 oil wells at that time, mostly in West Texas. Some of the investors George W. inherited were unusual: The company plane would fly the painter Andrew Wyeth from Delaware to Maine for the summer. Wyeth told the Cincinnati boys one time that he would like to meet their geologist. So Rea went along for the ride.

"I don't really know anything about painting," said Rea.

"I don't know anything about geology," replied Wyeth. They talked the whole way.

Despite George W.'s mediocre performance with Arbusto and Bush Exploration, he was smart about the people side of the business. He could sit in a meeting and cut right to the weak aspect of a pitch with a few pointed questions. He would remember details about a technical problem that had come up months earlier. No one could snowball him. He just had too good a memory.

He had the right sort of guys around him too. If he were ever inclined to lose his head and pay more for land than it was worth just because there was a hit nearby, accountant Mike Conaway and Paul Rea would rein him in. George W. knew when to give up on a dry well. Some oil people would just keep buying the rights, layer by layer, hoping to hit a fortune a little further down. George W. knew when it was time to plug a well and move on.

Rea and George W. frequently had to travel north for investor meetings. He learned a little more about public speaking then; how to give a fifteen- or twenty-minute talk in front of all of those financial advisers and tax attorneys.

But he never entirely lost his impetuous side. Rea remembered one time he was waiting for George W. at the airport in the predawn hours to go on one of those business trips. The cross street closest to George W.'s home at 912 Harvard would turn into a river when a storm hit, since there were no sewers in Midland. The night before the business trip, there had been a torrential downpour.

George W. pulled out of his driveway in the darkness and sped straight into the flood. The car stalled. He couldn't open the door because the water was so high. His biggest fear was soaking his suit, since it was—as far as anyone could tell—his only one and reserved for those out-of-town meetings. He rolled down the window, took off his jacket, his shirt, his tie, his pants, and then climbed out of the car in his underwear. He waded through the water and dashed across his neighbor's lawn to his own home.

His neighbor, Murray Fasken, who was a bank president, happened to be up early that morning. He looked out the window to see George W. racing across his lawn in his underwear. He later asked George W. what had happened. Fasken said he had thought maybe some husband had come home and caught him with his wife.

—

For a year, prospects were looking better, if not exactly soaring. The price of oil was still declining and the tax refund incentive had diminished with the restructuring of the tax code. Still George W. managed to gain some interest from investors simply through the strength of his personality and his tireless pursuit of business.

In 1984, he went back to Andover for his twentieth reunion. Several classmates noticed that he wasn't quite himself. His lighter side seemed to have dissipated. He was in more of a confessional mode. He admitted that he had been terrified of failure when he had been at Andover because of how much his father cared about the school.

It had been two decades since John Kidde last saw his former roommate. When they met again, they threw their arms around each other. The next sentence out of George W.'s mouth was a thank you. He wanted Kidde to know how much he appreciated the $250 donation that he had made to the 1978 campaign. Another classmate remembered George W. getting loud during dinner and Laura trying to shush him. "That's enough now, George," she would say.

"Let George be George," he replied.

George W.'s uneasiness about his future would only deepen in the next months. In 1985, a barrel of oil started selling for a little more than a movie ticket. The countries of the Middle East began overproducing, and the buzz in the oil industry was that they were flooding the market to drive out the U.S. independent producers. The smaller oil operations that had sprung up during the boom of the mid-'70s and early 1980s started closing one by one. That would make the nation even more dependent on foreign oil.

George W. had watched his father flourish in the oil industry, starting out as a tool pusher and working up to become a founding owner of one of the first, most sophisticated offshore drilling companies in the world. George W., on the other hand, was saddled with debt. Although he lived outside the limelight in Midland, he still was a known entity as the son of the vice president. George W.'s failure would be noticeable to the larger world, and he needed an escape route that would not cause his father any embarrassment.

Investors started backing away from the industry. "We couldn't afford to continue doing what we were doing," accountant Mike Conaway told the *Washington Post*. "No one wanted to invest. . . . Business as usual was not an option." Investors didn't need a write-off that large, and without cash, an independent oil producer had no possibility of drilling.

—

As a child, George W. had attended the Presbyterian church in Midland and the Episcopal church in Kennebunkport with his family. After he and Laura married at the First Methodist church, he began going to services there every Sunday. He was now an active member of the congregation, helping Don Evans with the church's building committee, among other responsibilities. Around the time that oil prices reached their nadir, George W. began taking Bible study classes. His spiritual epiphany didn't exactly coincide with the very bottom of the market, he has said, but he admits it came pretty close. "I believe my spiritual awakening started well before the price of oil went below $9 [per barrel]," he has said. "[But 1986 was] a year of change when I look back at it. I really never have connected the dots all the way."

David Maraniss of the *Washington Post* found that George W. was quick with the wisecracks, even during his religious studies.

What is a prophet? the teacher asked the class one day.

"That," said George W., "is when revenues exceed expenditures. No one's seen one out here for years."

One day, the teacher talked about his own insecurities, having grown up with the pressures of being a "PK—a preacher's kid."

"You think that's tough?" George W. joked. "Try being a VPK!"

Despite his joking, George W. was trying to wrestle seriously with the moral lessons in the Bible.

Since his teenager years, George W. had considered the Reverend Billy Graham a friend. One time George W. and his mother were debating whether or not a person needed to accept Jesus Christ into their lives if they wanted to get to heaven. George W. came down on the side that such allegiance to Christ was necessary. They called up Reverend Graham to settle the dispute. He told them that George W. was correct, but chastised him for trying to play God.

Reverend Graham and his wife, Ruth, visited the Bush family in Kennebunkport for a weekend every summer over a number of years. Graham would preach at the Bush's two churches—St. Ann's and First Congregational. Then at night, the whole family would gather to ask him their most personal spiritual questions about life and death. Such communal expressions of faith were not unusual for the Bushes. George W.'s grandmother Dotty read out loud from the Bible every morning, and she was known as much for her spirituality as she was for her competitive spirit on the tennis court.

One night in Kennebunkport, during the summer of 1985, a family roundtable with Graham led to George W.'s epiphany. Graham's ministry stresses the need for a person to invite Jesus Christ into his or her heart. A person needs to feel humbled enough to make the request, he has said. George W. apparently understood the message that beautiful summer night. He later met with the preacher for further discussion.

George W. began maturing in a multitude of ways. He had always been quick-tempered, impetuous, and sarcastic, but those coarse edges began to be smoothed. He did not just study the Bible—he clearly immersed himself in the task of understanding its message; he would talk to his friends about lessons he learned in the scriptures. He seemed more confident and less cocky. He had always had a tough temper. If he missed a shot on the tennis court or golf course, he'd blow up. The moment wouldn't last long, but he'd react. "That used to be his biggest

fault," said Charlie Younger. As George W. began to study the Bible
and take Reverend Graham's teachings to heart that fury began to cool.
"I know I'll never be perfect," George W. said. "All I can do each day
is to try to do my very best, and Billy helped me see that."

—

At the end of 1985, Spectrum 7 made one last bid for success. The
company invested $1 million in stripper wells—rigs already set up by
another company that were slowly sucking the last oil out of a zone.
The original company would have figured that the amount of oil eking
out of those old wells was not worth the cost of operation. Spectrum
7 figured it had ideas for streamlining the work to the point where it
would be profitable.

The plan never worked, and the company started looking for a
savior: Not just for another operator to buy them, but to drop a life
preserver so they could clamber up and take over the boat. Hugh and
Bill Liedkte, who started Zapata with George W.'s father, had merged
upward until they were the titans of Pennzoil. Spectrum 7 started
searching for just such a situation: a company where, for example, the
CEO had just died and left his business to his wife or kids and no one
wanted to learn the oil and gas business. Paul Rea and George W.
found a couple of prospects but nothing worked out.

By the beginning of 1986, Spectrum owed the banks a staggering $2
million. The company could still sell its interests to pay back the loans,
since the company had $4 million in resources. By March, however, they
lost another $400,000. The wells weren't relinquishing substantial
amounts of oil. Not long after the posted loss, George W. asked the staff
to take a 10 percent pay cut. He knocked his own salary down 25 percent.

He had to face the very real fear that the banks would start to call
his loan. The First National Bank, the largest privately owned bank
in Texas, had gone under three years earlier because it had made loans
projecting oil prices at $60 or $70 a barrel. No one could repay their
loans when they were called, and the price was down to $9.

The situation had gotten out of George W.'s control, and he wasn't
much for the roller-coaster lifestyle. He had always appreciated risk
taking; that was one of the qualities he most admired in his father. But
he seemed knocked off balance when business hit harder times. "I

don't think he likes the ups and downs," said Younger. "He likes the ups. The independent oil operator fit his personality when he came out here because it was booming, but I think when it started busting, it didn't fit his personality quite as well."

George W. wouldn't exactly get depressed. "He's never had two bad days in a row," Younger added, "but he was walking uphill into a headwind."

When a reporter came to interview George W. as the son of the vice president, he became what he most despised: a name dropper. "President Reagan. King Hussein of Jordan. Evangelist Billy Graham. Former Dallas Cowboys quarterback Roger Staubach. Houston Astros pitcher Nolan Ryan. Australian tennis star John Newcombe," the reporter itemized. "Names like those drop lightly from the lips of George W. Bush of Midland."

But George W. also described his own days, beginning at 6:45 when he awoke, arriving at work at 8:02, lovingly "watching the girls color" in the evenings, and reading spy thrillers and inspirational books until bedtime to keep his mind off his careening personal finances. He was treading water until someone came along to save him or until the price of oil started rising. Unfortunately, he didn't see that kind of reversal happening for another two or three years.

His employees said that if it were just his livelihood at stake, he could have closed down shop so he wouldn't have to carry the debt further. But George W. was afraid of what would happen to his staff. For the first time in his life, he had people counting on him—even their families relied on him—and he didn't want to abandon those responsibilities. He wasn't the type to take the staff out to lunch every day— he always needed that hour to exercise—but if anybody had a problem, he would sit down and figure it out with them. Or he'd just drop by their desk, sincerely ask them how they were.

—

That year, Mike Conaway's wife, Julie, was diagnosed with leukemia. George W. gave his accountant all the time off he needed. George W. took their boys to baseball games to get their minds off the trouble. When Julie was feeling better, he and Laura would invite the whole family over for dinner. Conaway never forgot the generosity.

He was excited to share his life with the staff too. When Vice President George Bush came to visit with the Secret Service hovering around the cubicles, George W. beamed with pleasure that his dad and his staff were getting the chance to meet. Charlie Younger joked that George W. was too cheap to throw Christmas parties, but in truth, he threw a party every year—he even held some at his own home. One summer in the mid-'80s, he told the staff that he'd like to take them up to Kennebunkport for a week. They could all unwind, enjoy that crisp sea air. He was excited about the idea, even started the real planning. But then, when money got tight, he figured he'd have to wait.

But besides George W.'s fears about the fate of his staff, he had to be gripped too by the possibility that he was wallowing in a pool of muck that would sully him forever. If, down the road, he wanted to run for office again—and most everyone thought he would—a business that tanked—his only entrepreneurial effort—would signal that he was a loser. His opponent and the lousy media would never care what happened to the oil prices that decade, or chalk the disaster up to the flukes of the business. They would just hammer him for having to bail out.

That's when Harken Energy Company from Bedford, Texas, came along. "[George W.'s] properties were pretty well encumbered," Harken's director, E. Stuart Watson, told *Time* a few years after his company bought Spectrum 7. "The banks hadn't foreclosed, but that was in the wind."

Harken had been acquiring smaller companies that year and must have found Spectrum 7 attractive for two reasons: First, because George W.'s company had enough prospects that if oil prices came back, the payout would be great. Second, putting the vice president's son on the company's board of directors was a draw. Even Watson acknowledged that benefit.

The acquisition of Spectrum 7 played right into Harken's plans to make itself over. When he was only 33 years old, Alan B. Quasha, the son of a prominent Filipino lawyer, headed up a group that bought the public company, which was running a losing series of drilling funds. Quasha decided to dump the drilling funds and, in 1986, he and a partner, oil man Mikel Faulkner, began gobbling up oil companies that were near bankruptcy from the crushed oil prices. Harken's main purchasing power came from $7 million that Harvard University invested from its endowment fund, and the rest of the acquisitions were done through stock trades.

Harken offered Spectrum 7 a swap. They would buy the company by paying out one share of Harken for every five shares of Spectrum 7. They would absorb Spectrum's debt and keep on a handful of the company's employees, if those workers were willing to relocate. George W. would become a director on the board of Harken and a salaried consultant out of the Dallas office for two years. His stock share would be around $530,000 at the market prices of the time.

When George W. broke the news to the staff, no one was overjoyed. Not only did it mean that their collegial office was breaking up for good, it meant that some of them were out of a job. Still, they didn't hold it against their boss. They knew something like this had to be done. Ultimately, George W. got on the phone and found a job for everyone who had lost their position.

—

Paul Rea always assumed that George W. would want to run for office again one day, but he feared that, when that time came, his friend's social drinking might pose a problem. Rea was attuned to the warning signs of alcoholism because his youngest son had struggled with the disease. His wife, in her concern, had become a counselor. Rea and his wife had stopped drinking in the mid-1970s.

Rea didn't think that George W. was necessarily an alcoholic. He never saw him imbibe in the daytime or really get out of control. But Rea could see how the drift might take place—that small shift that could change a social drinker who had three cocktails with dinner into someone with a problem.

Another friend asked George W.: "Can you remember a day when you haven't had a beer?" And George W. couldn't give him an answer.

"He would just get a little louder, a little more boisterous," said Charlie Younger. "He would never get mean. When he had a little alcohol under his belt, he had a few more answers than he normally had."

After evenings out with friends that even Laura described as "not particularly great," she would ask him to quit. She told the *Washington*

Post that he tried to reduce his drinking for about a year, but that he never seemed to be able to stop before he had downed four bourbons.

His personality would climb the Richter scale. "I would go from a three to a ten," George W. said about the uptick in his volubility when he drank. "And my wife told me, 'You're just a three.'"

That brand of spontaneity could be disastrous if political enemies of his father were looking for dirt. George W. had always been exceedingly careful to monitor his conduct so that his dad would have no public problems, his friends said. Drinking had become exactly that kind of liability. "His father was moving up the ladder," said Younger, "and George didn't want to do anything, truthfully, to embarrass his father and his family."

"When George [W.] drinks," Roland Betts, George W.'s friend from Deke who went on to become business partners with him, told the *Dallas Observer*, "he is very funny and very smart-mouthed. A couple of times he shot off his mouth in a political situation." Reportedly, he refused to disclose further details.

All George W. had to do was look at the political horror stories. His father had been a great fan of Wilbur Mills, the Democratic chairman of the powerful Ways and Means Committee. When Prescott Bush asked his former colleague Mills to appoint his son to the committee as a freshman, Mills did so, making George Bush the first neophyte to serve on that committee in 60 years. To George Bush, Mills was powerful, courteous, and fair.

Then Mills hit the bottle too hard, ended up splashing around in the Tidal Basin with a burlesque dancer, and eventually had to step down as the chair of the Ways and Means Committee. "I had great respect for Wilbur Mills during my years in Congress," wrote George Bush in his autobiography. "Twenty years later, I still do." Unfortunately, Mills's colleagues on the Hill and the constituents of his home state of Arkansas did not show such loyalty.

With George Bush serving as vice president, the family seemed under closer scrutiny than they had ever been before. Later that year, H. Ross Perot contacted George Bush to let him know that he had heard talk that two of Bush's sons were involved in improper activities. The vice president wrote back to Perot thanking him for his concern and telling him that all of his sons were good men and straight arrows.

When George W. was drunk, some of that bad temper he had worked so hard to quell would come to the surface. One night in April 1986, at a Mexican restaurant in Dallas, he was having dinner with a bunch of friends when he spotted Al Hunt from the *Wall Street Journal* at another table. The *Washingtonian* magazine had just come out with predictions of who was likely to win the Republican presidential nomination. Hunt had answered that it would be Jack Kemp. As George W. was leaving the restaurant, he approached Hunt. "You fucking son of a bitch," he spewed at him. "I won't forget what you said, and you're going to pay a fucking price for it."

Hunt wasn't sure who the cursing man was at first, and he had no idea what he was mad about. Then, from a few things the man said he pieced together that it was George W., angry about the Kemp prediction. Unfortunately, Hunt felt encumbered in responding because he was dining with his wife, Judy Woodruff, and their four-year-old son.

On another occasion, the *New York Times* reported that George W. went up to a dignified, well-dressed older friend of his parents at a cocktail party when he was very drunk. "So, what's sex like after fifty, anyway?" he said to the woman.

Other drugs, George W.'s friends say, were not a problem for him. "There was zero marijuana back then," said Younger. "Cocaine wasn't even a question. Nobody did drugs. You didn't see that in Midland. It wasn't a place where hippies would normally come, for every reason under the sun—including that [Police Chief] Darnell would run you out of town." Alcohol was a different story.

To celebrate the fortieth birthdays of a number of people from George W.'s set—including his own—he and Laura went up to the Broadmoor Hotel in Colorado for a weekend. The crew included Jan and Joey O'Neill III; Penny Royall, who had recently separated from her husband, L. E. Sawyer; Don and Susie Evans; and George W.'s brother Neil. They ate well and drank bottles of good wine. The evening became spirited, but no one remembered George W. becoming excessively drunk.

He woke up the next morning with a severe hangover—one that hampered his ability to run that day. Suddenly, he realized that alcohol did not mix with his energy level. It was holding him back. Without saying a word to the others, he just stopped drinking, cold turkey.

"He just said, 'I don't need it in my life anymore and I'm stronger than it is,'" said Younger. "I don't think many people would have or could have done it."

"I quit for the rest of my life," George W. told the *New York Times*, "and if you catch me drinking, it's not going to be a good sign for your old buddy George."

—

The Harken purchase of Spectrum 7 went through on September 30, 1986. Jim McAninch, the engineer who had joined George W.'s team with Arbusto, and Mike Childers, the landman who helped George W. with the 1978 campaign, stayed with the company.

George W. later told the *Dallas Morning News* that his business career had been a success thanks to "hard work, skillful investments, the ability to read an environment that was ever-changing at times and react quickly."

"As a result," he continued, "I have got a pretty good-sized asset base for a guy who started off fifteen years ago with not very much money."

The experience was not quite as financially positive for his investors. By 1986, George W.'s biggest supporter, Philip Uzielli had lost almost all of what he had put in. Still he wasn't angry. "[We] had a helluva good time," he reportedly said. "We were just very unlucky. . . . The oil prices went to hell."

George W. never seemed to acknowledge adequately the role of the carpetlayers in his life. He had been able to raise the capital for Arbusto with the help of his Uncle Jonathan. Philip Uzielli, a good friend of James Baker, had bailed him out at the right time. He had been saved from fiscal ruin by the merger with Spectrum 7 that Paul Rea helped facilitate; and Harken had taken a gamble on George W. because of, among other reasons, the power of his family name. While George W. was a smart, well-liked boss and colleague, his insecurities prevented him from giving credit where credit was due.

George W. was reluctant, in a way, to leave Midland. "There's a sense of camaraderie out there in the plains," he reportedly said. "When you step out there, your mind can see a long way. [If oil prices had not tanked,] I would not have left at all."

He put off the major responsibilities of working for Harken in Dallas so that he could move to Washington, D.C., to help out with his father's campaign. He still would be required to attend board meetings, but the fact that the company let him go suggested that his presence on a daily basis was not necessary for maintaining operations. "He was just itching to go," his friend Joey O'Neill told the *Washington Post*. "It was his hole card." He probably understood that politics suited him better than the oil industry. Since Spectrum 7 merged with Harken, George W. no longer had the power or responsibility of being CEO; he needed a new arena in which to test his abilities. He knew that he enjoyed campaigning from his work with Jimmy Allison and from his own 1978 effort. This presidential campaign would simply use all of those skills, but on a grander scale.

Friends knew the time was right for George W. to finally leave Midland, even if he was somewhat wistful. "I think he reached a point where he wanted bigger fish in his barrel," said Younger. "By that time he wasn't a social animal anywhere, so it didn't matter where he lived. He was looking to broaden his horizons. I think he was . . . maybe 'bored' is the right word."

X

THE AIDE REINCARNATED

Not long after Ronald Reagan was elected to a second presidential term, George Bush's good friend, Nick Brady, then serving on various Reagan commissions, sat down with the vice president to talk about what Bush wanted to do concerning the 1988 presidential campaign. According to Chief of Staff Craig Fuller, Brady quickly realized that his friend was not consumed by the desire to run.

When George Bush launched his first presidential campaign in 1980, he ran because he felt he was better qualified than, or at least as competent as, anyone else he had met in government. "I didn't see any Roosevelts or Eisenhowers running," he remarked in his autobiography. He also wanted to end President Jimmy Carter's liberal policies and tendency to blame Americans for bringing on their own problems, as in his famous "malaise" speech. At that time, George Bush had enough enthusiasm to propel him along the campaign trail.

But the 1984 campaign was tough on him. He was forced to walk a fine line between staying loyal to the president and defining his own positions in anticipation of the 1988 race. He had to gingerly campaign against the first woman to ever hold a spot on a presidential ticket. He found no graceful way to handle the historic predicament. As Geraldine Ferraro herself said, "[He] had to stand up to me, yet not be so aggressive he'd end up looking like a bully. At the same time, he could not be patronizing or condescending."

In the face of such gymnastics, George Bush floundered. The day after the vice presidential debates, he tried to toughen his image for a group of longshoreman and fell flat. "We tried to kick a little ass last night," he said. The press put Bush in a public headlock and submitted him to an unending pummeling.

Even in the years between his campaigns, George Bush did not fully relish the job of vice president. Ronald Reagan had mistrusted him before the 1980 campaign and never completely embraced him after. "I want to be very frank with you," Reagan reportedly told a friend before he put Bush on the ticket, "I have strong reservations about George Bush. I'm concerned about turning the country over to him." Despite the tenor of mistrust, Bush offered Reagan his unwavering loyalty after he was asked to be vice president. He never broke through to be a member of the president's true inner circle. His role was limited to conducting diplomatic missions, attending funerals, and occasionally chairing a policy meeting.

Bush so feared triggering Reagan's discomfort or suspicions about him, he trained his staff never to complain, gossip, joke about Reagan or his people, or object to any policy. He purposefully hired men and women who would placate Reagan's team rather than battle them. In a gesture of friendliness, Bush and Reagan met once a week for lunch, but Bush quickly discovered that the most important contributions he could provide were jokes or amusing stories. He set aside his briefings and readied new comic material each week.

One might have assumed that Reagan would take the lead in seeing that his legacy got carried on after his two terms of presidency by ensuring that George Bush won in 1988, but Reagan seemed uninterested in whether or not George Bush was elected to the White House. The president offered only lukewarm support up until the Republican convention in the summer of 1988. His staff would be of little assistance in Bush's efforts.

So in 1985, when George Bush sat with Nick Brady and considered the campaign hell that awaited him, he appeared cowed. He wanted to help the party and hoped to be a good vice president. Those were his main goals. But unlike 1980, when he was running against policies that he thought were intolerable, now he was campaigning from the cocoon of the Reagan administration. Bush had been loyal to Reagan's direction for the country over the past four years—even when he had minor twinges of disagreement—and Bush had no reason to believe there would be anything to strongly object to over the next four years.

Campaign strategist Lee Atwater believed George Bush would have no problem winning the party's nomination. But he knew how important it would be for Bush to lay out a "vision." In a memo to the vice president on December 19, 1984, Atwater set forth the one obstacle he could foresee: "What would be the purpose of a Bush presidency?" he wrote. "This question, which I guarantee is coming, is a close cognate of Roger Mudd's 'Why do you want to be president?' query that undid Teddy Kennedy in seventy-nine. The VP is forewarned that even an answer very much more glib and articulate than Kennedy's stumbling ramble will be judged insufficient by many eighty-eight echo chamberites."

Atwater offered no guiding political philosophy for the campaign, but, according to the consultant's biography, *Bad Boy*, by John Brady, he suggested a strategy that in its obtuseness underscored George Bush's predicament: "The VP's message needs to encompass the simultaneous desire of the American people for the status quo *and* for change, for continuity *and* innovation . . . an essential aspect of any effective theme is the quality of dualism. After all, life itself is based on dualities. Life and death. Black and white. Yin and yang. Heaven and hell."

"I agree with your conclusions," George Bush reportedly wrote back after reading Atwater's memo on Christmas Day. The question was, What could he actually do with that information?

At Nick Brady's meeting with the vice president, Brady pushed the idea of the presidency forward. He told Bush that people would like to put a campaign together for him. George Bush could accept that.

"He needs to be president, that's for sure," his cousin Ray Walker, a psychoanalyst, told the *Los Angeles Times* in the fall of 1987. "There's no choice for him really. For him, it's the absolute confirmation."

—

In 1986, the vice president told Atwater and Chief of Staff Craig Fuller that his son George W. was thinking about coming up to Washington to help with the presidential bid. Fuller was surprised by that news. Certainly nothing was unusual about a member of the Bush family pitching in; they were famous for their intense labors on behalf of the patriarch, stuffing envelopes, trudging through New Hampshire, and manning phones. But this suggestion that George W.—the blunt, hyperactive eldest son—actually camp out in the office full time was unusual.

As George W.'s childhood friend Joey O'Neill had pointed out, George W.'s working on his dad's presidential campaign was an ace in the hole. Who would question a son's desire to help his father in the most important competition of his life? Meanwhile, until election day, no one would wonder what George W. actually wanted to do with himself. Harken did not occupy enough of his time or attention to use up all of his energy. He would need to set a more consuming career path—but not until after November 1988.

Atwater was probably less taken aback than Craig Fuller at George Bush's announcement that his son would be on the team. In late April 1985, Atwater had directly proposed to George W. that he come serve as the campaign manager's minder. The occasion for the historic dropping of the glove was a special Bush retreat at Camp David initiated by Atwater to gear up for the 1988 race. There, family and staff bonded—as was hoped—during such friendly activities as screenings in the darkened presidential movie theater and intimate tête-à-têtes strolling through the burgeoning woods. The guest list included the candidate, his family members—including his brothers and sister—and the staff that had just been hired on to get George Bush elected to the presidency.

Since the beginning of his first term as vice president, George Bush had retained a casual, friendly group of employees. But with his election bid ready to launch, he had decided to oust that crew and bring in real fighters.

The notorious gentleman and kindly grandpa George Bush could be a tough son of a bitch when it came to getting rid of people, yet no one seemed to notice. "He fired more people than I have ever known anyone to fire," his press secretary Marlin Fitzwater recently noted, "and the amazing thing was they all ended up loving him." The regular pattern seemed to be that after sacking them, he would help find them a job, ensure they had enough money to get by, invite them to dinner, and follow up by regularly writing them notes. His message was: You might not work for me now, but you are still part of the political family. "I remember going to dinners at the White House after he became president," Fitzwater remembered, "and had the people there who were people he fired." Employing that system, he apparently left no enemies in his wake. This was the sort of gesture an essentially kind man felt compelled to make and a politician labored to do: Sand every hard feeling down to a smooth caress.

The new team that came aboard for Bush in preparation for the 1988 campaign was more of a wingtip shoe than house slipper crowd. (In fact such executive footwear hobbled Fuller during an early Kennebunkport retreat when he realized he had brought nothing else, and was forced to skitter along the rocky coastline when the vice president invited him out on walks.) In addition to Atwater and Fuller, the new group included Nick Brady, pollster Bob Teeter, media adviser Roger Ailes, and finance chair Robert Mosbacher Sr. The team playfully dubbed itself the G-6, a reference to the G-7, the group of nations that direct global economic policy.

On the retreat, the G-6 and the whole phalanx of eager, young staffers sat around a big table, while George Bush's wife, children, and siblings fired questions at them. The employees could immediately tell that this wasn't the usual sort of political family. Every professional politico had at some point in their careers endured the agony of a candidate's irritating relative: the crazy brother who constantly generated local headlines for disorderly conduct, the know-it-all daughter who hectored the staff with hourly calls until the campaign workers trembled at the bleating of the phone. Political handlers even had an aphorism for it, "The best candidate is a bachelor. . . ." In contrast, the Bush family was the political equivalent of a highly trained, precision Olympic water ballet team, all of them practiced at giving speeches for their father and comfortable "recreating" in front of the press to create human-interest copy and high-spirited photo opportunities.

"So what's your press strategy?" one of the kids asked Fitzwater. This wasn't like a candidate's relative asking how many friends he could pack onto the campaign plane. Some of the staffers came away thinking that the event was George Bush's way of showing the employees that they not only had to please the candidate but his ambitious, articulate, watchful family.

As the meeting ended and everyone filed out, George W. cornered Atwater. "How can we trust you?" he demanded. He was referring to the fact that other members of Atwater's consulting firm were working on Jack Kemp's campaign to win the Republican nomination.

"Are you serious?" Atwater replied.

"I'm damn serious, pal," said George W. "In our family, if you go to war, we want you completely on our side. We love George Bush, and by God, you'd better bust your ass for him."

Atwater offered his now famous challenge. "Why don't you come up here and watch?" he told him. "And if I am disloyal, you can do something about it." Nothing could have pleased Atwater more, many of the 1988 staffers believed, than being granted the opportunity to enchant the candidate's son at close proximity. Atwater always believed in his own brilliance; he would enjoy inculcating yet another disciple.

That's why Atwater probably wasn't altogether shocked when the vice president told him and Fuller that George W. was on his way. It was up to them to figure out exactly how George W. could fit onto the 1988 team. Neither of them had any ideas right away, but they must have suspected that George W. would be a human intercom into the Oval Office. How could he not be? At worst, they must have feared he would insert his own interests and ideas—however unschooled—into the campaign strategy. At best, he would keep the staff on its best behavior. Both Fuller and Atwater were happy to have him aboard. Who would turn down a potential surrogate campaigner—one who even bore the same name as the candidate, not to mention a striking resemblance to him?

As George W. aged into his forties, he looked something like the monkey version of his father, with no unkindness meant to George W. or simians. He had the same handsome features as his dad, but the face was a little rounder, the ears placed a little more obviously in the middle of his head, the lips thin. The mischievous spirit was a direct inheritance from his mother: His expression looked cocked and ready for a wisecrack. Although he would try to restrain himself on serious occasions, there was always an escape route for the joke to make its way

through. His face was prepared—eyebrows knit upward, mouth slop-
ing in a smirk, eyes glinting with the desire to go after the loping target—to just let it loose. What George Bush lacked in competitive fire
in those early days, his son more than made up for.

In late 1986, George W. started commuting between Midland and
Washington for meetings. He was able to find that free time because
his main duty for Harken was to help find financial investors, a task
that could be conducted on the road. In the spring of 1987, he and
Laura drove the family station wagon up to the capital with their five-
year-old twins and moved into a townhouse one mile from the vice
president's residence.

The decision to relocate wasn't without pain. George W. and
Laura still had considered staying in Midland, even after the Harken
deal spelled out that he would have to spend at least some time in
Dallas. They had bought a house in Midland from the Self family in
1985 and put a great deal of work into refurbishing the property.
When George W. realized that the Washington work would be full-
time, there was nothing for him to do but move the family up with
him, and that meant selling the Midland house. He couldn't afford to
own a home in both cities, and they still hadn't decided if they would
be returning to Midland or going to Dallas after the election. George
W. confessed to a friend that the decision to sell the Midland house
had been difficult.

But in the 1988 election, so much was at stake for him. He had
stumped for his father since he was a young man of 18, but this campaign was different. When he ran for president in 1980, George Bush
had been a dignified statesman and successful businessman daring to
compete for the highest office in the land; a failure at that level would
have been considered a win, just for having tried. But now George
Bush was vice president, in line to ascend to the highest office, and all
of the nation's media attention would be focused on his successes and
struggles. George Bush would be interspersing drop-ins in New
Hampshire with cabinet debates about what to do about Panamanian
dictator Manuel Noriega. The campaign was high powered and high
profile.

George W. cared more about the outcome than any of the people
paid to work for his father. He had been his dad's biggest fan since

boyhood—shaped in a large part by his mother's adoration for George Bush. His father had succeeded at every endeavor he had undertaken—from war, to baseball, to business, to politics—and maintained his gentlemanly demeanor throughout. By working on the 1988 campaign, George W. would be able to spend long periods of time with his dad; they would even reinstate the Sunday afternoon hamburger cookouts that had started back in Midland, but now with Laura and the girls. George W. also probably relished the opportunity to demonstrate to his father how much he had matured since finding spiritual salvation, giving up drinking, and taking on the responsibilities of fatherhood. He was ready to show his dad how much he could contribute.

In the past, George W. had felt the pressure—all internal—to live up to his father's standards as he traversed the same path. But after the big life changes he had undergone in less than a decade, he seemed ready to accept himself. "If ever there was competition with his father," Laura Bush observed, "it was certainly gone by 1988. He had given up drinking before we moved, and he felt more comfortable with himself. He had an opportunity most people never get—to work with his parent as adult to adult. They had time to work through any sort of competition."

George W. had liked Ronald Reagan; he had even given speeches after the election in 1980 touting the president's vigor, vision, and spirit. But he couldn't have been happy with the treatment his father received as vice president, relegated to a relatively impersonal role in the Reagan White House. George W. must have felt that his father was due the honor of finally making the difficult decisions and commanding the power of the presidency of the United States. All of Bush's hired guns certainly would now prefer to add a win to their resumés, but if the vice president lost, they could always shift the blame to the candidate; at least half the national press would back them up. But George W. wanted to see his father receive the final reward for a lifetime of diligence.

George W. also knew that if his father lost in 1988, his political career would be over. The campaign would be "it for Dad politically," George W. told the *Dallas Morning News* over a year before the election. "My own sense of things is this will be George Bush's swan song politically, win or lose. If he wins, he will have more glorious years in politics. If he doesn't, then he will look back and say, 'It has been a very interesting period in my life . . . and on to something unusual.' What it will be, I don't know, but it won't be the normal because George Bush is intellectually curious."

George W. moved into a cluster of offices down a long hall at campaign headquarters—next to Atwater, campaign aide Ed Rogers, and finance chair Bobby Holt, who hailed from Midland. At first, some of the staffers were suspicious about what kind of role the candidate's son would play. He was likeable, but it seemed clear he wasn't on a mission to buddy up to any of them. Would he be only a surveillance agent, reporting back watercooler discussions to his father? Would he lay back and do nothing, merely use his proximity to grant White House perks to his friends? "Senior adviser, they call me," he told the *Dallas Morning News*, "but when your name is George Bush you don't need a title in the George Bush campaign."

Before long, it became clear that he was there simply and exclusively for his father. He hung his Roger Staubach shirt on the wall and got ready for war. "We're going to win today!" he'd call out as he arrived for work at 8:00 every morning.

He became a kind of midpoint between Atwater and Fuller. He had more of a human touch than Fuller and was more socially mature than Atwater. George W. almost seemed refined compared to the campaign manager. While George W. was known as a terrible dresser with bad taste in sports shirts, Atwater rarely wore socks and never unknotted his ties, but instead just slipped them over his head. George W. could be frank in an interview, but Atwater took his candor to the extreme, even using the bathroom with the door open during an interview with journalist David Remnick. Most significantly, Atwater was a notorious womanizer while George W. was dedicated to his marriage.

But otherwise, the two men were remarkably alike. If they didn't get to run at noon, they were hell to deal with, all of that excess energy buzzing out of them in disruptive ways. Atwater was always jittery—his leg bobbed like a piston the whole time he talked. The whole room would hum around him.

Both of them were the good old boys around the office. George W. would seem even more Texan after he'd been on the phone with one of his Midland pals—his cowboy boots propped on the desk, a wad of chewing tobacco cradled in his cheek. His twang would pop like a banjo and he'd saunter around. "Junior'd always be *fixin'* to do something after one of those calls," a colleague noted to reporter David Maraniss. But Lee Atwater from South Carolina could out-country him any day, calling women "baby doll" and waxing poetic over his passion for rhythm and blues.

Like George W., Atwater had a mind for statistics. His brain was like a computer churning out the voting breakdowns in races going back decades. It was just like baseball: the percentage of losses, why the losers lost, and why the winners won. George W. soaked up that information. "He was the smartest guy around," Atwater reportedly said about his "alter ego." George understood the mathematical way of looking at campaigns. Sometimes it seemed as if they could read each other's minds. They didn't need to finish their sentences.

"When I was working for George W. in eighty-seven, he was still chewing tobacco, which is a pretty gross trait," Deborah Dunn, an assistant to George Bush, told the *Atlanta Journal and Constitution*. "I'd bring in his campaign itinerary, and stacks of material I'd already sorted through. He didn't want excessive detail. And by noon, three quarters of the stuff would be in the trash can, and when he'd go for his noon jog I'd be picking the stuff out of the trash can and I'd think, 'You couldn't have read this.' But he had, and picked out the facts and put it somewhere in his mind and moved on." Atwater could appreciate that kind of rapid thinking.

Atwater was as competitive as the Bushes, who even maintained a Ranking Committee for the tennis standings of their family and friends. They appreciated people who brought that kind of fire to politics. Every morning, around 6:30 or 7:00, Fitzwater would telephone the vice president to give him a rundown of what was in the papers. But Atwater couldn't stand to be left out of any aspect of the campaign and wanted to get there first. Before long, when Fitzwater called the vice president, George Bush would say, "Oh, yes, Lee and I already discussed that."

Despite the similarities between George W. and Atwater, there were many skills the Bush boy could learn at the campaign manager's knee. Atwater could smell the news coming months away, and with that prescience, ticked off responses even before there was a story to answer to. He would craft new ways of spinning the vice president's image. According to John Brady's biography of Atwater, the campaign manager tried to convince Bush to oversee a commission on the *Challenger* disaster so he could be seen on the news on a daily basis, and to start an investigation of U.S. nuclear facilities after the accident at Chernobyl. He wanted pictures of Bush in a hard hat, touring industrial sites. Both ideas were rejected by the vice president. The downside to creating staged projects for Bush was that, as time went by, the winning portrait that Atwater was crafting would look less and less like the real man.

George W. kept Atwater's focus on his father and on helping him win, rather than letting the strategist obsess about proving to other professional political consultants how brilliant he could be. George W. must have understood the power of loyalty—that enthusiasm for a specific goal that could be so defining, it could blind staffers to their own personal ambitions. In the one unifying mission, they would forget their infighting and status-seeking. They were *not*, George W. would frequently remind them, working to bolster their resumés. Their one task was to elect George Herbert Walker Bush to the presidency, and he would personally see to it that they were ousted if they ever lost that focus. He would play bad cop to his father's good cop. "If a grenade is rolling toward George Bush," he would tell the staffers. "I want you to jump on it." As in his Andover days, he would play both Godsquad member and head cheerleader simultaneously.

He would also serve as oracle for his father's desires. He educated the staffers about who his dad's closest friends were and what their histories were with the Bush family. Maybe an advance man had planned to keep the vice president in a holding room before a speech in Chicago. And say George W. got a call from a family friend who had expected to spend some quality time with their old buddy. George W. would let the staffer *know* that there was room for one more. He would tell the staffer to make it happen. Sometimes, after the elder George had gone out on a particularly grueling campaign swing, he would casually mention to George W., "You know, I'm getting a little tired out there," and George W. would go tell the schedulers to lay off a little. The old man was beat. Take it down a few. Like his mother, George W. insisted on knowing the justification for any decision about where he should speak and when. He never held back from voicing his opinions. If he didn't agree with an idea that a staffer floated, he'd let them know. "What the hell are you thinking?" he'd demand.

He would rarely if ever fall off message. "The father thinks the same," said Sam Skinner, who was George Bush's chief of staff in the early part of his presidential term. "George W. just speaks out more."

Indeed, he could get voluble—with Atwater particularly. Pete Teeley, recruited by George W. as press secretary, remembered getting into fiery arguments. "We had more than a few yelling matches," he told *Time*, "and sometimes you'd just have to leave him alone and come back at him later."

The vice president might not express a particular view as ferociously as would his son, but he was happy to have someone saying it. "George Bush wouldn't mind having a few other people pick up the sword and go to battle for him—as vice president or president," said Marlin Fitzwater. "And I think there's no doubt that he appreciated my battles with the press on his behalf and George W.'s on others." George W. was happy to be one of the soldiers.

—

George Bush always made sure he had those kinds of pit-bull personalities around him to balance his nice-guy demeanor. One such fighter, whose work overlapped only briefly with George W.'s, was the vice president's secretary Jennifer Fitzgerald. The young British woman had started working for Bush during his last year at the Republican National Committee and continued on with him in China as his gatekeeper. She was sophisticated, efficient, and reportedly well connected enough that she could introduce him to members of British parliament.

Bush seemed to enjoy her company, but many of his friends and staffers openly disliked her brusque demeanor and her seeming power to block him from granting favors and requests. No one could explain her sway over him, and so some started murmuring that sex was involved. It was too hard to imagine that she might be acting out George Bush's more honest responses to the entreaties of his colleagues. "I'm not saying she's Miss Popularity," Bush reportedly said in 1982. "She's doing what I want done. When you say no, particularly to friends, there's bound to be some level of frustration."

Nancy Ellis, George Bush's sister, dismissed the rumors of a sexual relationship in an interview with Herbert Parmet. "Dumpy little Jennifer," she said, "[was] like the most reliable, good person you know. We've all known her forever. She just absolutely adores George, as do all other people."

In late spring of 1987, Atwater and Teeter began hearing rumors out in the field about the allegations of an affair between Bush and Fitzgerald. The journalists were talking of little else. Some local reporter was bound to just pop off and ask the vice president about the buzz when he was on a rope line, the two men feared. Then if the vice president wasn't prepared, he might be caught off guard and say something odd. The staffers would be left with weeks of cleanup in the press. *Not that anyone had reason to believe the rumors were true* . . . .

The vice president had six intelligence briefings a week, so Fuller's plan was to slip in a short extra briefing just after the Saturday intelligence session to talk about campaign issues. Atwater and Teeter would join them, and the three men would just give the vice president a heads-up about the Fitzgerald rumor. Around 9:00 that morning, the aides sat down with George Bush on the front porch of the vice president's house to hash out the issue. They told the vice president what they had heard and asked him how to respond.

The vice president exploded, throwing in a selection of obscenities.

Just then, coming around the corner from her early morning constitutional, was the one person the aides did not want to see: Barbara Bush. The three men looked like they were a bunch of schoolkids caught leering over a copy of *Playboy*.

What are you talking about, boys? she asked amiably.

George Bush told her exactly what was being discussed. "Well, that's ridiculous," she said crisply. "The answer is N-O. Why are you guys even here?" Fuller told Barbara Bush biographer Donnie Radcliffe that her response was true to form. "You don't have to be delicate or dance around the point with her," he said. "That was just another affirmation, of course, and we then had a kind of sense that they were fine and they were going to take the thing head-on."

Clearly, within days, a family discussion had taken place, and

George W. became tangled in the talks. Atwater was apoplectic since he had received as many as 50 calls about the rumor in a single day. He felt that when the question really surfaced, it was going to rupture the campaign. After meeting with George W., Atwater called *Newsweek* to settle the matter and had an off-the-record lunch with reporter Howard Fineman, according to John Brady's biography of the campaign strategist.

Atwater told Fineman that George W. had asked his father point-blank about the issue. "You've heard the rumors," he said George W. had demanded of his father. "What about it?"

"They're just not true," George Bush told his son.

So, said George W., "The answer to the Big A question is N-O." He added: "They're trying to undermine one of my father's great political strengths—the strength of our family."

Almost none of the staffers would have wanted George W. publicly to field that question. If they had known of the plan earlier, they say, they would have stopped it. Bar was annoyed that her son had been put in the middle. "He opened the door for other people [to ask questions]," she told the *Houston Post*. "But I understood it. If it had been my mother and father, I would have spoken out too." Yet 24 hours after George W.'s quotations ran in *Newsweek*, the press backed off the story for a while.

It was to a certain extent a brilliant public relations move, since it drew such a direct connection between the rumors and the effect they might have on the family. The item also highlighted the fact that political strategy was behind the gossip. "The whole story shifted to whoever was putting this out was a dirty trickster, and this was vile, etcetera," Atwater observed.

But what seemed even more remarkable was the extent to which George W., in even daring to ask his father that question, had been able to objectify him. After decades of stumping for him, getting up to pitch him at country club luncheons and elementary school assemblies, of standing in for radio interviews, George W. had learned to view George Bush as a candidate, not just a dad. Of course, George W.'s ability to ask that question spoke to his faith in his father as well: He trusted that his father would give the answer he wanted to hear and that the response would be true.

Days after the *Newsweek* item ran, George Bush and his rival for the Republican nomination, Senator Bob Dole, reportedly negotiated a cease-fire on rumor-mongering. Atwater would later observe, "There were some [Jack] Kemp people who were masquerading as Dole people—a double whammy, that's a great technique. I'm Kemp, right? I want to get it out. I get a 'twofer' if I get the rumor out to fuck Bush and I also get the Dole people fucked in the process because they're being blamed for the rumor." Perhaps part of Atwater's brilliance was to leak the story of the cease-fire, citing only the Dole campaign's participation, thus implicating Bush's chief rival in mudslinging.

James Baker let George Bush know that he needed to move Jennifer Fitzgerald out of the White House. She was sent to his New York campaign office and was, according to Parmet, kept "on the payroll out of [Bush's] own pocket."

One of George W.'s main roles on the campaign had evolved into media gatekeeper—to sift through the requests and determine who would gain access to his dad. "Give me one good reason why I should let you talk to George Bush," he would say to reporters with an arrogance that annoyed them.

He fielded the tougher questions posed to the campaign staffers by the press. For example, when the media noted that George Bush was showing poorly in Iowa leading up to the caucuses, George W. candidly speculated to an Associated Press reporter that the factor that had damaged him had been the Iran-Contra scandal. The story "tends to confuse voters," he said. When Texas Agricultural Commissioner Jim Hightower stung his father with the jab that George Bush's idea of a good farm program was *Hee Haw*, George W. lashed back in the press, "He's a funny little fellow, that man."

The campaign had been working for weeks with *Newsweek* on their cover story to coincide with the Veep's official announcement kicking off his campaign on October 12, 1987. There had been a great deal of discussion about what photographs of the vice president were available. The *Newsweek* crew had requested something sporty. Then, two weeks before the deadline, Fuller was accompanying the vice president to a black-tie State Department dinner when he received a call from one of Bush's advance people who wanted to know where Fuller wanted the *Newsweek* cameras set up.

Fuller told the staffer that he hadn't approved a photo session and the plan had to be scrapped. He was immediately suspicious. Why would *Newsweek* be planning a cover picture of the vice president in *black tie*, in a *decorative* room of the state department?

The day of George Bush's big announcement the article's author, Margaret Warner, traveled with the Bushes on the plane. "George [W.] was giving her grief about the story we haven't seen," the vice president observed to his diary. "He asked if on the *Newsweek* cover, is the word 'wimp' on it? Margaret seems a little uncomfortable."

The answer was revealed that day as *Newsweek* hit the stands, and across the nation—on every newsstand, corner kiosk, airport lounge, dentist's coffee table—George Bush's picture ran under the headline, "Fighting the Wimp Factor." (Perhaps some subliminal effect of frailty was added too by the skyline, "The Latest on Cholesterol: How to Head Off Heart Disease.")

The photograph showed the vice president behind the wheel of his cigarette boat, *Fidelity*. Such a candid could have made him appear rugged and adventurous; but instead, the staff at *Newsweek* had selected a shot in which his mouth had taken a slight downward turn, as if he were cold, as if the wind were batting him just a little too hard. Any suggestion of machismo appeared contrived; he looked like a blue blood who financed Broadway musicals.

The premise of the story, by Margaret Warner, was that although George Bush boasted an impressive resumé and high approval ratings, he would have a hard time making it to the presidency, since the public perceived him as weak. The story explained this plight in a sympathetic tone, but the message was still there.

In the Bush view, Warner had violated the code of decency. She had been invited up to Kennebunkport and chummed around with the family. They couldn't believe that she had dared to write such negative spin. George W. went crazy.

When Margaret Warner called him, he let her have it. Reportedly, he said: "This is disgraceful. You spent all this time to write a two-page article, and it had the word *wimp* in it seven times about George Bush?" He claimed that she blamed her editor.

"Then you ought to quit," George W. recalled telling her. "You ought to quit if that's the kind of journalistic integrity you have."

She said later that when George W. called to chew her out, she had stood up to him, telling him that she thought that only the title was "unnecessarily cruel."

"It was a fair look at why Bush had this persistent image problem," she told *Texas Monthly*, "that he was, to put it delicately, something less than his own man. The campaign, George W. included, didn't like to admit it."

It is hard to fathom how much George W.'s defensive fury wore on him over all of the decades of his father's public life—to take such criticisms of his father forever to heart and react with such passion. He had held onto his disgust at Reverend William Sloane Coffin, who he believed slurred his father after the 1964 race. He had been infuriated by the Trilateral Commission conspiracy theories that had questioned his father's patriotism during his own 1978 race. During the 1992 campaign, George W. would summarize the pain of a lifetime watching his father be publicly pummeled. "I love politics," he told the *Dallas Morning News*, "but it has taken a little bit of a toll because I've got such a vested interest in my dad. It's hard to be a joyful participant in a mud-wrestling contest when someone you really care about is getting mud wrestled."

Many of George W.'s friends would vouch that he was able to bear the slights directed at him much more easily than he could endure those aimed at his father. Perhaps because he had traced his father's path so closely, he felt the criticism of that life more deeply. George W. had endured the educational rigors of Andover and Yale; tried to commit to marriage at a young age; flown planes for the military; worked the oil fields, and run for public office. He knew how difficult all of those efforts could be, what it showed about a man to not only live that life, but to excel at it. George W. himself hadn't even attained the high standards his father had set. He must have found it hard to believe that any wimpy journalist could match his dad's accomplishments, let alone try to tarnish them.

But perhaps too that defensiveness was touched off precisely because the journalists had pierced the vulnerability of George W.'s own subterranean perceptions. He would always have to face the fact that George Bush was a better father than campaigner. George Bush was a nicer man than most politicians, than most CEOs. He could scrap with the best of them, but he lacked a killer instinct. In fact, his gentleness caused even his old patron Richard Nixon to turn against him. The former president told Bush biographer Herbert Parmet in 1984 that Jack Kemp, not Bush, would be the best choice for president. Nixon had advised political consultant Ed Rollins to tell Ronald Reagan that he should let it be known that whichever Republican campaigned the hardest in the midterm elections of 1982 would be the vice president on Reagan's ticket two years later. "Make George a little paranoid," Nixon suggested to Rollins. He thought that was the only way to summon Bush's more ferocious side.

George W. knew the agony that his father had endured to serve his family and his country. He had been felled in a London hotel room by a bleeding ulcer when he was building his oil empire. He had lost weeks and months away from his wife and children when on the campaign trail. He had weathered the indignity of Watergate, put up with the nastiness of the Reagan staff when he first joined the White House team, worked diligently in the utter isolation of the outpost in China, and now the reporters were questioning his strength, his toughness? The media had revealed itself once again as an enemy.

The Bushes maintained a grudge against particular journalists. George Will had gone after George Bush from the moment his name first came up for the CIA post. Will was a good friend of Nancy Reagan and had, according to Bush biographer, Herbert Parmet, listened while she dished about the vice president over lunch. Will went on to write in 1986: "The unpleasant sound Bush is emitting as he traipses from one conservative gathering to another is a thin, tinny 'arf'—the sound of a lapdog. He is panting along Mondale's path to the presidency." George W. would later explain to *D* magazine that he believed that Will was "on a personal vendetta for having been denied social access to the White House."

Garry Trudeau would skewer George Bush as the Invisible Man in his "insidious *Doonesbury*" strip, as George Bush called it; and columnist Robert Novak, who originally had praised George Bush as a young candidate, began to grow more critical over the years.

But many reporters assigned to the Bushes grew to like the family a great deal. They were more fun to cover than most political personalities. They played more games, joked more readily. One of those bewitched on the trail was David Beckwith of *Time* magazine. He won their respect during a Kennebunkport picnic when, in a game of horseshoes, he piled a ringer on the vice president's ringer.

According to press secretary Sheila Tate, Beckwith kept a book of George Bush's malapropisms to tease him with. A favorite line was born when George Bush was supposed to say in a public forum that he was for the death penalty for drug kingpins and instead said he wanted the death penalty for those "narked up terrorist kinds of guys."

One night after the 1988 election, Marlin Fitzwater remembered, Beckwith came over to his hotel room when the press secretary was still working for Reagan and the Gipper was on vacation. Beckwith told Fitzwater that he wanted to be named Bush's press secretary. Fitzwater didn't have the heart to tell him that he had already been approached by a Bush adviser to take the post. When the announcement was made a few days later, Beckwith said nothing. He eventually left *Time* and went to work in Dan Quayle's press office and briefly many years later for George W.'s team for 2000.

—

George W. turned himself into a perfect medium for the messages the staff wanted conveyed to the president. He would ask the employees their opinions on how the work was going, what issues the president should be paying attention to. Then, he would relay the ideas to his father. As far as anybody could tell, he didn't inject himself into the dialogue. He was an honest broker. He would go see his father and suddenly the channels of communication would start moving again. If he came with a message for a staffer, that person would know that what George W. said was the truth, straight from the vice president.

After George W. had made one of his rounds, his father would seem more at ease. He knew what was on the minds of his staff without having to ask them himself. Other men had played this role for him in the past—former campaign manager Jimmy Allison Jr., and commerce secretary Malcolm Baldrige, to name just two. But they had both died before George Bush won the presidency (Allison of leukemia in 1978; and Baldrige in a rodeo accident in July 1987). Now his son was filling their place, not as an adviser, but as someone who understood how power germinated in the grandest hothouse of them all.

George W. matured in those years of presidential campaigning. In earlier times, he would have heard the first syllable of a problem and be barking out the solution before he had time to think. But in the 1988 campaign, he lost that impetuousness. He would hear out a staffer's problem, and then, instead of shooting off a response, he'd ask another person to state the difficulty as they saw it. He might even ask a third person for their input, and he wouldn't interrupt. He'd hear them through.

He was starting to seem like his father in that way—that tendency his dad had of never giving direct instruction when one of his staffers came to him with a mess. George Bush would ask the staffers what *they* thought they should do. There was a double edge to the technique. The staffers suspected that he wasn't just playing the role of some Zen master looking for the cricket to find its own wisdom; he wanted to see if the staffer was going to make a mistake.

Now George W. was sitting back more and listening. Andy Card, who was then Reagan's liaison for the governors and later Bush's deputy chief of staff, got the impression that George W. had taken that approach because he'd seen how unappealing the "know-it-alls" were. He didn't want to be one of those big mouths who never stopped talking long enough to learn anything.

—

In the months leading up to the convention, a power struggle broke out between Press Secretary Pete Teeley and Chief of Staff Craig Fuller. Teeley complained that he didn't have enough access to the candidate and resigned his post. He then began only scheduling the activities of Bush's campaign surrogates—primarily the family members. George W. let the press know that the problems weren't as deep as they seemed. "There's not a bunch of discord in our campaign," he said. "I know, because I'm sitting there and I'm the eyes and ears for [my father]."

Still, everyone was relieved when Jim Baker finally came over from the Treasury Department to head up the troops to help defeat the Democratic opponent Michael Dukakis. As to the delegation of power, George W. suggested to the press just what Baker's arrival meant: It would serve to downplay the role of the G-6. "We also have the G-1, me; and the B-1, Barbara Bush," he explained. "George Bush will not be pigeonholed by one collective group of people."

That sort of self-promotion could at times be among George W.'s biggest personality flaws. Many campaign staffers told journalist David Maraniss a few years after the campaign that George W. tended to "act out a bit."

"His father puts such a high premium on modesty and submersion of ego," one associate said, "that George [W.] was trapped. He never quite felt his father appreciated everything he was doing for him, so he became a little louder when his dad wasn't around."

Early on Tuesday afternoon, August 16, George W. sat by his father's side at a hotel in the convention city of New Orleans as George Bush called Dan Quayle to let him know he was the pick for vice president. They talked for over 15 minutes.

"I've thought long and hard about this decision and I'd like you to join me on the ticket," George Bush told the Indiana senator. He added that Quayle had been his first and only choice.

Bush had confided the choice to Fuller, Baker, and a few others in the commander's bedroom at the base upon landing that day. Although most political observers were surprised—even shocked—when they found out Quayle had been selected—no one in the know should have been very surprised. Two of Bush's top advisers—Ailes and Teeter—had worked closely with Quayle, and he filled a number of criteria: He would make history by being the first baby boomer selected for a national ticket; he had proven his electibility by crushing legendary Indiana politician Birch Bayh in the 1976 senate race, plus he had a good record on labor issues and other substantive domestic legislation; he was considered less moody and headstrong than Dole, more charismatic than Kemp. And Atwater liked him, particularly as a representative of the next generation.

"[John] McCain and I tingled when we heard the choice," enthused John Sununu, who that day was informed by George Bush that he had been a contender for the slot, but Quayle had gotten the nod.

McCain confirmed his support for Quayle. "I can't believe that a guy that is that handsome would not be of some benefit to Bush in attracting the support of women," he said.

Reportedly, Ailes wrote in a memo to Bob Teeter: "Dan Quail [*sic*] looks like Robert Redford—only he is better-looking. He symbolized youth in the future of the Republican Party."

But some staffers on the campaign believed that Bush's selection of Quayle was the vice president's attempt to show the world—and more important, the Reagan people—that he could win on his own. He wanted a null set in the second slot of the ticket.

Quayle was a hearty cheerleader. He oozed enthusiasm that day as he welcomed George Bush's steamboat to a rally in Spanish Plaza. "Let's go get 'em," he cheered.

"Well done, Danny," Bush commended him.

That Tuesday night, Fuller was standing on the convention floor when he noticed Lisa Meyers from NBC fluttering nearby. "We've got him! We've got him!" she kept saying excitedly into her headset. Suddenly, Fuller realized she was talking about him. Within seconds, Meyers was on the air asking him about Dan Quayle and the draft issue. At first, Fuller thought the question was a slam-dunk, since he had been prepared to talk about the fact that Quayle had served in the National Guard during the Vietnam War. But he started to get the feeling, from her manner, that she had more on the story than he had. As soon as Meyers transferred back to Brokaw, Fuller went to find some of the campaign people. They needed to get to the bottom of the story.

The emergency meetings about Quayle started that night with Baker, Atwater, Ailes, Teeter, and Brady. Not only did they have to worry about an allegation that Quayle had used family influence to gain a slot in the National Guard, but they had to field another story involving a controversial party in Florida in 1980 attended by a former lobbyist and *Playboy* model named Paula Parkinson. Two congressmen who also attended had fallen into a political quagmire about that event. Since Quayle had been an unusual pick from the start, the campaign staffers were unprepared for all the minutiae the press picked up. Those meetings led right up to George Bush's own nominating speech on Thursday night.

George W. was put forward to the media the next day to field the Dan Quayle criticism. "My view is that I was in the Texas Air National Guard myself and I am proud to have served," he said, pointing out that Lloyd Bentsen's son had been in the same unit. "I want you all to remember that [Dan Quayle] didn't go to Canada."

That next Sunday, John Sununu went on ABC's *This Week* with David Brinkley and criticized Bentsen for helping his son get into the Guard. Sununu referred to an article that ran in the *Boston Globe* as evidence that Bentsen had stepped in for his son. Comparing the Bentsen situation to Quayle's, he said, "There was not a special slot as there is in the Bentsen case, where a slot became open and Senator Bentsen ran to get his son to fill that," he said. "I think there's a difference between having someone speak for you and having someone move you up on a list or into a special slot as there was in the Bentsen case." The charge, however, was erroneous, since the story had made no such claim.

Bentsen countered that his son had met Lieutenant Colonel Walter Staudt—the same man who had accepted George W. into the National Guard—at the party of a friend in the 147th National Guard fighter group. Bentsen said he had been recruited as a fiscal accounting officer. George W. and the rest of the campaign were compelled to back him up.

—

On the night of George Bush's nomination to the presidency of the United States, George W., as the head of the Texas delegation, put his father over the top in what he described as "one of the most emotional moments of my life." With the Lone Star flags waving behind him, he bequeathed the 111 state delegate votes to his dad. "For a man we respect and a man we love," he said choking up, "for her favorite son and the best father in America . . . the man who made me proud every single day of my life and a man who will make America proud, the next president of the United States."

At the convention, George W. solidified his own public standing, conducting over 200 interviews, primarily with the Texas press. A year before, he had confessed to a newspaper: "I really haven't lost my desire to be in office."

He became the media darling, more relaxed than his father, less tongue-tied. They both could joke around, but George W.'s cracks would come out smoother. In 1992, when his father refused to be interviewed by Dan Rather, they sent George W. instead. "You're not as bad as people say you are," George W. had joked in closing. He could be that way. Just having fun. But underneath it all was that unspoken history, of how his father had exchanged heated words with Rather on the air just after the Iowa debates in January 1988. How Rather had tried to sandbag him about Iran-Contra, and how the Bush team had unleashed its phone bank on the network. (In fact, George W. had loved his father's outburst; he had commended his father for showing "naked emotion" on television.) How a group of about of 100 Bush delegates had staged a 40-minute rally against Rather from the convention floor, including screams of "Wimp!" up to the CBS control booth. How Rather wouldn't let up on calling Dan Quayle *J. Danforth* Quayle, as if he were some kind of elitist. How Sheila Tate had tried to reason with Rather's producer to just stop using the initial, but they refused. But George W. just joshed his way through the whole thing.

"George W. Bush is our Ann Richards," remarked a prescient Republican from Texas in 1988, as he watched the vice president's son during one of his interviews.

Still, it wasn't obvious that George W. would be a political player in his own right. He seemed more natural than his father, but that ease seemed to suggest that he was a normal person, not a star. His style could pale on camera in the way that a beautiful actor without makeup can and a politician never does. When George W. fielded questions, his head would jerk back a bit as if he were dodging the ghost of a physical blow. He had that look of a man who has worked out so much he feels uncomfortable in a chair, like his body was never meant to be bent that way—it was intended to be pole vaulting.

"My horizons are limited because I'm only interested in one George Bush's political career and that's my dad's," he explained to the Texas press people when they would push him about whether or not he would run, adding, "One George Bush at a time."

—

For the last few months of the campaign, George W. toured Houston, San Antonio, Tyler, and Dallas with Senator Phil Gramm. He appeared with Ronald Reagan at a rally in Mesquite. That fall his father did not appear at a single event geared to minority constituents, but George W. was sent to give a speech to black entrepreneurs in Houston. The professionals kept telling him how great he was on the campaign trail, how the people just warmed to him. And he felt it. It felt good to be out there shaking hands, joking a little with all the party stalwarts and undecideds. After the campaign, Atwater was going to be heading to the RNC as chairman, and his main mission was candidate recruitment. He had his eye on George W., as did Karl Rove, who was helping the Bush campaign as a consultant. "Governor Bush sounds nice," George W. acknowledged.

But he also seemed to feel some ambivalence about the time that the campaign had taken away from his family. He already had missed so much, being away from Laura and the twins on the long circuits he flew for his father, introducing the regional honchos for his father's campaign effort.

The more likely candidate from the family seemed to be Jeb, who was secretary of commerce for 1987-'88 in Florida. He seemed more serious, more interested in policy, more polished.

By early October, George Bush boasted a strong lead in the polls across all 50 states. Atwater had drilled Dukakis with so many negatives over all of those months. The Bush campaign had hammered at the story of Willie Horton, a convicted murderer in Massachusetts who had been furloughed for a weekend during the Dukakis administration. While he was out, Horton tortured a man and raped the man's girlfriend. The Bush campaign blamed Dukakis's liberal crime policies for the incident.

Atwater used campaign ads to attack Dukakis for the pollution in Boston harbor. Then the Democratic candidate sealed his defeat during the second presidential debate. "If Kitty Dukakis were raped and murdered," Bernard Shaw of CNN asked, "would you favor an irrevocable death penalty for the killer?" Dukakis glossed over the personalization of the question and went directly to his policy statement on the death penalty. The reaction from both the press and civilians was horror at his robotic response.

In Bar's diary in the last weeks of the campaign, she chastised Dukakis for going negative in the campaign. "Dukakis, or his supporters, have called George a racist, liar, and adulterer, silly and effeminate. I truly believe that George has run on his record, and Dukakis has run away from his." Her entries have the giddy quality of the final number in a musical, when all the cast is whirling around the stage, belting out different harmonies. The Bush production included the multitudes of family and friends around the country, feverishly campaigning to the last to win her George the White House. "George, Laura, Phil and Wendy Gramm at the foot of the steps [of the plane in Houston]," she wrote about her arrival with her husband for the events of election day. "The Gramms have been so great, so supportive. They were so excited. We, because of the gloom and doomsayers, were very nervous. They were almost high!"

Although Dukakis pulled closer in the polls in the days leading up to the election, he could not catch the vice president. George Bush won 40 states in the electoral college and 53.4 percent of the popular vote. "I can't explain it," Bar wrote in her memoir, "but there was a difference in the air; a difference in how George—and I—were treated. Everything had changed."

—

With victory on election night came the unpleasant task of fielding the barrage of requests for appointments to the new regime. Craig Fuller headed up the operation and George W. helped on the "scrub team," sifting out the friends who had remained true and deserved appointments from the hangers-on who should be set adrift. People were coming from every direction, exploiting security access to pass on resumés to the White House; cabbies were pushing their CVs on Bush staffers. The telephones rang constantly with reporters on deadline calling to find out if it were true that so-and-so was on the short list, and no one had ever heard of so-and-so. Hundreds of powerful government employees were in limbo waiting to hear about their fate, and the tension was tremendous.

The president needed a new chief of staff and he had grown weary of inside-the-Beltway types during his years in the White House. He thought perhaps John Sununu could fill that role. The former governor of New Hampshire had been dubbed the "delivery man" for helping Bush win the state's primaries when it looked like he had no hope. Sununu had put armies of supporters marching through the heavy snows to knock on doors campaigning for Bush; he had even manned the phone lines at the press office.

In the spring of 1988, Bush broached the subject with Fuller of what his plans were for the chief of staff position if he won the presidency. "If I win, what would be best for you?" he asked Fuller. The chief of staff told him that he had been in the White House compound too long and needed to get out.

On Election Day, Fuller conducted the final intelligence briefing with the vice president. When they finished, Bush told him that he thought he would pick Sununu to fill the post. Fuller's first thought was that Sununu seemed too partisan for George Bush. The fit didn't seem right. When Baker heard, Fuller said, he felt the same way. But Bush made the appointment.

—

"What's gonna happen to me?" George W. wondered aloud. He knew that he had no interest in staying in Washington, D.C. His work there was done with his father's election and transition. Atwater believed that just as a campaign's fate could be read in the successes and failures of past races, the hurdles that George W. faced could be predicted by the past. He asked Doug Wead, who had served as Bush's adviser from the conservative religious community, to put together a report on the lives of the children of presidents. The results laid out in the 44-page document weren't encouraging, including higher rates of alcoholism, divorce, and suicide than could be found in the general population.

Franklin Roosevelt Jr., for one, had been born into a family of six kids—four sons, a daughter, and a sibling who died at a young age. His brother had been an elected official in Florida and another son had gone out West. Franklin Roosevelt Jr. himself had run for governor from his home state and lost. "I do remember Junior looking at that and groaning, 'Oh, great,'" Wead recalled to the *Texas Monthly*.

Early in the fall, George W. received a fateful call from his Spectrum 7 partner, Bill DeWitt Jr. The Cincinnati moneyman had heard that the Texas Rangers were up for sale. The current owner was Eddie Chiles, the same man who had flown Bar and Robin up to New York during the worst days of George W.'s sister's illness. If George W. could work out a way to buy the team, he would be granted a popular and vast public forum from which he could run for governor. Professional baseball also had the advantage of being a business unregulated by the federal government, so there would be no conflicts of interest with his father. Even better, the ownership of a baseball franchise would be the fulfillment of that childhood dream that George W. and Terry Throckmorton had entertained in his pennant-plastered room back in Midland. In fact, the Rangers were the reincarnation of the Washington Senators, the same team George W. had gone to see with his father and Randy Roden back in childhood.

The work on the 1988 campaign had done much for George W. Besides revealing his own political skills, he had earned a new respect from his father. Now his father turned to him, not just for joking banter, but for full-fledged advice. He had become, to some extent, one of his father's wise men.

"It's the first son syndrome," Joey O'Neill told *Time* magazine. "You want to live up to the very high expectations set by your father, but at the same time you want to go your own way, so you end up going kicking and screaming down the exact path your father made. George didn't learn to channel his energy until middle age, and he didn't feel real comfortable until he went to Washington. He hated Washington, but it charged him up."

When George W. got back to Dallas, he took the energy of the capital with him, but focused that power on his local mission. Marvin remembered finding his brother a changed man when he called him down in Texas. Only weeks before, George W. had been barking orders and bouncing off the walls as he helped sift through the transition mayhem.

"I hear so-and-so might be involved in the administration," Marvin told George W.

Reportedly, George W. replied: "I don't give a damn. People down here in Texas don't care about that stuff, Marvin."

XI

THE MOUTH

OF THE TEXAS RANGERS

If investment strategy is destiny, then the most important day in George W.'s life was during the late winter of 1989 when Major League Baseball Commissioner Peter Ueberroth put the finishing touches on negotiations allowing George W.'s investors to buy the Texas Rangers. If any observer was foggy on the significance of that contract, its meaning was spelled out by Karl Rove, who was advising George W. on a possible campaign for the governorship in 1990. "Ownership of the Texas Rangers," Rove told the *Dallas Morning News,* "anchors him clearly as a Texas businessman and entrepreneur and gives him name identification, exposure, and gives him something that will be easily recallable by people."

But ownership of the team was not merely a political strategy, it was the continuation of a family legacy. Going back generations, the Bush clan had been more than just weekend athletes and diehard sports spectators. In 1923, George W.'s great grandfather George Herbert Walker started the Walker Cup tournament for golf—which pitted American against British athletes. The idea had been given to him by his best friend Dwight Davis of St. Louis, who had so enjoyed his own sponsorship of the Davis Cup tournament for tennis.

236

George W. would not be the first in his clan to invest in a Major League Baseball Club, nor was he the first to be assisted by a municipality in the building of a stadium. In 1959, when a group of baseball enthusiasts was creating the Continental League to compete with the American and National Leagues, Davis had been convinced by George Herbert Walker's son—named as a junior but known better in Bush family life as Uncle Herbie—to invest in a team for New York. Uncle Herbie was the same relative who had originally helped his beloved nephew George Bush start Bush-Overbey Oil back in Midland.

In the venture, Davis had paired Uncle Herbie with a rich, flamboyant grandmother from Kentucky and New York, among other residences. Mrs. Charles Shipman Payson, who had a taste for heavyweight boxing and horse racing, put up most of the money. New York's mayor at the time, Robert Wagner, was so excited at the possibility of hosting a new professional ball club that he authorized the city's baseball committee chairman, William A. Shea, to pledge $12 million toward building a new stadium in Flushing Meadows, Queens—today's Shea Stadium.

The Continental League never got off the ground, but the New York Mets, as the team would be known, was snapped up by the National League. Payson paid $4.5 million for 89 percent of the stock, and Uncle Herbie owned 6 percent. A third investor, Donald Grant, anted up the rest.

George W. remembered how much his great uncle loved his involvement with the team. He'd only given up his interest in 1977, shortly before his death on November 27. "There is no New York Mets fan who cares more about their success that I do," Uncle Herbie wrote in a statement upon his retirement from the club, while he was nursing an ulcer. "It has been a great privilege for me to have been one of their owners since their franchise came to life in 1960. Because, however, of some recent health considerations and my current disposition to pull back in several areas of activity where I have been active heretofore, I came to the decision several weeks ago to dispose of my ownership interest in the Mets.

"I am currently following the activity by radio from my summer home and I look forward to many visits to Shea Stadium after my return to New York in September."

When George W. and his family gathered with Uncle Herbie each summer in Kennebunkport, the whole extended clan would be expected to watch Mets games. Across the lawns, they would hear the calls of "Metsie!" and "Yogi!" as his uncle's dogs, named after the team and a manager, were summoned. "This guy had a fabulous time with [the team] and also made a lot of money with it," George W. recalled to a reporter. "It kind of caught my attention when I was a kid, and I've always wanted to be involved with baseball. I recognized early on I couldn't be a player."

—

It must have felt like a hearty portion of America was high on George W. just after his father's presidential election. Maybe George W. wasn't a household name yet, but everybody who was somebody in the Republican Party—all the strategists, pollsters, fund-raisers, so many of the Republicans leaders he had met in cities across the country over the previous 18 months, when he was stumping for his dad—all loved him. They told him how he had that magic with people. His friends had seen it as far back as high school, but now even he could clearly recognize the power of that special touch.

He was going back to Texas. There never really was any question that he would head home—anyone who really knew him was sure of that, since he was most comfortable in the Lone Star State. Sometimes his dad's friends would try to put a heroic spin on the choice: See, he wasn't the kind of guy to just grab a free ride from his father, mooch a government post himself. And to a certain extent that was true; George W. would hate a Washington coat-and-tie job, and he was savvy enough to understand that the media would never just let him settle comfortably into a nepotistic post.

But what those friends of George W. might not acknowledge was that, *of course,* he was going home to Texas. For one, he needed to earn the $120,000 Harken would be paying him in consulting fees in 1989. Over the last year he had made money from them as a consultant without devoting much time to the company's work.

More important, George W. had big plans for his political future. He had been bitten by the campaigning bug and most of the people who worked with him could see that he was pretty keen on running for governor in 1990. "If I ever ran [*sic*]," he told the *Dallas Morning News* in August 1987, "I'm going to get tagged on running on my father's name, regardless of how wonderful a person I am or not. So I would rather have that tag if he were in office rather than out."

Now with his father in office, he needed to head back to Dallas to see what could be put together for the gubernatorial. One did not win Lone Star constituents sitting around downing martinis and chewing steak at the Palm in Washington, D.C.

Before George W. left Washington, however, he managed to imprint his statehood on the American consciousness. During the inaugural festivities, he dashed among events, shaking hands and accepting campaign encouragement hurled at him by all the Republicans gathered around D.C.'s punch bowls. He assured the press that his parents had already bestowed their blessing on him for any campaign he might undertake. His consultants had scheduled him to deliver Lincoln's birthday speeches in over a dozen Texas counties when he returned home.

On inauguration night, the president and Bar put in an appearance at all of the balls, including the one thrown by Texas. The president pointed out that his son, George W., a proud resident of the state, was the only Bush family member in the crowd. Earlier, father and son had stood with the rest of the clan in the parade reviewing stands, gazing out over the sea of 300,000 spectators. As the University of Texas Longhorn Marching Band high-stepped by, blaring a rousing version of "The Eyes of Texas," and the Texas float followed, featuring a pair of massive, pink, spangled cowboy boots and plastic yellow roses, a beaming George W. pulled out a ten-gallon hat and, in a picture-perfect gesture, placed it firmly on his head.

—

Bill DeWitt Jr. had heard back in the summer of 1988 that Eddie Chiles was trying to sell the Texas Rangers. For years, when DeWitt and George W. would travel for Spectrum 7, they would take in a baseball game and talk about how great it would be to own a team one day. George W. had dreamed of buying the Houston Astros since his teenage years in that town, so when the Texas Rangers came up for grabs, DeWitt thought of George W. and put in a telephone call.

"His first reaction was, 'That sounds great,'" remembered DeWitt. "[He said,] 'I'm not going to have a lot of time to work on it during the campaign. Why don't you work on it and I'll obviously spend some time on it too, and once the election is over, we'll try to get the thing done, if it works out.' So I knew a lot of people in Major League Baseball and worked with the ownership committee; talked about what we had to do to put a group together, and expressed interest. I was more on the MLB side than on the seller's side, and when George started to focus on the project, he was the contact with Eddie Chiles."

DeWitt's own interest in Major League Baseball ran deep, since his father had been a legendary executive with the St. Louis Browns and the Cincinnati Reds. DeWitt also had a bit of a track record with sporting franchises, having partnered in the past in the ownership of Cincinnati's hockey team, the Stingers. DeWitt was only one of the suitors that Chiles was letting into his parlor.

Eddie Chiles was a tough, irreverent multimillionaire who looked a little like Jimmy Cagney in his later years. He had made his fortune in his own lifetime, starting with an entrepreneurial effort in his boyhood planting cotton seeds in the vacant lots of Itasca, Virginia. By the time he reached adulthood, he owned the Western Company, a vast offshore oil operation and the world's largest supplier of rigs. He became a folk hero in 1977, when he clawed an airhole through the Carter malaise with a blitz of radio and television advertising featuring his voice and strident views on the increasing intrusiveness of the federal government. Inspired by the line in the movie *Network*, "I'm mad as hell and I'm not going to take it anymore," Eddie "I'm Still Mad" Chiles became a well-known curmudgeon.

In 1980, Chiles increased his investment in the Rangers from 50 percent ultimately to full ownership, which had not been at all difficult for him, because his business was flying high with 4,500 employees and a stock price of $32 a share. But by the middle of the decade, the oil bust had dragged Western down to a stock value of $1.75. Chiles knew what trouble looked like: He had weathered baseball's ups and downs, including a couple of losing seasons. "I never did contemplate selling [the team]," he said. "But I was in a blue funk, a dark blue funk about baseball." Now, facing bankruptcy—and beginning to battle ill health—he had no choice but to try to unload the franchise.

Edward Gaylord Jr., the man who would become a major figure in the tangled negotiations that finally allowed George W.'s group to purchase the Texas Rangers, made his first appearance in the saga in February 1985. The entertainment tycoon was based in Oklahoma, but had financial interests around the country—from the Grand Ole Opry in Nashville, Tennessee, to KVTV (Channel 11) in Dallas. His other Texas investments included large real estate holdings in Far North Dallas and a publishing house that specialized in farming books.

With Chiles desperate for financial salvation, Gaylord tried to help him out by buying one third of the team. The Major League Baseball owners' group—which needed to approve every sale or investment—voted him down, apparently out of concern over his ownership of a cable company called Gaylord Broadcasting. A good portion of the money to be made in baseball came from the licensing fees that television stations paid to the owners for broadcast rights to the games. Ted Turner had set the rest of the owners on edge by flooding their local markets with Atlanta Braves games through his Turner Broadcasting System. He reaped the big national advertising dollars, while they scrambled to maintain their local revenues. Although Gaylord's operation was far smaller than Turner's, the owners' committee thought the circumstances were similar enough; the vote was thumbs down.

That's when Commissioner Peter Ueberroth first stepped in on behalf of Gaylord and Chiles. He overrode the vote and allowed Gaylord to be a minority investor.

Meanwhile the oil business continued to stagger along. Chiles, now in even more desperate straits, announced a year later that he was selling all of his interest in the Rangers to Gaylord and that the deal would be final in September of 1986. "I can see two more years [of the Western Company]," Chiles said. "I can last two more years. If this goes on any longer, I don't know whether any of us will be around. . . . There are no lights at the end of the tunnel," he said. "If there is, it's the headlight of a train coming toward you." The *Dallas Morning News* started running human-interest stories on the new owner, Gaylord, as if the purchase were official. But the owners' committee balked again, voting against Gaylord at one of their official meetings. This time Ueberroth did not overrule the group's vote, but he did demand that they immediately commit to official ownership criteria so that no prospective purchaser would be publicly humiliated that way in the future.

In the summer of 1988, Chiles approached two men—Frank Morsani, a car dealer in Tampa, Florida, and Bill Mack, a developer from New Jersey—to buy the team. He was desperate to sell and had decided to cast his net beyond the borders of Texas. Morsani and Mack had tried to buy a minority interest in the Minnesota Twins in 1984, but the owners never replied to the bid.

The two men were interested in the Rangers provided they could either move the club to Tampa or create an additional expansion team down there. Morsani had always been civic minded, and thought that the city could use a baseball team as part of its urban development. Morsani claimed he had made clear to Chiles and later Ueberroth the possibility that he would move the team from the get-go. By late August, Morsani and Mack had signed a contract with Chiles and forwarded a copy to Major League Baseball's legal counsel. Chiles wrote Morsani a letter saying that he was glad they'd been able to work out a deal. Now the plan needed to be approved by the owners' committee.

When Bobby Brown, the head of the American League at the time, learned of the agreement, he warned Chiles that the owners' committee was unlikely to approve the deal with the Tampa group and he should look for local interest.

Chiles seemed then to have panicked. He told a local paper that he hadn't realized the Tampa group might want to move the team and he hoped Gaylord would nullify the purchasing agreement by exercising his right of first refusal as a minority investor. Gaylord made his bid in September. Of course, the offer had no chance of being approved. Morsani's group claimed they never were notified by Chiles that their deal was off.

Gaylord's letter of proposal included the unusual stipulation that if the owners' group turned him down, then he would sell his minority interest to the Tampa group, probably in an attempt to see which devil the owners' group most feared—an owner of a cable television business or a group that might relocate the team.

—

Soon after George W. talked to DeWitt, he called Roland Betts in New York City. His old pal from Deke had crafted a remarkable career after graduation. Betts had won a draft deferment by becoming a teacher in Harlem, written a book on the plight of inner-city schools, then turned himself into a mogul, financing some 63 Walt Disney Company movies, including the *Little Mermaid* and *Beauty and the Beast*, through his Silver Screen Management. His friend Roy Blount Jr. described the financial rewards of such business ventures in his book *Be Sweet*. He wrote: "The value of all the films together Roland told me at his house in Santa Fe (zestfully furnished six-bedroom faux-adobe with four-hundred-year-old doors imported from Pakistan and Afghanistan, a kidney-shaped pool, mountain views, lots of painting and sculpture, and a leased orchid plant) has been estimated at a figure that I am not at liberty to disclose, but let's just say a shitload." After working as a film financier, Betts, through Silver Screen, had gone on to build a 1.7-million-square-foot sports fantasy land on the Hudson River piers in Manhattan that became the bustling health club Chelsea Piers.

George W. told Betts about the Rangers deal and how the Mack family had wanted to buy the team but that the owners' committee was worried about authorizing the sale. Betts was interested in partnering with George W., as was his Silver Screen colleague Tommy Bernstein. George W. rustled up other contributors, such as his cousin, Craig Stapleton, and his father's friend, Fred Malek, who was an executive at the Marriott Corporation and former political aide to Nixon. DeWitt was simultaneously assembling willing baseball partners among the Spectrum 7 investors out in Cincinnati.

In December, George W. visited Chiles to try to make a deal. "I walked into his house," George W. recalled, "and said, 'I would like to buy the team. I'm serious about it. I'll put together a group of people to buy it. I want you to give me serious consideration.' And therein began the courtship."

Chiles wrote a letter to Brown. "George [W.] Bush contacted me yesterday and asked me to turn over the financial records of our club," he explained. "As you know, he was contacted by the committee and asked to look into the possibility of buying the Texas Rangers Baseball Club." Chiles went on to state that based on his discussions with

George W., he did not think the president-elect's son had enough money to buy the club, apparently even with his team of investors.

Morsani and Mack learned about George W.'s bid from the newspapers. Morsani said they had no hard feelings against him personally—after all, Morsani had been friendly with Jeb Bush when he was commerce secretary in Florida. But Mack met with Brown that month to let him know he was still interested in buying a team, whether in Tampa or another city.

As late as December 28, Chiles was still urging Brown to get the owners to accept Gaylord as the Ranger's purchaser. George W. had tried to talk to Chiles again, but Brown told him that Chiles could be more of a handicap than an asset in trying to buy the team. At that point, the bid clearly began wending its way through the ownership committee exclusively. George W. and DeWitt were expected to present a letter of intent to purchase the Rangers at the ownership committee meeting just a few days after George Bush's presidential inaugural, although Chiles said he hadn't received any formal or semiformal bids except Gaylord's.

Ueberroth told the press that he became involved in helping to find new owners when he heard Gaylord's bid would be rejected. He had proved how much he believed in local ownership for ball clubs when he intervened in 1985 to find Pittsburgh investors for the Pirates. In 1988, he was friendly enough with the Bush family that he might want to help George W. with his financial package. Almost a year before George W. began pitching his plan, Ueberroth was discussed in the press as a possible appointee to a Bush administration, since he and the vice president had been friends for years.

A *Newsday* article on February 28, 1988 seemed to be one of those commonly leaked "inside scoops" that cover the desires of an ambitious person who wants his name considered for some higher post. A top television executive was quoted as saying, "Mark my words. If George Bush becomes the next president of the United States, Peter Ueberroth will become one of his top cabinet members—Secretary of Labor, or Transportation. Along those lines, Ueberroth and Bush are fairly close. . . . I am convinced that he would jump at the chance." In the weeks leading up to the Republican convention, George Will, traditionally a Bush critic, put Ueberroth on the short list for exciting vice presidential nominations. A leading California state senator wrote a letter to the editor also urging Bush to choose Ueberroth. Reporters declared that Ueberroth planned to head into politics once his term as baseball commissioner expired on April 1, although Ueberroth denied any interest.

On January 21, the day after George Bush's inauguration, the owners' committee planned to meet and vote on the Gaylord bid. George W. visited with Gaylord beforehand to say, very diplomatically, that he was not trying to step on any toes; he would wait until the vote was in before pursuing his own offer. Gaylord was rejected once again.

But Chiles still held out hope for the friend who had helped him through two tough situations—when he was broke and when he needed an out from the Morsani and Mack agreement. The day after the vote, Chiles told the press he was excited to be the owner of the team for the coming summer, he hadn't been approached with another serious offer, and he planned to wait to see if Gaylord would force the owners to hold a special meeting to vote before looking around for another buyer. He also said he'd had lunch with George W. but that the president's son had no serious offer to give him. As to a bid by other prospects, such as former Rangers executive Larry Schmittou or Fort Worth auto dealer Roger Williams, he wasn't interested.

A few weeks later, on February 6, Ueberroth postponed the owners' meeting in Chicago to review Gaylord's situation. He said if a new buyers' group could not be found, he would exercise his best interest of baseball provision and approve Gaylord. On February 9, the head of the ownership committee, Jerry Reinsdorf of the White Sox, sent a letter to Ueberroth about the George W. offer, copied to Brown. "There is plenty of out-of-town money if we need some," he wrote. "This appears to be a doable deal if we can get control of the franchise by, A, voting Gaylord down and your controlling Eddie Chiles."

Brown said he thought the reference to "controlling Eddie Chiles" had to do with Chiles's struggle with Alzheimer's disease. "There were times he made rational statements," Brown explained in a deposition for a lawsuit later brought by the Tampa group against Major League Baseball because of their regularly frustrated attempts to buy a team, "but there were other times when he didn't recall things that had happened in the immediate past and his behavior actually was erratic. And I have a feeling that that's what he was talking about, that it was difficult at the time to know exactly what he was digesting in the way of information and what you could rely on when he told you he was either going to perform or what he had heard."

On a business trip to Cincinnati, George W. told the press that it "would be a travesty" if Gaylord's bid was rejected, but that if the owners turned the offer down, and he were lucky enough to get the team, he would leave Texas baseball operations as they were. Chiles had said years earlier that "I hope and pray every night I can keep that managerial team in force until the day I die." Four days later, Eddie Chiles was admitted to the hospital for "routine tests." He said he hadn't heard from Ueberroth.

Ueberroth traveled to Dallas with Brown, Reinsdorf, and the Major League Baseball general counsel Ed Durso on February 14, to meet with five groups of potential investors. They talked to George W., but told him he didn't have enough local money to win approval. They also met with Raymond Nasher, a banker from Dallas, who had been a Rangers shareholder before Chiles became involved, and with a local real estate developer named Trammell Crow.

Later in the day, the baseball commissioner met with Ed "Rusty" Rose, the reclusive president of Cardinal investments of Dallas who had gone through Harvard Business school ten years before George W. "The Mortician," as he was known locally, had won acclaim for acquiring dead companies and setting their financial juices flowing.

Another meeting, which was picked up by the press, was with Richard Rainwater. In just fifteen years, the young investment genius had reportedly parlayed $50 million of the Bass family's financial holdings into nearly $4 billion. His own largest interests were with Energy Service Company and Wolverine Exploration in Texas. His skill as a rainmaker was well known. He would call up partners still dizzy from the payouts he had brought them and demand, "How does it feel to be rich?"

Brown had been trying to convince Rainwater to buy the Rangers for some time. One Fourth of July, the American League president ran into him and his two baseball-fan sons on Nantucket and tried to push the idea. He would check in every so often to keep the idea alive. When Brown, who was a longtime family friend of the Bushes, heard that George W. was interested in the team, he called Rainwater again to urge him to reconsider.

During the Dallas meeting, both Brown and Ueberroth pressed Rainwater not to reject George W.'s request to pair up on the purchasing—"out of respect for his father," the baseball commissioner urged, according to a source close to the negotiations.

George W. said he read about the meeting between Rainwater and Ueberroth in the paper and decided to call the financier. At that point, Rainwater was more receptive. "The commissioner's a better salesman than you are," George W. recalled Rainwater's telling him. They met with Betts and Stapleton at Rusty Rose's house in Highland Park in Dallas. Rainwater said he would come in on the deal if Rose would agree to be general partner. Betts said he would only sign on if George W. was a general partner.

The two chosen candidates for general partner met for almost five hours and hit it off.

—

Just over a week after Rose and George W. had their meeting, Ueberroth announced that their group had been hand-picked to buy the team. Morsani and Mack were the backup. That night, Chiles was among the hosts at a Republican dinner honoring George W. at the Fort Worth Worthington Hotel. George W. described Ueberroth as the architect of the deal. The rest of the group purchasing the team, he said, were a "good group of Texans," but would not say who they were or how many they numbered. He also said that he hoped Gaylord would stay a part of the deal.

On February 24, Ueberroth said he wanted the deal done in ten days and suggested he might approve the sale without turning it over to the owners' group for a vote. Gaylord countered that he might exercise his right of first refusal. "If they won't let me sell it to Gaylord," Chiles said, "I won't sell it to anybody."

On March 9, the owners' group met in Fort Lauderdale and rejected Gaylord's bid, ostensibly because they feared his television reach. "That reasoning was kind of silly, and not valid in my opinion,"

Gaylord told the *Dallas Morning News* a few years later. "But I've never been one to dwell on why they really did it." A year later, Reinsdorf would underscore the random nature of the decision when he put his White Sox on the superstation WGN. "That was something, wasn't it?" said Gaylord. "And that's just like him, too."

About a week later, on March 17, George W. signed the purchasing agreement. They held a press conference the next day—even before the owners' group had voted on the transfer—to make the announcement. The only names officially associated with the effort were George W. and Rose. Gaylord was still on board though, won over by George W.'s personal appeal. The press was aware that George W.'s financial contribution was lower than the other investors, however. When he was asked why he had been made general partner even when his contribution had been so small, he snapped back, "Because I put the deal together. I thought of it, worked it, and I was the one Eddie wanted to sell to."

The statement seemed strange. Of course he deserved some credit, but full credit? Even he had previously acknowledged that the original idea came from DeWitt, that Ueberroth had been the architect who united him with Rainwater and Rose, and that it would be a travesty if the team wasn't sold to Gaylord.

The boast also belied the physical reality of a melancholy Eddie Chiles, who attended the press conference with his wife. He watched from the sidelines as reporters hailed the new chiefs, wearing his Texas Rangers cap long after the new owners took off theirs. "They rejected my friend Ed Gaylord, who is a perfect man for the job," Chiles said. "They didn't have any good reason for doing it, but they did it anyway." He added: "Next to getting Mr. Gaylord [the sale to the Bush-Rose group] is the finest solution that could be made."

Years later, Peter Ueberroth would also try to correct the misconception that George W. had single-handedly crafted the deal. "George W. Bush deserves great credit for the development of the franchise," he told the *New York Times*. "However, the bringing together of the buying group was the result of Richard Rainwater, Rusty Rose, Dr. Bobby Brown, and the commissioner."

It would seem that George W. had once again missed the presence of the carpetlayers in his life, that as he careened through his career he had failed to notice the people smoothing his way. Perhaps with the press arrayed before him, the camera lenses focused, the reporters' pens hovering over the blank pages of their notebooks, he had sensed that he—a man who had been browbeaten out of boasting by his family—might be ready for some recognition. His father rarely bragged, but then he didn't have to. Everybody in the world seemed hell-bent on blowing his horn for him. He had achieved distinctions that bore precise titles: Distinguished Flying Cross, Phi Beta Kappa, team captain, one of the Five Outstanding Young Texans, congressman, and on and on, right up to president.

George W.'s accomplishments were harder to define: He could only list head cheerleader, fraternity president, and first lieutenant, a commission that would forever be marred by the fact that he received the promotion on his father's 1970 election day. What kind of awards were handed out for fun guy, loyal friend, good old boy, caring neighbor? You couldn't run on those resumé lines. With his boast about the Rangers' financing, George W. frankly seemed to have lost his head, and because everybody around him liked him so much as a guy, they started to believe that version of events too. Until the claim became scripture: George W. put the Rangers deal together.

"For those who believe I'm from a pampered lot and have been handed everything, I will never win their vote," George W. said after a month's reflection. "That's one of the problems with being the son of George Bush. But open-minded people will realize the Rangers deal was not an easy thing to put together, nor was it easy to organize my father's campaign."

—

Peter Ueberroth stepped down as Commissioner on April 1. He was replaced by A. Bartlett Giamatti, the head of the National League and before that, the popular president of Yale. The selection of successor was made almost a year earlier and Giamatti had gradually been acclimated to the business of Major League Baseball. He brought over one of his best friends, corporate powerhouse Fay Vincent, as the second in command—the same man who had worked as a roustabout for George Bush's oil company and who had put in money in Arbusto when it was first launched.

On April 18, the owners approved the Bush and Rose group by

conference call and George W. Bush officially became a partner in the
ownership of the team and a managing general partner.

The total cost was $75 million for 86 percent of the team, with the
only partners officially named at that time being George W., Rose,
Rainwater, and DeWitt. The rest were silent partners, a status until
then never used in sports franchises. Those unidentified figures held
the right to fire George W. and Rose. "I have nothing to hide," George
W. told the press, which wondered about the oddity of power resid-
ing in the hands of mystery owners. "I am not ashamed of any of these
people in the group. . . . We wouldn't have been approved if there were
any doubts about them." He would go on to provide a more complete
list in early June.

Perhaps one of the reasons for not identifying the partners right
away was the fact that Roland Betts was apparently the largest individual investor by a slight fraction. Ueberroth had insisted in February
that no investor from outside Texas could contribute more than the
largest in-state investor.

The financing as listed in a document provided in discovery for the
Morsani and Mack lawsuit included $2.5 million from Rainwater; $6
million from Silver Screen management, the company owned by Betts
and Bernstein; and $10 million from the Airlie Group, "a new part-
nership founded by Richard Rainwater but now to be run under the
direction of Morton Myerson of Dallas and Dort Cameron of
Connecticut." Meyerson was listed as a general partner along with
George W. and Rose. Some Bass family members also signed on.

George W. borrowed his $500,000 contribution from the United
Bank of Midland, where he had previously served as director. Later
he would invest a bit more to bring his share to $606,302 or 1.8 percent
of the team.

Thomas Schieffer, one of the investors that George W. brought
aboard, believed that his outreach was intended to make the ball club
more representative of the community after the reign of Eddie "I'm
Still Mad" Chiles. Schieffer had worked as an aide to Governor John
Connally when he was in college, been elected to the state legislature
in 1972 as a Democrat, and had worked for the Mondale campaign in
the previous election cycle. George W. brought aboard Comer
Cottrell, the CEO of a hair product company named Pro-Line Corp.,

the biggest minority-owned business in the area, and a contributor to his father's campaign. Cottrell at first told him that he didn't have the money to invest, but George W. told him that was no problem. Later George W. would say that Cottrell was the first black owner in any Major League partnership, although the publicity director of Major League Baseball disputed the assertion.

The Bush family put its promotional talents to work for George W.'s team. In early May, Bar flew down to throw out the first pitch in Arlington. She wore a Rangers jacket and brought her granddaughters a puppy to be named "Rangerette," in an echo of Uncle Herbie's tradition.

George W. was pleased by her theatrics. "I've just noticed that there's a little more showmanship in Mother, and that she's good at it," George W. told the First Lady's biographer about her appearance at the stadium. The following month, President Bush advised his granddaughter, Barbara, to christen the dog Spot Fletcher, after her favorite player, shortstop Scott Fletcher.

That was one of the family's great skills. When the press asked George W.'s partners which of his assets was most valuable, Rose said "star quality." Rainwater tipped his hat to George W.'s great public relations sense, including his insistence that the president wear a Rangers cap on a Maine fishing trip. The Rangers president, Mike Stone, said he appreciated the public relations tie to the White House.

—

The weekend after George W. held the press conference about his group's purchasing intent, he got back on track considering the governor's race. He went to Austin for a series of policy briefings on everything from taxes to prisons. "He wants a campaign based around new ideas," said Karl Rove, "and by the end of the weekend there was a list of sixty-eight policy proposals and new ideas that came out of those brainstorming sessions."

Betts—who put the biggest stake into the Rangers, with $3.63 million—said that he had only signed on to the Rangers deal on the stipulation that George W. not run, according to the *Dallas Observer*. "If you're gonna run for office now, then I'm not going to do this," he recalled telling his friend. "Build the Rangers. Build a stadium. It's gonna be a showstopper. Then you run."

But his friend began to appear more regularly in the press, even submitting to a feature article in April in *Texas Monthly* talking about his campaign. "If I run, I'll be most electable. Absolutely. No question in my mind," he said. "In a big media state like Texas, name identification is important. I've got it."

When asked about his attraction to politics, he brought up the big picture. "I want to affect the lives of people," he told the magazine. "I want to make life better. I think politics is an arena where you can do that."

Then Bar stepped in—the person who could quash his dreams quicker than anyone in the world. Hailed as one of the most popular women in America at the time, she had other ideas for her eldest son. Over a White House luncheon of salmon, veal, and honey ice cream with strawberries, she saw fit to put down George W.'s uppity desire to run, saying to a Texas reporter that she thought he should concentrate on baseball for the time being.

Apparently George W. was furious. "Mother's worried about my daddy's campaign affecting my race," he said. "Thank you very much. You've been giving me advice forty-two years, most of which I haven't taken."

A little later, he softened. "I love my mother, and I appreciate her advice, but that's all it is, advice. . . . I view this as an expression of love and worry and concern about her little boy." Still, the damage was done. How could he attempt to launch a campaign as an unproved talent when even his own mother—the beloved matriarch—thought he was too green? He tried to put on a brave face. "I don't know what I'm going to do yet," he said.

He had always struggled with Bar's sharp-tongued quality. "My mother's always been a very outspoken person who vents very well," he told the First Lady's biographer. "She'll just let it rip if she's got something on her mind. Once it's over, you know exactly where you stand and that's it. She doesn't dwell on it or hound you or anything like that." But this time, her candid nature had its effects.

George W. held on to the possibility of running through the rest of the spring, still not ending speculation. He emphasized his dominion over his wife and children. "When I figure out what is best for my family," he said referring to whether or not he would enter the campaign officially, "I'll let them know."

In August, he ended the speculation, saying that he had decided not to pursue the governorship and instead to concentrate on the Rangers and his family. He told the press that he had not consulted with his parents about the decision. "I'm sure [my mother] will be happy," he acknowledged.

Luckily, for George W., the Rangers started the new season with the best record in the team's history. In August, when Nolan Ryan struck out his five-thousandth batter, George W. sat in what would become his seat for every game played in Arlington during his tenure, alongside the home team dugout. He chatted with Giamatti, who had flown down for the occasion, and spat his chewing tobacco into a hole he had dug in the ground in front of him. Every time Ryan got to two strikes on a batter and hurled the ball toward the plate for the third, the whole stadium would go bright white with the camera flashes anticipating that historic moment. Then, at 8:51 P.M. the batter swung for the third strike and the stadium went wild. President Bush had taped a congratulations, which aired on the JumboTron, and up in Kennebunkport, where the satellite frequency had been switched to pick up the game, his father celebrated for George W. This was the glory of the game.

George W. considered the new venture his best potential political asset for a race down the road. Sure, he wanted to make money, and he loved the sport. But he acknowledged the power of his new enterprise. "The job has very high visibility, which cures the political problem I'd have: 'What has the boy done?'" Bush told the press. "Well, I'm the businessman who came to town and, at the very minimum, kept the Rangers from moving out."

XII

THE PRESIDENT'S ENFORCER

B y the time the 1992 presidential campaign rolled around, George W. had created a full life for himself down in Texas. He owned a respectable home in a neighborhood of elaborate estates in North Dallas. His twins were now active eleven-year-olds. He and Laura helped local charities with his celebrity presence, and most importantly, he was running the Texas Rangers for a $200,000 salary, plus the money made as a partner. In George W.'s few years of ownership, his group pushed through the financing for a gorgeous stadium in Arlington that would, when it was built in 1993, boast real grass and a suite of executive offices set into the middle rows so that all a Texas Rangers employee need do was swivel his or her chair around and gaze out the plate glass windows at the boys warming up for a game to be reminded why baseball was beautiful.

But before the franchise built to that bucolic climax, George W. experienced some of the tumult that comes from playing in the higher levels of power, and he became even tougher than he had been in the past. Before his father actually announced his intention to seek reelection in 1992, he enjoyed the enormous prestige and perks of the presidency, but he witnessed the downside of governing too, the media attacks and internal scuffles that were part of occupying the highest office in the land. Instead of letting the ugliness glance off of him without wounding, President George Bush seemed unable to avoid a certain disillusionment.

Some observers would say that George Bush got hurt exactly because he felt most comfortable as a follower rather than a leader, and under the press barrage, he lost his bearings. "He always placated his father," Ray Walker, his cousin and a psychoanalyst, told the *Los Angeles Times* when George Bush was first seeking the White House. "Then, later on, he placated his bosses. That is how he relates—by never defining himself against authority."

"If you have a history of deferring to somebody up the line," continued Walker, "of saying, I'm not really free to have my own moral position—that's not going to change when you become president. . . ." He went on to say that he expected Bush to govern by opinion polls or be led by strong advisers.

George Bush didn't exactly live by opinion polls, as his successor Bill Clinton would, but he did trust too much in their strength. When he soared to the heights of national popularity on the heels of the Persian Gulf War, he seemed to believe that the buoyancy would last forever. "The big lesson I learned in 1992 is that you can't rest on your laurels and hope the voters will reelect you out of gratitude," George W. told the *New York Times* two years later, when he was running for governor of Texas. "That doesn't work. Incumbents have to project into the future, offer a fresh vision. My father didn't do it, and [Ann Richards] hasn't either."

George W. would never have been able to offer that kind of critique of his father in earlier decades. Back then, he loved him almost blindly. Although his adoration for his dad did not diminish during the 1992 campaign, he witnessed, in his daily contact with Chief of Staff Jim Baker and on the trail, certain frailties in his father's leadership: an inability to take command of his campaign staff, a lack of bold ideas, an absence of a fire to win.

For the first time, the fact that George Bush enjoyed a reputation as the kindest, most gentlemanly politician in Washington did not greatly matter. The presidency was not a reward for good service, but a job for which the voters hired the man or woman who could best solve their problems and change their lives. Even George W. could see that his father had failed to make the case that he was the person who wanted to do the work. George W. himself wanted another term for his father, not because of a fierce ideological belief, but because he revered his dad. Once, when asked how he was able to have a close friendship with a Democratic friend and business partner, he reportedly explained, "I'm not a highly partisan person, but I'm a fierce warrior when it comes to my father. I'm in it for love, not power. That gives you a different perspective."

As to Walker's prediction that George Bush would need to be led by strong advisers, George W. became one of his father's toughest allies. He was called to deliver tough messages to the staff, stump through Texas, and try to infuse competitive passion into his father in the waning days of the campaign. He became the president's enforcer—the ego that his father lacked and the energy his father needed. "He's a credible individual in his own right, but he's also a solid salesman for his father," Ernie Angelo, the Midland resident who was at that time the National Republican Committee member from Texas, told the *New York Times*. "He has as good a feel for the issues as anybody on the campaign. In fact, I wish he was running the campaign."

Simultaneously, in 1992, another good man long connected with the family, Fay Vincent, was under fire. As the commissioner of baseball, he absorbed the fury of the owners' group over the escalating franchise budgets caused by collective bargaining. The attacks on both Vincent and George Bush crescendoed almost at the same time in the early fall, and George W. was faced with the pain of watching them both be brought down as he stood by, helpless to save these people he loved. He fought to the end for Vincent, even after the commissioner had been given a vote of no confidence by the owners' group. For his father, he tried his best to direct the reelection effort, but he couldn't rescue him from defeat on election night. Instead, he would have to redeem his father's reputation by running his own taut campaign for governor two years later. Horrifying as it was to admit, George W. probably realized that he might not be as good as his father at baseball, academics, or the oil business, but he was a better politician—the thing George Bush cared about most.

—

For a time, George W. found baseball to be an almost idyllic business. After the deal went through in the spring of 1989, he spent his workdays on the phones at his cluttered North Dallas office with its simple "GWB" on the door, arranging tickets for friends (almost never for free, they would find) and taking calls from the Oval Office. Whenever there was a home game, he would slip on his Rangers jacket and drive the half hour to the stadium at Arlington. He would chat up the ticket takers, greet the ushers by name. Every few feet a fan would wave him down, to give him a bit of advice on a proposed trade or accept a compliment. "Why, you're just as pretty as your mother," George W. might say to a young fan.

Then he would stroll to section 109, row 1, seat 8, which was nestled against the dugout. Maybe he would bring Jenna or Barbara along for some father-daughter time. It would be like those special sessions that he had with his old man which his father dubbed "Lad and Dad." George W. would get the bat boy to bring over a bag of sunflower seeds for snacking. He was a showman, demonstrating for the public how much fun could be had at a Rangers game. "Folks see me sitting in the same seat they sit in," he observed somewhat indelicately to the press, "eating the same popcorn, peeing in the same urinal." The folks would be compelled to buy season tickets too.

Nolan Ryan, a baseball legend who had been playing since 1968 and was a friend of George W.'s father, would come out of the dugout and lean against the wall to joke around with George W. until the game started. Tom Schieffer, one of the partners, and Rusty Rose, the other managing partner, would be at the stadium too, and the three men often congratulated each other on how great it was that grown fans could get paid to regularly watch nine innings.

There would be so many magical nights out at the stadium. One steamy Texas evening, George W. hosted baseball commissioner Fay Vincent and the game went into extra innings. Vincent was starting to feel the strain of so much time out in that simmering heat. Palmeiro was coming up to bat. So George W. called him over. "The commissioner is really tired," he said. "Will you get us the hell out of here."

"I'm going to try," Palmeiro answered, laughing. He went up and hit a homer and ended the game.

George W.'s work in the back office was soaring too. Tom Grieve, the vice president and general manager, assessed George W.'s skills. Reportedly, he said, "He's high-strung to the point where you'd worry about his being impulsive and making snap judgments," Grieve said.

"But after you get to know him, you realize it's just a high energy level. He's a solid businessman with long-term goals for the team. He's very calm—and not prone to panic."

The business of baseball was certainly on the right track, since the owners were assured of the franchise's growth by their plans to build a new stadium. Even before the purchase of the Rangers was completed, George W.'s group had been wooed by officials in both Arlington and Dallas to construct a more modern facility in their cities. The group knew even before the paperwork was signed that the team could never be profitable in the old Arlington stadium. Most of the seats were located in the outfield, on hard benches that could try the patience of any fan. The owners needed to build a new venue, with better high-priced seating and easier commuter access from nearby Dallas and Fort Worth.

George W. proved his political brilliance, even in the business world, by taking steps that assured the successful creation of the stadium and protected him from future criticism. He had laid the foundation by stocking his investor team with powerful people of all persuasions, including Democrats and minorities. Because every interest group was represented, critics wouldn't be able to claim that a particular clique had been granted special favors when the inevitable public-private partnership was forged for financing the construction.

Although that diversity was a plus in dodging attackers, George W. must have recognized the benefit of putting another partner into the lead on making the major stadium decisions. George W. could not afford the political fallout if any of his choices smelled of conflict of interest, payoff, or just failure, so he appointed Tom Schieffer stadium czar. With Schieffer guiding the project, George W. could claim credit for helping to build the grand new facility, but avoid heavy fire if the project fell into enemy territory. At first Schieffer was unenthusiastic about the idea of taking on the task. Although he had enough savvy to organize large Democratic events in the past, he doubted that putting together the stadium effort would be a pleasant experience. His wife finally convinced him to take on the challenge. "You have the opportunity to build a baseball stadium and you're going to turn it down?" she demanded incredulously. He agreed to be the point man.

The group took another precaution to blunt criticism about how they handled proposals from different cities. George W. no doubt understood how destructive intercity rivalries could be from his 1978 campaign in West Texas, when the Midland and Odessa antagonism spilled far beyond the confines of football games. When choosing the stadium site, George W.'s group didn't immediately rule out Dallas, nor did they really dally with any suitor other than Arlington. Although Dallas officials suggested that they would put up a bid, George W.'s team did not greatly excite their hopes.

Mayor Richard Greene of Arlington presented his proposal in March 1989, entitled "Arlington Forever," which set out the case—including evidence of $50 million in annual revenues generated by the ballpark—for why the Rangers should always call his city home. Later, Greene said that Arlington was willing to build a $102.5 million stadium for the team. Rather than using that proposal as a bargaining chip with Dallas, George W.'s group remained quiet about its plans. The Dallas city council would never be able to complain that they had been toyed with or used, and fans would feel little disappointment when the team simply chose to stay in its current home city.

George W. and his group realized that raising the money to build the stadium through tax dollars required a vote to build consensus. He must have recognized that he would suffer in the future if a half-cent tax increase was ramrodded through without strong public support. He had learned his lesson from his father's vow of "No new taxes" at the 1988 convention and the subsequent uproar two years later when he agreed to an increase to help address the federal deficit: Tax hikes could be lethal for a politician. George W.'s group asked the city's residents to vote on a special referendum. Voters turned out in record numbers and the tax increase passed in January 1991 by two to one.

Finally, the deal itself was masterful in that the city covered the bulk of the construction bill, yet George W.'s group could eventually own the stadium for the price they paid to lease the property. The final agreement stated that the Rangers would stay in Arlington if the city kicked in $135 million for construction. George W.'s group would pay the extra $30 million, but none of that money would come directly out of their pockets. They would take a loan for part of the cost and raise the rest through a $1 increase in ticket prices. Better still for the partners, they could purchase the stadium, 12 years after the deal was inked, for $60 million. As it was, they paid the city $5 million per year for leasing, and that money could be applied to the purchasing cost. That meant that by the end of the 12 years, George W.'s group could acquire the stadium for nothing.

More importantly, for George W. in the future, the decision to go ahead with the project was speeded up past the original timetable, thus making the stadium a useful campaign asset for George W. in 1994.

—

For a man who started in the West Texas oil business with nothing but the remains of an educational trust fund to invest, the scale of the deals George W. was now associated with were shockingly large. Harken Energy Corporation—where George W. was still an investor, director, and consultant—had also drastically increased its area of influence. On January 30, 1990, Harken won a potentially lucrative offshore drilling contract near the island nation of Bahrain in the Persian Gulf. The site was cradled between the world's largest oil field in Saudi Arabia and the world's largest natural gas field off the shore of Quatar.

The deal had come together somewhat capriciously. In April 1989, a representative of the Bahrain government was looking for a company to lease their offshore oil rights. According to *Time,* they had "suddenly and mysteriously broke[n] off promising talks with Amoco." The Bahraini official telephoned 66-year-old Michael Ameen, a veteran of Mobil's ventures in the Middle East, a U.S. citizen, and allegedly a man who worked for the CIA, for advice. The Bahraini official told Ameen, then retired from the oil business but working as a consultant to the U.S. State Department, that the Bahraini government was looking for a boutique company that would consider the country's offshore oil fields its biggest enterprise. Reportedly, Ameen said he was stumped as to whom to suggest for a candidate.

Coincidentally, the next call Ameen took was from David Edwards, a Little Rock banker who had recently started his own investment firm after departing the massive Arkansas securities company, Stephens Inc. In 1987, when Edwards was still at Stephens, he had worked with Harken in putting together a large foreign investment to buoy the Texas company. George W. and Paul Rea had gone down to see bank president Jackson Stephens to talk about financial assistance during a time that Harken was going through a bad spell.

Stephens put together a plan where the United Bank of Switzerland (UBS), an institution that didn't usually do business with U.S. companies, would invest $25 million in Harken in exchange for a portion of the company's stock. As it turned out, UBS was tied to the Bank of Credit and Commerce International (BCCI), the "criminal enterprise," as Manhattan District Attorney Robert Morgenthau later termed it, that tried to illegally take over First American Bank in Washington, D.C., using Middle Eastern money. At the very least, the top officials of BCCI tried to gain influence over the most powerful individuals in the United States by financing many of their business deals. The bank had numerous ties to former members of the CIA, and some investigators came to believe that the institution was a money-laundering operation for the agency.

David Edwards—who, coincidentally (in the small world of politics), was a friend of Bill Clinton—and his brother Michael had been the main contacts for Harken during the transactions with UBS. The loan from the Swiss bank appeared to help Harken a great deal; the company's revenues went from $4 million in 1986 to a staggering $747 million in 1988. In the year the loan went through, Harken paid $36 million for a chain of gas station and convenience stores called E-Z Serve; at that point the chain looked like a good investment, although it would end up draining Harken. Still, after the first half of 1989, Harken management projected annual revenues of $1 billion, and George W. had become the third-largest insider stockholder through stock options and low-interest loans that the company extended to him. Clearly, the UBS influx of cash was just what the company had needed. Now, Edwards recommended Harken to Michael Ameen as the company that could take on the drilling deal in Bahrain.

According to the major players in the deal, Harken officials reportedly won over the Bahraini government by putting on a geological presentation that meticulously analyzed the region's mineral assets—Harken proved to the Bahrainis that the Texas company would make up for its small size and lack of experience by diligently doing its homework. The Bahrain government officials said they felt reassured that the Texas company would consider their licensing its biggest deal, and gave them the contract. In January 1990, Harken signed the drilling lease with Bahrain. After news of the agreement came out, industry analysts registered surprise that such a small company could secure a deal of this magnitude. Skeptics wondered if Bahrain's motive in choosing Harken was simply to please the president of the United States, whose son was the company's largest insider stockholder.

While such a suggestion was dismissed at the time by George W.'s friends and Harken officials as foolish and insulting to the Bahrainis, historically, the Bushes' relationship with the Bahraini government had been unusually friendly. In 1986, Bahrain sent the Reagans a mere four dozen roses, but the Bahraini officials showered the Bushes with a full $83,000 worth of gifts—over 70 percent of the total value of presents the Bushes received that year from all other world leaders combined. As reported in a 1987 article in the *Washington Post*, Amir bin Sulman al-Kalifa gave Bar a $40,000 18-karat gold Audemars Piquedt diamond watch; a Vacheron & Constantine watch worth $2,500; an 18-karat gold choker, a gold diamond ring, gold earrings, and gold bracelet worth $22,200. Crown Prince Hamed bin Isa al-Kalifa bestowed a turquoise and pearl necklace worth $9,500. George Bush received fewer offerings, but still benefited from Bahrain's largesse. The amir sent the vice president a $15,150 18-karat Rolex presidential diamond dial watch, diamond ballpoint pens, and gold and diamond cuff links. Those more elaborate gifts were forwarded on to the General Services Administration, where they were either sold or sent on to the Smithsonian. But George Bush did keep a $3,000 silver and gold box for the vice presidential home.

The month that George Bush received those gifts he spent 10 days on a trip to Saudi Arabia, Oman, North Yemen, and Bahrain to talk about strategic, military, and commercial issues related to the Iran and Iraq war, which had begun to threaten the interests of those neighboring countries. But George Bush also said that he wanted to talk about how to "stabilize" global oil prices to protect U.S. interests. That remark triggered national confusion in the United States, since the official economic policy of the Reagan administration was to allow the free market to set its own course. Government officials and industry experts grew alarmed that Bush seemed to be implying that he hoped for price fixing.

Bush eventually clarified that he would not actually ask for oil prices to be set at a particular level, but he would urge the oil producers of the Middle East to avoid a "free fall." An administration official told *Platt's Oilgram News* at the time, "Texas is screaming," and all George Bush would have to do is pick up the phone and talk to his son in Midland—who at the time, was scrambling to find a savior for Spectrum 7—to be sure of the terror in the state.

On that trip in April 1986, George Bush met with Sheik Isa Bin Salman al Khalifa of Bahrain to discuss Iran. "We don't want to see Iran shift the balance of power in the area, nor threaten any of the countries of the GCC [Gulf Cooperation Council]," he told the *Chicago Tribune*. The small countries of the area had become worried that fighting would spread to Kuwait after Iran attacked Iraq's Faw Peninsula. Bush disclosed that the United States was pursuing a new plan for peace in the region but that he was "not at liberty" to provide details. Bahrain offered to act as a mediator between Iran and Iraq. Later, stories would surface that the United States was shipping arms to Bahrain.

Although George W.'s name was probably not the only factor that secured the deal in Bahrain, it is hard to believe that his family connections did not help him, given the excessive displays of generosity the Bahraini government had shown to his father just four years earlier. George W. and Harken officials later insisted that George W. opposed the idea of drilling in Bahrain from the first, and there is no reason to doubt that account is true. He knew his way around offshore drilling—his father was a pioneer in the industry, creating the first offshore well in Kuwait's waters—and he didn't think Harken was up to the challenge, since the company had never drilled offshore or internationally. The work was complicated: The drilling would take place 13,000 to 20,000 feet under the ocean. According to the agreement, Harken would have to drill six wells in three years.

Geologically, the site looked unbeatable—cradled as it was between the richest oil reserves in the world. But Harken knew that a dry hole had recently been drilled on adjacent territory, which was never a good sign. Still despite these harbingers of trouble, the company had weighed the risks against the potential for unprecedented profit, and Harken had gone ahead and made the deal. The company planned to start drilling in October 1990.

By the summer, that plan was threatened by the increasing tensions in the Gulf. In order "to earn all of the acreage rights under the agreement," Harken was required to drill an exploratory well within two years of signing, making the last buzzer January 1992. With Saddam Hussein threatening war, the deadline posed a problem. Harken's only protection if battle began was a U.S. military presence in tiny Bahrain. Luckily, an agreement between the United States and Bahrain allowing permanent American and multinational military bases there was signed the same year that the contract was inked.

The other major problem was that Harken itself didn't have enough money to finance the drilling. But as soon as they had the contract in hand, the company went looking for investors to put up the almost $13 million to drill the first well. Paul Rea took some investors from Midland out to the site, but they were not persuaded. Eventually a number of potential investors came forward, and from them Harken chose Bass Enterprises Production Company, which certainly was suitable, since it was one of the largest investment companies in the country. George W. also was tangentially connected to the Basses since Richard Rainwater, George W.'s partner and one of the biggest investors in the Rangers at the time, was the financial adviser who had multiplied the Basses' fortune many times over for them. With new consideration for the hostilities in the region, the group moved their target date and planned to drill the first hole in early 1991.

Most investors would perceive the fact that the Basses were backing the Bahrain expedition as good news, but inside the company, the overall picture wasn't as rosy. That fact would play into media criticism of George W. in later years, when critics would contend that he knew about the trouble and used the information for insider trading. Once Harken had the big Bahrain deal, the company decided to restructure its operations into three parts: gasoline retail, natural gas pipelines construction, and drilling contracts. For the time being, shareholders would only be able to purchase rights to retail and pipelines. The drilling contracts would be offered later. That spring, George W. sat on a three-member "fairness committee" intended to monitor whether the company's restructuring would hurt stockholders, a position that reportedly gave him access to detailed reports of the ailing financial condition. Advisers from Smith Barney, Harris Upham & Company had warned the committee that only radical action could save the company, which, despite its revenues, was showing large debt. In May 1990, the committee met for the first time.

A month later, in June, a Los Angeles broker named Ralph Smith from Sutro and Co. tried to buy Harken stock. He approached a couple of the company's officers but only George W. took him up on the trade. Before George W. made the transaction, he consulted with a Harken lawyer on ethics to make sure the deal, if consummated, was above criticism. The deal was cleared and approved. "Listen, I was the president's son," George W. reportedly said. "I was very sensitive to the scrutiny. I felt like liquidating the stock for personal reasons, but I was also fully aware that any deal I did was going to be fully scrutinized."

On June 22, he liquefied $848,560 worth of his Harken stock—a total of two thirds of his interest—at $4 per share. This turned out to be an extremely fortuitous transaction; eight days later, the company showed a second-quarter loss of $6.7 million, but that news was not yet reported publicly.

A month later, the United Arab Emirates, located just slightly south of Bahrain, asked the United States for military help because of concern that they might need protection from Saddam Hussein of Iraq, whose saber rattling had intensified. On July 23, the United States posted two tankers and a cargo transport offshore to soothe that nation's anxieties. Eight days later, the *Washington Post* reported that large numbers of Iraqi troops had moved to the border of Kuwait—less than 200 miles north of Bahrain—an escalation of a territorial dispute that had grown increasingly volatile. After Iraq invaded Kuwait on August 2, the price of oil in the United States shot up. But the official report of Harken's net loss came out on August 22, causing the price of their stock to drop to $2.37 a share. The price would not bounce back to $4 until June of 1991. In all ways, the timing of George W.'s sale of stock had been lucky.

That transaction bothered George W.'s critics, coming as it did just days before officials in the company became aware of the significance

of the company's losses. George W. protested that he had known nothing about the bad news and instead thought he had sold into the good
news that the Basses were investing in the Bahrain drilling. (Of course,
he had also claimed he considered the overseas offshore drilling deal a
bad idea, so he might have predicted that the Bahrain deal was not
altogether good news.) He had wanted to pay back the $500,000 loan
that he had taken out from United Bank of Midland to buy the
Rangers. "I didn't need to pay it off," George W. told the *Washington
Post*. "I did it because I just don't like to carry debt."

Critics would later say that George W. hadn't filed the appropriate
paperwork, implying that he had disguised the timing of the sale. In
fact, he had filed a form announcing his intention to sell, but the
Securities and Exchange Commission could not find a separate form
for use by a company's internal sellers until March of 1991. George
W. claimed he had filed the paperwork, and the SEC ultimately decided to stop its investigation.

On January 16, 1991, at 7:00 P.M. EST, the United States launched
Operation Desert Storm, its 38-day air and ground war against Iraq.
That night George W. was among the first to call his father to offer his
support.

Bahrain had required in its agreement with Harken that the first
well be drilled by January 1992. The rest of the company seemed in
utter disarray. "Their annual reports and press releases get me totally
befuddled," Phil Kendrick, a founder of the company and at the time a
small shareholder, told *Time* in October 1991. "There's been so much
promotion, manipulation, and inside deal making. It's been a fast-
numbers game." Just a few months short of the deadline, Harken's
engineers put down its first exploratory pipe near the Jarim Reef off
the coast of Bahrain. The stock price shot up to $8 and hovered there—
until the news came out that the well was a dud. George W. had been
right about the outcome of the Bahrain project, but still he had prof-
ited with his early stock transaction.

—

As for George Bush, the adulation that surrounded him during the
Gulf War would slowly but surely quiet to a grumble of discontent.
Even Richard Nixon could see the collapse coming. According to

Quest for the Presidency 1992, an annal of that campaign written by a group of *Newsweek* reporters, Nixon told a young friend in the spring of 1991 that George Bush's chances were doomed. "Bush will be defeated when he comes up for reelection," he reportedly observed to the friend. "Popularity from foreign-policy accomplishments is fleeting. If the economy is bad in the fall, he will be defeated—and the economy *will* be bad."

But in early 1991, George Bush held at the heights of an 89 percent approval rating—a demonstration not only of Americans' ability to pull together in support of their leader during times of military crisis, but also a clear acknowledgment that the voters admired George Bush's handling of foreign affairs. Coincidentally, global diplomacy and military matters were exactly the part of being president that George Bush enjoyed the most.

While George Bush was pleased by the response of average Americans to the war, he was irate that the media did not even fully allow him that moment of glory. Pundits lambasted him for not taking the war to its full conclusion—driving Saddam Hussein from power—and George Bush hated them for their criticism. On March 13, 1991, he dictated to his diary a description of the commentary he'd received at the hands of the fourth estate: the "sniping, carping, bitching, predictable editorial complaints."

That bitterness toward the press was greatly out of proportion to the Bushes' attitudes toward other attackers, particularly political opponents. The family was expert at making their journeys through some of the darkest corridors of ego, greed, betrayal, and sabotage seem nothing but blissful. They loved to come off as benign and victimized, and could hide well the Machiavellian schemes that were being acted out by them behind the scenes or on their behalf. They never liked to acknowledge that politics could be an ugly business. Publicly, the only real punching bag for their frustrations was the press, which they usually viewed as antagonistic.

"Sometimes I really like the spotlight," George Bush dictated to the diary, "but I'm tired of it. I've been at the head table for many years, and now I wonder what else is out there."

Unlike some other politicians who could brush off negative criticism, George Bush would take the wounds personally. That's why it was surprising that he reentered the political ring again and again. He always would insist that "public service" drove him into politics, that he felt a need to give back because he'd been granted so many advantages. Frequently, his friends and supporters complained that the media's inability to understand that notion was a symptom of its own cynicism. But the obvious retort was that one can easily serve the public through anonymous endeavors without launching a multimillion-dollar popularity campaign to rise to the post of commander in chief. Unlike Eisenhower or Goldwater, George Bush was not drafted into the campaign. He was not begged to run, he chose to. He was not driven to seek higher office by any strongly held political belief. In the past, he had seemed driven by a need to be "best boy" because he would receive acclaim for being on top, without ever violating his mother's admonition not to brag—others would announce his accomplishments for him.

He also had that famous Bush energy to work off, and nothing so consistently absorbed that freneticism than politicking and governing. But at age 67, with the Gulf War ended, he felt something like lethargy. He had begun losing weight and had trouble sleeping. "I don't know whether it's the anticlimax or that I'm too tired to enjoy anything, but I just seem to be losing my perspective," he dictated to his diary. On March 18, 1991, he recorded: "For some reason, my whole body is dragging and I'm tired. I don't understand it." He went for a checkup at the hospital in Bethesda and the doctors found nothing wrong. But in early May 1991, after experiencing shortness of breath while jogging, George Bush was rushed to the hospital and ultimately diagnosed with Graves' disease—a malfunction of the thyroid. Although the doctors treated the disease with medication, George Bush seemed drained of his usual vigor.

For his staff, the blush of popularity following the war had been intoxicating, but instead of capitalizing on the good feeling by pushing an agenda forward, they virtually froze. "We were so spoiled by the adulation that we lost perspective," said Ron Kaufman, the White House political liaison. The administration squandered its political capital.

Unfortunately, the 1992 campaign was doomed almost from the start by an untenable arrangement of egos, and George Bush had lost one of his most important advisers. In March 1990, Lee Atwater, who was then head of the Republican National Committee, was diagnosed with a brain tumor. His biggest fear, according to his biographer, John Brady, was that he would go from being one of George Bush's closest advisers to a nonentity; so immediately upon diagnosis he began working with Mary Matalin to put the spin on the story that the illness was merely a temporary hitch.

In July, George Bush and George W. went to visit Atwater at his home, according to Brady. "You know, I really thought that I might have an insecure relationship with President Bush," Atwater reportedly prayed into his tape recorder that night, "and I always worried about it. But look, Lord, you made sure that that was one of the strongest relationships I had. And what a way to find out."

In late February, as George Bush ended the Gulf War, Matalin called Atwater to wish him a happy fortieth birthday. According to Brady, Atwater told her that Bush and Sununu were up against a bad economy for the next election and didn't have a plan to deal with it. About a month later, on March 29, Atwater died of brain cancer at George Washington Hospital. So many of Bush's former staffers would talk about how Atwater might have saved them in 1992, shown them some campaign model from earlier in the century that would have fixed their path. They wondered if maybe he might have understood a way to diminish the impact of Ross Perot's third-party candidacy—the historic first of a presidential contender who did not need matching federal funds to compete.

Chief of Staff John Sununu did little to fill in the functions of that fallen Bush soldier. He had become distracted by his own political concerns. He always seemed to have had an almost a pathological need to say the wrong thing on national television. His attack on the service of Lloyd Bentsen's son in the Texas National Guard had been just one example in the way it had put George W. in an uncomfortable public position. Only two days into George Bush's presidency, Sununu had appeared on CBS's *Face the Nation* to talk about the White House's proposal to pare down the federal deficit, which soon would be delivered to Congress. He touted the fact that the plan included no new taxes. But then he hit the clanger. How long would that vow of no tax increases hold true? his interviewer asked him.

"As long as the climate of this country is appropriate for that commitment to stay in place," said Sununu, which suggested that George Bush's word was good, but only for the moment. It implied that the president would shift course at whim.

On the Hill, Sununu made few friends with his belligerent manner. The White House staffers found him hotheaded and domineering. Before long, the media had him in their crosshairs. In April 1991, the *Washington Post* and *U.S. News and World Report* uncovered the fact that he had taken an air force jet to Salt Lake City and then to Vail with two guests in December 1989; after three days, the plane flew back and picked them up, at a total taxpayer cost of $30,000. Sununu probably could have turned the incident into just a bit of political trivia if he had simply apologized and reimbursed the expense, but instead he decided to stonewall, asserting that there was nothing wrong with what he had done. The media began to dig and before long had burrowed deep enough to kick up $500,000 in trips. Sununu's only explanation was that he was abiding by a 1987 White House directive that had authorized the national security adviser and chief of staff to use military aircraft for transport so that they would always be in touch and protected.

By the end of that summer, the White House staff was petitioning George W. to join the anti-Sununu bandwagon. He demurred. "Sununu is loyal to George Bush and that counts for more than you think," he said, according to reporters from *Newsweek*.

The Sununu problem was in many ways typical of the Bush administration's propensity to isolate itself from the American public's real concerns. In fact, the White House staff seemed frequently unable to translate any understanding they had of the nation's worries into appropriate action or words. The imperiousness with which the chief of staff dealt with the travel issue seemed to confirm the suspicion of the average citizen that President Bush was alienated from their needs.

It was not that George Bush lacked compassion—nor did members of his family. He prided himself on visiting sick friends, writing notes to people he met along the campaign trail who needed a lift, offering transit on Air Force One to political colleagues—even Democrats. In terms of his political career, he had reached out to troubled constituencies over the course of his terms in office, listening to the concerns of war protesters although he might not have agreed with them, trying to bring more Latinos into the arena of Texas politics. But the truth was, for George Bush to be able to understand problems and offer compassion, he needed to actually *know*—however briefly—the people who had the worries. He never seemed particularly good at imagining suffering, and the voters seemed to sense that about him. He was better when confronted face-to-face with their struggles.

"I think George would be absolutely marvelous with the poor, don't you think?" his sister Nancy Ellis had asked her husband, Sandy, during a 1987 interview with the *Los Angeles Times*.

"Certainly, he cares in the religious sense," Sandy observed. "He knows it's right to have that concern. But I'm not sure what kind of *feeling* he has for the poor. It wouldn't be a priority for him. It wouldn't be where the resources go."

"Well, I didn't mean to say he'd be as dedicated as, say, Ted Kennedy," Nancy reportedly went on to remark. "But, really, he'd be marvelous."

People who live and work in the White House say that the place can be confining, both physically and mentally. Bill Clinton would later refer to it as a prison, and a former Reagan staffer spoke of how she didn't need a winter coat the entire time she worked there since she rarely went outside. Almost from the first days of George Bush's presidency, the white walls started to close in on him. As early as spring 1989, George W. started to notice his father's isolation. "He calls a lot," said George W. down in Dallas, "and lately I sense a little bit of a feeling that [he] feels a cocoon beginning to develop around him. He's always asking us to bring the girls to the White House, or to come to some state dinner, or to Camp David for the weekend. His family is how he stays in touch with reality."

If Sununu had been a more personable chief of staff, perhaps the Bush administration's alienation might have been lessened. But he tended to stop communication as it was headed into the Oval Office. He had his own strong political opinions that he used as a sieve for proposals. Staffers began complaining that nominations for key government posts were being sandbagged by the chief of staff. William Safire, the syndicated conservative columnist, stated the situation bluntly: "He is widely perceived to be a pompous ass . . . because he has repeatedly demonstrated arrogant asininity."

On Halloween, October 31, 1991, President Bush sent out a confidential letter to eight or ten people on his staff, including Sununu. The ostensible subject of the memo was how to approach the campaign as a whole in 1992, but the underlying issue he wanted to resolve was what to do about his chief of staff. "I have asked son George to very quietly make some soundings for me on 1992," he began. "I'd appreciate it if you'd visit with him on your innermost thoughts about how to best structure the campaign." He went on to assure each of the staffers that George W. would share his findings only with him.

The assignment proved that George W. was now a player in his father's eyes. "He had a different view of me, as a person who could perform," George W. reportedly said about his new stature. "He relied on me to do things."

Before George W. could get to Washington, he received calls from numerous staffers lobbying for Sununu's dismissal. According to reporters at *Newsweek*, Sununu finally lost George W. as a supporter by humiliating the president in full view of the press. The president had made a speech proposing various initiatives to help the American economy, including one suggestion that banks lower the penalties they charged credit-card holders when they were overdue on their payments. Wall Street was shaken by the offhand remark because the banks relied so heavily on those fines to make a profit. It was soon clear that the proposal needed to be retracted gracefully, and Chief of Staff Sununu took it upon himself to do the dirty work. But when he tried to push the matter aside, he only made the situation worse. "The president ad-libbed," he reportedly said in a dismissive tone—making it seem that when the president had an idea of his own, it was likely to be a bad one.

Clearly, Sununu had not only failed to dive on the grenade, he had practically thrown it into the president's face. This was the type of disloyalty that George Bush and his family abhorred, and it quickly brought out George W.'s rabid spirit. "We have a saying in our family," he said, according to the *Newsweek* reporters. "If a grenade is rolling by The Man, you dive on it first. The guy violated the cardinal rule."

George W. arrived in Washington two days before Thanksgiving, and a day before the president was scheduled to give a televised speech. The draft of the talk was loaded with more palliatives for the troubled

American workers. "I know people are hurting," the president was scripted to say repeatedly. "I'm thinking of you." Here was yet another sign that the staff had failed to understand the need for strong presidential action to address the sagging economy and alleviate fears. Instead the Bush administration was offering bromides to the American public.

Reportedly, Sununu was looking forward to meeting with George W., since he took the president's memo at its word—George Bush's son was sent to discuss restructuring the staff for 1992 and Sununu had his own ideas how to do that. But after 15 minutes of chitchat about the warm feelings that the Bush family had for Sununu, George W. finally said, "John, a lot of people are saying the problem is you." He suggested that the chief of staff go have a talk with the president about the issues of concern as he saw them and consider resigning.

George W. liked to say that he was instrumental in the firing of Sununu. There is no doubt his task was freighted with symbolism—he now was an agent of his father's will. "I was very happy for him," said Andy Card, Sununu's deputy. "It was a great testament to his relationship to his father. I felt it showed he had grown up, and it confirmed that I had grown up too."

For Sununu, George W.'s advice was less definitive. He had only taken the situation halfway to resolution.

For over a week, Sununu stayed on, submitting himself at staff meetings to President Bush's gibes about his bad relations with the staff and the Hill. When that teasing did not provoke a more frank discussion between Sununu and the president, George Bush privately turned to Card, a man respected for being loyal to both him and the chief of staff, to get his reading of the situation. "Well, Mr. President," Card said, according to Marlin Fitzwater's memoir, "right now there is a feeling he's worrying more about his own situation than about yours."

Sununu was scrambling to ensure his own survival. He decided that his only problem was that the staff members loyal to him had not yet spoken to the president. He lobbied them to push his cause, and some followed through over the weekend. On Monday, December 2, he contacted three of his closest supporters—Card, C. Boyden Gray, and Dorrance Smith—and urged them to go argue his case with the president. They went slinking down to the Oval Office and told the president why he should keep Sununu, the aide once affectionately dubbed "the deliveryman" for helping George Bush win the New Hampshire primary in 1988 when he had no hope of pulling through. The president listened to the whole argument. Then he asked the trio, What do you really think?

They told him they thought Sununu's problems were too distracting for him to do a good job.

So the president told them it was now their task to take that message back to Sununu. Card, as loyal friend and colleague to both the president and Sununu, was assigned to bear the message. Card ended up being the man to officially resolve the situation after George W. was long gone.

Sununu resigned the next morning, December 3, accompanied by the effusive praise of the president. George Bush, always the gentleman, could not fail to make Sununu the hero as he departed.

A 1992 account of the Sununu incident in the Texas magazine *D*, suggested that George W.'s role was much larger than it appeared in accounts given by key participants from the White House staff. The profile, apparently reported with the cooperation of George W., said that he had three weeks of conversations with Sununu, urging him to leave. George W. then, according to the article, declared the event one of the highlights of his life. "It's just not that often that you can do something really meaningful to help the president of the United States," he said.

There was something a bit unsavory about George W. gloating over his role in the dismissal of one of his father's key advisers, especially since most staffers agreed that Sununu had been so pivotal in even getting his father into the White House in the first place. Then, too, George W. had inflated his role once again—as he had in assessing the reasons for his success in the oil business and his skill at putting together the investors to buy the Texas Rangers. In this case, he exaggerated the impact that his words had on the chief of staff. Obviously, Sununu planned to seek second opinions after he met with George W. back in November of 1991, and he did. It was Andy Card who had been forced to do the dirty work.

—

By early 1992, George Bush showed a lead of 60 to 20 against his Republican rival Pat Buchanan in a direct match-up. That was the good news. The looming problem was the polltaker reportedly found that 36 percent of those voters were willing to cast protest votes against Bush. He had not shaken the perception that he was out of touch with the concerns of the average American, and Buchanan was slamming him in the press every opportunity he got.

One proclamation that Sununu had made early in the 1992 campaign season would prove to be a fateful warning. Watch out for Bill Clinton, he had said. He could see the Arkansas governor had that magic, that drive.

By January of 1992, George W. had acknowledged Clinton as the front-runner on the Democratic side, but suggested that the poll numbers might change after people "scrutinized his record." The Bush campaign, he said, wouldn't start to dissect Clinton until later in the year. As the primary season moved in March toward the state of Texas—where George Bush's Republican primary win was more meaningful for its home-turf resonance than its strategic importance— George W. acknowledged that the southern states would be a challenge in the general election if George Bush ended up facing Bill Clinton. He'd be the first Democrat since Carter who can "talk Texan," said George W.

In early April, Hillary Clinton tried to reverse all the damaging rumors that had circulated about her husband's womanizing. She told *Vanity Fair* magazine that Bush had always been protected by the establishment press and that his alleged affair was "apparently well-known in Washington." There would be no reply from the White House. Within days, President Bush reminded his staff to "stay out of the sleaze business."

A few days later, George W. arrived in Washington for another powwow and the press picked up on it, solidifying the eldest son's reputation as a political player. "He is one of his father's closest confidants and he keeps very close tabs on both the White House and the campaign," explained press secretary Torie Clarke. "He was here talking to and listening to all the key players and getting an outlook on the rest of the year." He also took in a Baltimore Orioles game with his dad. A few days later, his father was annoyed that the press thought he had been called to the White House to help sort through the campaign problems. He snapped at the suggestion. Perhaps the competition between father and son was veering in the other direction, with the father now jealous of George W.'s reputation as a tough strategist.

By June 1992, George W. had an easier spin on the relationship. "What I try to do is help him laugh and relax," he said. "I talk to him in terms no one else can. Talking about baseball is really good for him. It's important for the president to find proper outlets. But we also talk politics."

—

On April 25, 1992, George W. climbed onto a front-end loader and tore a strip of asphalt out of the old Arlington Stadium parking lot to symbolize the beginning of construction on the new home for the Texas Rangers. "That's not quite as straight as I wanted it," he said.

That quote, as simple as it was, epitomized what the press—particularly the sports press—came to love about George W.: He was able to approximate the behavior of a normal person even when cameras and tape recorders were trained on him. What he said for broadcast was pretty much what the average person would say if they were alone with good friends in the same situation. His commonness made him remarkable. Where another politician might have offered some bromide about a *new start*, or the *vision* they had for the place, George W. made a crack about his handiwork. That made for good television.

Most public figures answered questions with words that seemed like they'd been soaked in water overnight. In Texas, which was—as George W. himself pointed out—media saturated, his off-the-cuff quality was more valuable than money, intelligence, or good looks. In fact, all of America was obsessed with such people, those who could pretend that a hot light wasn't beaming into their eyes and a fuzzy microphone wasn't stuck under their chin, and just behave *candidly*. George W. could do that. He was used to the spotlight from a very early age; he was "a guy who never met a camera he didn't love," as he admitted to a reporter.

By the spring of 1992, George W. would have preferred that the focus shift away from him. The Texas Rangers was praised for being a well-managed business, with its low athlete salaries and a good attendance draw; of 102 professional sports franchises it was rated twenty-third for business success. But the situation on the field was gloomy, since baseball turned out to be an industry like any other, troubled now and then by greed, laziness, and backbiting.

Two years into owning the team, Eddie Chiles was asked if he ever had second thoughts about buying the Rangers. "Not only second, but third, fourth, and fifth," he reportedly said. "We have a saying in the oil business. I'm like that caught rat. I'm no longer interested in the cheese, I just want to get out of the trap." Blackie Sherrod, the legendary sportswriter for the *Dallas Morning News*, noted that in early 1992, George W. and his crew seemed to be getting to that point of despair.

With fans paying the big bills to erect a new stadium for the Rangers, the team needed to start winning. At the time, the team was, George W. admitted, "mired in mediocrity." But even as the team continued to lose, he maintained his vigil by the dugout through every home game. He didn't leave until the last out, no matter how bleak the situation got. At yet another losing game in May, he was one of 1,000 fans still watching during the ninth inning—the remnants of a crowd of 20,000.

Then, from up in the rafters came the bellow, "George! More pitching!"

A few minutes later, the man called out again, "George! More pitching!"

There was nothing for George W. to do but turn around, smile, and wave. But the guy kept yelling throughout the game. The next day in the office, his partners mimicked that chant to needle him.

George W. laughed it off, but it summed up the downside of their management situation. Here was the frustration of the fans and the need for more talent on the field. George W., as the public face of the Rangers, would be called to task. "Our antennas are quivering," he told a reporter. "It's not been a pretty picture. . . . If I feel this way, I know our market does. I'm frustrated, puzzled but patient." Now baseball, a business that had once seemed ideal from those days as a boy trading Topp cards, was showing its own challenges.

George W. and his partners would have to start restructuring the

ball club, which meant firing people. When George W. first took over
the team, Sherrod pointed out, he would proclaim his devotion to
what he called "the best organization in all of baseball" in speeches at
country club luncheons and civic meetings across the state. Then he
would reverently list off the top command: "Mike Stone, the president;
Tom Grieve, the general manager; and Bobby Valentine, the manager."
By late 1992, these men had all been fired. At a press conference, in
September 1990, he had personally announced the firing of Mike Stone
effective in two months. Stone became infuriated that George W.
tripped up their carefully orchestrated plans for his resignation by hiring a headhunting firm before his scheduled departure date (He resented George W.'s "marketing schtick," he told the press, and was
cleaning out his desk within hours of his comments appearing in the
newspapers.) Two years later, George W. fired Bobby Valentine, one of
the most famous loud-mouthed managers in baseball, who, when told
of his dismissal, was transformed into a saddened figure who elicited
public sympathy. And a little later, friend Tom Grieve was axed by
Schieffer and Rose with George W.'s blessing when he was on the campaign trail for his father.

From 1989, when the Bush group purchased the team, to 1992, the
payroll budget had increased 131 percent to $30 million dollars. That
dramatic increase was mainly the result of collective bargaining, which
made all franchises pay competitive salaries to players. The richest
clubs set the pace by offering huge contracts, and the struggling clubs
had to match the prices or miss out on decent players. The policy was
killing most of the franchises. "You take out the top five teams, and
clubs are hemorrhaging economically," said George W. in September
1992. "People react from economic fear and what you are seeing is
pure fear. F-E-A-R. People are fearful of the consequences of their
own behavior in the past and fearful of a future where our industry is
going to lose a lot of money."

"Maybe George was a little sorry to see the other side of baseball,"
acknowledged Tom Schieffer. "But George is pretty realistic about
things. I guess it's being an adult. You kind of wish Santa Claus really
did exist."

For most members of the Bush inner circle, Ross Perot will forever be condemned for his kamikaze effect on the election of 1992. Those Bush advisers believe that the reason the Texas billionaire popped in and out of that campaign—staying long enough to hammer at Bush's public image, gather constituents from among the Bush camp, stealing some and dropping others in Clinton's lap—was because of his personal animosity toward George Bush. In politics, the size of that type of grudge was unusual since it was so grand, but the fact that it existed at all was regrettably common. "It is not that unusual," said Robert Mosbacher Jr., who was chair of Victory 1992 for Bush. "Personal vendettas and egos unfortunately represent a disproportionate part of what motivates people to get in and out of political contests. If you reduced it all down to the people who were just running because they wanted to make the country better, it would be pretty slim pickings."

Jim Oberwetter, the longtime fund-raiser and head of the Texas campaign for George Bush in 1988, remembered the first time he had an inkling that there was bad blood between Bush and Perot. Oberwetter was riding in a car with Bush, who at the time was still vice president. "So," George Bush began meticulously, "what is my friend Ross Perot doing?"

Oberwetter thought the question was odd. Bush never seemed to enjoy a great friendship with Perot and, if they had been close, Bush never would have added that epithet. Oberwetter told him that he hadn't heard much from Perot lately. But it stuck in his mind.

Perot had been furious with Bush for years. Back in the early 1980s, Perot had been going through a receiving line for Reagan when he paused in front of the president to register his concerns about the issue of prisoners of war still lost in the jungles of Asia. He asked Reagan, if he, Perot, a common citizen, took it upon himself to find definitive proof that soldiers were still alive over there, would Reagan agree to follow up on the matter. Perot said Reagan assured him he would, and then Bush followed up on the conversation later. "Perot took that as a presidential directive to acquire information," said Craig Fuller, former chief of staff to Bush.

Because of George Bush's friendship with Perot from the days back in Texas, he volunteered to meet with Perot on the issue and asked Fuller to sit in. Fuller was to take the materials Perot offered as evidence and have them evaluated for their authenticity and significance. According to Fuller, the defense department did examine the materials and concluded that a large number of the claims contained in them were the work of conmen who had tried to peddle similar leads in the past in exchange for money.

In the 1992 campaign, Oberwetter was again appointed to oversee the Texas effort for Bush. He began to realize in early 1992 that Perot would be running. While he was familiar with Perot from Dallas—Oberwetter was the vice president of governmental and public affairs for the massive Hunt Oil Company—he decided that he should read up on him since he would be often called upon to compare the two candidates from Texas.

Oberwetter soon grew alarmed at what he described as the "[Perot] penchant for investigating and, in my view, tormenting the lives of some with whom he disagreed." He did not fear that Perot was capable of physical violence, but worried that one of Perot's supporters might be inclined to harm him or his family. He warned his wife that "some of the people who looked up to him on the POW/MIA situation and other supporters might take umbrage. . . . We alerted our children to take care with respect to any approach by strangers and to be on heightened awareness."

He also cautioned the staff at his campaign headquarters. "Frankly, from the beginning, we smelled danger and feared setups," he said. In other quarters, Perot had already made a bold effort to find damaging information on George Bush, according to Gerald Posner in his biography of the millionaire, *Citizen Perot*. For example, in 1991, Perot allegedly flew an associate to talk to an inmate who claimed to have shuttled Bush to Paris before the 1980 election. The alleged aim of the rumored Bush trip was to secure Iranian assurances that the U.S. hostages would not be released until after Carter had been defeated; the alleged strategy became known as the October Surprise. The day that the investigators arrived at the prison, however, the inmate had a heart attack, so the talks were thwarted, according to Posner.

In that climate, Perot became enraged when Oberwetter was quoted in the *New York Times* in late March as saying about Perot: "as smart as the guy is, he has never run for public office before and that can be a very dangerous thing in politics. . . ." Obwerwetter began having talks with George W. about the situation.

That summer Oberwetter became the target of an FBI sting operation in which he was offered audio tapes of Perot. He turned them down and was found innocent of any wrongdoing. He later testified to a House Judiciary Subcommittee: ". . . it is my belief that Mr. Perot and an agent (or agents) he hired . . . were participants in an elaborate effort to entrap me. . . ."

According to the *Newsweek* reporters, Perot suspected George W. was behind his bad press.

—

At the beginning of June, Bush's pollsters were alarmed to find that their candidate had dropped from a comfortable two-to-one lead in May over both Clinton and Perot. Now Perot was in the lead, Bush was in second place, and Clinton trailed by only 4 percentage points. The president was growing irritable, snapping at the staff. The campaign people and White House personnel began blaming each other for failing to put together a strategy to save the situation.

By June, George W. was commuting to the White House every other week to buck up the staff. "My job is to encourage them to do their jobs," he said. "I'm a single agenda man. My agenda is George Bush, and I make sure everybody else's is the same. Their job is to make sure this man gets elected. I'm pretty good about reminding them of their mission."

The president was reportedly "despondent" about Perot's campaign. In the middle of that month, Texas Republicans held their state convention. Winning that state would be crucial to victory in November, and the party was nervous about having two homegrown candidates vying for the nomination. Chairman Fred Meyer tore into Perot. "I just don't think he knows enough about how a democracy is supposed to operate," he said to the crowd, and added later, "Mussolini ran in 1923 [in Italy] to get the trains to run on time."

George W. attended the state convention but refused to blast Perot.

Less than a week later, the *Washington Post* reported the story of how Perot had allegedly investigated two of the Bush sons. Tom Luce, an aide to Perot from Dallas, claimed that the report was based on distortions. But George W. weighed in. "If the [claims] are true," he said. "I would be very worried to see him in the presidency. What we don't need is an enemies list and abuse of power." He also took steps to protect himself. He announced a couple of days later that he would be resigning from the board of Harken in order to spend more time on his father's campaign. He acknowledged that he hoped to avoid conflict-of-interest charges and that he did not want to stand in the way of Harken's overseas interests.

When Perot withdrew from the race on July 16, both Clinton and Bush called him to try to secure his endorsement, and their campaigns set out to woo away his supporters. Bush ran full-page ads in major papers across the country. On July 29, George W. accompanied ex-Perot aide Tom Luce, who he had been courting since the day after Perot's withdrawal, for an overnight stay at the White House, following a lecture by Truman biographer David McCullough. When Ross Perot jumped back into the race just before the election, Luce refused to join him.

At the end of July and into August, the president's poll numbers had sunk from their high of 89 percent after the Gulf War to a dismal 29 percent. The campaign was in complete disarray. In the year leading up to the convention, several staffers had approached George Bush with the idea of getting rid of Dan Quayle and putting in a fresh face as a way to generate some new excitement among the voters for a second term, but they had been furiously turned away by Bush. Now, in the days before the convention, word began circulating that the only salvation for the Bush presidency was to dump Quayle before the cavalcade arrived in Houston for the Republican celebration.

The political operation polled other possible candidates for the vice president. "The door is shut, but it isn't locked," a Quayle adviser admitted on *Evans & Novak*. They reported that the leading contender to replace the vice president was Governor Carroll Campbell of South Carolina, who at the time was a rising young star and an aggressive supporter of the president in his home state. He had also been a friend, as well as a candidate, in Lee Atwater's stable back when Campbell was first running for office in South Carolina during the '70s. Back in 1988, he had been put through the background checks for the vice presidency, before Quayle was chosen, which meant Campbell had been, from the first, one of the leading candidates for the post. Evans and Novak reported the intriguing fact that Campbell was scheduled to meet with George W. in Washington the same week that all of the rumors were flying, which suggested the campaign was pursuing other options. The president finally put a stop to the speculation by assuring Quayle that he would not be removed.

With no shakeup happening on the vice-presidential front, the only hope for President Bush to win was to turn ferocious on the trail. He would have to show now that he wanted the victory more than anything. George W. was more than happy to describe his father's competitive passion to voters, even if the President didn't show any signs of having the will to win. "I have seen the look in George Bush's eye and there's fire in the belly," George W. insisted in an interview at the convention. "The key thing for [my dad] is to become a fighter. To engage. He needs to come and fight back, and I think he will. . . . The issues ought to be jobs and peace and who best can do that. And I think that is where George Bush is going to try to elevate the debate, and if there is a fair hearing, we'll win that." George W. seemed to grow more understanding of the divide that existed between who his father was and how the public perceived him, and now he was willing to explain it instead of just lashing back.

George W. seemed to be developing an understanding that he could love his father as a good man and ferociously defend him, but that some situations his father might find himself in, particularly those involving power dynamics, might be out of George W.'s control—in particular the colliding forces that were making the 1992 campaign such a treacherous one. George W. was learning this same lesson on a different front too. Just as his father was headed into the home stretch of the election, another man George W. greatly admired was enduring a test of fire. Fay Vincent, the commissioner of baseball, had riled the ire of the Major League Baseball owners' group, and now his job hung in the balance. The situation seemed to be excruciating for George W., who loved Vincent from the days in Midland, and was seeing him destroyed in the arena George W. adored most: baseball. The incident would put George W.'s loyalty to the test.

Vincent would never forget that summer in the mid-'50s when he and his high school friend William "Bucky" Bush went down to Midland to work as roustabouts for George Bush's oil company, Zapata. Vincent and Bucky had even stayed for a couple of weeks with "Poppy," Bar, George W., Jeb, and baby Neil. Then they rented a rat's nest apartment with one bed in Odessa.

George Bush played baseball with them, tried to find them dates, and promoted them as stars all over town. On their last day of work, he called them to his office and said, "Hold up your hands." Bucky and Vincent did as they were told. "Thank God," George Bush said. "I got you boys through." Roughnecks usually lost fingers on the machinery. George Bush even paid for Vincent's train ticket to Dallas and arranged for him to fly back home with one of the Bushes' friends. Vincent thought George and Bar were two of the greatest people he'd ever met. Vincent would tease George W. "You have to be a very good owner and behave or otherwise I'll tell people about your Little League career," he would say. Vincent added, smiling, "It was not distinguished."

That first year up at Williams College, Vincent fell from a window ledge and damaged his spine. He would have a disability for the rest of his life, slowly negotiating his way through the world with a cane. By the time he became commissioner of baseball, he was still a hulking man but gave off an aura of gentleness, with his softened Northeast accent and level gaze.

Despite his almost Buddhalike calm, he had been a titanic business force for decades, having run Coca-Cola and Columbia Pictures. In 1989, he arrived at Major League Baseball with his best pal, Bart Giamatti, the former president of Yale. They had dreamed of working together for years, often joking that they would run a cafe and bookstore; Vincent would handle the numbers and Giamatti would sit dreamily at a table, smoking cigarettes and talking cantos with the enchanted patrons.

Giamatti had taken a job as head of the National League in 1986, and when the post of commissioner of baseball was offered to him after Uebberoth announced that he would be resigning early, Giamatti asked Vincent to come over as his number two, which Vincent accepted.

Although several scuffles with the players and owners occurred on their watch, Giamatti and Vincent worked happily out of the New

York office for five months. The worst of the trouble was negotiating Pete Rose's lifetime ban from baseball. They finished that business in August 1989.

Just days later, on Labor Day weekend, Vincent flew Giamatti out to Martha's Vineyard. They had a great time talking about the upcoming season; they were so happy that the Rose business was behind them. A couple of hours after Vincent had gone on to his own place in Hyannis, he got a call from Bobby Brown, the American League commissioner, that Giamatti had suffered a massive heart attack. Vincent knew Giamatti was dead.

The owners voted him in a couple of weeks later. When Vincent was in Milwaukee at a big press conference to announce the appointment, President Bush called him. No one at the event was aware that the two men had known each other for 30 years. Bush congratulated him. "If I had known you were going to be commissioner back in Texas I would have treated you much nicer," he said.

"Mr. President," Vincent replied, "if I had known you were going to be the president of the United States I would have been nicer to you." The president laughed.

The two men continued to socialize occasionally. They were at a baseball game in Los Angeles one time, when President Bush asked Vincent, "How's my son treating you as commissioner?"

"He's pretty good," Vincent said. "Some days he's better than others."

"Is he giving you any trouble?"

"No, once in a while," Vincent joked.

The president suggested they call George W., but he was on Dallas time and seemed to have been awakened by the call. "George, I'm sitting here with the commissioner," President Bush said. "He tells me once in a while you're a pain in the ass."

"Tell him to drop dead," George W. retorted.

Vincent apologized later. "Look, it could have been worse," he joked to George W. "I could have talked to your mother."

"Don't do that," George W. said, continuing the banter. "Don't go to her."

Those were the better days. In rapid succession, Vincent dealt with the suspension of George Steinbrenner from the Yankees' day-to-day operations, an earthquake during the World Series in San

Francisco, and ugly labor negotiations between the owners and the players. He also had to contend with the titanic personalities of the owners group. The variety and speedy accumulation of problems seemed to echo the sorts of struggles that regularly crop up in political campaigns.

Even under the best of circumstances, a baseball commissioner could count on having scuffles with the owners' group, and Vincent was not working in that ideal scenario. It was a wonder that conference rooms vast enough could be found to accommodate all the enormous egos involved with that particular committee of about 100 people that convened four or five times a year. The men and women who bought Major League teams usually had a good chunk of disposable cash on hand and were accustomed to wielding a big stick in their home cities. Of course there were some well-intentioned souls in their midst. But others of the more tyrannical breed seemed shocked that they kept running up against their mirror images in the owners' association. They would listen to presentations by the group's lawyers on an issue. Then there would be an attempt to hold discussion. Owners would play to the gallery. *We're going to get them this time, if we just stick together. . . .*

Many began grumbling about Vincent. Some of the American League owners thought he had been unfair when Major League Baseball divided up $190 million generated by new expansion, and they had received less than the National League. Other owners saw him as too fierce an advocate for the players and wanted him out of the way for labor negotiations that were probably coming up in December 1992. In the late 1980s, the owners had gotten busted for colluding on setting players' salaries, and been forced to pay $280 million. Their credibility had been seriously damaged for future negotiations. They knew Vincent was likely to encourage them to put off a real fight for a longer cooling-off period. Jerry Reinsdorf of the White Sox, in particular, was gunning for him. Vincent started reading the nasty rumors about him in the paper. He let it be known that he did not plan to leave quietly. "I will not resign—ever," he stated in a letter on August 20.

On September 3, the owners held a special four-hour meeting in Rosemont, Illinois, to discuss what to do about Vincent. Some owners got up and blasted him for refusing, before the labor negotiations began, to relinquish the commissioner's "best interest of baseball" power, which had been upheld twice in federal court. Others were furious at the way he had realigned the National League and at his stance against superstations. Still others were irate about the division of expansion fees. Bud Selig, of the Milwaukee Brewers, also began to take a major part in leading the insurrection.

George W. stood up, gave a long, impassioned speech in defense of Vincent that left no doubts that the Texas Rangers would fight for his survival. George W. said that Vincent was an intelligent and honorable man, and Major League Baseball should be happy to have him as commissioner—to let him go would be crazy. "You know they were making allegations that I was everything from a pederast to a thief. George defended that," said Vincent. "What I admired was, it wasn't politically in his interest to do that. It was a real act of courage, because they were going to win and he was going to have to deal with them. But he did it anyway. I had other guys on my side who never opened their mouths, who were supposedly great friends of mine, and they did vote for me, but they never got around to speaking."

Among other potential weapons, the owners have the power to approve or deny the sale of a team. Vincent felt that if George W. had come to him and told him that he couldn't take on the other owners— because of approval he needed for the stadium or for the eventual sale of his interest—Vincent would have been disappointed, but he would have understood. But George W. never let him down. By the end of the meeting, 18 of the 28 owners asked for Fay Vincent's resignation. Bill White, the president of the National League, called Vincent to tell him of the decision. Vincent said he would not resign.

The following weekend was Labor Day. It was the third anniversary of Giamatti's death, and Vincent went to Martha's Vineyard. He had hired Brendan Sullivan, who represented Oliver North, to take his fight to court. It would be great, he thought. A big public battle with the owners—how could he lose?

George W. talked to him that Friday and encouraged him to attend the meeting in St. Louis on Thursday. "Look, Fay," he said. "What you should do is come out and give one of your famous speeches. You could turn that audience. Come out and have a program. Make it very crisp, very strong. People will back you. They are embarrassed by what they did." George W. spent the weekend fishing at his country house in Athens, but he kept calling out to lawyers and to the eight other owners who had supported Vincent. He told Reinsdorf and the others that they'd better change their votes or face a long court battle. "I'm prepared for a fight and he's prepared for a fight," he told them.

But over the weekend, Vincent had a change of heart. He called George W. on Monday morning. "George, the problem is, if I win I lose," he said. "If I turn them all around, I have to go work for them. I can't go to the meeting. It would make me sick to my stomach. These are guys that turned on me.

"But I'm a lucky guy," he added. "I have all the money I need. I don't need this. I'm going to resign."

"Don't do that," George W. told him. "You have to be very strong. You tend to be a little laid back. Come on and make that speech and be very strong, you'll pull it off."

But that day, Vincent announced his resignation. "He didn't want to go out mud wrestling," George W. explained. "It got to be a very personal thing. I think it would have become very nasty if he had gone to the mat. He decided not to. I'm disappointed."

That remark about mud wrestling from George W. was interesting, in that he echoed the concept a little over a month later when talking about his father in the 1992 campaign. "It's hard to be a joyful participant in a mud-wrestling contest," he told the *Dallas Morning News*, "when someone you really care about is getting mud wrestled."

Vincent later heard that two of the main owners who were campaigning against him met coming into the hotel for the owners' meeting in St. Louis and gave each other high-fives. Schieffer said, despite the fact that George W. had gone up against Reinsdorf, the head of the committee, and Selig, who would go on to serve as baseball commissioner, he suffered no fallout. "What George [W.] understood is nobody stays mad at you for being loyal to your friends," said Schieffer. "Most people look at that behavior and while they might be mad at you at first, say, 'Gee, I wish I had a friend like that.'"

George W. and his father called Vincent after he had announced his resignation. "[President Bush] called me the day I got in and he called me the day I went out," said Vincent. "And it was the day that I went out that I remember most fondly because that's when I was feeling very low and I felt that I had been defeated. Of course, politicians understand that because they've been through it." Vincent thought George W. might have remembered how Vincent had invested $25,000 when Arbusto was just getting off the ground. "I don't know what the equation was for George," said Vincent, "but that was a time when he needed some help and he was trying to get his business going. So I can't say I'm totally surprised that he would be very loyal because I think he has been through some tough times."

"He's a noble man," George W. told the press about his friend Vincent. "It's a hard concept for people to grasp. It's called principle, integrity. He was willing to sacrifice himself for the good of the game."

That statement seemed so much like the kind of thing George W. would say about his father and like a requiem for both George Bush and Vincent. His father was being crushed by an array of pugilistic forces—in this case, Perot, Clinton, and the economy. Leading up to Election Day 1992, George W. underwent a crash course in the ugly grappling that goes along with the pursuit of power. In that process, he must have developed a remarkable tolerance for gazing at the worst sides of human nature. When discussing Vincent, an unhappy George W. gave the clear-eyed assessment: "He made a lot of tough decisions, and because of that he was not popular. But someone's ox is always going to be gored." He had learned, through his own experience and especially through seeing politics through his father's eyes, how power worked.

—

In late October, George W. was running hard for his father through Texas, hitting 17 cities in just three days. When he wasn't onstage in some Lone Star town, he was chewing an unlit cigar, wearing his eel-skin cowboy boots with the embossed state flags. That year, none of the Bushes were faring well in campaigns. His 10-year-old twins, Jenna and Barbara, had competed at their school for Student Council treasurer and secretary respectively. Jenna played off an Uncle Sam theme and Barbara tried the slogan "Elect the lean, mean, green, fighting machine," a reference to the school's colors. They had both gone down in defeat.

Aides to the president felt George W. was aching for some larger campaign shake-up. "George W. wanted something done more dramatic than what his father would do," said Chief of Staff Samuel K. Skinner. "He thought people were letting his father down." The most controversial figure had become Dick Darman, whose economic initiatives other staffers criticized as being too weak for the circumstances; and George W. thought he should go.

In the world of opposition research, the president's people had tried desperately to get Clinton on the draft issue. They also wanted to paint him as a communist sympathizer by releasing his passport information to show that he had traveled to Russia when still a Rhodes scholar in England. Jim Baker helped get the passport story out there. But George Bush was frustrated by how easily the press were shaken from the scent.

By spring, President Bush was warned that he was probably being targeted by the special prosecutor for the Iran-Contra investigation, Lawrence Walsh. Republicans already considered the effort a partisan investigation, but George Bush's special counsel confirmed that he thought Walsh was headed toward Bush. On October 30, just days before Election Day, the trap fell on Bush, but as a peripheral figure in another indictment. The timing could not have been worse for the campaign, since Bush had been closing the gap in the polls.

In Washington, D.C., Walsh entered a reindictment of former Defense Secretary Casper Weinberger, which included documents asserting that George Bush had known about the arms-for-hostages trade of Iran-Contra. The "smoking gun"—as Al Gore would call it—was one of Weinberger's handwritten notes from a January 7, 1986, meeting in which he and Shultz registered their objection to the plan, and George Bush approved the idea. Bush had always claimed that he was "out of the loop." As it turned out, voters cared more about that credibility issue with Bush than they did about any of the character issues his campaign had tried to slap on Bill Clinton. When news reached the Bush campaign plane, George W. turned to Mary Matalin and said decisively, "It's all over." Coming when the news did, no one seemed to even focus on whether or not George Bush could answer why that memo existed when he had said he never weighed in on the scheme.

Even with that devastating news, George Bush continued fight-

ing and showed good humor with his staffers, but his public campaign
style grew more shrill. The president's best qualities had always been
his gentlemanly manner, his sense of humor at times of difficulty, but
in the torment of the 1992 election, he was starting to lose that tone.
He started calling Al Gore "the Ozone Man," as a jab at his environmental positions. At another point, he dubbed the two men on the
Democratic ticket "bozos." Clinton, clearly enjoying his comeback,
turned his opponent's agitation to his advantage.

"He calls Al Gore 'the Ozone Man,'" Clinton said to a crowd in
Pittsburgh who had stood in the rain to see him. "Well, there's a guy
back there with a sign that says, 'I Love the Ozone Man.'

"Then he called us 'bozos.' Well, all I can say is Bozo makes people laugh and Bush makes people cry. And America is going to be
laughing on Tuesday."

Even George W. was disappointed that his father had stooped to
the 'bozos' crack. "George Bush probably uttered ten thousand words
yesterday," he said from Oklahoma. "I wish the emphasis would have
been on peace and prosperity and competency and experience and
doing the right thing for America."

The next day, the president's stump speeches had the liberated ring
of a man going down in defeat. Perhaps he was undone by the sight
of a plane circling above one of the events on that Halloween, trailing
the banner: *Iran-Contra Haunts You.*

"Today is Halloween, our opponents' favorite holiday," he told a
crowd in Wisconsin. "They're trying to scare America. . . . Every day
is going to be Halloween. Fright and terror!" At another stop in
Oshkosh, he yelled. "Fright and terror! Witches and devils everywhere!"

Even the attendance at the election-night event in Houston was
sparse. George W. kept getting word of how bad the returns were
while he was standing on the dance floor of the hotel with the president's dear friend from the days of the Martini Bowl, Bob Blake.
"Come on," he finally said to him, when the accumulation of difficult
news could only spell defeat. "Let's get out of here. I don't want anyone to see the two of us in tears."

Bar posed the pertinent question to herself in her memoir: "Why
did we lose? George Bush says it was because he didn't communicate

as well as his predecessor or successor. I just don't believe that."
George Bush seemed more at peace with the outcome than his family
did. Bar blamed the media for its lopsided coverage of her husband.

Perhaps even more painful to the Bushes than the incoming criticism during the campaign from overt adversaries like Ross Perot and Bill
Clinton or even Lawrence Walsh was the lack of loyalty in the
Republican Party itself, to a man who had given such long service to the
party. Torie Clarke, the campaign press secretary, was horrified how
politicians who had worked with George Bush for decades and benefited from his kindness were running scared and would not support him.

That four years was George Bush's swan song in political life, and
it was hard for staffers and family members to send him back into civilian life. No decision would provide George W.'s beloved father more
solace than knowing that his son—in fact his *sons*, including Jeb—had
looked at his life in public office and decided to emulate it. "They
know it's ugly, and they're still willing to do it," Bar said in an interview with *Greenwich* magazine. "In a way, that sort of vindicates our
life. It makes me feel, well, it wasn't as bad as I thought it was going
to be. They didn't say, 'Oh, we'll never get into politics, it ruined our
lives.' It did touch their lives enormously. But in spite of that, they felt
strongly that they wanted to serve their country."

XIII

GOVERNOR GOOD GUY

George W. surveyed the wreckage of his father's 1992 aspirations and realized he needed to undertake a massive project to blunt the pain: He would go running. It was the Bush tonic for sadness, for the crushing disappointment of defeat. Sign up for a marathon and wash the agony away with flushes of endorphin high. He went to see the Dallas fitness guru, Dr. Ken Cooper, to get himself ready for the White Rock Marathon. On the northern edge of Dallas, in a setting that most resembled a turn-of-the-century sanitarium with quiet brick buildings set off from a geometry of running paths, George W. trained for a race that would not end with an election day.

Unfortunately, just before the big event, George W. developed a respiratory infection and had to sit out the competition. But he had established a simple fact in his mind. He *would* run again—on the roads of Dallas and later on the campaign trails of the great state of Texas.

—

When George W. finally began breaking the news that he planned to run for governor against Ann Richards in 1994, many of his friends just laughed him off. He had started floating the idea in the press in early 1993, but the more serious discussions began taking place about six months later. Charlie Younger remembered his talking about the idea up at Walker's Point in June, when the Young One and his wife

293

were honeymooning there. The newlyweds were sitting on a seawall with Laura and George W. looking out to the ocean. George W. told his old buddy from Midland about his plan to become the governor of Texas in 1994.

"It kind of floored me," said Younger. "My advice was, you're crazy—wait four years."

Since 1990, when Richards had handily beaten Texas oil man Clayton Williams for the governor's seat, she had been happily ensconced in Austin. The residents of the Lone Star state seemed smitten with her tough-talking, motorcycle-riding ways. She had even enchanted the national press, not least with a crack against George W.'s own father. At the 1988 Democratic convention, she had become the party's darling by uttering the now famous line, "Poor George, he was born with a silver foot in his mouth." The crowd at Madison Square Garden roared its approval, and she became a bona-fide star.

The Bushes took the criticism personally, as they usually did. "I was in Kennebunkport with the family and for some reason settled down to watch Ann Richards's (she's now the governor of Texas) ugly, devastating attack on George," wrote Bar in her autobiography. "I watched about ten minutes and turned off the tube with a sick feeling in my stomach. How naive of me to think that I was going to enjoy watching people trash George for three days! It hurt." During the 1990 gubernatorial campaign, George Bush paid a special visit to Texas as president—with all of its attendant press attention and pomp—to campaign against her, just months before the election. Bar and George probably did not mind the fact that now their eldest son was planning to drive Richards out of office.

But like all of George W.'s friends, Younger feared what would happen to the "bombastic Bushkin" if he went up against Richards. "You've got a popular incumbent Democrat that you can't beat," continued Younger. "It would be suicide. You've got a good life going . . . just don't ruin it." All of George W.'s friends knew that he loved his job running the Rangers; the new stadium was under construction and many of the team's management problems now seemed to be resolved. The money that George W. made as a salaried employee of the club furnished the family with a comfortable life, including a North Dallas home with three fireplaces, a library, pool, arbor and guest house. Laura seemed happy with her friends and philanthropic work, and Jenna and Barbara were lively 11-year-olds with a full array of buddies and extracurricular activities in Dallas. George W.'s Midland friends knew enough from the ups and downs of the oil patch not to upset a happy existence like that for a run at a long-shot deal.

But George W. felt troubled by the management of the state of Texas and thought he could do something about it; he thought that there were wasted opportunities for economic growth. Looking at the structure of his campaign that followed, one can surmise too that he had a few other reasons for running: He had always wanted to get back into politics, and with the stadium set for completion just months before the election, he not only had the bank account necessary, by family credo, to run; in addition he now had the tangible accomplishment that he could show voters. But he also could use the 1994 election to settle old scores. The campaign too offered a great opportunity to condemn publicly a couple of his father's biggest critics: Ann Richards and Bill Clinton, and in fact George W. could use Texas voters' distaste for Clinton as a weapon against Richards.

With all of those factors probably feeding into his motivation, George W. was confident of his potential for success. "I can beat her," he insisted.

"What makes you think that?" Charlie Younger asked.

George W. just repeated the statement. "I can beat her."

"I always thought he had some secret poll going," said Younger, "but I don't think he did, because he later admitted that name recognition was very important and that he had name recognition throughout the state. Not for who he was, but who his dad was." As George W. had recognized when he considered running for governor in 1990, in media-saturated Texas, name recognition meant more than anything.

That famous name had probably helped him at Andover, Yale, in the Texas Air National Guard, and the oil business. It had hampered him when he ran for Congress in 1978, when the Establishment politics that George Bush represented had fallen out of favor. By 1990, George W.'s well-known moniker helped raise interest in his candidacy for governor, but ultimately stopped him in his tracks when his mother decided that if her son ran for governor, President George Bush would suffer at the polls in 1992. Now, with his father out of office, George W. decided to capitalize fully on the power of the family.

He called his mom to let her know his plans. "Mother, I've made up my mind," he said. "Laura and I are fixin' to announce for governor."

"You can't win," she replied curtly, according to his own accounts of the discussion.

"I told her, 'You've been reading the *Washington Post* too long,'" he said. "'Come back to Texas and live. Start paying taxes like the rest of us. Start worrying about schools, shirk the Secret Service, and walk outside your house and see how you feel.'" He claimed in stump speeches to have found another convert in her. "She moved back here for six months," he said, "and now she's beginning to realize what everybody else is: I can win!"

George W. acknowledged that Ann Richards was well liked, but insisted that she was an ineffectual leader who had never adequately focused her agenda. She was like a cheerleader without a team, and as soon as the voters of the state became aware of that fact, he thought, they would flock to him as the alternative. There was more to running Texas than "funny sound bites," he said, launching his first vague salvos that the state had not been managed efficiently. A Texas poll conducted in July showed that while 58 percent thought Richards was doing an excellent or good job as governor, only 33 percent said they were very likely to vote for her in the next election. When these same polls pitted her against various Republican contenders, only George W. placed well, although 25 percent expressed confusion over which George Bush was being discussed.

His challenge was to show up her weaknesses rather than fight her on the basis of her strengths. "I don't have to erode her likability," he told the *New York Times*. "I have to erode her electability." And that's exactly what he did. Even in the late summer of 1994, her favorability rating would remain 54 percent, a high figure for a governor of a major state; and yet George W. was gaining on her in head-to-head voting predictions.

Before he formally announced, though, George W. decided he needed to clear the Republican field. He contacted each of his possible opponents in the party to let them know that he would be running.

Tom Craddick of Midland; former Perot adviser Tom Luce; and Bob Mosbacher Jr., the longtime family friend and compatriot on the Bush bandwagon in 1970—all were contacted and eventually bowed out of the contest. The last two exited on August 30, the same day Mosbacher met with George W. Only one quixotic candidate remained: 42-year-old Louis Podesta, a freelance writer who had never been to a political event or contributed to a campaign and planned to run on a Goldwater platform. He was an asterisk on the list.

George W. began to promote himself as a candidate with a character-building education in the oil industry and Major League Baseball. "My business experience will enable me to provide the strong, independent leadership our state needs from its governor," he said in September. He presented his professional career as unquestionably successful, although he had endured as many failures as accomplishments.

The next month, a poll showed that he was only eight percentage points behind Richards.

After the baseball season had ended with its accompanying distractions, George W. announced his candidacy for the governorship of Texas on November 8, 1993, a full year before the election. In a series of speeches that day in Houston, San Antonio, Austin, and Dallas, he began to outline his platform to the 300 supporters gathered at the Loew's Hotel in the final stop on the four-city swing. "Instead of sitting on the sidelines watching baseball," he told a reporter a few days later, "I want to abandon the sidelines and get in the middle of trying to improve my state. It's time for my generation to accept responsibility." George W.'s speechifying always showed less good-old-boy joking than he displayed when working a roomful of voters. He was usually businesslike in his delivery and issue-oriented. This seven-page declaration was no exception—less inspirational than programmatic, addressing the need for stricter crime initiatives, less government control over education, a reassessment of the juvenile justice system, and the importance of the free market. He presented himself as a manager politician as compared to his gentleman politician father; George W.'s would be a governorship with an agenda, and an intimate one at that, addressing issues of safety, the schooling of children, and the pocketbook. Every voter likely harbored one of those concerns.

While announcing for governor was a historic moment for George W., it was not a first for the Bush family. Jeb had decided almost a year earlier to run for governor in Florida and had publicly announced his intentions in June. Among the Bush boys, he had always been considered the more likely candidate because of his serious and long-standing interest in policy issues. While George W. often adopted his father's positions whole cloth, Jeb wrestled with them from an early age. He even considered resisting the draft, when he was in his early twenties. "He came down on the side of being drafted," Bar explained, according to biographer Donnie Radcliffe. "We kidded him that we'd back him whatever."

But like George W., Jeb had found his father's life a model worthy of emulation. He married at age 21, which even to his mother seemed significant. "He and Columba reminded me so much of George and me," Bar wrote in her autobiography. "Jeb was just twenty-one, a year older than his father had been, and Columba was my age, nineteen, and they still had college to finish."

In 1986, when, like his father, he was chair of his county's Republican Party—in this case in Dade, Florida—he called the vice president to talk about the possibility of entering the race for Congress. Perhaps, behind the scenes, his mother had given her 33-year-old son the same chastisement that she had delivered to George W.: This is not your time; you must let your father have his day. But publicly, the story went that his father had simply asked Jeb the practical questions: Could he afford two houses—one in D.C. and one in Miami? Could his family handle the strain?

In January 1993, Jeb called his father to tell him that he planned to run in 1994. Reportedly the retired president told him: "Go for it." Both of his parents were touched that he would still want to play in the political arena after all they had seen of its darker side. George Bush also must have been pleased at the match-up of his son against the incumbent governor, Lawton Chiles; he had been the other primary target, alongside Ann Richards, of George Bush's mid-term campaigning in 1990.

Jeb was actually the first Bush boy to use the benchwarmer terminology in his announcement. "We were taught never to sit on the sidelines," he said. His political persona was much more conservative than his brother's, almost aggressively so. He dubbed himself a "head-banging conservative," whose great gift to office would be the "healthy disrespect I have for government." He planned to wipe out welfare, social services, and educational systems that no longer worked. He seemed to distance himself from his father's country club Republicanism and gave credit to his mother for instilling in him a contrarian's energy. "Barbara Bush always liked to challenge authority," he noted.

From the sidelines, former President George Bush brimmed with emotion. "There is no way I can possibly describe the feeling of pride that I have in my boys," he wrote to a reporter. "Last year was not pleasant for any of us; and now, knowing what lies ahead, they are both willing to try. I am very proud of them both."

But Jeb seemed less happy that his brother had jumped into 1994 campaigning simultaneously. "It turns into a *People* magazine story," he quipped. But he also admitted that he had no control over his brother. That fact was underscored when George W. began lifting material from Jeb's speeches. Maureen Dowd, reporter for the *New York Times*, noted that Jeb's pitch included the line: "I am running for governor not because I am George and Barbara Bush's son; I am running because I am George P. and Noelle and Jeb's father."

An echo resounded from Texas. "I am not running for governor because I am George Bush's son," George W. said. "I am running because I am Jenna and Barbara's father." His political consultant, Karl Rove, confessed to the thievery. "George heard Jeb use the line and thought it was so good, he stole it," he told Dowd. "He admits it."

This wasn't the first time George W. had stolen family political pitches. In 1978, he had lifted his father's line from 1964, that his one regret was that he hadn't been born in Texas, but at the time he thought it was more important to stay close to his mother and "she happened to be in New Haven, Connecticut."

In the early stages of the campaign season, most political observers thought Jeb would be the victorious Bush in November 1994. His opponent incumbent, Lawton Chiles, was vulnerable, plus, "Jeb is a better politician than George," Pete Teeley, former press secretary for George Bush's 1980 campaign, told the *Boston Globe* at the time. "Jeb's got his feet on the ground. He doesn't suffer from the ego problems of George. But I remember when George came up to Washington as a full-time volunteer for his old man in eighty-eight, he was willing to do anything. There was no group too lowly for him to speak to." That energetic pursuit of votes would make George W. victorious.

He ran hard throughout the state. "I am a whipper in rural Texas," he told *Dallas Observer* reporter Miriam Rozen. "People in small-town Texas want attention, and I've got the energy and drive to go see them and shake their hands."

His strategy, crafted by Karl Rove, was to fly under the media radar for as long as possible and appeal directly to the constituents. Although the Bushes could boast a few friends in the media, George W. inherited his dislike for reporters directly from both his mother and father. All three had been particularly incensed by the press's handling of George Bush in 1992, and George W. himself was probably in no hurry to get back in front of a reporter's microphone. George W. had fared better with the sports reporters who covered the Texas Rangers, but political questions were tougher to navigate, and George W. was a relative novice on the statewide issues of Texas. Rove thought it best that the new candidate get some practice fielding questions out on the trail before allowing the media to write profiles dissecting his campaign.

George W. was still stiff when giving speeches, but with a day's supply of breath mints at the ready, he had a knack for interacting with voters, especially kids. Many of his campaign events promoted his concern for education but had the added benefit of putting him in adorable situations with young Texans. At one campaign stop at an elementary school, two of the kids misheard his name and called him George Washington, to the press's delight.

—

Out on the trail, George W. was introduced as "a Yale graduate, a fighter pilot, a man who worked in the oil business in Midland." He also pointed out that he was the kind of man who "knows what it means to meet a payroll." This was his father's resumé too, during losing Senate races in Texas in 1964 and 1970. So why did the same pitch win the governor's seat for the Bush son some 30 years later in 1994?

To a great extent, his father had been cannon fodder for his son's war. George Bush's campaigns had helped set up the infrastructure that decades later, in 1992, allowed Texas to send two Republican senators to Washington for the first time since Reconstruction. Back when George Bush was running the Harris County Republican party in 1962, he described his responsibilities to his friend Lud Ashley. "My job is primarily an organizational job since the Republican Party has quite a few unorganized precincts," he reportedly said. "So far I like it a lot, and although it takes a tremendous amount of time, I think it is worthwhile." By 1994, those chores had helped shift the politics of the state to favor the Bush family party.

But George W. also gets credit for structuring a brilliant campaign. He knew from his father's presidential race in 1992 that nothing was softer than popularity numbers, recalling that President Bush's own approval ratings had nose-dived after the Gulf War, primarily because the average citizen could not associate him with any major political endeavor. George W. had learned that a good personality could carry a candidate into office, but it could not keep him there.

George W.'s strategist, Karl Rove, had first cut his teeth on political campaigns as far back as 1973, two years after the Colorado native dropped out of the University of Utah. He ran successfully for the presidency of the College Republicans National Committee, headquartered at the RNC. Lee Atwater had been his campaign manager, and when Rove and his rival, Robert Edgeworth, tied for victory, George Bush, who was then head of the Republican National Committee, decided the race in Rove's favor. Rove won some level of infamy as the head of the College Republicans for organizing conferences to teach dirty tricks campaigning, including searching the opposition's garbage cans for memos and lists of contributors. According to a biography of Atwater by John Brady, 19-year-old Rove even adopted a false name to get into a Democratic headquarters in Chicago to steal a sheaf of letterhead. In a move reminiscent of the George W. beer bash debacle, Rove printed invitations to an opening at the city's headquarters, advertising "free beer, free food, girls, and a good time for nothing" and sent them to a hippie commune, a rock concert, and soup kitchens.

The dirty tricks campaigning came to light in the course of Watergate-era reporting. In August 1973, George Bush told the *Washington Post* that he would "get to the bottom" of the charges. After a month-long investigation, Bush decided that Rove was clean.

Rove had admitted that he had been involved in the "prank," and contended that the charges were part of an attack by rival College Republicans. That must have been a good enough explanation for George Bush, because he hired Rove to work as an assistant at the Republican National Committee. Rove met George W. in 1974 when the Harvard Business School student was home on vacation. "I was supposed to give him the car keys whenever he came to town," Rove said. When George Bush left the CIA after Carter's inauguration and went back to Houston, he hired Rove to work in his office. In 1978, George W.'s Republican primary opponent for the congressional race, Jim Reese, accused him of using Rove, a "Rockefeller Republican," to mastermind the campaign. Rove continued working for George Bush through 1980, when the Houston businessman was on the presidential ticket with Reagan, before going out on his own with a consulting and direct-mail fund-raising business. Rove gained prestige by getting Republican Bill Clements elected as governor of Texas in 1982, and seventeen years later he helped sweep Republicans into office in every major post in the state.

The first task George W.'s 1994 gubernatorial campaign faced was to identify the issues uppermost in the minds of 18 million people living in Texas. Leading up to 1994, the state's economy had been in fairly good shape since it had diversified its industries after the oil bust in the 1980s. Unlike the rest of the nation, which had obsessed about the downturn during the 1992 election, Texas had weathered the worst crisis.

The big issue for Texans was crime, brought to a head by a series of grisly teen murders that regularly made the nightly news. When George W.'s campaign began to play upon this burgeoning fear, Richards's camp accused him of using the "weak woman" strategy—emphasizing crime issues when facing a female opponent to take advantage of the fact that some voters automatically perceive a woman as being softer on punishment strategies. The tactic more likely came from the Bush team's usual bag of tricks. Six years earlier, Lee Atwater had boosted George Bush's campaign by publicizing the case of Willie Horton. Now, Atwater's protégé, Karl Rove, would do the same for George W. using violent crime in general.

George W. sat down with a Dallas district judge, Harold C. Gaither Jr., to compose a series of solutions. "He knew right off the bat that this was going to be a hot issue," Gaither told the *Dallas Observer*. The candidate's 17-point proposal included lowering the age at which a minor could be tried as an adult from 16 to 14; taking fingerprints and mugshots of every kid brought in for a misdemeanor; making youth criminal records available to the public; and boosting the bed count at the Texas Youth Commission by 3,500. For dramatic effect, the plan was printed on paper with a screened silhouette of a policeman grabbing a kid by the neck.

"Texas is considered the third most dangerous state in the nation," the candidate told voters in his television ads. "No wonder, because in the last three years, seven thousand seven hundred criminals have been released early from prison." While Ann Richards would later contest the validity of most of George W.'s crime statistics for her term in Texas, George W. had obviously hit a chord with the state's voters.

The ad showed what appeared to be surveillance footage of a man pointing a gun at the head of a woman in a parking lot. Then the scene cut to a cop pulling a blanket over her corpse. The event was actually staged. "It was just my sound man accosting the makeup woman," Don Sipple, George W.'s campaign guru, told the *Washington Post*, "but it looks very real."

George W. formulated a strategy for a "war" on rapists, child molesters, and other sex offenders; he would not offer them parole under any circumstances. His press secretary, Karen Hughes, finally admitted to *Dallas Observer* reporter Miriam Rozen that the governor actually had little power over most early releases since they are required by court order. But, she said, George W. would fight for the prisoners to be kept in tents or barracks until their prison sentences were up. At the time, politicians around the country were campaigning on the idea of making prison tougher on criminals, with proposed chain gangs, the elimination of television, and restricted visitation rights; the idea of the tents for parolees fit right into that political vogue.

George W. said that violent crime was up 6 percent from the year that preceded Richards's time in office in 1990 to the current year of 1993. "Violent juvenile crime is exploding," he told the voters, explaining that there had been a 52 percent increase in that category over the three-year period. He planned to shift $25 million from drug rehabil-

itation for adults in the prison system to "community-based" programs for juveniles.

When Rozen challenged his use of the word "thugs" when referring to young criminals, George W. explained, "I tend to speak off my
gut. There are thugs and there are not thugs. There are nice little kids
lost for all kinds of reasons who need to be surrounded with love, who
can be saved. And then there are those *thugs* who walk into people's
homes *and blow people's heads off.*"

Richards could only try to contradict his statistics. She pointed out
that from 1992 to 1993, violent crime was down by 5.5 percent; and
that all crime had declined to 1985 levels. She said that she had cut
prison release by 45 percent since 1990 and parole requests to 29 percent. Meanwhile, she had doubled minimum sentences for violent
offenders. Prisons had proliferated. Despite Richards's ready responses, George W., as the challenger, held the advantage when talking about
crime issues. When confronted with the differing statistics from
Richards and George W., voters might throw up their hands in confusion, but they would believe the images they saw on the nightly news.
The local programs always gave airtime to grisly murders. George W.
must have learned from his father's use of Willie Horton as an issue in
the 1988 presidential campaign that Americans' flat-out fear of crime
could generate extraordinary negative ratings for an opponent.

George W.'s other major priority was to improve education across
the state by offering school boards "total local control." Unless the students in a particular school system failed a standardized Texas test, all
decisions would rest in local hands, including class size, teacher com-
pensation, and academic requirements. When a reporter asked a question about a particular element of the proposal, George W. cut them off.
"There's *no* detail," he said. "That's the wonderful thing about it."

He also promised to change the financing for education, which in
Texas was built on a "Robin Hood" model, whereby wealthier communities kicked in funding for poorer schools. In fact, his daughters'
own fate would not be decided in the public school system, a fact that
exposed him to criticism. "We chose to send them to private school,"
he told the *Observer,* "because we thought this would be a better place
for them to reach the standard of excellence that our family has set for
our little girls."

The other hot issue was welfare. Republicans across the nation had decided to make reform a major goal. George W. put a tougher Texas spin on the proposals, suggesting that bounty hunters be used for fathers who "cut and run." He also pushed to end the policy by which a woman would receive $38 a month more in welfare payments for each child she had; he planned to require the identification of fathers before the state would bestow benefits, and hoped to end welfare payments after two years, except for families with children under three years of age or those who were physically or mentally incapacitated.

"I'm not sure that punishing a newborn child is any kind of solution," Richards countered. According to the *Washington Post*, George W.'s aides were thrilled with her "bleeding heart" response, since they believed it would get her in trouble with voters. In that election cycle, the nation as a whole had become enchanted with the Republicans' message of personal responsibility and fiscal discipline—a sentiment that would, in November, elevate the revolution's father, Newt Gingrich, to speaker of the house, ushering into the Congress a new Republican majority.

The Texas Republican platform had been written in Fort Worth by a committee heavily stacked with religious conservatives. George W. chose to ignore the document's principles, and campaign only on his own views, which were far less controversial. How many people could say, after all, that they were *for* sex offenders getting out before they served their sentences? What percentage of voters would be so attached to the idea of state control over the schools that they would attack his proposal for local control?

Some of his views would have raised greater controversy—particularly nationally—if he had campaigned on them. When questioned, he told a group of constituents that he supported the existing Texas laws that outlaw sodomy, but he did not include these particular views in more public speeches. "I don't campaign on that," he explained. "I am not campaigning on that at all." He understood that making such hot topics wedge issues could only hurt him, since they would stir up the national press and alienate middle-of-the-road voters. He opposed abortion, but spoke publicly only about his support of parental notification for minors, which was more generally accepted.

Down in Florida, Jeb gave stronger voice to conservatism. "As governor," he said, "I'll sign the death warrants that Lawton Chiles hasn't." He supported a ballot initiative that would deny homosexuals specific protections under state civil rights laws. When he was heckled for that view at one campaign stop, he retorted, "I don't believe we need to create another category of victims."

—

George W. called his father every couple of weeks to talk during that campaign, but refused to acknowledge any dependence on him. When a reporter asked, "What do your parents think about you running?" He snapped, "I didn't ask their advice."

But he was facing a sassy, sharp-tongued, white-haired grandmother, so what was he to do but bring in her Eastern twin for the battle? He invited Bar to campaign for him, but did not ask his father to help him publicly. It wasn't that paternal support would hurt him: His father was popular in Texas—in 1992, he had won the state, and for that matter, Florida—but George W. could not afford to have any confusion about whether he was running on his father's record or his own. He mentioned his father in a speech delivered on George Bush's undisputed home turf—a rally at College Station, home of the presidential library—but in most public talks he would only refer to his famous mother. The tactic served multiple purposes. Not only would he de-emphasize the notion of political nepotism, he would remind people of how much the American public loved his mother, and he would show himself to be a man who respected the power of women, so Richards would have a hard time running a gender-based campaign.

He also would concede the personality contest. Although he could be a joking, smiling campaigner when pressing the flesh, he tended to remain businesslike in his speeches. He left the smart-alecky comments to Richards.

In 1990, against Clayton Williams, Richards had been masterful at playing to the thigh-slappers while still keeping her composure. On several occasions, Williams had gone too far and spewed off-color comments that badly damaged his standing. On one occasion, he predicted that he would "head her and hoof her and drag her through the dirt." He compared rape to Texas weather, saying, "If it's inevitable, relax and enjoy it." At one of the debates, a miffed Williams refused to shake Richards's hand. She just purred like a prairie cat. "Well, I'm sorry you feel that way about it, Clayton," she said. The audience roared its approval.

But something had happened to Richards's cool since 1990. On the trail, her attacks on George W. seemed oddly personal. In one speech, she tried to portray George W. as a man compelled into politics by vanity. "You just can't wake up one morning and decide you want to be governor," she told a crowd in Alice, Texas, in the spring of 1994. "You can't just be looking in the mirror shaving one morning and say, 'O Whee! You're looking good, you're looking real good—[she then made a kissing sound]—You're so good you ought to be governor.'"

At Texas Girls State, she lectured the teens on the need for independence, but the message took a dark turn. "I cannot tell you what a pitfall it is to count on Prince Charming to make you feel better about yourself and take care of you," she said, perhaps referring to the sting of the end of a 30-year marriage some years earlier. "Prince Charming may be driving a Honda and telling you that you have no equal, but that won't do much good when you've got kids and a mortgage and he has a beer gut and a wandering eye. Prince Charming, if he does ride up in a Honda, he's going to expect you to make the payments."

Perhaps the sweltering heat of Texarkana in mid-August had gotten to her this time around. "You just work like a dog, do well, and all of a sudden, you've got some jerk who's running for public office telling everybody it's all a sham and it isn't real," she said. "And he doesn't give you credit for doing your job." She started referring to him derisively as "Shrub."

George W. shamed her for her fit of pique. "The last time I was called a jerk was at Sam Houston Elementary School in Midland, Texas," he said, employing the kind of suavity he had witnessed in Bill Clinton when his father was hurling around the "bozo" epithet. "I'm not going to call the governor names," he added. "I'm going to elevate this debate to a level where Texans want it."

He later told the *Washington Post* that this moment was a turning point. "I think the dynamics of this campaign changed when she called me a jerk," he reportedly said. "People didn't like that, and they began to say, Wait a minute. If you base your whole reason for being on a personality, and the personality goes sour, well, I think it undermined the 'Reelect-Ann-Richards, she's-larger-than-life' feeling."

His campaign standards included not running a negative campaign on personal issues. Both candidates had acknowledged giving up drinking—he through his fortieth birthday vow, she through the 12-step system. In 1990, Richards's primary opponent had raised allegations that she had used illegal drugs. George W. said he would not pursue similar avenues of assault, since he wouldn't answer those questions himself. When confronted with the question by reporters, he said, "Maybe I did, maybe I didn't. How I behaved as an irresponsible youth is irrelevant to this campaign."

Behind the scenes, he could still be a bit of a hothead. The attention paid to Karl Rove sometimes seemed to eat at him. Once, after an event had ended and reporters were still asking Rove questions while George W. was free to walk away, he snapped, "Is the Rove news conference about over?"

On another occasion, George W. had given a speech in which he criticized Governor Richards for destroying her office's phone records. His mention of the incident seemed confused, however. "He muffed it," Rove reportedly told Brian Berry, Bush's campaign manager at the time. When George W. called for a postmortem of the event, Rove tried to broach the subject.

"You did good," said Rove, "I think you could have done better..." He was stopped by the voice on the other end, the *Dallas Observer* reported.

"I got it confused," Rove corrected himself. "You did great."

—

The blessing and the curse of running as a Bush would affect both Jeb and George W. on the trail. Both did extremely well with their fundraising—George W. even raised $1 million on a single night early in the campaign—and that could be largely credited to the vast network their father had established. Jeb was even able to forgo public funding of his campaign since he had done so well.

But they also would be hit by all of the old George Bush legacy issues. Maureen Dowd, then on the campaign beat for the *New York Times*, reported how at a stop in St. Petersburg, Florida, Jeb delivered a tough speech to the employees about how he would like to abolish the Florida department of education and crack down on teenagers who carried guns. "You're familiar with the Skull and Crossbones Society?" a secretary named Jackie Miller reportedly asked him. "I mean, Skull and Bones."

"Yeah, I've heard about it," he said.

"And you're familiar with the Trilateral Commission and the Council on Foreign Relations?" she continued.

"Yeah," he said.

"Well, can you tell the people here what your family membership in that is? Isn't your aim to take control of the United States?" The charge must have been wearying to Jeb, since it had been cropping up since 1978, but also there was a tinge of irony. The one Bush who briefly had been a member of the Trilateral Commission had been drummed out of the presidency and was now in retirement in Houston, playing with the grandkids, working on a book about diplomacy, and helping guide the construction of his presidential library in College Station, Texas.

—

The Texas Rangers had been leading their division; George W. hoped they would take it right to the World Series. But then the players' strike began. That kind of put a damper on the last few weeks of the campaign.

Even leading up to election night, George Bush thought that Jeb would be victorious and George W. would need to be comforted. On November 8, those fates reversed, and the retired president in Houston called his son in Austin to offer his congratulations for a victory of 54 percent to 46. "You've made me proud," he reportedly told George W.

The new governor-elect's friends from Midland, his high school buddies, his major supporters from across the state were gathered at a hotel in Austin to watch the returns. Dennis Grubb remembered how the excitement built as people got word of the good returns. Then he remembered the whole room starting to buzz. A kind of electric field filled the hall and the people in the crowd looked at each other in a daze, as if they had been shot with stunguns. A screen came down and showed the winning projections. George W. would win, 54 to 46 percent. People were screaming when a beaming George W. and Laura took the stage.

In his usual style, George W. was the first to leave the party, at 11:00. Grubb remembered wanting to leave a message for his old friend from Midland that night when he got back to his hotel room. He called George W.'s room at 11:30 and the new governor picked up.

"Can you believe it?" Grubb asked him.

"It's pretty hard," marveled George W. All of a sudden they couldn't talk the way they used to.

A few months later, Tom Schieffer, the president of the Rangers, went over to George W.'s house in Dallas to say good-bye on the day the family was heading off to Austin. The movers had already come and gone. While they were chatting, Schieffer kept getting choked up. He wished he could stop, but he couldn't.

"Come on, Schieff," George W. said, slapping him on the back. "There's no reason for that."

"Yes, there is," Schieff said. "It's not going to be the same anymore."

George W. smiled. "Of course it is," he insisted, putting his arm around him. "It will be exactly the same."

A month or two later, Schieffer got a call from the governor. George W. told him that he had just gotten back from hunting on a friend's ranch. When they were driving back along a dirt road toward the house, they came across a group of Mexican kids who had raced out, excited to see the governor. They had never seen a governor before and they were just beaming.

"You know, Schieffer," George W. said. "You're right, it's not the same."

XIV

THE CONTENDER

In 1980, George Bush had tried to snare the Republican presidential nomination with a slogan that would capitalize on the long dutiful career he had enjoyed in public office since he first won the chairmanship of the Harris County Republican Party in 1963. The pitch would encompass all that he had learned schmoozing with party poohbahs in every little hamlet across America when he was head of the Republican National Committee. It would encompass the secrets he had unearthed as head of the CIA, the delicate diplomatic dances he had done in China and at the United Nations.

In short, this slogan would set him apart from all the fly-by-night candidates who thought they could just jump from a governor's mansion into the White House—namely Jimmy Carter, the incumbent president who had annoyed the American people by failing to unravel the Machiavellian undercurrents of Washington and take a firm U.S. position in international affairs; and California Governor Ronald Reagan, the favorite candidate for the GOP that year, who lacked foreign policy experience. "You see," George Bush said in a speech to the Foreign Corespondents Club in Hong Kong, in 1978, just as he was gearing up for his own run, "my thesis is that the United States won't elect a person totally unfamiliar with foreign affairs, totally running against Washington and how Washington works."

That's why he hit on the slogan: "Elect a president we won't have to train."

As the presidential election in 2000 neared, that worry—that anyone who occupied the White House should have enough experience and expertise to negotiate their way through the complicated domestic and international issues of the modern day—had begun to plague George Bush's eldest son, George W. Bush. In early November 1999, the governor of Texas faced Andy Hiller, a wily television reporter from the NBC-affiliate in Boston, who decided to launch a pop quiz at the leading Republican candidate.

Who are the leaders of Chechnya, Pakistan, India, and Taiwan? George W. was asked, and he froze. He could only offer a reply to the question of Taiwan's president. "Yeah, Lee," he replied cryptically.

As for the general of Pakistan, he responded, "General. I can name the general. General." George W. offered the last response light-heartedly—showing off his quick, boyish, if roguish, charm. But his ignorance about the identities of those leaders caused many Americans to register concern, particularly the members of the press. Thomas Friedman, an editorial columnist for the *New York Times*, suggested he be given a more extensive quiz that would expose his broader vision. Maureen Dowd wrote dismissively that even "Lee" was probably a lucky guess.

The pop quiz was, to be sure, something of a cheap shot on the part of the media although the subject matter rated far above trivia. After all, each of the regions named is a hotspot with nuclear capabilities. Questions about broader diplomatic vision would probably have been more appropriate, but the quiz indicated a significant issue of George W.'s candidacy. The Boston reporter was grilling a man who could still remember the 1954 starting lineup of the New York Giants; who could memorize the names of his 50 fraternity brothers within days; who was able to recall the names of campaign volunteers from two decades earlier. If George W. had failed to identify those foreign leaders, the problem was not that he had a mind unaccustomed to detail. It meant that he had probably never paid attention to those subjects; he had no natural curiosity about Chechnya or Pakistan or Taiwan. He did not curl up at night with foreign policy treatises, nor perhaps, even a substantial news magazine, since those leaders were certainly in the news at the time.

In that lack of innate interest in foreign policy matters, he would be the polar opposite of his father, who had felt most passionately about the international affairs of the country. His father fared poorly on a pop quiz thrown at him on the trail in 1992, when he was asked the price of a quart of milk or loaf of bread. George W. was by far a candidate more interested in domestic issues, and he had come to that passion having won praise as the governor of Texas. The only guide the voters in the race for 2000 would be able to use to determine whether or not George W. was the kind of candidate who would need to be trained was contained in the four and a half years George W. had spent in the governor's mansion before heading out on the campaign trail for the presidency.

—

In each stage of George W.'s life, as he followed his father's path, he ended up with fewer accolades for his efforts. The baseball business alone had been the most satisfying and had given him a launching pad for his run for governor. With the win in 1994, he had established himself as a more disciplined candidate than his dad. Just days before George W. was voted into office, he told the *New York Times* what he had learned from watching his father's defeat two years earlier. "Bill Clinton drove the agenda against my father," he reportedly said. "My father let Bill Clinton decide what issues the two of them were going to talk about. That was a major mistake, and I wasn't going to let it happen this year."

George W. had picked his four issues before the race began—education, juvenile crime, welfare, and the importance of the free market—and hammered at them until voters knew where he stood. The result was that he had added a new name to the list of differentiations between the two George Bushes. It was now not just George and Georgie; or George Senior and Junior. With George W.'s election in 1994, friends and colleagues of the Bush family also could clarify which George they were talking about by saying President Bush or the governor.

George W.'s political strategy had not only snagged a clear victory, it had set a map for governing. The main task of a governor, according to the nation's governors themselves, is to be a manager. George W. seemed to survey his beloved Texas with the eye of a Harvard Business

School graduate. "People that have made a lot of business deals care about the bottom line," Representative Rob Junell, a Democrat, observed about George W. to the *New York Times*. "What they're concerned about is, let's close the deal. He's a pragmatist. If there's a problem, he wants to know [what] is the best way to solve it."

Texas, the second largest state, offered plenty of challenges in terms of the number and diversity of its constituents, but the governor's power to affect its fortunes is limited. The legislature only meets for 140 days once every two years, so the rest of the term the governor mainly uses his or her office as a bully pulpit to push pet issues. As governor, George W. could encourage legislators to introduce bills promoting his favorite causes, but he could not ensure that they would be put to a vote.

He did have the power to veto legislation (a two-thirds vote would be needed to override) and convene special legislative sessions to address particular bills that had not yet been settled. He could appoint the secretary of state, the parole board, and members of commissions and task forces, thus distinctly marking the management of the state. To oversee that distribution of jobs, George W. appointed his old friend from Andover and Yale, Clay Johnson, a decision applauded by many who knew the man once nicknamed "Opie." Johnson, formerly the chief operating officer of the Dallas Museum of Art, would not be swayed to award favors to beseeching friends and acquaintances. "It was brilliant to put Clay in there," said George W.'s friend, Charlie Younger. "He's totally loyal to George and he's very capable and is the Iceman."

George W. put to use the lesson that he had learned at Andover: Friendliness and enthusiasm could corral people into getting projects off the ground. Within days of George W.'s 1994 victory, he jump-started his term by traveling to the capital to meet with legislators to explain his agenda and gather feedback. By inauguration day, he had already sat down for one-on-one discussions with the leading voices in the Texas state house, as well as with 29 of the 31 state senators. Since the Democrats held the majority, he could not afford to play partisan politics, so he wooed legislators across party lines.

The most important Democrat, the man who could drag George W.'s agenda to a complete halt if he so chose, was Lieutenant Governor

Bob Bullock. Some political observers would note that George W.'s plan was blessedly close to the policy points that Bullock wanted to address, so resistance would be unlikely. But a personality clash could have changed that equation. The Texas political legend—a "Machiavelli in cowboy boots," as his friends described him—possessed the power, through the authority of his office, to choose which legislation went up for a vote, who would speak to support or bash the bill, and in what order. He selected the committee chairs and the membership of each subgroup. Bullock was a big personality, a recovering alcoholic who had been married five times. He had a vicious temper and would employ renegade techniques to achieve the results he wanted. He was famous for locking legislators in his office until he was able to establish consensus.

In George W.'s early days in office, the new governor noticed that one of his top aides had a Bullock bumper sticker plastered to his car, but did not sport a Bush one as well. As George W. remembered the incident, he mentioned the oversight to the aide, pointing out that the staffer worked for him, not the lieutenant governor, and should show suitable allegiance.

The aide replied, "Governor, you're new here. You just don't understand. Everybody works for Bullock."

George W.'s friend from Midland, Charlie Younger, remembered George W. telling him how Bullock was a tough old son of a gun, but that he intended to make him an ally. "He said, 'I'm going to break him down and win him over and charm him.' I guess like a snake charmer,'" said Younger. "He kept knocking away and obviously they ended up with a great relationship."

Not only did George W. stop by Bullock's Austin office to visit and hash out issues, he would call when the lieutenant governor was in retreat at his ranch in Llano, a little over an hour's drive from the capital. By the end of the first legislative session, Bullock extended an invitation to George W.'s legislative aide to attend all of the meetings at the capital—an unusual act of graciousness.

Bullock and George W. proved to be a powerful combination. Bullock understood the intricacy of crafting laws, the nuances of political infighting. George W. knew the direction he wanted the state to take. "With him, it is the vision thing," Republican state senator Teel Bivins told the *National Journal*, "that's his strong suit, looking to where he wants to go. In terms of legislative craftsmanship and the twists and turns to get there, that's his short suit. He says, 'My job is to set the goal, and your job is to figure out the details of how to get there.'"

George W.'s understanding of policy mainly came from reading summaries, not treatises. He would virtually commit policy memos to memory and then pick them apart in meetings, searching for the weak spot that the memo's author was trying to hide. His approach as governor sounded remarkably similar to his manner at meetings back at Arbusto when he could effortlessly dissect a salesman's half-baked pitch.

The four main points George W. ran on in 1994 had been reform of education, juvenile justice, welfare, and tort payouts. He managed to address each during his term. He encouraged legislators to pass a bill lowering the age at which a minor could be tried as an adult. He appointed a stern parole board that cut down on approvals by 8 percent. George W., who had been lucky so many times in the past, was fortunate again in that first term: A decrease in crime nationally, a phenomenon mainly attributed to the strong economy in the second half of the decade, was also reflected in Texas itself. During the term, the state would boast the lowest crime rate in history.

But George W.'s lack of attention to detail could sometimes work against him, as some of George W.'s 1994 campaign promises simply could not be fulfilled because of legal barriers. He had vowed to end parole for child molesters and murderers. Four years later, he was still unable to make that change, primarily because his goals collided with the Constitution. The courts ruled that parole was guaranteed in the basic rights provided for therein. Gary Mauro, the land commissioner and George W.'s Democratic opponent in the 1998 campaign for governor, would use that failure as a weapon against George W. But Mauro missed the larger point and made the mistake of promising the same policy change, saying that he would make sure the paroles were ended. George W.'s error in pushing the issue in the 1994 campaign was that, while he had the political capital to make the policy happen, he had not studied the fine legislative print to know that what he was proposing was impossible because of the court order.

Likewise, George W.'s plan to lock up juveniles picked up for carrying illegal firearms met a quick end when it turned out that rural counties did not have appropriate detention centers to hold the youths.

George W. had originally campaigned on an education plan that, he boasted, included "no detail," just a complete shift from state control to local dominion over education decisions. He ended up offering a package of programs that moved the system more slowly than expected. From Governor Ann Richards he had inherited a comprehensive testing program that gauged student achievement not only by grade, but by race and gender. The data could be used to focus attention on failing schools, but he also used testing to end the social promotion of students who failed to meet the state standards.

He increased the number of charter schools—which encouraged local innovation. He was proudest of his 1996 reading initiative, which required that all students be literate by the third grade. Perhaps he was inspired by the struggles of his own brother Neil, who had moved along through the early years of grade school without anyone discovering his severe dyslexia. Only when he stayed home sick one day did Bar notice the problem and begin trying to make up for lost time. With the new system of testing and tutoring, no child would be able to slip through without learning the basics of reading at an early age.

None of George W.'s new initiatives actually cost the state significantly more money. When George W. arrived in office, Texas ranked 35th out of the 50 states in spending on education, and at the end of his first term the position was the same. But his biggest education challenge was to change the funding model in Texas. The state operates on a Robin Hood formula where wealthier communities pay higher property taxes to fund education in poorer schools. George W. campaigned in 1994 on the promise that the structure would be modified to something more equitable if he were elected. With that vow, many voters in upper-middle-class communities were more than happy to support him. Once he took office, he offered to cut property taxes by $3 billion a year, and make up the money by increasing the state sales tax by a half penny and levying a fee for professional partnerships, including accountants, attorneys, and doctors. Democrats cheered the idea, but the state Republican Party chair, Tom Pauken, was furious with the proposal, calling it a "Democratic tax hike."

George W. ignored Pauken's anger and went out on the trail, drumming up support. When the legislature was in session, the governor rarely campaigned publicly for his own issues, since he believed such efforts politicized the debate. But on this agenda item, he made an exception.

In the end, George W.'s plan was defeated and many supporters of the governor's race for 2000 praised the day. The legislature devised its own strategy to cut property taxes by $1 billion. George W. blamed his setback on his colleagues' lack of imagination. "The status quo is a powerful, powerful force in the face of a noncrisis situation," he told the *National Journal*. "We had no crisis, and oftentimes government is reactive as opposed to proactive."

Still, some of George W.'s wealthier constituents in Texas were annoyed that he failed to deliver on that election-year promise to abolish the Robin Hood structure. Tax reform advocates complained that he had signed a pledge during the campaign not to raise sales taxes and then violated the oath by proposing just that. George W. argued that he was responsible for the largest tax cut in the state's history, since he had signed the $1 billion reduction. Further, he explained that although he had proposed the sales tax, his bigger property tax cut would have more than offset the effect on Texans' pocketbooks. But if he had gotten the tax proposal passed, no matter how he justified the idea that the financial rewards to taxpayers would be greater, he would have been hit with the George Bush curse, some of his supporters believe. George W. would have his own "no new taxes" debacle to live down.

As for welfare, during George W.'s first term, monthly rolls decreased by half to 474,755. That reduction was remarkable, but credit had to go not only to the welfare-to-work program, but to the vibrant national economy that was lifting the fortunes of so many Americans. The state's programs that funneled welfare recipients into jobs were not considered among the nation's best, and the minimum wage—which overrode federal minimum wage standards primarily for farm work—had held at a steady $3.35 an hour throughout George W.'s term.

George W.'s call for tort reform seemed to have been influenced by the values he developed in Midland. He was so impassioned about the need to rein in lawyers, both in what they charged their clients in fees and what they demanded in tort payments in the courts, that he put the matter toward the top of his agenda for the first legislative session. With Bullock, he negotiated a limit to the amount that courts could order in punitive damages. George W.'s annoyance with attorneys was probably fostered during his days as an oil man in West Texas. "Lawyers were a necessary evil," observed his childhood friend from Midland, Randy Roden, who returned to the town as an adult. "You just made the deal and then got the lawyers to draw up the documents and hoped they didn't cause too much trouble. If [the transfer of mineral rights] didn't involve title to land, even though it involved large sums of money, the oil men probably wouldn't have used lawyers."

Of course, as governor, George W. would be forced to address issues beyond his four main campaign proposals. While he was not a member of the National Rifle Association, he did oppose gun control beyond those laws already on the books. As far back as September 1988 his main political adviser, Karl Rove, understood the importance of such a position in Texas. When George Bush was running against Dukakis, Rove told the press, "Texas values include rugged individualism and, by God, the right to keep and bear arms. And some goofy governor from up north who wanted to register BB guns is not our kind of guy."

Not long into his first term, George W. signed a law legalizing concealed weapons. In his home state, such a position meant strong support from voters. But in the wake of the carnage in Littleton, Colorado, among other shooting tragedies, George W. became vulnerable to criticism about this issue when he was on the trail in 2000. Several people were killed in a Fort Worth church by a gunman in the summer of 1999, and George W. quickly cut short a campaign trip through Michigan to get home to Texas. He announced that the blame fell on "a wave of evil" spreading across the country. A week later he proposed appointing "gun prosecutors" to enforce existing laws.

George W. was almost an amalgam of his parents' views on abortion. His father was pro-life, his mother quietly pro-choice. She refused to discuss her disagreement with her husband with the press. Once, when giving an interview in April 1989, she was happily conversing on a myriad of topics until she and the reporter came to a question about whether or not she and the president discussed their differing abortion stances. "What I talk [about] to George Bush is none of your business," she barked.

Like his father, George W. was pro-life, but, like his mother, he remained rather reticent on the subject. Fortunately for him in the late

1990s, abortion was no longer being used as a wedge issue in the same way it had in previous campaigns. A national poll conducted by the *Dallas Morning News* in May 1999 showed that over half of the Americans surveyed "want the next president to leave most abortion laws alone." Many pro-life forces had become disgusted by the violence committed against abortion doctors in the name of their cause and had toned down their rhetoric. Pro-choice supporters seemed relatively quiet about the piecemeal restrictions being placed on abortion state by state, and in fact, according to the survey, most Americans favored parental notification.

George W. declared himself pro-life, but was far from a radical on the issue. He supported the ban on partial-birth abortion, and pushed a bill through the state legislature in 1999 that required a minor to gain parental consent before undergoing the procedure. But he had stated that he abides by the *Roe v. Wade* decision as the law of the land and would not use abortion as a litmus test when appointing Supreme Court justices, should he win the presidency. "The United States Supreme Court has settled the abortion issue: There will be abortions in Texas and the rest of the United States," he said. "I believe that the best public policy is to encourage fewer abortions through strong adoption laws and by sending a clear abstinence message to our children."

He had allowed his prison board to decide most death penalty issues for him. In February of 1998, Karla Faye Tucker was put to death, the first woman executed in Texas since the Civil War. Her case had gained international media attention because the convicted pickax murderer had become a born-again Christian while in prison. George W. refused to intervene in her execution, saying that he had appointed people he trusted to that board and that their decision would be appropriate for him.

In another case filled with high emotion, George W. refrained from traveling to Jasper, Texas, after James Byrd Jr., a black man, was decapitated after being dragged to his death by several white men. George W. did not visit the city while tensions were high, explaining that he thought such grandstanding would be unseemly. Critics chastised him for not taking the occasion to make stronger statements about race issues, and were even angrier when he failed to push for a hate-crimes bill to move through the legislature. The legislation died in the senate during the 1999 session before reaching his desk; an event that some observers credited to friendly politicians who did not want to see the governor forced to sign a bill that included language making anti-gay violence a bias crime—a policy conservative Republicans would be likely to abhor.

Like Bill Clinton, George W. refrained from employing the easy tactic of creating a common enemy within his constituency to galvanize his support. He did not spout anti-gay, anti-immigrant, or even anti-Democrat rhetoric. When he was asked about the Texas sodomy law on the 1994 campaign trail, he admitted that he supported the existing statute prohibiting such conduct, but three years later, when a debate arose at the Texas Republican convention about whether or not a gay group could set up a booth, he asked for an end to the "name-calling." When Republicans launched a national crusade against immigration, demonizing Mexicans in particular, George W. wrote a *New York Times* op-ed article calling for the criticism to stop. He refused to campaign against Democratic incumbents during his term in office because those politicians had all helped him get legislation passed.

During the 1994 campaign, he had set off a flurry of criticism when he repeated to a reporter that his view of salvation was that one needed to commit one's self to Christ. "It was, of course, picked up and politicized," he told the *New York Times*. "You know, 'Bush to Jews: Go to Hell.' It was very ugly." Then, he added one of those candid comments that made him such an unusual politician in the modern era. "It hurt my feelings," he said.

If Bill Clinton was any gauge, then this tendency to take a stand on various issues, but not too loudly, could help George W. win over more conservative Democrats. Even the Christian Coalition had changed its strategy in the last few elections to get more like-minded candidates elected to office; the idea was to address education and the pocketbook issues first, then start discussing the more volatile morality debates. George W., as a pragmatic rather than revolutionary conservative, subscribed to this plan naturally.

———

Back in 1988, when George W.'s father was running for president, the eldest son hopped aboard a fishing boat with the candidate for an interview with Walt Harrington of the *Washington Post*. The three men were out on the Saco River in Kennebunkport, when Harrington brought up how George Bush had been raised a child of privilege. He wanted to discuss how that reality might affect George Bush's understanding of the struggles of the poor. George W. reportedly interrupted him. "This sounds, well, un-American to George Jr., and he rages that it is crap from the sixties," Harrington wrote. "Nobody thinks that way anymore!"

By the time George W. became governor, however, he seemed to have sprouted concern for the powerless and disenfranchised. His efforts focused on education, particularly in rural areas predominantly inhabited by new immigrants. By the time he ran for president, his platform was dedicated almost entirely to the need for "prosperity with a purpose"—maintaining a strong economy that could finally reach down to the poorest Americans, that could go toward investing in sound education for all.

Like his father, George W. tended to sympathize with people after he had met them, having little ability to imagine the predicament that some American citizens might face. At one point during his governorship, he visited a prison and came into direct contact with some of the "thugs" he had campaigned against so fiercely in the 1994 campaign. After he had toured the facility and heard from the prison authorities about their programs, George W. asked the young inmates if they had any questions. One teenager raised his hand. "What do you think about me?" he asked.

George W. choked up. He told the young man that he and the state of Texas cared about him, but that the teen needed to be punished for what he had done. Despite the firm statement, the message was a far cry from the "thug" rhetoric he had spewed a few years earlier. By 1998, George W. had become a more mature candidate because of the extended contact he had had with his state's own citizens.

How did he transform himself from a candidate primarily concerned with protecting the oil industry in 1978 to one more eager to campaign for children and the working poor? Certainly, his wife Laura's interest in childhood education and reading initiatives must have greatly affected his priorities. But his religious epiphany in 1985 and the spiritual work that followed changed him too.

"He wants faith to be vibrant," Reverend Anthony Evans, an adviser and friend to the governor told the *Boston Herald*. "He believes government should serve God's interests. Government can hand out money and such, but government can't express love. People need an anchor for hope and stability."

George W.'s proposed social programs—such as teen education to promote saving sex for marriage and faith-based drug and alcohol counseling—reflected this interest in government's creating a kind of moral compass.

—

There was almost no transition from George W. running for reelection to the governor's mansion in 1998 and the presidency in 2000. He didn't just campaign for statewide office, he auditioned for a bid for the White House. Soon after the 1996 election, a Republican pollster conducted a national survey to test the top contenders who might ostensibly face the likely Democratic nominee, Al Gore, in the next presidential race. George W. placed far above the rest of the pack. In the United States—as in media-saturated Texas—name recognition meant everything. Republicans frustrated by the back-to-back presidential defeats in 1992 and 1996 came courting George W. to consider a run for 2000.

For the 1998 campaign in Texas, George W.'s opponent was Land Commissioner Gary Mauro, and from early on, most observers believed that he would offer George W. no real challenge. One hundred of the state Democratic leaders crossed party lines to endorse George W. Most importantly, Bob Bullock, the diehard Democrat, stated that he could not in good conscience campaign to remove a qualified governor from office. He endorsed George W., defying not only his own party, but his personal relations: Bullock was godfather to Mauro's daughter.

On another front, George W. had more good news. The Bush/Rose group sold their interest in the Rangers to Tom Hicks on June 16 for $250 million. George W. received $14.9 million, which included the extra 10 percent he was guaranteed if the partners earned back their initial investment. With that windfall, he could claim that he not only built a stadium for the area, but he proved himself to be a savvy businessman in his own right. He could also be assured that if his pursuit of the presidency fell apart, he would have plenty of personal wealth to cushion his fall from politics' highest echelons. But he parted from baseball filled with some regrets. He had resigned his direct participation just after the election in 1994. "Baseball's still a huge issue with me because it helps define part of my identity," he told the *New York Times*. "It speaks to the person who likes to go watch 70 baseball games, and speaks to the issues that are important to me and the fans. It was a huge tug, deciding to not be involved with shaping a sport, shaping a way of life."

On the campaign trail, he refused to confirm or deny his plans to run for president in 2000, despite the fact that the national press was hovering. "I don't know whether I'll seek the presidency or not," he told the *Dallas Morning News*. "I told the people of Texas if that bothers you when you go into the voting booth, then make that part of your consideration. I understand the consequences of not making up my mind." Still, he added, "I don't think there would be all this speculation going on if the people didn't think I was doing a good job as governor."

Laura too was noncommittal. "We haven't thought through anything specifically about George running [for president]," she told the *Dallas Morning News*. "I really haven't. Plus, I'm busy. I don't have a lot of time to spend going over every decision. And George and I, actually, neither one, are the types that do that. We don't agonize over decisions. We just do things."

Despite George W.'s successes as governor, some of his friends began wondering if he would run for president for the simple reason that his current duties left him with so much excess energy. Both George Bushes had pep that needed to be spent and what better way than shaking hands, hopscotching across the country, and negotiating the ins and outs of power shuffles. Certainly, this was preferable to a life of quiet contemplation. George Bush, when he was president, once outlined his frenetic vacation plans at Walker's Point to the *Washington Post*. "I'll play a good deal of golf here, a good deal of tennis, a good deal of horseshoes, a good deal of fishing, a good deal of running—and some reading," he said smiling. "I have to throw that in for the intellectuals out there."

Being governor wasn't exactly a full-time job. As described in *Texas Monthly*, George W. arrived at the office by 8:00 A.M.; then left for a run at the track at 11:40 and returned at 1:30. He would play video golf or computer solitaire until 3:00. "There were days when [the legislature] weren't in session, to be honest with you, he was looking for something to do," said Younger. "He would go out and burn some energy. Go jog or do something to kill time." Reportedly he carried an electronic device that kept him continuously updated on the Texas Rangers' stats.

His scheduled appointments, according to *Texas Monthly*, never lasted five minutes more than their designated allotment; when the time was up, an aide would knock on the door. If George W. thought the subject matter was important enough, he might wave the staffer away for another five minutes, but when the second knock came, the visitor would be shunted out. The magazine also noted that official dinners at the governor's mansion would never last past 9:00 P.M., at which point George W. could brutally make his point: "Okay, you're outta here."

That blunt style served him well when trudging through the bureaucracy of a large state. *Texas Monthly* described a meeting with George W. and a group of university chancellors who had come calling to win $1 billion more from the state budget for higher education. George W. asked them, "Would you accept five hundred million?" They immediately agreed.

He then told them that he had been kidding about the $500 million, but since they acquiesced so quickly to a budget cut of 50 percent, they would have to come back to him with a justification why they needed the money at all.

To the press, that mischievous sense of humor could be endearing, as when he jokingly provided leads to a *Texas Monthly* reporter by reeling off a list of sordid gossip items swirling about him, such as the rumor "I bought cocaine at my dad's inauguration." At other times, he just came off as abrasive. He blew up at a reporter who had the audacity to pull out a pad and pen and start taking notes at a scheduled photo opportunity, then followed the reporter around to make sure he didn't start writing again. He has been known to be curt. "Get outta here now, go play in traffic," he once told another local reporter.

On election day, November 3, the Bushes celebrated double victories as Jeb beat Lawton Chiles in Florida and George W. defeated Mauro. In Texas the returns were 69 to 31 percent. Political observers noted how Jeb had learned a few lessons since the 1994 campaign from his older brother. "[George W.] ran on four or five items or whatever it was," Jeb told the *New York Times*, "and he stayed focused on that. And that is a great lesson in politics." Jeb also recognized how George W.'s upbeat approach worked better with voters than the "headbanging" rhetoric that Jeb himself had employed in 1994. The public preferred the "optimism" that George W. offered.

. With that 1998 reelection, George Bush's eldest son became the first governor in Texas history to be returned for a back-to-back second term. That event made the already heated speculation about his run for president even more feverish. His father had been the first vice president since Martin van Buren to be elected directly to the presidency. If George W. were to win the highest office in the land he would be the first son of a president since John Quincy Adams to ascend to the White House.

Despite the fact that George W. was fighting a nasty case of the flu at his second inaugural ball, he seemed to settle back and enjoy himself more. Perhaps his enemies could view his first election to the governorship as a fluke—as the hand-me-down of his father's legacy. But there could be no doubt that his reelection was reward for his own performance. Finally, he could feel that he had earned power on his own merits.

In a 1999 interview with the *National Journal*, George W. discussed the success of his friendly, bipartisan approach. "You think you can take your style in Austin up to Washington?" the reporter asked him.

George W. seemed almost plaintive in his reply. "It's not just me," he said. "That's the point I'm trying to explain to you. It's an administration." He had grown to like the fact that governing was not a solo operation. He enjoyed the fact that he had, by his own assessment, attracted a staff of bright, enthusiastic people to government. He seemed to recognize that he was just head cheerleader; the real players were in the field.

His response seemed so different from the attitude he had demonstrated when he claimed full credit for his financial windfalls out in the

Midland oil fields with Spectrum 7 and Harken. He seemed more mature than when he grabbed full credit for putting together the Texas Rangers deal at the press conference announcing the purchase; he was finally more honest than when he claimed to have been the individual who fired George Bush's chief of staff, John Sununu. After more than four years in the governor's mansion, he had learned that he didn't have to author every detail of a project to gain accolades for his skill as a team leader.

Just after the inaugural in 1999, George W.'s friends noticed the atmosphere around their friend becoming a little more rarefied. He was under the media's microscope, working harder as he sandwiched in meetings with presidential campaign advisers, under pressure to make that year's legislative session one that he could run on.

He began to smooth over any tattered feelings he might have left behind over the years of drinking and smart-aleck responses. He sent Don Evans to talk to former lieutenant governor Ben Barnes about what he remembered about George W.'s admission to the Texas National Guard.

In the spring of 1999, Al Hunt, of the *Wall Street Journal*, received an unexpected call from George W. The governor apologized for blowing up at the journalist back in April 1986 at the Mexican restaurant in Dallas; he had been ticked off because Hunt had picked Kemp as the probable 1988 Republican presidential nominee for the *Washingtonian Survey*. George W. said he was sorry he had cursed out Hunt in front of his four-year-old son. He went on to say that he had just been defending his father.

"I did not go to any lengths to point out that he really wasn't defending his father," Hunt recalled later. "[My choice of Kemp] was far more benign than that."

Was the apology that of a good man or a politician? The timing certainly appeared suspiciously strategic, an effort to sweep up past faults before the reporters started to call not just his friends, but the people he had wronged over the years.

Hunt accepted the apology, but saw no reason to stop relating the story when asked about the incident. A few months later, *Washington Post* reporters Lois Romano and George Lardner Jr. interviewed the governor for a series of long profiles; they questioned him about the

1986 encounter. George W. told them that they should ask Hunt about the event. When they told him that Hunt had recalled the incident to them, George W. said he could not recall "what was said." The *Post* reporters asked why Hunt received the apology after such a long delay. "I heard he was angry about it, and it began to weigh heavy on my mind," George W. explained to the reporters. "I would have done it earlier had I realized I had offended him."

—

Traditionally, Republicans have honored the diligent party servant when picking their presidential nominee. George Bush was of that mold, as was Bob Dole. Unfortunately for the party, those candidates could not excite the electorate enough to secure either of the last two elections for the GOP. Clearly, the party was looking for a winner in 1999; whether George W. had earned the honor through a lifetime of achievement or dutiful labor was beside the point. "He's at fifty percent in the polls" among Republican voters, Scott Reed, who headed Dole's campaign in 1996, told the *Wall Street Journal* in May 1999. "Half the people who are for him can't exactly tell you why. They know his name, they liked his father, they think he's going to win." For the first time in his life, George W. was drafted into service—this time to run for the presidency.

Charlie Younger believed George W. struggled with the choice. "It hasn't come easy," Younger said. "He's made some gut-wrenching decisions to even go, and he's had pressure on him from a lot of people telling him he had to do it, [otherwise] he may not have done it. I know that somebody like George Shultz has pressured him and told him you've got to step forward. We need you. The country needs you. The minister at his last inauguration, Mark Craig, gave a prayer breakfast before the inauguration day. He was quoting a couple of biblical verses about leadership and his mother said he's really trying to talk about you, George."

—

George W. would likely be facing Al Gore if he ran in 2000. Both were sons of revered political men, but as far as George W. was concerned, the similarities ended there. At the 1998 Alfalfa Club dinner in

Washington, D.C., he joked with the crowd. "Can you imagine how much it hurt," he said, "to know that Dad's idea of the perfect son was"—pause— "Al Gore?"

On a more serious note, George W. defined the distinction between him and the vice president once again by geography, just as he had clarified the nuance between him and his father. "I think there's a huge difference [between Al Gore and me]," he told *Texas Monthly*. "And I think the difference can be described by the difference between being raised in Midland and being raised in Washington." Which is to say that the most important moment in making him the kind of politician who could work personal magic on the campaign trail, who could understand the travails of middle-class, rural, and suburban voters was when his father pointed the nose of his 1947 Studebaker toward the prairies of West Texas.

George W. had first campaigned against Gore in 1984, when George W.'s friend from Yale, Victor Ashe, was running for senator from Tennessee. George W. rolled along the trail for a seven-city swing that kicked off the campaign. He accused Gore of trying to portray himself as a friend of Ronald Reagan in his television advertisements, when he had no basis for making the link. "An obvious political ploy will not hunt in east Tennessee or Tennessee as a whole," he reportedly told a cheering crowd in Sevierville. "It is certainly not going to hunt with the two people I represent. I can assure you there is only one candidate in this race who is supported by President Reagan and Vice President Bush, and that is your next U.S. Senator, Victor Ashe." Gore won that race.

George W. also had, of course, campaigned against Gore when the senator from Tennessee was on the ticket with Bill Clinton in 1992, but at that time, the focus of the Bush aggression was not the "Ozone Man." They were looking to topple Bill Clinton's steamroller course up the polls. One hint of what the strategy might become as the 2000 election approached is contained in one of Bar's diary entries from 1992: "I can't understand [Clinton] picking another southerner from a small state. Al has a good military record and a very nice family. He is a liberal and a demagogue. Neither he nor Clinton have ever been in the private sector. They are just professional politicians. They have made their living in politics. Amazing."

Despite the heated atmosphere of the campaign, George Bush,

ever gracious, officially offered his blessing to Bill Clinton after the election. As Bush prepared to leave the White House for the final time, he left a note in the drawer of his Oval Office desk to let the new president know that he was rooting for him. That was before the Monica Lewinsky scandal.

In George W.'s lucky life, perhaps no event was so pivotal as Bill Clinton's dalliance with Monica Lewinsky. In the Restoration comedy or national tragedy that followed, the nation's love affair with its president cooled and voters began looking for options other than Clinton's hand-picked successor for their next president. The scandal also gave George W. license to be disgusted with the man who defeated his father for violating the Bush clan's Family First motto.

On August 17, when President Clinton was still giving his testimony in front of the grand jury, George W. vented some of his long-held fury for the man who had, in his opinion, defiled the office that his father held so dear. George W. offered the comment that he "felt embarrassed for the country" because of Clinton's actions.

Lanny Davis, George W.'s friend from Yale and, at that time, an aide to Bill Clinton, was appearing on television with Brian Williams that afternoon. When the clip rolled showing George W.'s comment, Davis became irate. "I was just in a state of pique," said Davis. "I was mad at Clinton, I was mad at everyone, and I thought that George was piling on. I sat on the set with Brian Williams beating up on me about Clinton being a liar and I didn't know if I wanted to be where I was. And my old friend George Bush just couldn't resist piling on—that was my reaction. I thought, give me a break, George, can't you just hold fire for a couple of hours?"

"I was in college with George Bush Jr.," Davis said to Williams on the air that day. "And if we start seeing smug, sanctimonious comments from political officials, especially Governor Bush, throwing stones in glass houses, I think everyone is going to be at risk." Davis said later that as soon as he made the remark, he regretted it. The telephone switchboard at the studio lit up with callers eager to hear the sordid details of life at Yale.

When Williams came back on the air after a commercial break, Davis apologized to George W. and said he had meant nothing by his comment. Soon after, Davis ran into a good friend of both President

Clinton and George Bush. "I said, 'Look, I don't think my writing George Bush now would do him or me any good because if someone got a hold of it in the middle of all this public stuff I'm doing for President Clinton, it would blow it up all over again. But I hope you'll give a message to him that I hope he'll forgive me and I still consider him a good friend.' Time passed and I believe it was right after the impeachment vote where I got a handwritten note from George saying, 'President Clinton should be very proud of what you did for him,' 'I admire greatly what you did,' or something like that."

The message was vintage George W.: He might not respect Bill Clinton, but he honored Davis's loyalty to the president, as well as his own bonds of collegiate friendship from long ago. George W. had no problem maintaining those friendships across party lines.

But George W.'s feelings for Bill Clinton himself were apparently a different story. Some of the most staunch supporters of George W.'s campaign for 2000 would not let America forget the turmoil that Bill Clinton put the country through by indulging in the affair. They said that George W. needed to enter the race to help lift the national moral climate. "Reverend Graham has told [George W.] that he has to do it," said Charlie Younger. "Because of where America is today."

Many friends and supporters of George W. believed that's why he had been able to break all records for fund-raising—accumulating over $50 million in the first six months. The voters would rather have someone they could trust than a policy wonk. Given the fact that George W. was a rather unknown quantity in the early stages of the campaign, the supporters had to have been inferring a hereditary honesty descended from George W.'s father.

Oddly enough, the field for 2000 began filling with other nemeses of George W.'s father from his many years in public service. By the fall of 1999, Pat Buchanan, one of George Bush's toughest opponents from the campaign seven years earlier, began threatening to launch his own effort for the election at the turn of the millennium. In 1992, Buchanan had upset George Bush's efforts in the New Hampshire primary by arriving early in that crucial state and drilling his populist message directly against the president. "Patrick J. Buchanan handing the baton, the proverbial political knife, off to Ross Perot," George W. told the *New York Times* in 1998. "The kind of isolationism and nativism and very harsh attacks against George Bush. You die a death of a thousand cuts in the political process."

When Buchanan began expressing his disgruntled views of the GOP, George W. first sought to appease him by begging him to stay in the party, saying that the tent was big enough for all views. He then confessed to the press that he thought that Buchanan's rumblings, and Perot's encouragement of them were all part of a vendetta against the Bush family. In 1994, Perot had tried to chip away at George W.'s support in Texas by endorsing Ann Richards; and this new alliance, George W. believed, was a way for Ross Perot to deliver yet another attack on George Bush by toppling his son. In late 1999, Buchanan left the Republican Party to run on the Reform Party ticket with Ross Perot's blessing.

—

In the post-Lewinsky era, George W. drew a line between the kind of bad behavior a politician needs to reveal and that which he doesn't. Bill Clinton violated the public trust by engaging in the affair with the White House intern while in office and then by not revealing his transgressions. George W. believed that his own wild antics did not need to be discussed because they existed in the past and because he had always been faithful to his wife. He answered questions about his more reckless days with the statement, "When I was young and irresponsible, I was young and irresponsible." As rumors circulated about youthful drug use, he refused to answer the specific queries, saying that he did not want to set a bad example for young people—including his two daughters—by itemizing past transgressions. He suggested that the lax moral climate of the era in which he came of age was to blame for whatever indulgences he might have committed.

Many of his supporters—and friends, including Lanny Davis—congratulated him on limiting his responses. "The issue for George [W.] is, will he set important ground for the future in really breaking this scandal-machine culture that his father speaks so eloquently [about]," said Davis.

In the fall of 1999, George W. still had been successful in keeping the media at bay. But some of his friends theorized that he also needed to keep talk of his wild side to a low whisper to cast his persona in the mold that American voters most love: the Comeback Kid or the Underdog. He needed to be perceived as a man who had lost his way at one point, and—through religion—quit drinking, found focus, and would eventually ascend to the presidency. Without that plot point, his story would be that of a privileged young man who was given a good deal of assistance from family friends and acquaintances until he found his niche in the governor's mansion. For the sake of the narrative of the American Dream, George W. needed to be the Prodigal Son, lost at some point, in some way, so that the public could feel that he earned the presidential nomination and perhaps the White House itself.

—

Before George W. hit the trail for 2000, he required some work polishing his views on national issues. He viewed himself almost as the politician-as-entrepreneur, a man who risked innovative thinking to solve problems. He considered himself a political conservative, but spontaneous enough to devise solutions outside of the rigid dogma.

Back in 1990, when he was considering a run for governor, he traveled to Austin to cram on statewide issues with a bunch of policy experts. From the time he first began working toward a run for the presidency, he maintained a regular schedule of policy meetings where he gathered disparate voices in the Republican party to hash out issues. According to many of those who attended, George W. took great glee in assembling the most diverse group he could find and then letting the discussion fly for several hours. He would ask hundreds of specific questions, demonstrating the same intense curiosity that he displayed when campaigning on the backroads of West Texas.

His biggest stumbling block to date has been his command of the details of foreign policy. He dubbed the Kosovars "Kosovians," and the Greeks "Grecians." But he has been consulting with such advisers as former Secretary of State George Shultz and a former member of Bush's National Security Council, Condoleeza Rice, to formulate a coherent international strategy. He has been focusing his concerns on China, which he considers a "competitive partner," and Russia, which he believes should be held to higher accountability before the United States continues to prop up its economy. He staunchly opposes the kind of global intervention Bill Clinton engaged in with Haiti and

Rwanda, and what his father undertook in Somalia. In a George W. administration, the vital—as opposed to humanitarian—interests of the United States would need to be proved before military action could be justified.

Most of George W.'s friends have said that despite the joy he feels in accepting the challenge of a presidential campaign, if he were to choose his time to run for the highest office in the land, it would not be in 2000. He worries about his teenage daughters and what effect the spotlight might have on them, and he frankly has enjoyed being governor of Texas. If he wins, he will be leaving his home state at least two years earlier than he would like.

But he has said that he believes that if he does not run now, he probably will never have another shot. At one point, he turned to the Bush's old family friend, Fay Vincent, for his counsel on whether or not he should launch such an ambitious pursuit. "My advice to him was that when he was eighty-five and on a screened porch and looked back," said Vincent, "if he didn't run, he would regret it. But for some magical reason the stars all lined up for him. Who could have predicted this ten years ago? It just happened. He is a very lucky guy in that sense. And you can't fail to take advantage of that. And as I said, my analysis is, even if you don't make it you will be much happier having tried. At least when you're on the porch, you took a shot at it. You failed. That's the way it is.

"But otherwise you sit on the porch and wonder infinitely."

NOTES

Chapter I

11   The war "was against imperialism and against facism ...": David Frost, "George Bush on God, War and Ollie North," U.S. News & World Report, December 14, 1987.

14   "What you'll find about George Bush ...": Barry Bearak, "Team Player Bush: A Yearning to Serve," Los Angeles Times, November 22, 1987.

15   "For one thing, Barbara, young George ...": George Bush with Victor Gold, Looking Forward: An Autobiography (New York: Bantam, July 1988), p. 43.

15   "The biggest difference between me and my father ...": Patricia Kilday Hart, "Don't Call Him Junior," Texas Monthly, April 1989.

16   "George's mother was a formidable and strong ...": Peggy Noonan, What I Saw at the Revolution: A Political Life in the Reagan Era (New York: Random House, 1990), p. 303.

17   "The boys were more scared of him ...": Herbert S. Parmet, George Bush: The Life of a Lone Star Yankee (New York: Scribner, 1997); Parmet's interview with Nancy Bush Ellis, November 12, 1992.

19   "God's therapy" he called his autobiography ...: G. Bush with Gold, Looking Forward.

19   George W. would later say ...: Donnie Radcliffe, Simply Barbara Bush (New York: Warner Books, 1989), p.140.

21   "slightly spoiled little boy ...": Barbara Bush, Barbara Bush: A Memoir (New York: Scribner, 1994), p. 35.

22   In the frantic last weeks before giving birth ...: B. Bush, Barbara Bush: A Memoir.

25   Every morning ...: Author interview with oil man from Midland.

25   "If I had to go talk to somebody ...": Author interview with Terry Throckmorton, August 5, 1999.

25   At First Presbyterian ...: Ed Todd, "Teacher Was Popular with Presbyterian Youth," Midland Reporter-Telegram, January 20, 1989, p. 11.

26   "You have two choices in life ...": B. Bush, Barbara Bush: A Memoir.

26   "All my life, I'd worked ...": G. Bush with Gold, Looking Forward.

28   Not that George Bush ... So much for the bond of the man's word ...: G. Bush with Gold, Looking Forward.

Chapter II

30   "I'm either going to lie on the bed and look at books ...": Patrick Crimmins, "Houses reflect developing status of young family," Midland Reporter-Telegram, January 20, 1989; B. Bush, Barbara Bush: A Memoir, p. 49.

31   "You should take her home, make life easy ...": B. Bush, Barbara Bush: A Memoir.

31   "You could never live with yourself ...": Barbara Bush interviewed by Amy Cunningham, "'I made up my mind, she'd be happy'," reprinted in the Midland Reporter-Telegram, January 20, 1989, from Texas Monthly, February 1988.

31   He ran to ask his teacher if he could go see his mother ...: David Maraniss, "The Bush Bunch," Washington Post Magazine, January 22, 1989.

32   Robin had died ... It wasn't fair ...: George Lardner Jr. and Lois Romano, "A Sister Dies, a Family Moves On; Loss Creates Strong Bond Between Mother, Son," Washington Post, July 26, 1999.

33   They had been so strong ...: Ibid.

33   "At least it wasn't your firstborn ...": Ibid., p. 46.

34   As Dottie Craig said ...: Julie Hillrichs, "No Frills Style Familiar to Midlanders," Midland Reporter-Telegram, January 30, 1998.

34   "One way she'd be spinning around like this ...": Radcliffe, Simply Barbara Bush, p. 120.

34   "[The death] was a sad and disturbing ...": Author interview with Randy Roden, August 2, 1999.

34   "Nobody's trying ...": Ibid.

35   "I have to be with my mother ...": Radcliffe, Simply Barbara Bush, p. 120

35   In a letter to his mother ...: Ibid., p. 48.

36   "It was gruesome ...": Author interview with Terry Throckmorton, August 12, 1999.

36   George W. played sandlot football ...: Author interview with Randy Roden, August 2, 1999.

36   During the spring ... Author interview with Austine Crosby, June 17, 1999.

37   George W. would later recall on of the most poignant moments of his life ...: Pamela Collott, "The Son Rises," Texas Monthly, June 1999.

37   He came up with the idea of pasting the Topps cards ...: Author interview with Terry Throckmorton, August 2, 1999.

37   "Dear Mister, I sure do hope you make the All-Star Team ...": Ibid.

38   "There's no way you could get Mickey ...": Ibid.

39   George Bush loved the camp so much ...: Author interview with Tex Robertson, June 12, 1999.

39   The family never coddled the kids ...: Author interview with Fay Vincent, July 16, 1999.

39   The telling moment for Fay ...: Ibid.

40   "I was surprised ...": Author interview with Jim Oberwetter, July 29, 1999.

40   "Don't be ridiculous ...": Parmet, George Bush: The Life of a Lone Star Yankee, p. 23.

40   "My grandmother is an unbelievable ...": Radcliffe, Simply Barbara Bush, p. 136.

40   "We need a doll house ...": B. Bush, Barbara Bush: A Memoir, p. 48.

40   "We need a legitimate ... Her peace made me feel strong ...": Ibid.

42   "I want to be an ambassador ...": Ed Todd, "Then, A Handshake Was a Man's Bond," Midland Reporter-Telegram, November 28, 1989.

42-43 ... she would later say ... It meant he could enter politics ...: Barbara Bush interviewed by Amy Cunningham, "'I made up my mind, she'd be happy'."

43   ... he was drinking sake with his friend C. Fred Chambers ... His plan was to be a senator ...: G. Bush with Gold, Looking Forward, p. 71.

44   Baine and Mildred Kerr found a 1.2-acre lot ...: Collott, "The Son Rises."

44   "One day at Kinkaid ...": Ibid.

44   "I had moments where I was jealous ...": Radcliffe, Simply Barbara Bush, p. 128.

45   "She'd say, 'Alright' ..." Ibid., p. 129.

45   "I don't think that's any good ...": Lardner Jr. and Romano, "A Sister Dies, a Family Moves On."

45   "Once he had to drive his mother ...": Ibid.

45   "'Don't you think he ought to talk about this ...'": Ibid.

Chapter III

46   "Congratulations, son ...": Lardner Jr. and Romano, "A Sister Dies, a Family Moves On."

47   It would help him springboard ...: Author interview with L. E. Sawyer, June 25, 1999.

47   The higher score meant ...: "Well Begun Is Half Done," Time, October 26, 1962.

48   One legend ...: Author interview with Peter Schandorff, July 8, 1999.

49   "The spirit of man ...: "Well Begun Is Half Done," Time, October 26, 1962.

49   "Last weekend was the greatest ...": B. Bush, Barbara Bush: A Memoir, p. 56.

49   "Without a great deal of effort ...": Author interview with Randy Roden, August 2, 1999.

50   "It's a natural challenge ...": Ibid.

50   "He was a real quiet man ...": Author interview with Peter Schandorff, July 8, 1999.

50   "He was sort of like" ... His tone left no room for talking back ...: Ibid.

51   Some of the dorms had working ...: Author interview with L. E. Sawyer, June 25, 1999.

51   Randy Roden remembered ...: Author interview with Randy Roden, August 2, 1999.

52   "The biggest crime we could commit growing up ...": Radcliffe, Simply Barbara Bush, p.129.

52   "The ratio of dollars spent for educating a white child ...": Steve Finch, "Bill Higgs, Mississippian Attorney, Talks On Horrors of Segregation," The Phillipian, Phillips Academy newspaper, April 17, 1962.

53   If there were any group ... burger joint until curfew ...: Author interview with Peter Schandorff, July 8, 1999.

53   "Don't you think that's true, Herbie? ... Yeah, I think that's right ...": Author interview with John Kidde, June 28, 1999.

53 George W.'s other big buddy ... Author interview with Don Vermiel, August 3, 1999.

53 George W. was a near-jock ... didn't fit him ...: Author interview with Tom Eastland, August 5, 1999.

54 And George W. could keep right up ...: Author interview with John Kidde, June 28, 1999.

55 But before he got expelled ... the young French teacher ...: Author interview with Tom Eastland, August 5, 1999.

56 "They're running scared ...": Ibid.

57 "He was unembarrassable ...": Sam Ellis, "When George W. Bush Was the Stickball King," Boston Globe, June 20, 1999.

57 "Today my daughter graduates ...": "Well Begun Is Half Done," Time, October 26, 1962.

57 "He did not lay back ...": Author interview with Tom Seligson, June 25, 1999.

57 "Everything has turned into numbers ...": Cummisky, "The Voice of the NEGO."

58 "I wish ...": Ibid.

58 By the time I graduated ...: Author interview with Tom Seligson, June 25, 1999.

58 "Last year the student was lost ...": The Phillipian, October 15, 1963.

58 "We're going to work hard next year and try to make it an honor to be a cheerleader ...": The Phillipian, May 28, 1963.

59 "He just loved being in the midst of stuff ...": Author interview with Randy Roden, August 2, 1999.

59 He'd made varsity ...: Author interview with Don Vermeil, August 3, 1999.

60 The next week, inspired by a teacher's speech ...: "Mike Wood Picked '65 Head Cheerleader; Bush's Boys Instruct New Megaphonemen," The Phillipian, May 6, 1964.

60 A boy once got kicked out of church because under his suit and tie ...: Author interview with Peter Schandorff, July 8, 1999.

60 The cheerleaders would get everyone chanting ...: Ibid.

61 His lecture that day ran long ...: The Phillipian, October 22, 1963.

61 The Phillipian came to the cheerleaders' defense ...: Ibid.

62 "I didn't know what George would do ...": Author interview with Dan Cooper, August 24, 1999.

62 Tom Seligson remembered looking out his dorm ...: Author interview with Tom Seligson.

63 Randy thought they were talking about Sean Kennedy ...: Author interview with Randy Roden.

63 "[George W.] was very upset about the tragedy ...": Author interview with John Kidde, June 28, 1999.

64 "What the hell is this?" ...: Ibid.

64 "My parents gave this to me ...": Ibid.

64 "I see no hope of John getting ...": Ibid.

64 ... once Benedict put up that challenge, he'd been forced to prove him wrong ... appealed to the ...: Ibid.

65 "He came home and he was real ticked off ...": Ibid.

66 "He got it read because ...": Ibid.

66 "Have we come to the point in our life as a nation ...": "Rockefeller Under Fire, Bush Urges That He Withdraw," U.S. News & World Report, June 24, 1963.

66   "There is a philosophy that is the basis ...": Interview notes from Herbert Parmet research.

67   "He's such a hateful warmonger ...": Author interview with Randy Roden, August 2, 1999.

67   Still the New York Times review ...: "One Senator's Manifesto," New York Times Book Review.

68   He introduced the rest of the commission ...: "Stickball High Commission Prevents Plans; 'Tweeds' Denies Underworld Connections," The Phillipian, April 15, 1964.

68   Rumors about Lucky Luciano: Ibid.

68   "I don't consider anyone who's been deported ...": Ibid.

69   "George took responsibilities ...": Author interview with Tory Peterson, August 19, 1999.

69   "Somebody's got to be at the bottom ...": Author interview with Peter Schandorff, July 8, 1999.

70   The tea dances thrown by the clubs were a slight improvement ...: Author interview with John Kidde, June 28, 1999.

70   She kept up with George W. for a time ...: Author interview with Debbie Taylor Smith, August 4, 1999.

70   "first upperclass to eat in an unproctored ...": Pot Pourri, 1964.

71   "There were no crusades ...": Ibid.

Chapter IV

73   "If you were in politics ...": Parmet, George Bush: The Life of a Lone Star Yankee.

75   "There is a Christian innocence ...": "Team Player Bush: A Yearning to Serve," Los Angeles Times, November 22, 1987.

76   "We should repackage our philosophy ...": George Bush, "The Republican Party and the Conservative Movement,", National Review, December 1, 1964.

76   Celebrating second-term victory: "Bush Says Ideal GOP Candidate for 2000 Race Should Be Upbeat," Dallas Morning News, November 20, 1998.

76   When George Bush first moved his family ... like Borneo and Trinidad: "Senate hopeful 'Texan' Bush feels at home," Dallas Times-Herald, June 4, 1964.

76   He even drilled...: "A Well of a Deal," Common Cause, March-April 1991.

76   As GOP Chairman of Harris County ...: Ibid.

77   George Bush's whole point...: "Harris County GOP Chief May Oppose Yarborough," Dallas Times-Herald, September 11, 1963.

78   She insisted that her children brag about the team's accomplishments...: "Bush Opens Presidential Library," Midland Reporter-Telegram, November 7, 1997.

78   He was setting out on the road...: Richard Ben Cramer, What It Takes (New York: Random House, 1992).

78   So he used Bentsen's desertion ...: "Bush Reports GOP Views on LBJ Role," Dallas Times-Herald, January 10, 1964.

79   "He reminds me of Stassen ...": "Bush Jabs Cox, LBJ, Yarborough," February 7, 1964.

79   "I'm pleased to detect ...": "Senate hopeful 'Texan' Bush feels at home," Dallas Times-Herald, June 4, 1964.

79   Amazingly, even after...: "Bush Opens Presidential Library," Midland
        Reporter-Telegram, November 7, 1997.
79   Cox returned the favors...: "Two Drilling Contractors Making Political
        History," Dallas Morning News, May 31, 1964.
80   On April 13th, he brought up charges...: "Bush Raps Estes Ties of
        Candidate," Dallas Times-Herald, April 13, 1964.
82   You have served your country well...: "Race Bias Scored in Prayer at Yale,"
        New York Times, June 11, 1962.
83   "Connecticut is home to Senator Prescott Bush ...": Author interview with
        Lanny Davis, July 30, 1999.
83   George W. and his friends ...: Author interview with Robert McCallum, July
        12, 1999; Yale Daily News Reunion Issue, May 27-30, 1993.
83   "Let's rock and roll ...": Lois Romano and George Lardner Jr., "Following
        His Father's Path, Step by Step by Step," Washington Post, July 27, 1999.
84   "the darling of the John Birch Society ...": G. Bush with Gold, Looking
        Forward, p. 78.
84   The night before the election ... Yet the broadcast that night featured ...:
        Author interview with Martin Allday.
84   "It was just nervousness-like ...": "Bush Admits Loss, Congratulates Foe,"
        Dallas Morning News, November 4, 1964.
84   At the Hotel America ...: Ibid
85   "George Bush ought to pick up his baggage ...":"'He Beat Me Fair and
        Square,' Bush Admits—Now Back to Work," Houston Chronicle,
        November 4, 1964.
85   "I just don't know how it happened ...": Ibid.
85   "I literally ate for days after ...": Author interview with Martin Allday.
85   "My father had a great disappointment ...": Romano and Lardner Jr.,
        "Following His Father's Path, Step by Step by Step."

Chapter V

86   "So he couldn't backslide ...": Author interview with James Lockhart.
87   He just personalized what people said about his father ...: Author interview
        with Kenneth Cohen, August 5, 1999.
87   "I knew your father ... Maintain the wound ...: Romano and Lardner Jr.,
        "Following His Father's Path, Step by Step by Step."
87   "George W. is not duplicitous ... right to the other team ...: Author interview
        with Robert McCallum, July 12, 1999.
88   "We could play like we discuss books and stuff around the dinner table ...":
        Maraniss, "The Bush Bunch."
88   "big secret was how smart he was and he didn't want anybody to know it
        ...": Author interview with Lanny Davis, July 30, 1999.
89   "unprintable activities with young women ...": Author interview with
        Lanny Davis, July 30, 1999.
89   "I was eighteen or nineteen at the time ...": Radcliffe, Simply Barbara Bush.
89   "I'd be surprised if George didn't ...": Author interview with Russell
        Walker, August 19, 1999.
89   "Marijuana didn't really appear until senior year ...": Ron Rosenbaum, Yale
        Class of 1968 Reunion Book.
89   "He just didn't have his heart in making money anymore ...": G. Bush with
        Gold, Looking Forward, p. 89.

90   "Bush his strongest and [his opponent] weakest ...": James Allison and Harry Treleaven, "Upset: The Story of the Modern Political Campaign," February 1967.

91-92   "12 Basics of the Bush for Congress ...": Ibid.

92   "Okay gang—pile in! ...": Ibid.

93   George Bush's effective advertisements ...: Ibid.

93   Briscoe began criticizing Bush for overspending ...: Ibid.

93   "Gosh, Mother and Dad ...": Parmet, George Bush: The Life of a Lone Star Yankee.

93   "I have been elected to practice law ...": Dallas Morning News, November 9, 1966.

94   "And today, with TV taking them into everybody's home right along with Johnny Carson ...": Allison and Treleaven, "Upset: The Story of the Modern Political Campaign."

94   "I'm wondering if I said the right words ...": Ibid.

94   Bush's stage directions: Ibid.

95   "only a cigarette burn": Romano and Lardner Jr., "Following His Father's Path, Step by Step by Step."

95   "I don't know if I still have it ...": Author interview with James Lockhart.

95   "Such practices imperil the reputation of the house, the worth of the IFC ...": Yale Daily News, editorial, November 3, 1967.

95   George W's practices as president of DEKE: Romano and Lardner Jr., "Following His Father's Path, Step by Step by Step."

97   The engagement to Cathy Wolfman: Houston Chronicle, January 1, 1963.

97   "Personally," he told him, "I think you are too young ...": Author interview with Donald Ensenat, August 1, 1999.

98   Arguments about Vietnam: Author interview with Robert McCallum, July 12, 1999.

98   "[Quarrels] came back to visit on leave ... George was much more forgiving ...": Author interview with Robert Birge.

99   Birge recalls George W.'s passion for fighting in Air Force: Ibid.

99   "George W. and I had no objection to military service ...": Author interview with Donald Etra, July 1, 1999.

100   "I knew he was going to be in a military air program ...": Author interview with Robert McCallum, July 12, 1999.

100   Reagan whispered to an aide that the Yale students were "surprisingly quiet and receptive ...": Tom Herman, "Politics," essay in Yale 1968 Class Reunion book.

101   Rosenbaum uncovers secrets of Skull and Bones: Ron Rosenbaum "The Last Secrets of Skull and Bones," Esquire, September 1977.

102   Skull and Bones German slogan: Ibid.

102   "It's a much smaller group ...": Author interview with Robert McCallum, July 12, 1999.

102   Bones members shared first their biographical histories: Rosenbaum, "The Last Secrets of Skull and Bones."

103   "He was much more introspective than Strobe ...": Author interview with Robert Birge.

103   "When you got to know him as just another student ...": Ibid.

103   George W. being escorted down the field with a cop holding each arm: Author interview with Donald Ensenat, August 17, 1999.

104   "I frankly am lukewarm on sending more American boys ...": "Houston

GOP Lawmaker Plans Junket to Vietnam," Dallas Morning News, September 17, 1967.

105   "When I came home I read about the shelling of Danang ...": Parmet, George Bush: The Life of a Lone Star Yankee.

106   George W. explained that he had decided on the National Guard ...: "Bush received Quick Air Guard Commission," Los Angeles Times, July 4, 1999.

106   "Governor Bush did not need and did not ask ...": "Texas Speaker Reportedly Helped Bush Get Into Guard," Washington Post, September 21, 1999.

106   Deposition states that Bush asked friends for help in getting Jr. in National Guard: "Bush Resists Call to Testify in Lawsuit," Reuters, July 30, 1999.

106   George W. was also subpoenaed in the lawsuit against GTECH: Ibid.

107   George W. letter to Barnes: "Bush Friend Pushed For Guard Slot," Washington Post, September 28, 1999.

107   Jim Lockhart turned to Senator Humphrey for assistance with Navy OC3: Author interview with James Lockhart.

108   "George W. and I knew it would change the fabric of the school ...": Author interview with Kenneth Cohen, August 5, 1999.

108   That year George Bush only managed to win 3 percent of the "Negro or Latin" precincts: Author interview with Martin Allday.

109   George W. says he wants to fly "just like his daddy": "Bush Received Air Guard Commission," Los Angeles Times, October 29, 1999.

109   "Nobody did anything for him ...": Ibid.

110   Another 150 applicants for all the Texas Air Guard posts, including ground crew, waited on a list ...: Ibid.

110   "George W. was stunned and horrified like the rest of them ...": Author interview with Donald Etra, July 1, 1999.

110   "Maybe George W. despaired for his father's safety ...": Author interview with Kenneth Cohen, August 5, 1999.

110-111   Until last Wednesday morning I hadn't expected ... in order of seniority ...": Kingman Brewster Jr., "The Pall of Negativism," speech, June 9, 1968.

111   "As long as the United States continues to wage its war in Vietnam ...": "Statement Blasts War Draft," Yale Daily News, May 10, 1968.

112   "It wasn't said in passing ...": Romano and Lardner Jr., "Following His Father's Path, Step by Step by Step."

112   "Don't cut this off just because you might die or something ...": Author interview with Britt Kolar.

Chapter VI

114   He would be given a discharge ...: Military Records, September 3, 1968; George Lardner Jr. and Lois Romano, "At Height of Vietnam, Graduate Picks Guard. With Deferment Over, Pilot Training Begins," Washington Post, July 28, 1999.

115   "I, George Walker Bush ...": George W. Bush military records, Department of the Air Force Statement of Intent.

115   That's when he was, by his father's own description, lost ...: "Team Player Bush: A Yearning to Serve," Los Angeles Times, November 22, 1987.

115   While George W. acknowledged how aimless ...: Ibid.

116   "A total Nixon man ...": Parmet, George Bush: Life of a Lone Star Yankee, p. 157; Ehrlichman notes of meetings with the President, November 17, 1972, Fenn Gallery, Santa Fe, NM.

116 "Doubt if you can do better than Bush ...": Ibid.

116 ... take Nixon's daughter on a date ...: Pete Slover, "'Irresponsible Youth,' No Real Scandal," Dallas Morning News, November 15, 1998.

116 Rose would continue to recommend W. for a promotion ...: George Lardner Jr., "Bush Friend Pushed for Guard Slot, Ex-Speaker Testifies," Washington Post, September 28, 1999.

117 Lieutenant Colonel Walter B. Staudt greenlighted George W. for advancement ...: Confirmed by Lt. Col. John Stanford, Public Affairs Officer with the Texas Air National Guard.

117 "I've never heard of that ...": "Bush Received Quick Air Guard Commission," Los Angeles Times, July 4, 1999.

117 The Los Angeles Times discovered documents itemizing standards for promotion in pilot training ...: Ibid.

117 George W. just answered in the negative ...: From "Application for a Commission for Training Leading to a Commission or for Flying Training in Officer Grade," May 28, 1968.

118 George W. wrote none in those boxes: Ibid.

118 David Beckwith reportedly insisted that W. was quickly accepted ...: "Bush Received Quick Air Guard Commission," Los Angeles Times, July 4, 1999.

118 Staudt staged a second swearing-in ceremony ...: Lardner Jr. and Romano, "At Height of Vietnam, Graduate Picks Guard. With Deferment Over, Pilot Training Begins."

118 "We were looking for someone to get the media on and of the plane ...": "Inside the Beltway," Washington Times, June 25, 1999.

119 "I've got someone in mind ...": Ibid.

119 "How much will we have to pay him ...": Ibid.

119 Gurney's views: Mike Morgan, "Fifth Collins-Gurney Clash Echoes First," Miami Herald, October 22, 1968; Georgia Marsh, "Vote Drive Zooms to 115-mph Pace," Miami Herald, October 1968; John McDermott, "Gurney Tactics: Link Foe to LBJ-HHH Liberalism," Miami Herald, October 1968.

119 He believed that the U.S. needed to go in "hot pursuit "...: Ibid.

120 In Gurney's case ...: McDermott, "Gurney Tactics: Link Foe to LBJ-HHH Liberalism"; Georgia Marsh, "Johnson's Credibility Gap, Law and Order Stand Raked," Miami Herald, October 25, 1968.

120 Gurney did not disclose the fact that a good portion of his missed votes ...: Morgan, "Fifth Collins-Gurney Clash Echoes First"; McDermott, "Gurney Tactics: Link Foe to LBJ-HHH Liberalism."

120 "followed a national trend ... to deeper conservatism ...": John McDermott, "Gurney Defeats Collins with Big-City Showing," Miami Herald, November 6, 1968.

120 He told his supporters at his election night celebration ...: Ibid.

121 George W.'s father traveled from Washington to pose with them ...: Lardner Jr. and Romano, "At Height of Vietnam, Graduate Picks Guard. With Deferment Over, Pilot Training Begins."

121 George W. seemed to be the only guardsman ...: Confirmed by David Hanifl, another trainee at the time.

121 Usually, the air force would not train a recruit ...: Author interview with David Hanifl, July 15, 1999.

121 "Basically we knew George was there ...: Author interview with David Hanifl, July 15, 1999.

121 "You had to pass a lot of tests ...": "Bush Received Quick Air Guard Commission," Los Angeles Times, July 4, 1999.

122 "How do you read this crap?": Author interview with David Hanifl, July 15, 1999.

122 "I thought George W. was pampered ...": Ibid.

122 Hanifl considers not ever flying with W. a lucky coincidence ...: Ibid.

123 Senior instructors seemed to seek out contact with George W.: Ibid.

123 George W. revealed to some of the other pilots that he had taken a plane up ...: Ibid.

123 About half of George W.'s pilot training group flunked out ...: Author interview with David Hanifl, July 15, 1999.

123 George W. was special to the most powerful people ...: Ibid.

124 Bush described Nixon as "kind of pulled back ...": Parmet, George Bush: The Life of a Lone Star Yankee, p. 157.

124 "It's hard to say no ...": Los Angeles Times, November 22, 1987.

125 Nixon's "tough and cold" personality ...: Parmet, George Bush: The Life of a Lone Star Yankee, p. 157.

125 George Bush boils over at protesters ...: Parmet, George Bush: The Life of a Lone Star Yankee, p. 79; Scott McCartney, Houston Post, June 26, 1988.

126 Allison stayed put on at RNC ...: Jane Marler Dees, "Bush Pays Tribute to 'The Aide'," Midland Reporter-Telegram, January 20, 1989.

126 "He told me he loved [flying] ...": Author interview with Don Etra, July 1, 1999.

126 Cathy Wolfman says George and Cathy drifted apart ...: Pete Slover, "Texas Governor's Ex-Fiancee Says She Has No Regrets and Sends Bush Good Wishes," Dallas Morning News, April 1, 1999; Romano and Lardner Jr., "Following His Father's Path, Step by Step by Step," Washington Post, July 27, 1999.

126 Other friends hypothesized ...: Ibid.

126 "I don't want to say ...": Author interview with Robert Birge, August 25, 1999.

127 "I loved [George] ...": Slover, "Texas Governor's Ex-Fiancee Says She Has No Regrets..."

127 "They were very nice ...": Texas Monthly, June 1999.

128 " I went to see him ...": Author interview with David Hanifl, July 15, 1999.

128 "His parents had the attitude that he had been isolated ...": Ibid.

129 The talk, almost from the start ...: "Team Player Bush: A Yearning to Serve," Los Angeles Times, November 22, 1987.

129 Bush felt he owed such a courtesy to Johnson ...: Parmet, George Bush: The Life of a Lone Star Yankee.

129 "Tweedledum" versus "Tweedledee": "Team Player Bush: A Yearning to Serve," Los Angeles Times, November 22, 1987.

130 "George Walker Bush is one member of the younger generation ...": From Press Release of the Texas Air National Guard, March 24, 1970.

130 "really neat ... It was fun, and very exciting ...": Ibid.

130 "I did [ask]—and I was told, 'You're not going' ...": Lardner Jr. and Romano, "At Height of Vietnam, Graduate Picks Guard. With Deferment Over, Pilot Training Begins."

131 "Lt. Bush's skills far exceed his contemporaries ...": Military Records, November 3, 1970.

131   He played all-day games of volleyball in the pool ...: Texas Monthly, June 1999.

132   "surrogate candidate": Military Records of George W. Bush, Application for Reserve Assignment, May 24, 1972.

132   they did not have to believe in the Republican platform ...: Author interview with Nancy Ippolito, September 27, 1999.

132   George W whipped off his shirt ...: Texas Monthly, June 1999.

133   the "vision thing": "Team Player Bush: A Yearning to Serve," Los Angeles Times, November 22, 1987.

133   George Bush puts forward his views on election day ...: Sam Kinch Jr., "Bush Proposing Department on Population-Environment," Dallas Morning News, October 17, 1969; "Bush Favors Lowering Possession Penalty," Dallas Times Herald, August 11, 1970; "Bus Unlooses Pitch to Latins," Dallas Morning News, October 15, 1970; Stuart Davis, "Bush Cites 'Can-Do' Philosophy as Main Difference," Dallas Morning News, October 31, 1970; Martin Casey, "Bush Urges Select Ethics, Conduct Committee," Dallas Morning News, March 16, 1967.

134   "And I'm for block grants, decentralization ...": Davis, "Bush Cites 'Can-Do' Philosophy as Main Difference."

134   "I hope I never get so blasé ...": Stuart Davis, "Bush Given Warm West Texas Welcome," Dallas Morning News, October 30, 1970.

134   Secret "Townhouse Operation" fund: "Team Player Bush: A Yearning to Serve," Los Angeles Times, November 22, 1987.

135   "Oh, no, it won't ...": Dees, "Bush Pays Tribute to 'The Aide'"; "Bush Wipes Tears Away," Dallas Morning News, November 5, 1970.

135   "I can't find anything to blame ...": "Bush Trying to Find What Went Wrong," Dallas Morning News, November 5, 1970; "'Too Many Dems': Bush Not Sure Why He Lost," Dallas Times-Herald, November 4, 1970.

135   "I've got a house, a wife ...": Ibid.

135   "I had a depth of feeling about being in the senate ...": "Focus," Dallas Morning News, December 27, 1970.

135   "George Bush doesn't get mad when he loses ...": Author interview with Jim Oberwetter, July 29, 1999.

136   "We weren't looking for someone ...": Lardner Jr. and Romano, "At Height of Vietnam, Graduate Picks Guard. With Deferment Over, Pilot Training Begins."

137   "Lt. Bush is very active in civic affairs ...": Military Records, May 26, 1972.

137   He was briefly suspended from flying ...: "Bush Received Quick Air Guard Commission," Los Angeles Times, July 4, 1999.

137   "Now the fellow in charge of that agency ...": Jon Nordheimer, "Sparkman Cites Service in Bid for Re-Election," New York Times, October 26, 1972.

138   Blount Billboards: Ibid.

138   "let them think it out for themselves ...": Radcliffe, Simply Barbara Bush, p. 131.

138   George W. told David Maraniss about trying to establish his own identity ...: David Maraniss, "The Bush Bunch."

139   "Oh, I'm not going ...": Robert Draper, "Favorite Son," GQ, October 1998.

139   "He wasn't that wild ...": Texas Monthly, June 1999.

139   George W. meets Jimmy Dean: Lardner Jr. and Romano, "At Height of

Vietnam, Graduate Picks Guard. With Deferment Over, Pilot Training Begins."

141   Bar begged Bush not to take the post if it was offered ...: "Team Player Bush: A Yearning to Serve," Los Angeles Times, November 22, 1987.

141   "being married to a centipede ...": Ibid.

141   "You can't imagine the tension ...": Ibid.

142   "While they were drinking Chivas Regal ...": Lardner Jr. and Romano, "At Height of Vietnam, Graduate Picks Guard. With Deferment Over, Pilot Training Begins."

142   "You know Harvard Square and how they felt about Nixon ...": Radcliffe, Simply Barbara Bush, p. 139.

142   "Yesterday was a real downer ...": Parmet, George Bush: The Life of a Lone Star Yankee, p. 172; George Bush to Thomas Ludlow Ashley, August 21, 1974, Thomas Ludlow Ashley Papers, MS-159, Center for Archival Collections, Bowling Green State University, Bowling Green, OH.

142   "[George Bush] thought he had it ...": "Team Player Bush: A Yearning to Serve," Los Angeles Times, November 22, 1987.

Chapter VII

145   "By the early 1980s, Midland was the richest town in America ...: David Pasztor, "Midland, Odessa Bury the Hatchet," Dallas Times-Herald, March 11, 1984.

146   "He has said that if he were to die tomorrow ...": Collott, "The Son Rises."

147   "'Anywhere else in America ... underneath that counts ...'": Author interview with Randy Roden, August 2, 1999.

149   "To learn the business ... shopping deals ...": Author interviews with L. E. Sawyer, June 25, 1999; Martin Allday, August 11, 1999; and Buzz Mills, August 2, 1999.

150   "I'm so glad that SOB ... to a reporter ...": Maraniss, "The Bush Bunch."

150   "He and George hit it off ... dogs at the racetrack ...": Author interview with Charlie Younger, July 13, 1999.

150   "'I bet I could beat ... he said ...'": Author interview with L. E. Sawyer, June 25, 1999.

151   "We'd go out in the boat ... manage the boat as well ...": Lardner Jr. and Romano, "A Sister Dies, a Family Moves On; Loss Creates Strong Bond Between Mother, Son."

152   "Donnie Evans remembers ... fly a Cessna ...": Maraniss, "The Bush Bunch."

152   "As Michelle, one topless waitress ... in having fun ...": Pasztor, "Midland, Odessa Bury the Hatchet."

154   "In late 1975 ... be a renegade agency ...": Parmet, George Bush: The Life of a Lone Star Yankee, p. 180.

154   "But George W. called ... want you home ...": Radcliffe, Simply Barbara Bush, p. 164.

154   "But Carter chose ... forced to resign ...": Parmet, George Bush: The Life of a Lone Star Yankee, p. 206.

156   "When one of George W.'s older ... George W. retorted ...": Author interview with Midlander.

157   "When young George W. Bush popped into the race ... overlapped with the U.S. congressional ...": Author interview with Kent Hance, August 7, 1999.

157 "What we need is decent representation ... first political campaign ...": Richie Reecer, "Bush to Be Candidate," Midland Reporter-Telegram, July 20, 1999.

157 "George W. had convinced Donnie ... aspired to public office ...": Author interview with Robert McCleskey, July 7, 1999.

158 "George W. implied that ... Midland oilman ...": Reecer, "Bush to Be Candidate."

158 "I'm idealistic enough to think some good ... George W. said ...": "George Bush Jr. Enters Race for Mahon's Seat," United Press International, July 20, 1977.

158 "The son of former CIA ... races by himself ...": Ibid.

159 "Three of us were diving under the couch ... supreme volunteer ...": Maraniss, "The Bush Bunch."

160 "Hance thought George W. seemed like a nice enough guy ...": Author interview with Kent Hance, August 7, 1999.

160 "Any time he ... out of there ...": Author interview with Charlie Younger, July 13, 1999.

161 "I would never have matched ... reveler and rambler ...": Ibid.

161 "Barbara Bush insisted ... recall the incident ...": Skip Hollandsworth, "Younger. Wilder?," Texas Monthly, June 1999.

162 "My personal explanation ... crossed at the right time ...": Author interview with Charlie Younger, July 13, 1999.

162 "We don't agonize ... after meeting ...": Todd J. Gillman, "Texas' First Lady Wouldn't Fight Run for White House; Laura Bush Said Husband Is Really Undecided," Dallas Morning News, February 1, 1999.

163 "I don't really like ... where we philosophize ...": Ibid.

163 "In general ... need to one of them ...": Ibid.

163 "When they were married ... insisted on truthfulness again ...": Kimberly Goad, "Laura Bush: Adjusting to the Spotlight, the First Lady Relishes Her New Role," Dallas Morning News, September 24, 1995.

164 "He promised never to ask her ... running with him ...": Ibid.; author interview with Ruth Schiermeyer.

Chapter VIII

166 Namely he used a few of his father's local contacts ...: Author interview with Martin Allday, August 11, 1999.

167 Later in the campaign, Hance made an issue of all the money ...: Lana Cunningham, "Bush Says Most Contributions Come from Within 19th District," Midland Reporter-Telegram, November 1978.

167 Media calls George W a carpetbagger: Midland Reporter-Telegram, May 30, 1978.

167 George W responds to the charge of being a carpetbagger: Ibid.

169 Hance/Blanchard debate: Author interview with Kent Hance, August 7, 1999.

169 1978 Congressional race between Bush, Sheats, Hickock, and Reese: Ibid.

170 "we're going to be polite and dignified ...": Ed Todd, "Bush Planning Run-Off Tactics," Midland Reporter-Telegram, May 10, 1978.

170 he said that Reese had "insulted the voters" ...: Ibid.

170 "We don't need Dad in this race ...": Ibid.

171 The farmers blamed the sudden about face ...: Nicholas Lemann, "Pointing a Finger," New York Times, January 7, 1979.

172   Ag movement tractors stop traffic: Washington Post, February 8, 1979.

172   The farmers back down when reporters agree to print their side: Author interview with Jay Harris, August 17, 1999.

172   "tooth and toenail on farm issues ...": Ibid.

172   Reese observed that George W got a few dirty looks: Author interview with Jim Reese, August 20, 1999.

172-173 Dialogue about Trilateral Commission ... Author interview with Kent Hance, August 7, 1999.

175   "The Trilateral Commission thing ...": Author interview with Charlie Younger, July 13, 1999.

175   The farmers in Hereford told Lewis that Bush said he wanted to take them on ...: Author interview with J. C. Lewis, August 18, 1999.

175   George W. defended himself saying ...: Lana Cunningham, "Bush (of Connecticut) Reveals His Single Regret," Midland Reporter-Telegram, June 2. 1978.

175   "George W's a personable young man ...": Carolyn Barta, "George W. Bush Trying to Hold Up Tradition in Runoff," Dallas Morning News, June 2, 1978.

176   Reagan gives another $2,000 to Reese: Lois Romano and George Lardner Jr., "A Run for the House; Courting a Wife, Then Voters," Washington Post, July 29, 1999.

176   "I'm not interested in getting into an argument ...": Ibid.

176   Post reports that Bush complained to Reagan: Ibid.

178   Hance and Bush help a guy with a broken-down car: Author interview with Kent Hance, August 7, 1999.

179   Bednard throws a "Bush Bash": Lana Cunningham, "GOP Candidate Bush Under Fire from Hance Camp," Midland Reporter-Telegram, November 3, 1978.

180   "This is the only place where we served beer ...": Ibid.

180   "Maybe it's a cool thing to do at Harvard ...": Ibid.

180   "That is harking back to my education ...": Ibid.

180   Hance owns Fat Dogs: Author interview with Ruth Schiermeyer, November 7, 1999.

180   Weiss tells of George W.'s spontaneity: Author interview with Mike Weiss, August 18, 1999.

180   "Ruthie, Kent Hance is not a bad person ...": Author interview with Ruth Schiermeyer, November 7, 1999.

181   Schiermeyer tells Hensely about Bednard's working for Hance: Ibid.

181   Hance says his "Bush Bash" didn't hurt George W.: Author interview with Kent Hance, August 7, 1999.

182   George W concedes to Hance: Jim Steinberg, "Hance, Citing His Legislative Experience, Wins Mahon Seat," Midland Reporter-Telegram, November 8, 1978.

182   "We got to be friends during the campaign ...": Ibid.

183   "When the Trilateral Commission that had absolutely nothing ...": Author interview with Ruth Schiermeyer, November 7, 1999.

Chapter IX

185   George W.'s uncle Jonathan helped put his nephew's drilling fund ...: Romano and Lardner Jr., "Courting a Wife, Then the Voters."

185 "I was running Columbia ...": Author interview with Fay Vincent, July 16, 1999.

186 Uzielli was also a close friend ...: Kevin Sack, "George Bush the Son Finds That Oil and Blood Do Mix," New York Times, May, 8, 1999.

186 "I originally invested in some wildcat drilling ...": Charlotte Anne Lucas, "Bush Has Fared Well Despite Firms' Troubles, Candidate Credits 'Hard Work, Skillful Investments'," Dallas Morning News, May 7, 1994.

187 "I think there were times they'd rather he maybe bit his tongue ...": Author interview with Ernie Angelo, July 14, 1999.

188 voodoo economics: Washington Post, March 26, 1980.

188 "A lot of the Reagan people here in Texas ...": Author interview with Ernie Angelo, July 14, 1999.

189 "[Bush] knew that he had gotten pretty out of character ...": Ibid.

189 "We very nearly had a rebellion ...": Ibid.

189 Speech by Angelo: Ibid.

191 "I didn't decorate nurseries ...": Dallas Morning News, January 31,1999.

191 John Kirwan thought George W. was worried that ...: Author interview with John Kirwan, November 12, 1999.

192 Uzielli put up $1 million ...: New York Times, May 8, 1999.

192 George W said that it was only after this investment that he found out "Uzi" was a close friend of James Baker ...: Dallas Morning News, November 16, 1998.

192 They barely managed to scrape together a sixth of that ...: New York Times, May 8, 1998.

192 George W's grandmother and Marvin's godfather contributed ...: Dallas Morning News, November 16, 1998

193 George W. had accumulated 4.7 million dollars' worth of investments ...: Dallas Morning News, November 16, 1998.

193 He turned to that bank for help ...: Dallas Morning News, May 7, 1994.

193 Rea contacts George W. for DeWitt: Author interview with Paul Rea, July 17, 1999.

195 He was given the titles of board director ...: Washington Post, July 30, 1999.

195 The Dallas Morning News discovered that George W.'s company performed far better for itself ...: Washington Post, July 30, 1999.

196 DeWitt said he liked the deal ...: Washington Post, July 30, 1999.

196 George W. knew when to give up on a dry well ...: Author interview with Paul Rea, July 17, 1999.

197 George W. runs across his lawn in his underwear: Ibid.

198 "We couldn't afford to continue doing what we were doing ...": Washington Post, July 30, 1999.

198 His spiritual epiphany didn't exactly coincide with the very bottom ...: Time, June 21, 1999.

199 George W. bible study jokes, according to Maraniss: Washington Post Magazine, July 30, 1999.

199 Billy Graham chastises George W. for playing God: New York Times, September 13, 1998.

200 "I know I'll never be perfect ...": From transcript of South Texas Billy Graham Crusade.

200 Spectrum 7's on last bid for success ...: Washington Post, July 30, 1999.

200 Spectrum's debt: Ibid.; Time, June 21, 1999.

201 "He likes the ups ...": Author interview with Charlie Younger, July 13, 1999.

201   George W. drops names: Janice Johnston, "Vice Pres's Son Favors Simple Life of His Native Land," Dallas Morning News, July 31, 1986.

202   "properties were pretty well encumbered ...": Time, October 28, 1991.

203   Harken's main purchasing power ...: Forbes, September 3, 1990.

203   His stock share would be $530,000 ...: New York Times, May 8, 1999.

203   "Can you remember a day when you haven't had a beer ...": C-Span Interview, June 1991 (Brian Lamb interview).

203   "He would never get mean ...": Author interview with Charlie Younger, July 13, 1999.

204   Laura tells Post about husband's drinking habit ...Lois Romano and George Lardner, Jr., "1986: A Life-Changing Year-Epiphany Fueled Candidate's Climb." Washington Post July 25, 1999

204   "I would go from a three to a ten ...": C-Span Interview June, 1991, Brian Lamb interview.

204   Mills hits the bottle too hard ... Washington Post May 3, 1992.

204   "I had great respect for Wilbur Mills ...": George Bush, with Victor Gold, Looking Forward: An Autobiography (New York: Bantam Edition, July 1988).

204   Ross Perot calls Bush with news of sons ... Gerald Posner, Citizen Perot: His Life & Times (New York, Canada: Random House, 1996).

205   George W loses temper at restaurant and curses at Washingtonian magazine ... Author interview with Al Hunt, July 15, 1999.

206   "He just said, 'I don't need it in my life anymore ...'" Author interview with Younger, July 13, 1999.

206   "I quit for the rest of my life ,,," New York Times, September 13, 1998.

206   "I have got a pretty good-sized asset base ...": Charlotte Anne Lucas, "Bush Has Fared Well Despite Firms' Troubles, Candidate Credits 'Hard Work, Skillful Investments',"Dallas Morning News May 7, 1994.

206   Uzielli loses almost all he invested ... Charlotte Anne Lucas, "Bush Has Fared Well Despite Firms' Troubles, Candidate Credits 'Hard Work, Skillful Investments',"Dallas Morning News May 7, 1994.

207   "By that time he wasn't a social animal ...": Author interview with Younger, July 13, 1999.

Chapter X

208   "[He] had to stand up to me yet not be so aggressive ...": Parmet, George Bush: The Life of a Lone Star Yankee.

209   "We tried to kick a little ass ...": Ibid., p. 298.

209   "I want to be very frank with you ...": Ibid., p. 243

209   He purposefully hired men and women ...: Ibid., p. 301

210   "What would be the purpose ...": John Brady, Bad Boy: The Life and Politics of Lee Atwater (New York: Addison Wesley Publishers, 1997), p. 136.

210   "I agree with your conclusions ...": Ibid., p. 136.

210   "He needs to be President ...": Barry Bearak, "Team Player Bush: A Yearning to Serve," Los Angeles Times, November 22, 1987.

211   "He fired more people than I have ever known ...": Author interview with Marlin Fitzwater, August 19, 1999.

212   The G-6 group members: Author interview with Craig Fuller, August 25, 1999.

213 "I'm damn serious, pal ...": Evan Smith, "George, Washington," Texas Monthly, June 1999.

213 Nothing could have pleased Atwater more ...: Author interview with Marlin Fitzwater, August 19, 1999.

214 He was able to find free time ...: Eric Pooley with S. C. Gwynne, "How George Got His Groove," Time, June 21, 1999.

215 "If ever there was competition with his father ...": Paul Burka, "The W. Nobody Knows," Texas Monthly, June 1999.

215 "My own sense of things is this ...": Sam Attesley, "George Bush Jr. Likely to Seek Elective Office--One Day," Dallas Morning News, p. 42.

216 "Senior adviser, they call me ...": Ibid.

216 but Atwater took his candor to the extreme ...: Brady, Bad Boy, p. 152.

216 Atwater was a notorious womanizer ...: Ibid., p. 153.

218 According to John Brady's biography of Atwater ...: Ibid., p. 143.

218 He wanted pictures of Bush in a hard hat, touring industrial sites ...: Ibid., p. 143.

219 Like his mother, he insisted on knowing the justification ...: Author interview with Craig Fuller, August 25, 1999.

219 "The father thinks the same ...": Author interview with Samuel K. Skinner, August 26, 1999.

219 "George Bush wouldn't mind having a few other people pick up the sword ...": Author interview with Marlin Fitzwater, August 19, 1999.

219 No one could explain her sway over him, and so some started murmuring that sex was involved ...: Parmet, George Bush: The Life of a Lone Star Yankee, pp. 239-240.

219 "I'm not saying she's Miss Popularity ...": Ibid., p. 241.

220 "Well, that's easy ... the answer is N-O ...": Interview with Anonymous; Radcliffe, Simply Barbara Bush , p. 208.

221 "The answer to the Big A question is N.O.": "Bush and the 'Big A Question'," Newsweek, June 29, 1987.

222 "There were some [Jack] Kemp people ...": Brady, Bad Boy, p. 156.

222 She was sent to his New York campaign office ... kept "on the payroll out of Bush's own pocket ...": Parmet, George Bush: The Life of a Lone Star Yankee, p. 241.

222 "He's a funny little fellow, that man ...": "Be It Odessa or Atlanta, It's a Long Way From Paradise for Bush: The View From Dallas," Dallas Morning News, July 22, 1988.

223 "This is disgraceful ...": Smith, "George, Washington."

223 He claimed she blamed her editor ...: Ibid.

224 "It was a fair look at why Bush had this persistent image problem ...": Ibid.

225 The former president told Bush biographer that Jack Kemp would be best choice for president ...: Parmet, George Bush: The Life of a Lone Star Yankee, p. 293.

225 "Make George a little paranoid ...": Ibid., p. 294.

225 "on a personal vendetta for having been denied social access to the White House ...": Ruth Miller Fitzgibbons, "George Bush, Too," D magazine, April 1992.

226 "narked up terrorist kinds of guys ...": Author interview with Sheila Tate, August 25, 1999.

226 according to press secretary ... "close to the family": Author interview with Marlin Fitzwater, August 19, 1999.

227   "There's not a bunch of discord in our campaign ...": Mark Nelson, "Bush Advisers Want James Baker to Take Reins," Dallas Morning News, June 14, 1988.

228   many campaign staffers ... "a little louder when his dad wasn't around": Marannis, "The Bush Bunch."

228   "I can't believe that a guy that is that handsome would not be of some benefit ...": Kevin Merida, "Bush Ends Suspense, Chooses Quayle," Dallas Morning News, August 17, 1988.

229   "Dan Quail looks like Robert Redford ...": Parmet, George Bush: The Life of a Lone Star Yankee, p. 344.

229   "My view is that I was in the Texas Air National Guard": Mark Nelson and Richard Whittle, "GOP Cheers Bush's 'Message to Michael'," Dallas Morning News, August 19, 1988.

230   the next Sunday ...: Carl P. Leubsdorf, "Sununu Chastises Bentsen," Dallas Morning News, August 22, 1988.

232   "If Kitty Dukakis were raped ...": Parmet, George Bush: The Life of a Lone Star Yankee, p. 355.

234   Fuller's first thought was that Sununu seemed to partisan for George Bush ...: Author interview with Craig Fuller, August 25, 1999.

234   "What's gonna happen to me now?": Smith, "George, Washington."

235   "It's the first son syndrome ...": Pooley with Gwynne, "How George Got His Groove."

235   "I don't give a damn, people down here in Texas don't care about that stuff ...": Maraniss, "The Bush Bunch."

Chapter XI

238   For one, he needed to earn the $120,000 ...: "Insider Sale by Bush's Son Questioned," Associated Press, Dallas Morning News, March 8, 1992.

239   "I'm going to get tagged on running on your father's name ...": Attlesey, "George Bush Jr. Likely to Seek Elective Office--One Day."

239   George W. pulled out a ten-gallon hat ...: Victoria Loe, "Lone Star Sparkles Among States at Inaugural Parade," Dallas Morning News, January 21, 1989.

240   "His first reaction was ...": Author interview with Bill DeWitt Jr., August 11, 1999.

240   Eddie "I'm Still Mad" Chiles became a well-known curmudgeon ...: Jack Z. Smith, "Eddie Chiles: Too Tough to Quit," Fort-Worth Star Telegram, November 3, 1985.

240   In 1980, Chiles increased his investment ...: Ken Stephens, "Chiles Steps Aside After Long Sale Saga," Dallas Morning News, March 19, 1989.

241   Peter Ueberroth overrode the vote ...: Kevin Sherrington, "Ueberroth to Search for Buyers," Dallas Morning News, February 10, 1989.

241   "I can see two more years ...": Frank Luksa, "Winning Rangers Still Own Chiles' Heart," Dallas Times-Herald, July 20, 1986.

242   In the summer of 1988 ...: Author interview with Frank Morsani.

242   Chiles wrote Morsani a letter ...: Ibid.

242   Bobby Brown warned Chiles ...: Deposition of Robert W. Brown, M.D., March 25, 1997.

242   Morsani's group claimed they never were notified ...: Author interview with Frank Morsani.

242 Gaylord's letter of proposal included ...: Letter from Ed Gaylord to Eddie Chiles on September 16, 1988, read into deposition of Robert W. Brown, M.D., March 25, 1997.

243 "I walked into his house ...": Kevin Sack, "George Bush the Son Finds That Oil and Blood Do Mix," New York Times, May 8, 1999.

243 "George [W.] Bush contacted me yesterday ...": Letter from Eddie Chiles to Bobby Brown, December 1988, read into deposition of Robert W. Brown, M.D., March 25, 1997, for Frank L. Morsani, individually, and for the use and benefit of Tampa Bay Baseball Group, Inc., p.182.

244 Although Chiles said he hadn't received any formal bids ...: Tracy Ringolsby, "Upbeat Chiles Back in Business Despite Rejection," Dallas Morning News, January 26, 1989.

244 "Ueberroth will become one of his top cabinet members ...": "The Absentee Commissioner," Newsday, February 28, 1988.

245 The day after the vote Chiles tells the press ...: Tracy Ringolsby, "Bush's Son Leads Group Interested in Rangers," Dallas Morning News, January 1989.

245 "There is plenty of out-of-town money ...": Letter from Jerry Reinsdorf to Commissioner Peter Ueberroth, February 9, 1989, read into deposition of Robert W. Brown, M.D., March 25, 1997.

245 Eddie Chiles's Alzheimer's disease: Deposition of Robert W. Brown, M.D., March 25, 1997.

246 Richard Rainwater reportedly parlayed $50 million of the Bass family's ...: Sam Attlesey, Cathy Harasta, "Likely Buyers Accustomed to Big Deals," Dallas Morning News, February 24, 1989.

247 "out of respect for his father": Lois Romano and George Lardner Jr., "Bush Earned His Profit, Rangers Deal Insiders Say," Washington Post, July 31, 1999.

247 Ueberroth announced that their group had been hand-picked to buy the team ...: Kevin Sherrington, "Gaylord Steadfast in Rangers Bid, Keeps Bush-Rose Group on Hold," Dallas Morning News, March 6, 1989.

247 "If they won't let me sell it to Gaylord ...": Kevin Sherrington, "If Gaylord Bid Fails, Chiles May Pull Team Off Market," Dallas Morning News, March 9, 1989.

247 "That reasoning was kind of silly ...": Randy Galloway, "Baseball's Balk of Gaylord Underlines Rangers' Plight," Dallas Morning News, March 8, 1992.

248 "Because I put the deal together ...": Kevin Sherrington, "More Than Meets the Name," Dallas Morning News, May 2, 1989.

248 "They rejected my friend Ed Gaylord ...": Stephens, "Chiles Steps Aside After Long Sale Saga."

248 "George W. Bush deserves great credit ...": Sack, "George Bush the Son Finds That Oil and Blood Do Mix."

249 "For those who believe I'm from a pampered lot ...": Ron Boyd, "Bush Brings His Soft Pitch to Hardball," Dallas Times-Herald, April 26, 1989.

250 The total cost of the team was $75 million ...: Sack, "George Bush the Son Finds That Oil and Blood Do Mix."

250 The financing as listed included $2.5 million from Rainwater ...: Exhibit A, document 955, read into deposition of Robert W. Brown, M.D, March 25, 1997.

250 Cottrell at first told him that he didn't have the money to invest ...: David

Moore, "Unlimited Partner," Dallas Morning News, September 12, 1989.

251 "If you're gonna run for office now ...": Miriam Rosen, "Young George," Dallas Observer, March 17-23, 1994.

252 "If I run, I'll be most electable ...": "Don't Call Him Junior," Texas Monthly, April 1989.

252 Barbara says her son should concentrate on baseball: "Mrs. Bush Advises Son Against Governor's Race," Dallas Morning News, April 28, 1989.

252 "I love my mother ...": Ibid.

252 "My mother's always been a very outspoken person ...": Radcliffe, Simply Barbara Bush, p. 129.

253 "I'm sure [my mother] will be happy ...": Sam Attlesey, "Bush Declines to Make Run for Governor's Seat," Dallas Morning News, August 2, 1989.

Chapter XII

255 "He always placated his father ...": "Team Player Bush: A Yearning to Serve," Los Angeles Times, November 22, 1987.

255 If you have a history of deferring to somebody ...: Ibid.

257 "Folks see me sitting in the same seat they sit in ...": Sam Howe Verhovek, "Is There Room on the Republican Ticket for Another Bush?," New York Times, September 13, 1998.

257 "He's high-strung to the point where you'd worry ...": "He Brings Star Quality and a Hands-Off Approach to the Texas Rangers," Dallas Times-Herald, February 25, 1990.

258 At first Schieffer was unenthusiastic about the idea of taking ...: Author interview with Tom Schieffer, September 7, 1999.

259 Greene said that Arlington ...: Catalina Camia, "Arlington Plays Hardball," Dallas Morning News, November 6, 1989.

259 George W.'s group asked the city's residents ...: Byron York, "George's Road to Riches," American Spectator, June 1999.

259 Better still for the partners ...: Ibid.

260 The Bahraini official telephoned 66-year-old Michael ...: Toni Mack, "Fuel for Fantasy," Forbes, September 3, 1990.

260 Coincidentally, the next call Ameen took was from ...: Ibid.

261 George W. and Paul Rea ...: Author interview with Paul Rea, July 7, 1999.

261 Stephens put together a plan ...: Stephen J. Hedges, "The Color of Money," U.S. News & World Report, March 16, 1992.

261 As it turned out, UBS ...: Richard Behar, "The Wackiest Rig in Texas," Time, October 28, 1991.

261 David Edwards—who coincidentally ...: David Armstrong, "Crude Dealings," Dallas Observer, August 8, 1991.

261 the company's revenues went from $4 million in 1986 ...: Maria Halkias, "Harken Expects $1 Billion in Revenues," Dallas Morning News, June 9, 1989.

261 In the year the loan went through ...: Hedges, "The Color of Money."

262 ... Harken was simply to please the president ...: Ibid.

262 As reported in a 1987 article ... necklace ...: Sarah Booth Conroy, "Gift to the White House: From Daggers to Jellybeans," Washington Post, March 5, 1987.

262 But George Bush did keep a $3,000 silver ...: Ibid.

262 The month that George Bush received ... those neighboring countries ...:

"Bush: Will He or Won't He Ask Saudis to Cut Production?," Platt's Oilgram News, April 3, 1989.

262 But George Bush also said that he wanted to talk ...: Jonathan Feurbringer, "Congress Splits Over Remarks by Bush on Oil," New York Times, June 9, 1986.

263 "Texas is screaming ...": Bush: Will He or Won't He Ask Saudis to Cut Production?," Platt's Oilgram News, April 3, 1989.

263 On that trip in April ...: Timothy J. McNulty, "Bush Stresses Need for Gulf Oil to Flow," Chicago Tribune, June 9, 1986.

263 Bush disclosed that ...: Ibid.

263 George W. and Harken officials later ...: Halkias "Harken Expects $1 Billion in Revenues."

263 According to the agreement ...: Hedges, "The Color of Money."

264 Harken was required to drill ... contract was inked ...: David Armstrong, "Crude Dealings," Dallas Observer, August 8, 1991.

264 The other major problem was that Harken ...:Hedges, "The Color of Money."

264 Paul Rea took some investors from Midland ...: Author interview with Paul Rea, July 7, 1999.

264 Once Harken had the big Bahrain deal ...: Toni Mack, "Fuel for Fantasy," Forbes, September 3, 1990.

264 That spring George W. sat on a three-member "fair committee" ...: Hedges, "The Color of Money."

266 On January 16, 1991 ...: Bob Woodward,"Hammered," Washington Post Magazine, June 20, 1999.

266 Bahrain had required ...: Richard Behar, "The Wackiest Rig in Texas," Time, October 28, 1991.

267 "Bush will be defeated when he comes up for reelection ...": Brady, Bad Boy.

268 "For some reason, my whole body ...": Parmet, George Bush: The Life of a Lone Star Yankee, p. 48.

268 "We were so spoiled by the adulation ...": Author interview with Ron Kauffman, July 28. 1999.

269 His biggest fear, according to his biographer ...: Brady, Bad Boy, p. 298.

269 In July, George Bush and George W. ...: Ibid.

270 "As long as the climate of this country ...": Marlin Fitzwater, Call the Briefing! (New York: Times, 1995).

271 "I think George would be absolutely marvelous ... But really, he'd be marvelous ...": "Team Player Bush: A Yearning to Serve," Los Angeles Times, November 22, 1987.

272 "I have asked son George to very quietly ...": Peter Goldman, Thomas M. DeFrank, Mark Miller, Andrew Murr, and Tom Matthews, The Quest for the Presidency 1992 (Texas: Texas A&M University Press, College Station, 1994), p.303.

272 He went on to assure each of the staffers ...: Ibid.

272 According to reporters at Newsweek ... it was likely to be a bad one ...: Ibid., p. 307.

272 "We have a saying in our family ...": Ibid.

273 "John, a lot of people ...": Ibid., p. 308.

273 "I was very happy for him ...": Author interview with Andrew Card, September 2, 1999.

273   "Well, Mr. President ...": Ibid.

273   Sununu was scrambling ... What do you really think? ...: Ibid.; author interview with Marlin Fitzwater, August 19, 1999.

274   A 1992 account of the Sununu incident ...: Fitzgibbons, "George Bush, Too."

278   He resented George W.'s "marketing shtick" ...: Kevin Sherrington, "Rangers Sink to Upsurdity with Stone Mess," Dallas Morning News, October 5, 1990.

278   "Maybe George was a little sorry ...": Author interview with Tom Schieffer.

279   "It is not that unusual ...": Author interview with Robert Mosbacher Jr., July 8, 1999.

279   "So, what is my friend Ross Perot doing?" ...: Author interview with Jim Oberwetter, July 29, 1999.

279   According to Fuller, the defense department ...: Author interview with Craig Fuller, August 25, 1999.

280   "[Perot] penchant for investigating ...": Testimony to the House Judiciary Subcommittee on Civil Constitutional Rights by James C. Oberwetter, delivered March 24, 1993.

280   "Frankly, from the beginning ...": Ibid.

280   For example ... very dangerous thing in politics ...": Ibid.

282   ... he would be resigning from the board of Harken ...: David Jackson and Maria Halkias, "Bush's Son Takes Leave to Aid Campaign," Dallas Morning News, June 24, 1992.

282   Back in 1988, he had been put through the background checks ...: Kevin Merida, "Running-mate Rumor Mill Revs Up," Dallas Morning News, August 16, 1988.

283   "I have seen the look in George Bush's eye ...": Sam Attlesey, "The 'Spin Doctor' Is In," Dallas Morning News, August 19, 1992.

284   That first year up at Williams college ...: Author interview with Fay Vincent, July 16, 1999.

284   The worst of the trouble was negotiating Pete Rose's lifetime ban ...: Ibid.

285   "If I had known you were going to be commissioner ...": Ibid.

286   Some of the American League owners thought he had been unfair ... he stated in a letter on August 20 ...: Ibid.

286   On September 3 ... also began to take a major part in leading the insurrection ...: Ibid.

287   George W. said that Vincent was an intelligent and honorable man. ... "but they never got around to speaking" ...: Ibid.

287   Vincent felt that if George W. had come to him ...Vincent said he would not resign ...: Ibid.

287   "Look Fay" ... "I'm prepared for a fight ...": Ibid.

288   "If I turn them all around" ... "you'll pull it off." ...: Ibid.

288   "He didn't want to go out mud-wrestling ...": Phil Rogers, "Beleaguered Baseball Czar Steps Down," Dallas Morning News, September 8, 1992.

288   Vincent later heard that owners ... how power worked ...: Author interview with Fay Vincent, July 16, 1999.

291   "Why did we lose?" ...: B. Bush, Barbara Bush: A Memoir, p. 498.

292   "They know it's ugly, and they're still willing to do it ...": James Keogh, "Barbara Remembers," Greenwich magazine, December 1994.

Chapter XIII

294   "It kind of floored me …": Author interview with Charlie Younger, July 13, 1999.

294   "Poor, George, he was born with a silver foot in his mouth …": Lois Romano and George Lardner Jr., "Father's Campaign, Baseball Provide Foundation for Own Run," Washington Post, July 31, 1999.

294   "You've got a popular incumbent Democrat that you can't beat …": Author interview with Charlie Younger, July 13, 1999.

295   "I can beat her …": Ibid.

295   "I always thought he had some secret poll going …": Ibid.

296   "Mother, I've made up my mind … I can win!": Miriam Rosen, "Young George," Dallas Observer, March 17-23, 1994.

296   A Texas poll conducted in July showed that while 58 percent …: Hugh Aynesworth, "Bush Son Targets Richards in Texas," Washington Times, September 1, 1993.

296   The next month, a poll showed that he was only eight percentage points behind Richards …: Skip Hollansworth, "Born to Run," Texas Monthly, May 1994.

296   "It's time for my generation to accept responsibility …": Claire Smith, "On Baseball," New York Times, November 17, 1993.

298   "He came down on the side of being drafted …": Radcliffe, Simply Barbara Bush.

298   Could he afford two houses …?: Maureen Dowd, "New Races (Their Own) for 2 Bush Sons," New York Times, November 30, 1992.

299   Karl Rove confesses to George W.'s speech thievery …: Dowd, "New Races (Their Own) for 2 Bush Sons."

299   "Jeb's got his feet on the ground …": Curtis Wilkie, "Bush Sons Push Same Themes in Texas, Fla.," Boston Globe, July 4, 1994.

301   Rove teaches dirty tricks campaigning …: Brady, Bad Boy, p. 38.

301   19-year-old rove even adopted a false name …: Ibid., p. 38.

301   Rove printed invitations advertising beer, food, girls and a good time: Ibid., p. 38.

301   Bush decided Rove was clean: Ibid., p. 38.

302   Rove admitted he was involved with prank: Wayne Slater, "Top Bush Aide Brings Aggressive Style to Effort: Strategist Dominates Presidential Bid, Observers Say," Dallas Morning News, March 21, 1999.

302   "weak woman" strategy: Howard Kurtz, "In 1994 Political Ads Crime Is the Weapon of Choice," Washington Post, September 9, 1994.

303   George W.'s 17-point proposal: Rosen, "Young George."

303   "It was just my sound man accosting …": Kurtz, "In 1994 Political Ads Crime Is the Weapon of Choice."

303   Violent crime issues and W.'s plans to combat them: Rosen, "Young George."

304   George W. talks about thugs: Ibid.

304   total local control: Ibid.

304   "We chose to send them to private school …": Ibid.

305   Welfare issue: Thomas B. Edsall, "Texas Democrats Fighting Back on Crime, Welfare, Family Issues," Washington Post, May 8, 1994.

305   George W.'s aides were thrilled with her "bleeding heart" response …: Ibid.

305   "I don't campaign on that …": Ibid.

306 Jeb's strong conservative speech: Kurtz, "1994 Political Ads Crime Is the Weapon of Choice."

306 "I didn't ask their advice ...": Rosen, "Young George."

306 "If it's inevitable, might as well enjoy it ...": Ibid.

307 Williams refuses to shake hands with Richards: Sam Howe Verhovek, "Texas Challenger Uses Thick Skin and a Smile," New York Times, August 22, 1994.

307 "Well, I'm sorry you feel that way ...": Ibid.

307 "You just can't wake up one morning and decide ...": Edsall, "Texas Democrats Fighting Back ..."

307 Lecture by Richards at Texas Girls State: Sam Howe Verhovek, "Family Becomes an Issue in the Texas Governor's Race," New York Times, June 22, 1994.

307 "She started referring to him derisively as 'Shrub'": Verhovek, "Is There Room on the Republican Ticket for Another Bush?"

307 "The last time I was called a jerk ...": Verhovek, "Texas Challenger Uses Thick Skin and a Smile."

308 "Is the Rove news conference about over?": Rosen, "Young George."

308 Rove reports that George W. "muffed" his speech: Ibid.

308 George W. even raised $1 million on a single night early in the campaign: Ibid.

309 Jackie Miller asks Jeb about Skull and Bones ...: Dowd, "New Races (Their Own) for 2 Bush Sons."

310 "Can you believe it? ...": Author interview with Dennis Grubb, August 26, 1999.

310 You're right, it's not the same ...": Author interview with Tom Schieffer, September 7, 1999.

Chapter XIV

311 George Bush's speech to the Foreign Correspondents Club...: "Bush Not Coy About Interest in Race Against Carter in '80," Houston Post, April 23, 1978.

312 "Elect a president we won't have to train ...": "Team Player Bush: A Yearning to Serve," Los Angeles Times, November 22, 1987.

312 Who are the leaders of Chechnya, Taiwan ...: "Bush Names 1 of 4 World Leaders in Questions From Reporter: Aide Notes Most People Can't Name Head of Chechnya," Associated Press, November 5, 1999.

312 "General, I can name the general ...": Ibid.

312 ... suggested he be given a more extensive quiz ...: Thomas L. Friedman, "George W.'s Makeup Exam," New York Times, November 7, 1999.

312 "Lee" was probably a lucky guess ...: Maureen Dowd, "Name That General," New York Times, November 7, 1999.

312 The pop quiz was ...: Author interview with Jane Anne Stinnett, November 12, 1999.

313 The main task of a governor ...: National Governors' Association, "Reflections on Being a Governor" (Washington, D.C.: Center for Policy Research, NGA, February 1981).

314 "What they're concerned about is ...": Carl Cannon, "The Book on Bush," National Journal, August 7, 1999.

314   The legislature only meets for 140 days once every two years ...: Paul Alexander, "All Hat, No Cattle," Rolling Stone, August 5, 1999.

314   He did have the power to veto legislation ...: Texas Office of the Governor web site (http://www.governor.state.tx.us/divisions/duties.html).

314   To oversee that distribution of job ...: Pot Pourri, Phillips Academy at Andover 1964 yearbook.

314   "It was brilliant ...": Author interview with Charlie Younger, July 13, 1999.

314   By inauguration day ...: James A. Barnes, "The Company He Keeps," National Journal, August 7, 1999.

315   Some political observers ...: Alexander, "All Hat, No Cattle."

315   "Machiavelli in cowboy boots ...": Texas Legislature Online, "The Legislative Process, Powers, and Duties of the Lieutenant Governor" (http://www.capitol.state.tx.us/capitol/legproc/ltgov.html).

315   He was famous for locking legislators in his office ...: Christy Hope, "Bullock's Passion, Vision Honored," Dallas Morning News, June 21, 1999.

315   "Governor, you're new here" ...: Ibid.

315   "He said, 'I'm going to break him down ...'": Author interview with Charlie Younger, July 13, 1999.

315   "With him, it is the vision thing ...": James A. Barnes, "The Company He Keeps," National Journal, August 7, 1999.

316   George W.'s four main points ...: Mark Murray, "Issues of the Day: Where Bush Stands," National Journal, August 7, 1999.

317   The data could be used to focus attention ...: Siobhan Gorman, "Bush's Lesson Plan," National Journal, August 7, 1999.

317   He was proudest of his 1996 reading initiative ...: Ibid.

317   Perhaps he was inspired by the struggles ...: B. Bush, Barbara Bush: A Memoir, p. 55.

317   Only when he stayed home sick one day, did Bar notice ...: Ibid, p. 56.

317   None of George W.'s new initiatives actually cost the state ...: Verhovek, "Is There Room on the Republican Ticket for Another Bush?"

318   In the end, George W's plan was defeated ...: James A. Barnes, "Bush, In His Own Words," National Journal, August 7, 1999.

318   Still, some of George W.'s wealthier constituents ...: Murray, "Issues of the Day: Where Bush Stands," National Journal, August 7, 1999.

319   "Lawyers were a necessary evil ...": Author interview with Randy Roden, August 2, 1999.

319   Of course, as governor, George W. would be forced to address ...: Sam Attlesey, "Bush Pushes Gun Question With Texans," Dallas Morning News, September 11, 1988.

319   Several people were killed in a Fort Worth church ...: "Bush Announces Initiative on Gun Crime," New York Times, September 26, 1999.

319   Once, when giving an interview in April 1989 ...: Carl P. Leubsdorf, "Mrs. Bush Advises Son Against Governor's Race," Dallas Morning News, April 28, 1989.

320   A national poll conducted by the Dallas Morning News ...: Todd J. Gillman, "Voters Not Taking Issue with Republican's Views, Lack of Familiarity Could Hurt Later, Experts Say," Dallas Morning News, July 25, 1999.

320   "The United States Supreme court has settled the abortion issue ...": Verhovek, "Is There Room on the Republican Ticket for Another Bush?"

320   George W. refused to intervene saying that he had appointed ...: Author interview with Charlie Younger, July 13, 1999.

320   George W. did not visit the city while tensions were up ...: Robert Draper, "Favorite Son," GQ, October 1998.

320   Critics chastised him for not taking the occasion ...: Christopher Lee, "Byrd Death Anniversary Observed: Demonstrators Fault State's Inaction On Hate-Crimes Bill," Dallas Morning News, June 7, 1999.

321   Like Bill Clinton, George W. has refrained from employing ...: Verhovek, "Is There Room on the Republican Ticket for Another Bush?"

321   During the 1994 campaign ...: Ibid.

321   "It was, of course, picked up and politicized ...": Ibid.

322   "This sounds, well, un-American ...": Walt Harrington, "What Makes George Tick?" Washington Post Magazine, September 28, 1986.

322   "What do you think about me?" ...: Draper, "Favorite Son."

322   George W. choked up ...: Ibid.

323   "He wants faith to be vibrant ...": Andrew Miga, "Faith Fuels Bush's Run for GOP Nod," Boston Herald, June 13, 1999.

323   He didn't just campaign for statewide office ... Michael Duffy and Nancy Gibbs, "Who Chose George?," Time, June 21, 1999.

323   For the 1998 campaign in Texas, George W.'s opponent ...: Stuart Eskenaz, "Bush's Free Ride," Dallas Observer, November 4, 1998.

323   The Bush/Rose group sold their interest in the Rangers ...: Ibid.

324   "I don't know whether I'll seek the presidency ...": Wayne Slate, Sam Attlesey, "Bush, Mauro Spar in Debate: Governor Questions Challenger's Promises; Democrat Accuses Him of Failed Leadership," Dallas Morning News, October 17, 1998.

324   "We haven't thought through ...": Todd J. Gillman, "Texas' First Lady Wouldn't Fight Run for White House; Laura Bush Said Husband Is Really Undecided," Dallas Morning News, February 1, 1999.

325   "There were days when [the legislature] weren't in session ...": Paul Burka, "The W. Nobody Knows," Texas Monthly, June 1999.

325   "He would go out and burn some energy ...": Author interview with Charlie Younger, July 13, 1999.

325   Reportedly he carried an electronic device ...: Burka, "The W. Nobody Knows."

325   His scheduled appointments, according to Texas Monthly ...: Ibid.

325   That blunt style served him ...: Ibid.

325   He then told them that he had been kidding ...: Ibid.

325   "I bought cocaine at my dad's inauguration ...": Ibid.

325   "Get outta here now, go play in traffic ...": Rosen, "Young George."

326   Jeb also recognized how George W.'s upbeat approach worked ...: Verhovek, "Is There Room on the Republican Ticket for Another Bush?"

326   "It's not just me ...": Barnes, "Bush, In His Own Words."

326   Al Hunt, of the Wall Street Journal, received an unexpected call ...: Author interview with Al Hunt, July 15, 1999.

327   Hunt accepted the apology ...: Ibid.

328   "I heard he was angry about it ...": Lois Romano and George Lardner Jr., "1986: A Life-Changing Year, Epiphany Fueled Candidate's Climb," Washington Post, July 25, 1999.

328   "It hasn't come easy ...": Author interview with Charlie Younger, July 13, 1999.

329   "Can you imagine how much it hurt ...": Verhovek, "Is There Room On a Republican Ticket for Another Bush?"

329   "And I think there's a huge difference ...": Draper, "Favorite Son."

329   "It is certainly not going to hunt ...": Phyllis Gilchrist, "As She Says Deficit Nation's Most Pressing Problem," United Press International, September 6, 1984.

329   One hint of what the strategy might become ...: B. Bush, Barbara Bush: A Memoir, p. 473.

330   As Bush prepared to leave the White House ...: Parmet, George Bush: The Life of a Lone Star Yankee, p. 510.

330   On August 17, when President Clinton was still ...: Verhovek, "Is There Room on the Republican Ticket for Another Bush?"

330   "I was just in a state of pique ...": Author interview with Lanny Davis, July 30, 1999.

330   "I was in college with George Bush, Jr. ...": Ellen Joan Pollock, "Empty Chatter: Behind the Rumors About George W. Bush Is a Culture of Gossip," Wall Street Journal, May 14, 1999.

330   Davis said later ...: Author interview with Lanny Davis, July 30, 1999.

330   When Williams came back ...: Ibid.

331   "I said, 'Look, I don't think my writing ...'": Ibid.

331   "Reverend Graham has told ...": Author interview with Charlie Younger, July 13, 1999.

331   "Patrick J. Buchanan handing the baton ...": Verhovek, "Is There Room on the Republican Ticket for Another Bush?"

332   When Buchanan began expressing his disgruntled views of the GOP ...: Allison Mitchell, "Rebel Buchanan Is Urged by Bush to Stay in GOP," New York Times, September 25, 1999.

332   He then confessed to the press that he thought ...: Richard L. Berke, "Bush Speaks of Perot and Buchanan Acting in 'Vendetta'," New York Times, September 30, 1999.

332   Bill Clinton violated the public trust by engaging ...: Katie Fairbank, "Beating the Bushes Reveals Little Trouble In Possible Presidential Candidate's Past," Associated Press, April 1, 1999.

332   "When I was young and irresponsible ...": Ibid.

332   "The issue for George [W.] is ...": Author interview with Lanny Davis, July 30, 1999.

333   He dubbed the Kosovars ...: Michael Duffy and Nancy Gibbs, "Who Chose George?," Time, June 21, 1999.

333   But he has been consulting with such advisers ...: James Kitfield, "Periphery Is Out; Russia and China, In," National Journal, August 7, 1999.

333   He has been focusing his concerns ...: Ibid.

334   But he has said that he believes that if he does not run now ...: Michael Mulvey, "Bush Says 2000 Race May Be His Last Chance to Seek Presidency," Dallas Morning News, January 21, 1999.

334   "But otherwise you sit on the porch ...: Author interview with Fay Vincent, July 16, 1999.

INDEX